Alice Hunt is I and History at the Univers ...mpton. She was awarded a Leverhulme Trust fellowship to research this book. Alice is also the author of *The Drama of Coronation* (Cambridge University Press) and has previously written about the Tudors and James I. She lives in Winchester.

Praise for *Republic*:

'A magisterial, compelling and eye-opening biography of Britain's great and extraordinary experiment.' Suzannah Lipscomb

'By restoring colour to character and excitement to event, Alice Hunt brilliantly reanimates this most extraordinary decade. It is a gripping tale of political and cultural crisis but also one of joy and hopeful innovation, told with eloquence and passion.' Malcolm Gaskill

'Whip-smart, witty and a dream to read, *Republic* gives a real sense of what it was actually like to live through Britain's most exciting decade. A superb achievement.' Jessie Childs

'As alert to nuance as to the big picture, invariably insightful, and storied with vivid set-pieces and character sketches, Alice Hunt's compelling narrative nails one of the most myth-laden decades of British history.' David Kynaston

'*Republic* is an eloquent, accessible and thrilling account of Britain's only radical republican experiment. It is essential reading for anyone who wishes to understand the country's past, present – and potential future.' Paul Lay

'A gripping account of one of the most exciting – and most misunderstood – periods in British history. I couldn't put it down.' Adrian Tinniswood

'A splendid guide to the decade that saw England's great experiment with radicalism, examining a heady world of "overturning days" with crisp, scholarly lucidity.' Lucy Moore

'An excellent introduction to the period; lively, erudite, and blending political, military, religious and cultural history in a way accessible to any reader.' Ronald Hutton

'Lively, engaging, yet also rigorous and searching, *Republic* offers a powerful reassessment of our century of revolution. Professor Hunt wears her learning lightly, but every page is informed by her profound understanding of a complex, controversial period in our history and enlivened by her sense that what happened then, matters now.' Anna Beer

'Vivid, fast-paced, revelatory: *Republic* inhabits one of the most elusive periods of British history with all the tension and jeopardy of a thriller.' Lisa Hilton

'An enthralling narrative of the rise and fall of Britain's republican experiment. Alice Hunt is an admirably deft guide to the turbulence of the 1650s, capturing the fizzing cultural dynamism of a period that's often dismissed as dour and complicated. Above all, she gives her story a tangible sense of uncertainty: nothing is inevitable, and you can't wait to find out what happens next.' *The Times*, Best History Books of 2024

'A thorough survey of politics, religion, warfare and culture in a tumultuous time, told through excellent set-pieces and character sketches.' Simon Heffer, *Telegraph*, Best History Books of 2024

'Post-regicide, the unstable politics of the 1650s proved exhilarating and hazardous. Hunt's *Republic* is a richly evocative cavalcade recounting one of the most extraordinary decades in British history.' Clare Jackson

'My favourite book of the year was Alice Hunt's *Republic*, because it brings alive a short but crucial period of history that has always fascinated me. Historians always skip over the year and a half between Oliver Cromwell's death and the restoration of Charles II – a period of extraordinary political chaos, when any number of Roundhead generals might have seized power. So why didn't they? And why did things work out as they did? This book is brilliantly researched and elegantly written. What's more, it really captures the era's sense of flux and possibility. I loved it.' Dominic Sandbrook, *The Times*, Favourite Books of 2024

'The 1650s are often neglected in favour of the dramatic events of the civil war-driven 1640s. Alice Hunt's *Republic* redresses the balance with aplomb as she charts the challenges of rule without a king. This lively book invites readers to "eavesdrop" on the republican revolution through the speeches, letters and diaries of the time.' Jackie Eales, *History Today*, Books of the Year 2024

'Hunt, in admirably clear and direct prose, attempts something . . . comprehensive, providing an earnest narrative, with each chapter devoted to a year of the republican experiment . . . *Republic* covers a lot of such ground, featuring a huge cast of characters.' *The Times*

'A fast-paced and enjoyable year-by-year survey of events . . . The lively narrative, interspersed with wry asides, presents a plethora of rich vignettes of notable episodes and personalities that bring this exhilarating period to life . . . Allow[s] us to look afresh at the republican era.' *Times Literary Supplement*

'Excellent . . . The author's primary aim is to rescue the 1650s as a revolutionary decade and to show that the period's politics cannot be isolated from the riches of its art, philosophy and science . . . Imaginative and intelligent.' *The Spectator*

'[A] splendidly dissident and engrossing history.' *Literary Review*

'A very good read . . . beautifully presented.' *BBC History Magazine*

'Instantly reminded me of the history books about the civil wars that I read as a boy – those which fired my passion for this entire period. *Republic* tells the story of eleven transformative years from 1649 to 1660. A beautiful narrative picks up the threads of civil war and weaves them into a compelling exploration of Commonwealth and Protectorate.' *Aspects of History*

'Alice Hunt's bold and stylish new history, *Republic*, reanimates the action of [1649–1660] once again.' *Unseen Histories*

'A picaresque narrative full of vivid vignettes . . . Her good eye for arresting quotations culled from contemporary authors and politicians is also evident throughout.' *Church Times*

'Hunt captures the essence of a republican decade: that it was a holy quest to create a new – and free – constitutional compact between the English nation and God.' *Irish Times*

'The 1650s are back. Against the backdrop of our new Carolean age, a flurry of books has appeared to illuminate our nation's brief flirtation with republican government . . . To their number we may add Alice Hunt's *Republic*, a year-by-year narrative of "a daring and unprecedented decade that deserves to be written about and understood as a distinct entity" . . . *Republic* is a book about novelty.' *The Critic*

REPUBLIC

Britain's Revolutionary Decade 1649–1660

ALICE HUNT

faber

First published in the UK in 2024
by Faber & Faber Ltd
The Bindery, 51 Hatton Garden
London EC1N 8HN

This paperback edition first published in 2025

Typeset by Typo•glyphix, Burton-on-Trent DE14 3HE
Printed in the UK by CPI Group (UK) Ltd, Croydon CR0 4YY

A CIP record for this book
is available from the British Library

ISBN 978–0–571–30320–5

MIX
Paper | Supporting
responsible forestry
FSC® C013604

Printed and bound in the UK on FSC® certified paper in line with our continuing
commitment to ethical business practices, sustainability and the environment.
For further information see faber.co.uk/environmental-policy

Our authorised representative in the EU for product safety is
Easy Access System Europe, Mustamäe tee 50, 10621 Tallinn, Estonia
gpsr.requests@easproject.com

2 4 6 8 10 9 7 5 3 1

For James, Florence, Mary and Jem

Contents

Dates and Quotations

All dates have been modernised, to reflect the new year changing in January rather than in March. The original spelling and punctuation have generally been retained in quotations from early sources, as long as the sense can be clearly understood.

Prologue: Execution

Exit the Tyrant

Inscription on the beheaded statue of Charles I, Royal Exchange

Early in the morning of 6 December 1648, soldiers began to gather around Whitehall. Some were on foot, some on horse. A pale light was beginning to show in the sky. It was cold, and the atmosphere was edgy. At the heart of the mass of buildings that sprawled along the Thames and made up the Palace of Whitehall was St Stephen's Chapel – the seat of the House of Commons. On that morning, standing at the top of the long flight of stone steps that led into the narrow medieval chapel was Colonel Thomas Pride, uniformed, hat in hand. He was waiting for the MPs to arrive, to take their place on their benches, to press on with what they had agreed the day before: to make a treaty with Charles I and end the terrible civil wars.

But the army, stoked by the radical and persuasive Henry Ireton, did not want to settle. Ireton, commissary general, had become convinced that the king against whom they had risked their lives on the battlefield could not be trusted to protect the people's liberties. He believed Charles was the 'grand Author of our troubles' and should be brought to justice for the blood he had shed.[1]

Pride's orders on that December morning were to hold the doors against those MPs who would block putting Charles I on trial. He had a list of the names of those who must be denied entry. Beside him stood the young army commander Thomas Grey, Lord Grey of Groby – a small man, mocked by Royalists as 'that grinning dwarf' – to help him identify the right men.[2] Here is a tableau of the time: Pride, a brewer from Glastonbury, who had risen rapidly through the ranks of Parliament's formidable New Model Army;

Grey, at his shoulder, the eldest son of the earl of Stamford, a Puritan peer. Both had been moved to take up arms against their king. Both were ready to confront, even imprison, MPs.

One of those turning up to take his place that day was William Prynne. He was a staunch Puritan – he had railed against stage plays, had lost his ears for slandering Queen Henrietta Maria, and had criticised Charles I's policies, arguing forcefully for the sovereignty of Parliament. Yet he was also among those who favoured a settlement; he yearned for peace. From the top of the stairs, Pride warned Prynne not to go any further. Prynne ignored him and carried on climbing until he reached Pride, who pushed him back down. 'By what authority and commission, and for what cause, they did thus violently seize on and pull him down from the House?' Prynne demanded to know. By way of answer, Pride showed him the soldiers standing by, armed with muskets, their matches already lit.[3] Cowed, Prynne was led to another part of the palace, under guard, to join the forty or so other MPs who had been gathered like swine. Over the next week, many more Members of Parliament were sent home by Pride, shuffling back through Westminster Hall, past all the little bookstalls, and off into the city or into their waiting coaches and home to the country. Others pusillanimously, or wisely, stayed away.

This shocking purging of Parliament, known to history as Pride's Purge, is merely the prologue to the drama that followed. For it was this radical, emboldened remnant, this tail of a Parliament – later known, derisively, as 'the Rump' – that declared itself 'the supreme power in this nation', above the House of Lords, above the king.[4] It was this 'clensed' Parliament – numbering only about a hundred MPs – that passed an act that enabled it to put the king of England, and Scotland, on trial for treason, leading to his conviction, death sentence and execution.[5] The Rump

Parliament then went on to abolish monarchy and the House of Lords, and usher in England's republic. For the next ten years, the country experienced the first and only republican rule it has ever known. As in many a tragedy, however, the protagonist who uses violent means fails to thrive. The political body that was born on that cold December morning was ambitious, but it was conceived in violence, delivered by the sword and branded, by many, as illegitimate.

The decade of kingless rule became possible that day, with Colonel Pride on the steps of Parliament. This beginning is the end of the longer story of conflict between king and Parliament. Many of the men Pride turned away on 6 December had been Members of the Commons since 1640 when Charles I, after eleven years of ruling without a Parliament (kings were allowed to do this, then), recalled them, hoping to raise money to fund war in his other kingdom, and native country, Scotland. Fighting on the northern side of the border had been triggered by Charles's tactless imposition of a new Book of Common Prayer in 1637: the Church of Scotland (the Kirk) did not want their liturgy dictated from Westminster, by a king they never saw, or by an archbishop of Canterbury, William Laud, whom they did not know. They did not want their forms of worship corrupted by the Anglican Church's taste for fuss and ceremony, which looked suspiciously Catholic, and they did not want bishops. To assert his authority, Charles mobilised troops. Back in St Stephen's Chapel in Whitehall, the newly recalled Members of Parliament took the opportunity to challenge Charles – and the rights of a king. Led by the committed parliamentarian John Pym, certain Members of the House were troubled by Charles's willingness to rule without Parliament, his immovable belief in his absolute and divine authority, and his unsettling readiness to fight in Scotland.[6]

In December 1641, Parliament presented Charles with a list of grievances about the state of the kingdom. It was long. Those behind this 'Grand Remonstrance', which included the forty-two-year-old Cambridge MP Oliver Cromwell, wanted Charles to get rid of those they believed to be malignant, corrupt counsellors, intent on sabotaging relations between king and people and destroying the English Church.[7] They worried about the influence of Charles's French, Catholic wife, Henrietta Maria, and they feared a Catholic plot. So they moved to strip Charles of a key royal prerogative: the power to raise an army. Yet, for Charles – as for all kings and queens before him – defending his kingdom was his duty; it was a promise he had made before God. The prospect of Parliament controlling the militia forced him to make a catastrophic mistake – the first of many. In January 1642, the king and about a hundred soldiers marched into St Stephen's Chapel, seeking to arrest John Pym and four of his troublemaking allies for treason. But the so-called traitors had got wind of the plan and fled through Whitehall's garden, into a waiting boat and up the river. And, as the news spread, the people of London turned against their king, rising up to protest what they saw as his violation of Parliament's privileges, and by extension their freedom.

No longer safe in his city, Charles fled Whitehall with Queen Henrietta Maria and three of their five children. Believing that they would soon be back, they packed little. Charles would soon have to request extra linen shirts from the Royal Wardrobe. He managed to retrieve the Great Seal, that precious little metal mould into which hot wax would be poured and turned into the very stamp of royal authority.[8] He fled to Windsor, then York, then Oxford. Parliament pushed through its militia bill, granting itself the power to muster forces of ordinary men in each English county. By the autumn of 1642, king and Parliament were at war. Both sides believed they were the guardians of the people's liberties and the English Church. Charles could not conceive of a king whose power was limited – then he would be 'but the Picture, but the Sign of a King' – and he believed that only chaos would come from disobedience and a rebellious Parliament.[9] But that this had ended in real conflict puzzled many. As the lawyer and MP Bulstrode Whitelocke recalled, the country 'insensibly slipped into this beginning of a civil war by one unexpected accident after another, as waves of the sea'.[10]

Battle after battle followed, across the kingdoms in places whose names are forever associated with the victories and losses of the Royalists (the long-locked cavaliers) and the parliamentarians (derided as 'roundheads' because of their short hair). First, in October 1642, was Edgehill, where 1,500 men were killed on a field. Locals soon reported seeing their ghosts and hearing their death groans. Then there was Marston Moor, in 1644, where Oliver Cromwell, now a rising military star, triumphed as the earl of Manchester's lieutenant-general in the Eastern Association army, joined by the Scottish army which had agreed to support the English parliamentarians. At Naseby, in 1645, Colonel Pride excelled and Henry Ireton's thigh was run through with a pike. In the middle of the wars, Henrietta Maria fled back to the continent, and to the Louvre in Paris, leaving her one-month-old daughter, Minette, in Exeter. All the while, the MPs sat on in St Stephen's Chapel, issuing Charles with proposals for settlement, directing the militia, passing laws that were never stamped with the Great Seal. And it was from within the Commons chamber that England's first standing, professional army – the New Model

Army – was created. This army, led indefatigably by its general Sir Thomas Fairfax – with the brilliant Oliver Cromwell as his deputy after 1645 – crushed the king's men.[11]

During those long and horrid years, the Palace of Whitehall stood largely cold and empty, apart from the white-hot Parliament house in its midst. It became increasingly dilapidated. The old masquing house, the queen's 'dancing barn', was torn down. The stained-glass windows in the chapel royal were stripped out.[12] In some of the palace's empty rooms and lodgings, former royal household staff continued to live, having nowhere else to go, while homeless families, seeking shelter, squatted in the dark corridors. In 1648, the Royalist newsbook *Mercurius Pragmaticus* reported that Thomas Fairfax himself had taken up residence in Whitehall, 'as if he meant to King it', along with his exhausted soldiers and sweating horses.[13] The palace was now a collection of musty smelling rooms that were once heavily perfumed and bustling with curly-haired nobility and richly dressed visitors. Anyone could wander into the presence chamber, and keep his hat on, and, why not, try out the throne. It was a 'Court without a Court', a 'Pallace without a Presence'.[14] Many of Charles I's splendid paintings and tapestries still adorned the damp walls. In the cockpit and revelling rooms, where jewels had once glittered in the candlelight and theatrical entertainments had awed princes, courtiers and ambassadors, painted panels and pulleys hung, useless. Where once the cries of gallants and liveried servants thronging at the palace gates could be heard, all was now 'as silent as midnight' and 'wrap'd up in the black mists of confusion, and desolation'.[15] Yet, throughout the 1640s, it was expected that the king, or at least *a* king, would return one day. The wars had set out to define, not abolish, monarchy. 'Though for a time we see White-hall / With Cobweb-hangings on the wall', the balladeer Martin Parker wrote, Charles will certainly, one day, 'enjoy his own again'.[16]

But Charles and his family never did return to live at Whitehall. At the end of 1646, after thousands of British lives had been lost, countless bodies maimed, women widowed and children orphaned, Charles was forced to surrender to the Scots. They handed him over to the English Parliament, who kept him in prison while they tried to reach a settlement. Meanwhile, Scotland began to doubt how the king was being treated, and Charles, captive in Carisbrooke Castle on the Isle of Wight, began to plot with and make false promises to the Scots in return for military help. This prompted another outbreak of bloody conflict in the summer of 1648. It was this second wave of civil war that convinced Henry Ireton, and other radicals in the New Model Army, that the only way to achieve peace was to bring 'capitall punishment' upon the king.[17] A formal treason trial would have the trappings of legitimacy, and if this could only come about through the purging of Parliament, then so be it. It was widely imagined that such a trial could, and probably would, end in Charles's execution – in regicide.

The next time Charles saw 'his own again' was on Saturday 20 January 1649, when he entered Westminster Hall to face sixty-eight appointed judges, seated on benches under the south window. Spectators crowded in at the other end of the hall and filled the public galleries above, some even teetering on the windowsills of the high gothic bays. The solicitor-general and chief prosecutor John Cook read out the charges. Charles was accused of levying war against his subjects, and of attempting 'to rule according to his Will, and to overthrow the Rights and Liberties of the People'. The king, now a defendant, sat in a red velvet chair, cloaked, clutching a cane, smiling. In defiance of the court's pretended power, he wore his tall black hat throughout. Those trying him also kept their hats on, for they no longer acknowledged his authority as king. At one point, the silver head of Charles's cane toppled off and rolled onto the floor. This was an 'ominous' sign, reported Gilbert Mabbott in his newsbook, *The Moderate*.[18]

Charles appeared three times in court, and three times he refused to answer the charge by pleading either innocent or guilty. He refused to acknowledge the authority of this court – a king would be judged by God, not his subjects. 'I would know by what power I am called hither . . . I would know by what authority,' he challenged, adding: 'Remember I am your King.'[19] Refusing to plead was tantamount to accepting a guilty verdict, and this meant that Charles would certainly be condemned to die. Charles knew this. He was either already preparing for martyrdom or hoping that the trial would collapse and the judges lose their nerve. They did not. On 27 January, the MP John Bradshaw, president of the court, read out the verdict. Charles was, Bradshaw pronounced, 'a Tyrant, Traitor, Murderer and Public Enemy to the good people of this Nation', and he was sentenced to death 'by the severing of his head from his body'.[20] He had reneged on his solemn promise, made at his coronation, to protect his subjects and, Bradshaw told him, if the bond between sovereign and subjects is broken, then 'farewell soveraignty'.[21] Fifty-nine MPs signed the parchment death warrant, including Oliver Cromwell, Henry Ireton, Lord Grey of Groby and Colonel Thomas Pride. And each of those fifty-nine sealed his black spidery signature with a bright red blob of wax.[22]

On 30 January, at two o'clock in the afternoon, Charles passed through the corridors of his former Whitehall home and entered the Banqueting House. He clambered out of a first-floor window onto a high scaffold draped in black cloth. It was bitterly cold and he wore two shirts underneath his cloak.[23] In the middle of the scaffold stood the axe and block. On seeing the block and how low he was being asked to stoop, Charles asked if it might have been a little higher. Colonels Hacker and Tomlinson, the supervisors of this grim ritual, stood by, along with two masked executioners. 'I am the martyr of the people,' Charles told the gentlemen of the scaffold, and anyone among the thousands of spectators who could hear him. 'Take care they do not put me to pain,' he said to Colonel Hacker, before asking the executioner, 'Does my hair trouble you?' He tucked his long, dark locks up inside his nightcap, and took off his cloak and doublet. He handed his George, the jewelled emblem of the Order of the Garter, to his chaplain, Dr William Juxon, with one word: 'Remember.' He then knelt down, laid his head on the block and stretched his arms out to the side. The executioner swung his axe; Charles's head fell to the floor, and took 'all Britain with him'.[24] He was, we remember, Scotland's king, and Ireland's too. Many in the crowd groaned, and some pushed forwards, seeking to soak up a drop of royal blood with their handkerchiefs. Charles's severed head was held aloft and shown to the stunned spectators.

This was a very public execution and, for those who staged it, legitimate for being so. A decade later, in 1660, Major-General Thomas Harrison, who had escorted Charles to London for his trial and signed the death warrant, defended the regicide when he said that 'the things that have been done, have been done upon the stage, in the sight of the Sun'.[25] The choice of Inigo Jones's classically inspired Banqueting House as the backdrop for Charles's last performance as king was a strategic one, for it was inside this glorious hall, first built for James I, that the Stuart kings had indulged in their most extravagant displays of monarchical power: Garter ceremonies, investitures, masques. And it was for this building that Peter Paul Rubens, commissioned by Charles, had painted the apotheosis of James I, Charles's father. In the central oval of the trabeated ceiling, an elderly James I, escorted to heaven by Justice in a flurry of crimson silk and chubby cherubs, still looks down on all visitors who are compelled by the hall's architecture to look up, and contemplate the divine right of kings. But the blow of the axe on that icy January day split open the idea of the sacred, divinely appointed and untouchable monarch.

The crowd that gathered outside the Banqueting House to gape at the fall of the king – and the monarchy – was mixed. Newsbook writers jostled with soldiers, courtiers, politicians and poets, and with men and women both curious and appalled. Philip Henry, a young man who had gone along to watch the beheading, was too far away to hear Charles I's words, but he saw the blow of the axe, and he heard 'such a Grone by the Thousands then present, as I never heard before & desire I may never hear again'.[26] Samuel Pepys, the great diarist, was fifteen years old when Charles I was killed. He skipped school that day to join the crowd, and was one of those who applauded the death of the tyrant king. 'The memory of the wicked shall rot,' he noted, quoting from Proverbs.[27] (Pepys would go on to serve the republic, working for the general-at-sea Edward Montagu – before both men switched sides.) The young poet Andrew Marvell, twenty-seven years old, may also have been outside the Banqueting House watching Charles's execution. In his most prophetic poem, written on Oliver Cromwell's return from fighting in Ireland in 1650, Marvell recalls the execution as 'that memorable hour', describing how Charles 'bowed his comely head / Down, as upon a bed', while soldiers stood round, clapping slowly.[28] Marvell, who had previously written an elegy on the death of a Royalist, Lord Francis Villiers (the duke of Buckingham's son), slain by a parliamentarian soldier, would go on to write panegyrics for Cromwell. Away from London, and abroad, men and women could read about the execution in one of the many newsbooks – the proto-newspapers of the time. In the small parish of Earls Colne in Essex, the Puritan clergyman Ralph Josselin confessed to his diary how his 'tears were not restrained at the passages about his death'. But for many God-fearing Puritans like Josselin, such upside-downness was all part of God's plan: 'The Lord hath some great thing to do, fear and tremble at it, oh England,' he wrote.[29]

Oliver Cromwell, the man who would go on to build England's republic, and then transform and lead it as Lord Protector, was not among the thousands of people gathered for the spectacle. At the time of Charles's death, Cromwell was apparently praying in a room in Whitehall, accompanied by Thomas Fairfax and other leading army officers. He did supposedly pay his respects later, however, when he went to visit Charles's body, which lay in a closed coffin in the Banqueting House. 'Cruel necessity,' Cromwell is said to have muttered, before stealing away.[30] It is hard to be sure exactly what Cromwell thought of Pride's Purge and the way the trial of the King had come about – the nature of Cromwell's private feelings is one of the great mysteries of the period – but he certainly believed that God had witnessed against Charles on the battlefield, and that the Lord was with them and had secured their victory for a purpose. As he wrote to Colonel Robert Hammond, who was in charge of guarding Charles I in Carisbrooke Castle in the autumn of 1648: God's 'presence hath been amongst us, and by the light of his countenance we have prevailed'.[31]

A few days after the execution, Charles's head was crudely stitched back on to his neck and his body embalmed and removed to St James's Palace, while Parliament decided where and how to bury him.[32] Even in death – perhaps more in death than in life – the body of an anointed king was (and still is, *pace* Elizabeth II) alluring, and its resting place, Parliament knew, would soon become a site for mourners and pilgrims. The former king could not be denied all dignity. He was buried in the royal vault in St George's Chapel, Windsor, the 'cradle' of England's kings as the poet John Denham had called it. Beyond the vault, the castle was now a squalid army lodging.[33]

This book is about what happened in England, Scotland and Ireland after the execution of Charles I. It tells the story of the lives of those politicians and soldiers who, once Charles was dead and the scaffold dismantled, retreated to Whitehall to work out how to rule a country without a king. It is also a book about those who resisted what was happening – including Charles I's son and heir (the future Charles II) plotting his revenge from exile in Europe – as well as those who wanted England to be even more radical, such as the fiercely intellectual poet and government employee John Milton.

At the same time, many men and women adapted to their new world and seized the opportunities and changes the 1650s offered. The Polish émigré Samuel Hartlib, for instance, became renowned for advocating reform, enterprise and innovation in everything from agriculture to banking. Charles I's favourite masque writer, William Davenant, staged England's first operas in the back of his London home, Rutland House. Women, too, found new roles and voices. At Swarthmoor Hall in Lancashire, Margaret Fell hosted spiritual gatherings for men and women who, it was said, shook and trembled during their meetings. Feared by the authorities and scoffed at as 'made up out of the dregs of the common people', these religious radicals – dubbed the Quakers – numbered sixty thousand by 1660 and really rattled the authorities.[34]

While politicians and army officers in Westminster argued with each other and among themselves about what a republic should look like, and what liberty of conscience really meant, English troops were sent to defend the regime in Ireland and Scotland, and the navy engaged the Dutch and the Spanish in battles at sea. They failed to seize Hispaniola from the Spanish but conquered Jamaica instead. Luxury goods from Asia and the Americas, meanwhile, flooded into London's markets; people shopped for silks, discovered the health benefits of drinking chocolate and enjoyed drinking coffee – and talking politics – in the city's new fashionable coffee houses. In Oxford, meanwhile, a group of young, enquiring scientists – Robert Hooke, Robert Boyle, Christopher Wren – began to meet and experiment, committed to scrutinising the world in new ways.

By the end of the 1650s, Cromwell was dead, his son Richard had abdicated and England's republican experiment, which had always struggled to secure legitimacy, fell apart. On 1 May 1660, Parliament voted to restore the monarchy and crown Charles II king. The events that brought Charles II back were swift and unexpected. If Cromwell had not died suddenly in 1658, and if his son had been different, or acted differently, then it is possible that the Stuart dynasty would never have been restored. Only weeks before Charles II was invited to return to England, many still thought that a restoration was inconceivable. The republican theorist James Harrington, for example, believed that even if the king were to return, it would not last. For him, and he was not alone, monarchy no longer suited England; things had changed. For the men and women who have left us vivid traces of their lives in diaries, letters, books and pamphlets, this period was certainly not an 'interregnum'.

England's republic – and it was England's, imposed on Scotland and Ireland – was short-lived. Its impact on British monarchy, politics, religion and culture, and on the story the British tell about themselves, however, has been lasting. Despite the notoriety of the decade's protagonist Oliver Cromwell, the republic is a period that history has generally suppressed, assigned to aberration, misrepresented or chosen to forget.[35] Yet the very survival of the monarchy has much to do with the fact that it was abolished by an act of Parliament in 1649. No one has wanted to repeat the constitutional confusion and conflicts that characterised the 1650s; instead stability and custom (oh, how Milton hated the tyranny of custom) have become tightly woven into Britain's cultural fabric. The republican experiment was dogged by the army coup that, in December 1648, barred the doors against elected MPs. It was not the last time in this period that soldiers would send MPs packing, showing their contempt for Parliament. The sovereignty of Parliament can still cause conflict between the Commons and the executive, the government: Brexit was a case in point. Today, Charles III is a constitutional monarch, but there are still moments when the royal prerogative makes the headlines. The dissolution of the Fixed-term Parliaments Act in 2022 means Charles III has regained the prerogative to dissolve and summon Parliament, albeit on ministerial advice. Certain bills still require

Crown consent, again albeit on advice, before they can begin their passage through the Commons and the Lords.

As for Britain's monarchy, just as the stitches fixing Charles I's severed head to his body could not hide the blow of the axe, the scars of this kingless decade are still there. Pull a little, look closely: the fabric is delicate. When Charles II was crowned in 1661, the dazzling, confident display of the 'restored' rather than the 'new' king clutching his freshly made regalia, and of his winding entourage (many of whom had been supporters of Oliver Cromwell), clad in silken robes, had a self-consciousness about it, and that quality has not gone away; the architects of Charles II's coronation knew that monarchy was not the only form of government, and that rebellion could raise its head again. Since then, of course, the political power of kings has been snuffed out, replaced by increasingly visible pomp and pageantry which enable Britain to tell a story about continuity, tradition and stability, connecting the country to a particular version of its history, a version in which the republic was a blip, an interregnum, a failure. We know – the current royal family certainly knows – that monarchy could vanish and melt away like Prospero's airy masques. Still, the majority consents to its presence, and as a nation, if not necessarily individually, Britain performs this assent at each royal wedding, jubilee, birth, death and coronation. Before the execution of Charles I and the period of the republic, however, the idea that a people *consented* to a monarch was radical, an idea advanced by the likes of John Milton and contested by those who argued, conventionally, that monarchs were divinely ordained. It was the nineteenth-century constitutional historian Walter Bagehot who pointed out that Britain's attachment to kings and queens was sentimental – irrational, even.[36]

Today's constitutional monarchy has its roots in the 1650s, when the questions of the power and prerogative of a single person, and of their relationship with the body of representatives – Parliament – and of the legitimacy of hereditary power, were debated and picked apart, endlessly. These were debates that constitute the greatest drama of the 1650s. Some of the best scenes on which we can eavesdrop are those played out in the Commons chamber – heated, exhausting, exhilarating and serious debates held long into the night, in flickering candlelight in old St Stephen's Chapel, minuted in the Commons journal, recorded by the clerk or a diarist, or described in a letter to be sent overseas. Sovereignty, single-person rule, one chamber or two, state involvement with the Church, religious toleration and liberty of conscience – these ideas and ideals drove men (and some women), and divided them, as did the perceived legitimacy of institutions and their rituals and symbols. It was in this decade that the emotional pull of monarchy was both powerfully articulated and robustly challenged, and in new and lasting ways. Distinctive and diverse ideas for a lasting republican settlement and what defined civil and spiritual liberty – and how these could be guaranteed in a government – were diligently developed and widely disseminated. Alongside the threads of continuity and in among the repeated pattern of royal rituals and customs in British national life, these alternative threads still run.

There, too, presiding over the seventeenth century and this decade in particular, is the scrutinising, restless Puritan mind and conscience, searching and rifling for meaning and intention, looking for God's purpose, making sense of the Bible. Out of this yearning came the diary, the autobiography and the biography – the kinds of primary source that make writing about this period so intimate and moving, sources full of introspection and storytelling, of protracted reflection on and justification of an individual's life, a life both buttressed and buffeted by providential thinking, and touched by politics and matters of state. We hear, loudly, voices that sound immediate and recognisable: confessional, agonising, doubting, mourning, self-justifying or politically robust and engaged, urgent, cynical and satirical, mocking or challenging. We also hear many voices that are strange and more remote: prophetic cries or apocalyptic ecstasies, declarations that England was an elect nation (what about Scotland, Wales or Ireland?), singled out by God, the chosen site for Christ's much-anticipated second coming – a belief shared for a while by the republic's head of state (the first commoner ever to hold this office), Oliver Cromwell.

What follows is a year-by-year account of the 1650s: a biography of a daring and unprecedented decade that deserves to be written about and understood as a distinct entity. Events moved so fast in this period that something cataclysmic happened each year, something that would thrust the republic and its people in a new direction. In some years, with the impact of sudden, unexpected reversals, it must have seemed that time itself was running backwards. Whichever way it ran, time in the 1650s was experienced intensely by ordinary men and women. Some felt they were living through biblical time and were about to witness the visions from the book of Revelation. Astrologers looked to the stars to predict what would happen during the next twelve months, publishing their readings in eagerly anticipated almanacs that sold in their thousands. Men and women began to record time in a new way, with the rise of the diary, carefully recording exact dates.

Above all, everyone knew that they were living through a particular kind of time, that they were witnessing profound historical change. Regardless of where their political sympathies lay, men and women in their conversations and writings reached for images of excess, or biblical images, or coined new words entirely. The

Royalist poet and clergyman Robert Herrick, turfed out of his Devon vicarage for his courtly connections, declared that he was writing 'of times trans-shifting'. For the poet Katherine Philips, married to a parliamentarian but loyal to her king, it was a 'scorching age'. And for a group of Londoners who believed Christ's second coming was imminent and wrote to warn Parliament, these were the 'overturning, overturning, overturning dayes'.[37]

I : REPUBLIC

Into Another World

1649

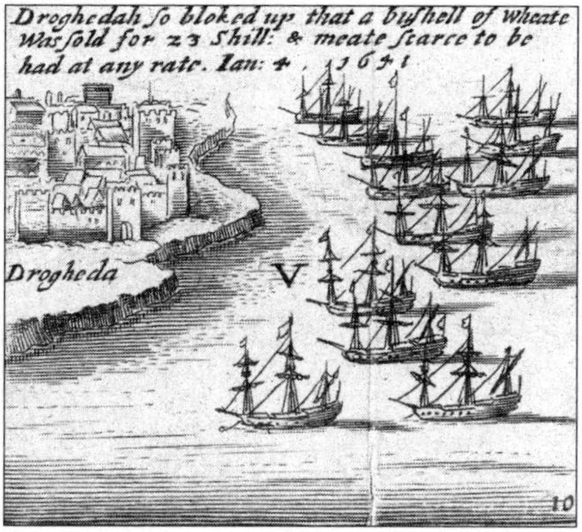
Droghedah so bloked up that a bushell of Wheate
Was sold for 23 Shill: & meate scarce to be
had at any rate. Ian: 4 . 1641
Drogheda
V
10

Old England now is grown perfectly new,
and we in another world.

Mercurius Pragmaticus,
12–19 June 1649

For some, 1649 was the first year of a new-found freedom. At the Royal Exchange in London, Charles I's statue had been beheaded, and now bore the inscription, 'Exit the tyrant, the last of kings, in the first year of England's restored liberty.'[1] For others, 1649 would always be the 'year of slaughter', and a time of mourning.[2] Loyal subjects predicted God's wrath. 'You must expect to have the thunderbolts of Gods anger throwne down upon you,' one such patriot told the MPs who had pushed through the king's execution.[3] The spilling of royal blood would not, he predicted, go unavenged. Even those who did not admire Charles I warned against his death. At the end of December 1648, the young and slightly wild prophet Elizabeth Poole, who had grown up among the bustling bookstalls around St Paul's, was visited by visions of how to cure the sick nation. Parliament had just heard the first reading of the act that would enable the king's trial. Senior army officers, some wrestling with their consciences, had summoned Elizabeth, and had listened to her. By all means bring the king to trial, she told them, but 'touch not his person'.[4]

No thunderbolts appeared to punish the men who had dared to touch the Lord's anointed. For those at the helm of England's new ship of state, 1649 was spent forging and legitimising a kingless regime, and defeating those who threatened it. It was an extraordinary year that saw England's ancient constitution of king, Lords and Commons – what the poet Andrew Marvell called the 'great work of time' – definitively rejected, and a rebellious Ireland overwhelmed by Oliver Cromwell.[5]

A week after Charles's execution outside Whitehall, the purged Parliament – that 'relique of a House of Commons' as the philosopher Thomas Hobbes called it – resolved that the office of a king was 'unnecessary, burdensome, and dangerous to the Liberty, Safety, and publick Interest of the People of this Nation'.[6] Parliament had already declared, the day before, that the House of Lords was also 'useless and dangerous, and ought to be abolished', and they now set about preparing the necessary acts of Parliament that would rid English government of hereditary right, in monarch or peer.[7] Any person who dared to proclaim Charles I's son, Prince Charles, or anyone else as England's lawful king would be guilty of treason. They had already squirrelled away the crown jewels, and locked them up.[8] On 14 February, the MPs elected their first council of state. Instead of a king and his privy council, this group of forty-one nominated men would be the country's executive body, responding to the House of Commons, and headed by a rotating president. John Bradshaw, the earnest, successful judge from Cheshire who had presided over the trial and delivered the death sentence, was elected as the council's first president. (Cromwell had initially taken the chair.) He was rewarded handsomely with land and properties. To his friend John Milton, Bradshaw was the epitome of integrity and fairness, his name synonymous with liberty itself. To his Royalist enemies, he was doing the devil's work.[9]

In May, an act of Parliament declared that 'the People of England, and of all the Dominions and Territories thereunto belonging, are and shall be, and are hereby Constituted, Made, Established, and Confirmed to be a Commonwealth and Free-State', which shall be governed by the 'representatives of the People in Parliament', 'the Supreme Authority of this Nation'.[10]

'Commonwealth' and 'free state' were the words with political currency that they chose to denote a state where people were not subject to a monarch. 'Commonwealth' carried an emotional charge, too, for it was a word used to describe a community or communities brought together by a principle of shared well-being and general prosperity. A 'free state', meanwhile, compared to monarchy, would encourage men 'to the study of wisdom, truth, justice', for those in government were 'chosen by their fitnesse, gifts, and abilities', and not their titles. Everything would be done 'for the general profit and welfare of the people'.[11] Within a year, prompted by an idea of Henry Ireton (he who was behind Pride's Purge), it was expected that all men over the age of eighteen in England, Wales and Ireland should sign the oath of engagement, and pledge their loyalty to this new Commonwealth.

The Commonwealth's council of state balanced soldiers, politicians, peers. It was a mixed group: not everyone shared the same feelings about the regicide, or agreed about what exactly the new republic should look like. Among the forty-one councillors nominated were the highest army officers, Sir Thomas Fairfax and Oliver Cromwell. Thirty-four councillors were also Members of Parliament, including Cromwell. Five were peers from the dissolved House of Lords, including the ageing Jacobean courtier Philip Herbert, fourth earl of Pembroke, nephew of the Elizabethan sonneteer Philip Sidney. In peacetime, Pembroke had entertained Charles I every summer in his Wiltshire home, Wilton House, showing off his collection of Van Dycks and Titians. But Pembroke became a parliamentarian and, as constable of Windsor Castle, had twice held Charles I prisoner. Pembroke, however, had refused to sit in judgement of Charles at his trial.[12] Similarly, Thomas Fairfax, who had triumphed on the battlefield, had withdrawn from the king's trial. Described by Charles I as the 'brutish generall' of the

New Model Army, which he had led from the age of thirty-two, Fairfax remembered the day of Charles's execution as 'the fatal day', and a day that, he hoped, time would blot out entirely.[13] Neither had the lawyer and MP Bulstrode Whitelocke signed the death warrant or watched the execution; he was, he said, 'troubled att the death of the King', and stayed at home all day.[14] Whitelocke had once written music for a royal masque performed at Whitehall, and a coranto which Queen Henrietta Maria reportedly loved.[15] But he was also a pragmatist, and he accepted his seat on the council of state. He continued to work for the republic all through the 1650s, sharing his work, pricks of conscience and private joys and griefs in journals and notebooks – which constitute one of our most valuable sources from the period.[16]

Others who might have expected to be on the council were not offered a seat. Henry Ireton, for example, who had argued so powerfully that Charles should be brought to justice was not given a place. Many MPs loathed him for having masterminded Pride's Purge, and he was too close to some of the most radical members of the army. On the other hand, the regicide Henry Marten, an MP and one of those 'fiery spirits' who had argued early on in the wars that Charles, and indeed monarchy, should be brought down, was given a seat.[17] Marten is remembered, perhaps unfairly, as a womaniser and a drinker. His contemporary the brilliant biographer John Aubrey said he was a 'lover of pretty girles'.[18] He allegedly (and almost certainly apocryphally) flicked ink at Cromwell, like a cheeky schoolboy, as they both signed Charles away to his death.[19]

The councillors of state agreed to meet daily, at 4 p.m. in Derby House, Westminster, with its pretty gardens running down to the bank of the Thames. They ordered a new mace for themselves, which would not be topped with a coronet, orb and cross, but with a design of English oak leaves and an acorn – symbols of the nation rather than of the monarchy.[20] They soon asked to sit in Whitehall Palace, instead of Derby House. As the executive branch of government, the council of state needed to be where power in England had long been: at Whitehall. Once there, they used Queen Henrietta Maria's presence chamber as their meeting room. 'We turned ourselves into a Commonwealth,' MP and councillor of state Sir Arthur Hesilrige said.[21] Hesilrige was another who had qualms about the legitimacy of the king's trial, and he refused to swear the oath of engagement. But he took his seat on the council and would go on to become one of the republic's loudest defenders. What exact form this Commonwealth would take was not clear. 'Everyone almost . . . endeavoured or expected to have his private fancy put in motion,' recalled Bulstrode Whitelocke.[22] To observers, it was troubling that those men whose job it now was to govern and to rebuild confidence in Parliament were at odds: 'If the workmen differ,' the newsbook *The Moderate Intelligencer* reported in February, then 'the building is not like to go on so fast, nor to be made so strong, as otherwise it might.'[23]

Certainly there were some workmen who had been preparing for a kingless constitution since before Charles I's trial and execution, whatever their private beliefs and scruples might have been. In late December 1648, Oliver Cromwell and Bulstrode Whitelocke, along with Whitelocke's friend and fellow lawyer Sir Thomas Widdrington (who was also Fairfax's brother-in-law), and William Lenthall (long-standing Speaker of the House of Commons, also a lawyer), had met occasionally in private to discuss a 'settlement' for England that did not include Charles, or even a king at all. The men, Whitelocke tells us, 'spake their opinions freely and faithfully'. On one occasion Cromwell received Whitelocke in Whitehall, where he lay 'in one of the Kings rich beddes'.[24] When they shared their ideas with some MPs, Henry, duke of Gloucester (Charles I's youngest son) was put forward as a possible successor on the grounds that he was young and malleable; others were 'wholly ag[ains]t having any king att all'.[25] Whitelocke describes staying up late with Widdrington, coming up with proposals and revolutionary constitutional ideas. Both Whitelocke and Widdrington were moderate parliamentarians, and not vehemently anti-monarchical, but England was in uncharted waters. Although it was possible in the early days of 1649 that the imminent trial of the king might *not* end with his death, or with the subsequent abolition of monarchy, they were prepared to imagine this scenario. The civil wars did not set out to kill the king and bring down monarchy but, by their end, a republican settlement was not only entertained but also, by some, desired. A full three weeks before Charles I's execution, a treatise called *The armies vindication* argued that monarchy was the worst form of government, and a free state the 'best'.[26] In March, it was Whitelocke who was charged with preparing the declaration that would establish, and defend, England as a 'free state'.[27]

Old England was put to death with foresight, and some ceremony. Parliament reworked familiar symbols and customs as it sought a legitimate transformation for England. Immediately after abolishing monarchy Thomas Widdrington and Bulstrode Whitelocke, as lord commissioners of the Great Seal of England, brought the seal, wrapped carefully in its embroidered purse, into the House of Commons, and laid it on a table.[28] This was the 1643 replica of the Great Seal that Charles I had kept close to him after he had fled Whitehall in 1642, but which Parliament later seized and destroyed when Charles surrendered. Before the chamber of silent MPs, a workman proceeded to smash it up, and then handed the broken pieces – splintered shards of Charles I's body – back to

Widdrington and Whitelocke for them to dispose of. Such ritual destruction was not in itself new; James I had taken a hammer to Elizabeth I's Great Seal to mark the beginning of his reign and his authority. But the Great Seal of the Commonwealth was something radically different. It conferred parliamentary, and not kingly, authority on writs, patents and official documents. In anticipation of this moment, before the trial in early January, a committee led by the fiery Henry Marten had come up with the design. Parliament's chief engraver, Thomas Simon, who had struck many a victory medal depicting Thomas Fairfax, had already been granted the commission, and was paid £200.[29] On one side, following the committee's design, Simon had engraved an image of the House of Commons in session, led by the Commons Speaker William Lenthall, whose office, when there was no king or no other executive, was by default the highest in the land. Coiled around the circumference of the seal were the bold, revolutionary words, 'In the First Year of Freedom, by God's Blessing restored', and the date 1648. (At this time the Julian calendar was followed and the new year changed legally on 25 March, not 1 January.) On the other side of the seal, Simon had engraved a map of England, Wales and Ireland, and the islands of Guernsey and Jersey, with some ships sailing to and fro. Scotland was not yet subsumed into England's republic so the archipelago looks, to modern eyes, decapitated.

The new seal clearly emphasised Parliament's authority, as a body of men who represented the people who lived in this Commonwealth. Gone – smashed – was the image, and the authority, of a king. At this point, Thomas Widdrington's conscience got the better of him, according to his friend, Whitelocke, and he chose to decline his reappointment as commissioner of this new Great Seal.[30] Whitelocke also resisted at first (so he said), but his excuses were dismissed by the House and he was duly sworn in as one of the keepers of the seal, along with fellow lawyers John Lisle and Richard Keble. With ceremony, care and reverence, they carried the new seal away and locked it up. All of the 'kingdoms old', as the poet Andrew Marvell would soon write, had literally been cast 'into another mould'.[31]

Whitehall needed renovating and clearing. The council of state needed to decide what to do with what Charles I had referred to as 'my Household stuffe which I leave behind me'.[32] Squatting families who had set up home in the empty palace during the wars were mostly evicted. New locks needed to be fitted, plumbing mended and the garden replanted for the use of the council, whose members worked, relaxed and ate in Whitehall, occasionally feasting on venison slain in neighbouring St James's Park. Edward Carter had been surveyor of the works at Whitehall since 1643, once the king had left, and he presided over returning the palace to a seat of legitimate, if novel, power. While the council requested a degree of grandeur, the orders were to keep the costs down. The timber used for repairs was felled in Windsor Forest, and the lead for new pipes was recycled from Windsor Castle.[33]

Immediately after Charles's death, his possessions had been kept under lock and key. Some royal plate had been destroyed, but the king's clothes, books, furniture and paintings were preserved. Anxious that the goods might be 'spoiled and imbezled, or made away with without advantage to the State, if due care be not had', all of the royal family's possessions were inventoried and valued. The council of state decided that they would keep, for their own use, up to £10,000 worth of royal goods. Two years later, however, in 1651, this figure had crept up to £20,000. Eventually they decided that they needed to retain £53,000 worth.[34] Necessity competed with greed. As Whitehall became staffed and populated again, bustling with committees, staff and their families, beds needed bed linen and lofty chambers needed curtains, carpets and tapestries to keep them warm. There were also, of course, the king's palaces and estates. It wasn't just the Palace of Whitehall that was retained for the use of Commonwealth men: Somerset House, St James's Palace, Hampton Court, Greenwich and Windsor were also reserved.[35]

The rest of the royal family's remaining property and goods were put up for sale. The money raised would settle the vast debts accumulated by the late king and pay the army. A sum of £30,000 would be earmarked for the navy, to protect the island's shores from rebel Royalist ships that were cruising around, such as those under the command of Charles II's cousin, Prince Rupert of the Rhine. On 4 July, Parliament passed an act for the sale of 'the goods and personal estate of the late King, Queen and Prince'.[36] Charles's household objects, clothing, fabrics, sculptures, tapestries and paintings were made available to anyone who could afford to buy them. Items deemed saleable abroad for higher prices, on account of their antiquity or rarity, were handed to merchants and loaded onto ships. Lists of creditors were drawn up to whom possessions and paintings would be given instead of money owed: tailors, drapers, musicians became owners of Leonardos and Titians. The great hall and additional rooms in Somerset House were then used to display the items on sale to the general public. The sight must have been astounding. Shrewd buyers and casual visitors had the chance, for the first time, to admire and acquire treasures from the Royal Collection – sculptures, paintings, tapestries – hitherto hidden inside the palaces and royal apartments.

The sale went on for two years, and was not officially closed until early 1654. Keen buyers could go back for several return visits, and many did, including foreign visitors. The young Dutchman Lodewijck Huygens admired Van Dyck's portrait of Charles I mounted on a white horse, available for £150.[37] Some art was bought for private homes; other works were passed on, and taken out of England. Some buyers sought royal relics, or images of the king, or his clothes; others were keen art collectors themselves. The Dutch painter Emanuel de Critz bought Bernini's bust of Charles I and installed it in his house in Austin Friars, surrounded by works by Titian, Giorgione and Correggio that de Critz also snapped up.[38] Major Edward Bass, one of the king's creditors, bought Raphael's prized *Holy Family*, which Charles I had bought from the duke of Gonzaga in Mantua. Bass sold it on to the Spanish diplomat Alonso de Cárdenas; it wound up in Madrid in Philip IV's collection. Bass also bought Charles I's coronation robes.[39] The republican army officer Colonel John Hutchinson spent £2,000 on paintings at the sale. He bought Titian's erotic *Pardo Venus* for £600, before selling it to the French ambassador Bordeaux a few years later for £1,200; other paintings he kept for himself, to hang in his country house.[40] Thomas Bagley, the king's former glazier, acquired Correggio's *Education of Cupid*, worth £800.[41] John Boulton was a London goldsmith who spent thousands at the sales, but on bits and pieces: gloves, purses, fans.[42]

The crown jewels, those 'Reliques of Superstition' saturated with the belief in sacred monarchy, were not for sale.[43] In 1643, the House of Commons ordered that the regalia – St Edward's crown, the sceptres, orb, spurs – should be inventoried and locked up. As they were preparing the inventory, irreverent Henry Marten and the parliamentarian and poet George Wither had supposedly taken out what Marten called the 'toys and trifles' of the iron chest in which they were stored. Wither had dressed up in the robes and crown and 'marched about the room in stately garb'.[44] In 1649, the crown jewels were valued again and then passed on by Parliament to the trustees of the sale (George Wither was one) with the orders that they should 'be totally broken; and that they melt down the Gold and Silver of them; and . . . sell the Jewels for the best Advantage of the Commonwealth'.[45] Rubies, emeralds and diamonds that had once glittered in crowns at coronations were stripped out and put on sale. The twelfth-century silver and gilt coronation spoon, into which the holy oil is poured when a new monarch is anointed, escaped being broken and melted down: it was not considered valuable enough. Clement Kinnersley, formerly Charles I's yeoman of the removing wardrobe before becoming keeper of the state's wardrobe, bought it for sixteen shillings and kept it.[46] At the Restoration, Kinnersley returned this spoon, the oldest object among the regalia, to Charles II. It has been used at every coronation since 1661.

The history of England's monarchy was woven into much of the stuff put on sale, into the fabric and furnishings: the initials of Anne Boleyn embroidered on a cushion, Henry VIII's enormous tapestries, Mary I's coronation dress, Elizabeth I's bed hangings. The memory of monarchy was preserved privately, individually. The Commonwealth needed money, but putting the goods up for sale was a powerful and irreversible accomplice to the political act of abolishing kingship. These goods were understood to belong to the state and therefore should benefit the state, both its politicians and its people. This big royal jumble sale removed hundreds of works of art from the clutches of the elite and put them in the hands of ordinary men and women who could, if they were able to afford it, own and appreciate paintings, tapestries and sculptures. In this way the sale was a great act of democratisation. It has sometimes been seen as indicative of the republican regime's attitude towards the visual arts – uncultured, destructive, boorish. With the passing of this act, one of the most extensive and valuable art collections of the time was broken up and dispersed, carelessly. Such a view is based on the clichéd and persistent view of the period's Puritanism: Puritans did not value or enjoy art, or music, or fine houses and fabrics. This too readily collapses a religious persuasion into a political one. It was possible, of course, to be a Puritan who had fought against the king but did like music and poetry (Cromwell was one of them, Fairfax another). It was also possible to be a Puritan who felt ambivalent about images but revered monarchy. It is easy, too, to overlook the forces of necessity. In a bankrupt nation reeling from years of war, it would have been bizarre for the council of state to have left palaces stuffed full of treasures to simply gather dust, or to wholly appropriate them for their own use and pleasure. Monarchy was not in abeyance. It had been abolished.

There were those who were hoping for something even more revolutionary for England. A faction known as the Levellers, who had emerged from the New Model Army, argued that the wars and the toppling of Charles I should open the way to a more thorough reformation of England's political, social and religious landscape. They railed against both the illegitimacy and the hesitancy of the new regime: 1649 was, for them, the 'yeer of the peoples pretended freedom, but intended slavery'.[47] For the committed Leveller and prolific pamphleteer John Lilburne – 'Freeborn John' with his neat moustache – and for many of his fellow soldiers who had risked their lives at Edgehill and

Marston Moor and watched friends die, Parliament, and not a king, should be the supreme authority in the land. But Lilburne and his fellow Levellers also wanted an agreement, a written contract, between the people and their representatives. They wanted annual elections to Parliament, and they wanted to extend the suffrage to all men over twenty-one. (To extend this to women was a revolutionary step too far.) They believed that all people, rich or poor, should have a say in how they were governed. During the discussions known as the 'Putney debates', held during the autumn of 1647 at the New Model Army's headquarters in St Mary's Church, Putney, on the south bank of the Thames, the 'valiant and faithful' Leveller Colonel Thomas Rainborowe uttered the famous words:

> I think that the poorest he that is in England hath a life to live, as the greatest he; and therefore truly, Sir, I think it's clear, that every man that is to live under a government ought first by his own consent to put himself under that government; and I do think that the poorest man in England is not bound in a strict sense to that government that he hath not had a voice to put himself under.[48]

Such calls for democracy may seem uncontroversial to us; not so in seventeenth-century England. Even those army grandees – Oliver Cromwell, as lieutenant-general, and his son-in-law Henry Ireton among them – charged with listening to the demands of their Leveller soldiers at Putney, and who had some sympathy with them, did not believe that *all* men that 'hath a breath and being' had the right to vote, for they did not own land: 'No person hath a right to this, that hath not a permanent fixed interest in this kingdom,' Ireton stated. For if you extend to all men the right to vote, why should these men not also claim the right to own land and redistribute property? 'The consequence of this rule tends to anarchy, must end in anarchy,' warned Cromwell.[49]

Levellers like Lilburne were religious Independents. This they shared with Oliver Cromwell. They were fiercely against the idea of a national Church, which is what the Presbyterian faction in Parliament wanted. Both groups were strongly Puritan, and united by their desire for deep reform of the Church in England and their criticism of Charles I and his rather Catholic style. Neither wanted bishops. But Independents went further, for they did not want any state involvement in religion at all – no church hierarchy and no guidelines on how to worship. They argued for liberty of conscience for all kinds of Protestants (but not Catholics), and for the right of parishioners to choose their own ministers. Their cries for tolerance were bold, and alarming, for the time.

At the end of 1648, Levellers' voices joined Ireton's as they called for the defeated Charles I to be brought to account. But they wanted his trial, and any future settlement of the country, to be ratified and legitimised by a Parliament that would properly represent the English people, and would fully adopt Leveller demands and reforms, as published in their 'Agreements of the People'.[50] In early 1649, John Lilburne felt betrayed by those he thought were on his side, but who now looked powerful and comfortable on the new council of state, and seemed reluctant to act. He wrote that 'that which perplexed me most was that I found promotion and promised hopes of gain had very much changed the principles, and cooled the zeal of three or four of my familiar acquaintance and friends, that not long before had been the valiantest, stoutest, ablest champions for England's liberties and freedoms that I know'.[51]

In February Lilburne presented his petition, *England's New Chains*, co-written with fellow Levellers William Walwyn and

Richard Overton, to Parliament. For Lilburne, the 'liberties and freedoms' fought for at such cost on England's battlefields were now threatened by a monstrous council of state that, once it got a taste for power, could easily become as 'absolute and unaccountable' as an anointed king. 'For where is that good, or where is that liberty so much pretended, so deerly purchased?' Lilburne opined.[52] Lilburne singled out Oliver Cromwell, and questioned his ambition over his revolutionary zeal. 'O Cromwell! whither art thou aspiring?' asked Lilburne.[53]

During the first half of 1649, the Levellers sent the government into a panic. According to the turncoat journalist Marchamont Nedham, the giddy activity of this 'hot-headed rabble' jeopardised the fledgling republic and put it into 'an utter Impossibility of Setling'.[54] The Leveller soldiers' distrust was made worse by the fact that the council was now preparing to send them back to war, to quash Royalist rebellion in Ireland. Across the country, tired troops began to mutiny, refusing to mobilise for Ireland unless they were paid and the terms articulated in their 'Agreements of the People' promised. At the end of March, on the publication of the second part of his angry and 'highly seditious' *England's New Chains*, Lilburne was dragged from his bed at his lodgings in Winchester House, hauled before the council of state and then thrown into the Tower. 'You have no other way to deal with these men, but to break them in pieces,' Cromwell is alleged to have said (by Lilburne). 'If you do not breake them, they will break you.'[55]

In May, the Levellers were decisively broken. During the night of 14 May, in the small wool-trading town of Burford in Oxfordshire, Thomas Fairfax and Oliver Cromwell rounded on more than a thousand mutinous soldiers, who were marching north across Salisbury plain towards Oxford. Cromwell locked nearly four hundred rebels in Burford's riverside church; others escaped into the night.[56] A few days later, the ringleaders Corporal Perkins, Corporal John Church, Cornet Henry Denne and Cornet James Thompson were taken outside to be shot, one by one, against the church wall. Corporal Church apparently stretched his arms out and looked his executioners in the eye before they fired, showing no fear or remorse. Denne, however, showed such penitence and readiness to die that Fairfax pardoned him on the spot. Only earlier that day, Parliament had passed a new Treason Act. Where once it had been treasonous to imagine the death of the king, now it was high treason to declare Parliament as 'Tyrannical, Usurped or Unlawful', to 'Plot, Contrive or Endeavor to stir up or raise Force against the present Government', or for anyone to 'stir up any Mutiny' in the army.[57]

Those executed in Burford churchyard, in front of their fellow mutineers who stood watching from on top of the church roof, were victims of Fairfax's and Cromwell's – and the government's – reaction to the perceived scale of army unrest. It had been provoked, so they believed, by Leveller leaders, from Lilburne's prison cell in the Tower. It was a 'sad spectacle', Fairfax reported back to Speaker Lenthall, but it was mutiny 'of so high a nature' that it risked ruining 'Parliament and Kingdom'.[58] It is interesting that he used the word 'Kingdom'. The Burford mutiny is often cited as an example of the regime's willingness to use illegitimate force, with the setting of a countryside church adding to the horror. Inside the church, one of the rebel soldiers foresaw the tragedy's place in history. Into the stone font, Anthony Selden carved his name and the words '1649. Prisner'. The font is still standing, as is Burford Priory on the other side of the high street, which belonged to Speaker Lenthall and which housed his art collection.

It was not just the men who were moved to protest. Just a few weeks before, early in the morning of 23 April, five hundred women, 'lusty lasses of the levelling party', clad in sea-green dresses, their colour of revolution, gathered outside Westminster Hall. There they presented their *Humble Petition of divers wel-affected Women*, calling for the release of John Lilburne and fellow Levellers William Walwyn, Thomas Prince and Richard Overton from the Tower.[59] Among these 'bonny Besses' were, probably, Elizabeth Lilburne, wife of John, Mary Overton, wife of Richard, and courageous Katherine Chidley, haberdasher and leader of these Leveller women. They were wives and mothers – poor, hungry, with small children to feed – but, above all, they were politicised women, 'equal unto men', they said, and moved to step 'beyond our compass' to express dismay with the Parliament they had supported in wartime, but which was now oppressing them. 'It is not your words, your declarations and acts of Parliament (as you call them) will feed or cloath us or our children,' they protested, 'while our husbands, servants and best friends are imprisoned by your Arbitrary warrants.'[60] Parliament responded by insulting them and calling on the troops to draw their pistols. 'You are desired to go home, and look after your own business, and meddle with your housewifery,' they were told.[61]

They did go home, but a few days later, on 29 April, more Levellers gathered in Smithfield, wearing black and sea-green ribbons, for the funeral of their fellow agitator Robert Lockyer. Lockyer had been shot to death by six musketeers for his part in a mutiny at Bishopsgate. On Fairfax's command, Lockyer was 'fetch't off like a Cock-Sparrow at the side of a wall' in St Paul's Churchyard.[62] A crowd of more than four thousand ordinary men and women had joined the soldiers to protest at the execution of the young Lockyer, and at a government ready to rule by the sword. The mourners processed through the City to Moorfields, following Lockyer's horse and coffin, upon which lay branches of rosemary dipped in blood and the martyred soldier's sword – a double-edged symbol of liberation and tyranny.

Meanwhile, in Surrey, a community of men and their families had set up shelters and huts on St George's Hill, near Weybridge. Led by the divinely inspired, bankrupt merchant tailor Gerrard Winstanley, these men called themselves 'True Levellers', but they were known as the Diggers. Winstanley and his band of fifty families took their spades, dug into the earth on St George's Hill and planted crops in the sandy soil: corn, parsnips and carrots. The threat to land and property ownership articulated by Henry Ireton at Putney back in 1647 was now being realised in the Diggers' belief that the land belonged to the common people. By living and working together, by sharing the treasures of the land, Winstanley claimed, they were restoring England to a prelapsarian Eden, as it was meant to be, before William the Conqueror arrived and created lords of the manor. The old world, Winstanley wrote, 'is running up like parchment in the fire, and wearing away'. As for the new government who tried to repress them, and succeeded, they could no longer see things aright: 'All men have stood for freedom . . . and now the common enemy is gone you are all like men in a mist, seeking for freedom and know not where nor what it is . . . freedom is the man that will turn the world upside down,' said Winstanley.[63] (St George's Hill is now a wealthy gated community with a golf club. Former celebrity residents include John Lennon.)

London's authorities reacted to the suppression of the Levellers by finally recognising the Commonwealth and the abolition of monarchy, and agreeing to a loan of £120,000. This would finance the unavoidable campaign in Ireland. On 7 June, Fairfax and Cromwell, along with Speaker Lenthall, John Bradshaw,

Bulstrode Whitelocke, Philip Herbert, earl of Pembroke, and other councillors, were invited to a summer banquet with Lord Mayor Thomas Foote. In the great hall of Foote's livery company, the Grocers, the regime's key players and politicians dined with London's aldermen and common councillors. Before they began to eat, the preacher John Owen delivered a sermon on deliverance, in praise of the crushing of the Leveller 'rebels', and in support of the imminent military expedition to Ireland.[64] There was no music or raising of glasses, but there was a lot of food. Leftovers were sent to local prisons and distributed among the poor.[65] Fairfax and Cromwell, meanwhile, were lavished with gifts of gold: plates, a large bowl, a jug.[66]

As for the irrepressible Lilburne, he was soon released on bail to comfort his wife, Elizabeth. Their eldest son had just died – as had many other Londoners at this time – from an epidemic of smallpox, and Elizabeth and two of their young children were also seriously ill. 'I earnestly beseech you, as bowels of men dwell within you, to make an effectuall and speedy Motion in your open House, for a few dayes liberty for me to go see my distressed Wife,' Lilburne pleaded in his letter to Henry Marten. 'For though I lie in a dungeon in fetters of iron at my coming back, I care not, so I may but see her,' he added.[67]

In the early days of 1649, across the Channel, at The Hague in Holland, was Charles I's eighteen-year-old son, Prince Charles. He had celebrated Christmas 1648–9 at the Dutch court, with his younger sister Mary, wife to William II, Prince of Orange and stadholder of most of the Dutch republic. Also there was his aunt, Elizabeth, James I's daughter and mother of Prince Rupert.

Elizabeth was also an exile, from Bohemia, the kingdom she and her husband Frederick had lost to Catholics in 1620. During the civil wars in England, the young Prince Charles had stayed near his father, even on the battlefield. He was twelve when he and his younger brother James saw their father fight at Edgehill, and tried to join in. In March 1646, in danger of being seized by Parliament, Prince Charles obeyed his father's orders to leave England, and he sailed from Land's End to the Scilly Isles. By the summer, he was reunited with his mother Henrietta Maria at St Germain, near Paris, as guests of the French court. Louis XIV was his eight-year-old cousin.

Charles's brother, James, had also made it into exile, and he too was at The Hague that Christmas. James had been held in St James's Palace since 1646, when his father surrendered. But in 1648 James outwitted his parliamentarian captors at St James's Palace in a well-choreographed game of hide and seek. He escaped from the palace and fled to Holland, disguised as a girl. The youngest Stuart child, Henriette Anne (Minette), left behind by her mother when only a few months old, was taken to France by her governess when she was two. Only the middle children, Elizabeth and Henry, remained in England. It was not unusual for royal children to live separately from their parents, and when Charles I and Henrietta left Whitehall in 1642, Elizabeth and Henry, then aged six and one, were living in St James's Palace – which soon fell into Parliament's hands. It was there that the children had been able to see their father the night before he died. Elizabeth herself reported that Charles I told his distraught daughter not to weep and grieve, for 'it was a glorious death he should die'.[68] They did not watch his execution. By 1650, these two young royal prisoners were in Carisbrooke Castle on the Isle of Wight.

1649

The news of Charles I's execution travelled quickly to the Dutch court. His family had pleaded for his life, in vain. On 5 February, Stephen Goffe, one of Prince Charles's chaplains, entered his rooms at The Hague, hesitated, and then addressed him as 'Your Majesty'.[69] On hearing these words, Charles knew that he was now, according to his birthright, king. He wept. He asked to be left alone for several hours. But then he began to plot his restoration.

From his place of exile, Charles II, ever the gambler, had been corresponding with leading Scottish and Irish noblemen sympathetic to his cause. Both Scotland and Ireland were appalled by England's execution of his father, for Charles I was their king too. In each, he was proclaimed king. Charles II immediately began negotiations with both kingdoms, seeking to make a deal in exchange for troops he could lead into England. Scotland was a separate country, which had shared its king with England since James VI of Scotland had been crowned James I of England in 1603, when Elizabeth I died childless. After initially joining with the English parliamentarians against Charles I in the civil wars, the Scots had later signed an 'engagement' with Charles I, promising to support him as long as he himself promised to establish a Presbyterian form of church government in England – which would, in turn, protect the cherished Presbyterian Kirk in their own kingdom. Scotland wanted to secure religious and political promises from their king, rather than topple monarchy. Two days after Charles I's execution, in Edinburgh, the Scots proclaimed Charles king, not just of Scotland but of England and of Ireland too, as was his right. But this announcement came with tough conditions that compromised Charles's power and tied him, as his father had been tied, to promoting Presbyterianism.

Ireland was also a kingdom under the Stuart Crown, but it was a colony. And it was overwhelmingly Catholic. Anglo-Normans had invaded in the twelfth century, and settled in the east, around Dublin (in an area known as the Pale), and in parts of the south. Large swathes of the mountainous west of Ireland remained in the hands of the native Irish. In 1541, Henry VIII had dubbed himself king of Ireland, and under his daughter Elizabeth I and her aggressive expansionist campaigns of the 1590s, the native Irish had surrendered. By then, of course, there was a religious dimension to England's violent foreign policy; Elizabethan and Jacobean Protestant settlers had expelled many of the Catholic descendants of the Anglo-Norman settlers (the so-called 'old English') and the native Irish Catholics from their lands. To many, including the political poets Edmund Spenser and John Milton, the Irish were wild and barbarous, and the country in need of civilising. Such was the early modern justification for colonialism. In 1649, James Butler, marquess (and future duke) of Ormond and, as lord lieutenant of Ireland, the most powerful man in Ireland at that time, declared Charles II king of Ireland. Butler was long-haired and loyal but he also had conditions for the young Charles: he should protect the native Irish and Anglo-Irish Catholics who lived there. Scotland and Ireland's proclamation of Charles II as king of all three kingdoms was a direct challenge to the English Parliament back in Westminster. They bridled, and prepared for war.[70]

No one was sure which way the wind would blow Charles II – west to Ireland, or north to Scotland. On 12 August, Walter Strickland, the Commonwealth's man in The Hague, warned Speaker Lenthall: 'It is thought here, that prince Charles will pass privately into Scotland or Ireland, in some Dutch ships.'[71]

Meanwhile, Charles II had written to Ormond in Ireland, promising him that he was on his way there. 'I am using all the means,' he wrote, 'and making all the haste I can possibly to you, that I may help you in that great good work you have with such discretion and so good success thus far advanced.' He signed off 'your most affectionate friend, Charles R'.[72] At around the same time, it is likely that Charles had also sent a message to Scotland, to the stern Archibald Campbell, marquess of Argyll and head of the Kirk party, suggesting that he would join forces with them.[73] Charles II was eventually persuaded by his close adviser Edward Hyde, future earl of Clarendon, that an invasion led from Ireland was the better option. Since March, Charles's dashing cavalier cousin, Prince Rupert, had been docked with his fleet in the narrow, sheltered harbour of Kinsale in the south of Ireland, waiting. In September, Charles II, his brother James and a pared-down court, including Clarendon, arrived on the island of Jersey. There they were hosted by the Royalist governor, Sir George Carteret, and they rode horses and messed about in boats while they prepared to sail to Ireland.

The situation in Ireland was beyond precarious. Ormond, as lord lieutenant, was managing a coalition of native Irish Catholics, old English Catholics and new English Protestants, who were bound, loosely, by loyalty to Charles I, and thus to his son. But this was a fragile and fraught alliance, forged out of Ireland's own brutal civil war in the early 1640s. Back in 1641, on the eve of civil war in England, Irish Catholics in Ulster in the north had rebelled against their English administrators in Parliament in Dublin. At that time, Ireland was a political tinderbox waiting to be lit. Under the leadership of Phelim O'Neill, members of the Catholic elite could see how Charles I's authority in England and in Scotland was being challenged, and they took the opportunity to air their own grievances about their lack of freedom to worship as Catholics, and the security of their prosperous estates. O'Neill was particularly wealthy and powerful. He and his fellow noblemen were not rebelling against Charles I, or against monarchy, but against religious policies and, in particular, the authoritarian governance of one of Charles's most loathed advisers, Thomas Wentworth, earl of Strafford, who had been lord deputy in Ireland until 1640. They were also frightened about what might happen to them – to their land and to their religion – should a zealously Protestant government become established in England. Their coup gathered steam, and Catholic risings spread beyond Ulster and beyond fearful landowners, engaging farmers and other working people. All of the latent hostility between the Irish (meaning both the native Irish and the 'old' Catholic English) and the new Protestant English was unleashed. Soon tales of the bloodthirsty and barbarous Irish were circulating. Gruesome, and exaggerated, reports of the bloodthirsty Irish rebels were read voraciously in England over the following weeks and months: stories of Catholic villains who tore off limbs, plucked out eyes, boiled children's heads, slaughtered newborn babies and ripped out the wombs from their Protestant mothers.[74] These rumoured atrocities provide the background to what would happen in Ireland during England's republic. Oliver Cromwell would later recall this Catholic rebellion to justify his own actions in war. Then, as it would become again, Ireland was a 'fresh bleeding nation'.[75]

The result of the 1641 rebellion was de facto independence from England. Led from Kilkenny in the south-east, a confederation of native Irish Catholics and old English Catholics came together and agreed to rule Ireland. It was in Kilkenny that James Butler, marquess of Ormond, descended from an 'old' English family but raised as a Protestant in England, had his family estates, including the great Anglo-Norman Kilkenny

Castle, which was seized in 1641. Charles I's increasingly desperate situation with his English Parliament saw the Catholic confederates in Ireland pledge loyalty to the king. The parliamentarian John Pym and his allies began to suggest that the king might even bring Catholic rebels over to help him regain political control. It was the possibility of Charles I using Catholic soldiers to fight a war in England that precipitated Parliament's militia bill, which would divest the king of military control. And it was this bill that pushed Charles I to raise his standard at Nottingham in 1642 and declare war. Ireland's tears, then, were soon to become England's. England's civil wars, and the republic that was to follow, cannot be understood without understanding the 'bleeding nation' that was Ireland.[76]

Following the outbreak of war in England, Charles I had urged Ormond, as lord lieutenant, to make peace with the Catholic confederates. He was especially keen for Ormond to secure their military support. Finally, on 17 January 1649, in the castle at Kilkenny, his former home, Ormond ceremonially proclaimed the articles of peace that he had agreed with the confederate supreme council. The terms of the peace were generous to the Catholics, granting them 'free exercise of the Roman Catholick Religion'. 'Perfect unity' was promised to all, and relief from the miseries and calamities of war and division.[77] In response, the speaker of the confederate assembly, Richard Blake, powerfully seconded this marvellous peace that 'wil cure these bleeding wounds, search to the very core, and pluck out all the splinters that remaine of them'.[78] When Ormond then proclaimed Charles II king a few weeks later, confederates as well as some Royalist Protestants could both cheer. For parliamentarian Protestants in Ireland, as for many back in England, the terms agreed with the Catholics, those 'bloody papists', were considered outrageous. 'No true born

Englishman', wrote John Milton, 'can so much as barely reade them without indignation and disdaine.'[79]

Back in Westminster, in the months following Charles I's execution, the council of state and Parliament turned their minds to Ireland. Some reinforcement troops had already been sent to help crush Ormond's Royalist rebels but Parliament now turned to Oliver Cromwell to bring Ireland back under English control. They sent him, as the poet Andrew Marvell noted, to 'tame' the Irish and, like a well-trained falcon, to bring back a kingdom to lay at the republic's feet.[80] So Cromwell, Fairfax's second-in-command, was made lord lieutenant of Ireland, and commander-in-chief of the army there. Cromwell had agreed that the Irish, as wild papists, even 'nott of any Religion', posed a great threat: 'all the world knowes their Barbarisme', he had said.[81] The Irish expedition would catapult Cromwell to greater fame, and to notoriety.

Cromwell, however, was initially reluctant to accept his commission, not wanting to leave England until money for himself and his soldiers was in place.[82] Cromwell's past successes had rested on such attention to preparation. Parliament agreed to divert funds from the sale of deans' and chapters' lands. Cromwell was given £100,000 in cash, and a salary of £2,000 a quarter while he was away, on top of his standard salary of £3 a day. This financial preparation meant that Cromwell would lead paid, well-fed troops who could pay their way while in Ireland. His soldiers could buy from, rather than plunder, the towns and villages they would tramp through.

On the night of 5 July, Cromwell hosted a farewell dinner at his house in King Street, Westminster, for his 'chief friends'.[83] Henry Ireton and his wife, Bridget (Cromwell's eldest daughter), were surely there: possibly Cromwell's wife Elizabeth, their second son Henry and their three other daughters, Elizabeth, Mary and Frances, too. Their eldest surviving son, Richard, lived with his wife's family in Hursley, Hampshire. On 11 July, on his way west, Cromwell and his convoy arrived at Windsor Castle. At Windsor, he met Bulstrode Whitelocke, who had retired for the summer to the royal park's desirable Manor Lodge, the tenure of which he had been granted that February. Whitelocke had been, since May, mourning the death of his beloved second wife and their unborn child, and at the lodge he took solace in the fresh air and in hunting the red deer. In the castle, Whitelocke and Cromwell prayed together, and asked for God's blessing upon their journey to Ireland. They listened to Colonels William Goffe and Thomas Harrison read out appropriate passages from the Bible to give them strength and hope. Cromwell, Whitelocke said, 'seemed to like well of his Counsell', and wished him to accompany him further.[84] From Windsor, Cromwell's train of six grey Flanders mares, eighty life-guard and milk-white flags then made its way to Bristol. They reached Milford Haven in Wales in early August. Cromwell's wife had also travelled there, to wave him off.[85]

On 13 August, aboard the *John*, Cromwell sat down to write a few letters. He had never been to Ireland before and he was not used to the sea (he would be really sick on the crossing). He wrote to Richard's father-in-law, Richard Major, to ask him to watch over his son while he was away. He hoped that Richard would not be swallowed up by family joys but would also 'minde and understand businesse'. Perhaps he could also 'reade a little historye, study the mathematicks, and Cosmografie', subjects fit for 'publick services for which a man is borne'.[86] He also wrote to his son's wife, Dorothy or Doll, a letter of concern and advice, for she had lately miscarried a child. 'I doe intierlye love you,' he wrote, and he entreated her to eschew worldly pleasures, and 'seeke the Lord'.[87]

Meanwhile, news had reached Cromwell and his soldiers of a sudden and unexpected parliamentary victory in Ireland at Rathmines, just outside Dublin – a victory that shifted the winds of fortune, and convinced the English MPs that God was, once again, on their side.[88] Determined to win Dublin from the parliamentarians, and anticipating that this was where Cromwell would land, Ormond had manoeuvred his troops and positioned them around the city, to the north and south. He had successfully stormed Rathfarnham Castle to the south of the city, wrenching it from parliamentary hands, and after also securing the ruined Baggotrath Castle, he was planning to refortify this to launch his attack on Dublin. In the morning of 2 August, Ormond had been resting in his tent at the Royalist camp at Rathmines. He was woken by stampeding horses and firing guns. Colonel Michael Jones, an Irish Protestant and the governor of Dublin, had planned a surprise morning attack and was advancing through the meadows and fields towards Rathmines. Ormond was not ready, and his men were dispersed on both sides of the River Liffey. In the battle that followed, Ormond lost about six hundred men, his artillery, a lot of money and his cabinet of letters and papers. A number of his Protestant soldiers defected to the parliamentary army, while others fled, including himself. It was a huge victory for the parliamentary army, and Ormond's defeat was soon the subject of cruel satire. A fictional dialogue between a cavalier and a roundhead trundled off the Dublin presses, suggesting that instead of making sure his soldiers were safe, Ormond was apparently playing cards, or sporting 'at Venus game' – to which the godly roundhead replies that this mattered not, for it was God who brought about Ormond's defeat, and Jones's triumph.[89]

God's victory meant that Cromwell could now cross and land safely at Dublin. So, on 13 August, 130 ships turned their bows towards the coast of Ireland and sheeted in their sails. They were carrying more than ten thousand men, horses, artillery and plenty of corn.[90] Not everyone wished the English soldiers and their commander a safe crossing. A disloyal subject bid Cromwell adieu with the following:

Come yee grim Furies of the Stigian Lake,
With hideous cryes, and make the welkin [heavens] shake,
Rouze Charon up, winds, Seas, and all implore,
To waft this Rebell to the Irish shore
[. . .]

His Exits come, Ireland the Stage must be,
Where he must act his latest Tragedie,
Where he his life shall spend in discontent,
And bid farewell to Englands Parliament.[91]

Two days later Cromwell's fleet anchored at Ringsend, on the mouth of the River Liffey just east of Dublin. On 15 August, Cromwell entered the city. A huge crowd had gathered to see him, and gunshots echoed around the walls. With his hat in his hand, Cromwell addressed the citizens: 'All those whose hearts affection were reall for the carrying on of the great work against the barbarous and bloud thirsty Irish and the rest of their adherents and confederates for the propagating of the Gospell of Christ, the establishing of truth and peace, and restoring that bleeding Nation to its former happinesse and tranquillity, should', he promised, and warned, 'find favour and protection from the Parliament of England'.[92] Not everyone in the crowd would have welcomed these words that talked about 'restoring' a happiness that had not existed in Ireland for a very, very long time. On 24 August, from Dublin Castle, Cromwell issued his 'Declaration' to 'all Ireland'. In this, he promised that his soldiers would adhere to the articles of war, that they would not rob and pillage innocent and uninvolved civilians, who would not be hurt, but could continue to live peacefully in their homes, and would be able to sell their goods and wares to his soldiers and know that they would be paid promptly for them, as long as they were 'behaving themselves peaceably and quietly'.[93] It was for this that Parliament had advanced, at Cromwell's insistence, the significant amount of cash, just before his ships left England.

But, just a few days later, Cromwell and his troops reportedly reneged on these promises. Drogheda was an important port, thirty miles north of Dublin, situated on two raised banks on either side of the River Boyne. It was positioned between parliamentary Dublin and the province of Ulster, where English Protestant and Scottish Presbyterian migrant communities – both Royalist – were under the leadership of the Ulster Scot Hugh, third Viscount Montgomery. Ormond, who had returned north with extra troops after fleeing to Kilkenny following his disaster at Rathmines, had fortified Drogheda; reports called the town 'impregnable'.[94] Cromwell's first move, then, would be to seize Drogheda. On 30 August, having despatched the artillery by sea, the army moved north, a force of more than twelve thousand men prepared to batter down the town's high medieval walls. They marched with colours flying, drums beating and trumpets sounding – the threatening, but oddly ceremonial, noises of approaching war and death.[95] Two battering guns and cannon were loaded off ships that had managed to sail up the Boyne. The guns were set up at the south-eastern corner of Drogheda, just next to St Mary's Church. The city rejected Cromwell's summons to surrender so the soldiers blasted the south wall until, by the evening of 10 September, they had made two openings. Late the next afternoon the holes were big enough for soldiers to clamber through. Trumpets and drums sounded the signal to storm. Behind the walls, inside the town, enemy soldiers waited in ready-made trenches in the streets. Nearly eight hundred parliamentary soldiers scaled the toppled medieval stones, but many were killed and they were forced to retreat. Further along, another possible entrance became choked with dead Royalist soldiers. So the parliamentarians tried again. Cromwell himself inspected the new breach and led his soldiers through the damaged city wall, shoving sweating horses through with them. This time, Cromwell's soldiers overwhelmed the enemy behind, and got into the church. 'God was pleased to animate them,' Cromwell later reported.[96]

The governor of Drogheda, Sir Arthur Aston, and about two hundred officers and soldiers had fled up to the fort on top of Mill Mount, a raised mound positioned just inside the walls of the city, in the bottom south-west corner. Aston was a one-legged veteran Royalist soldier. He had been governor of Oxford in the 1640s, where Charles I set up his court. It was Cromwell who gave the order to his men to 'put them all to the Sword', even though, supposedly, Aston and his men had dropped their arms.[97] One report tells of Aston being beaten to death with his own wooden leg. According to Ormond, despite the promise of quarter to soldiers who had laid down their arms, his officers and soldiers heard the words 'No quarter!' echoing through the streets.[98] In the rules of early modern warfare, if you refused to surrender you were refused quarter. As for those fleeing Drogheda, Cromwell ordered that no one who bore arms should be spared. But his soldiers could not be sure, amid the chaos and the terror, who bore arms and who did not. Many had fled up towers and into St Peter's Church, scurrying up the steeple. On Cromwell's order, the church was set on fire.

From the inside, the appalling cry could be heard: 'God damn me, God confound me; I burn, I burn.' Cromwell wrote that he thought a hundred people died in that church. In the siege overall, Cromwell lost not quite one hundred of his men.[99]

Drogheda had been cracked open like a 'potter's vessel', reported one contemporary newsbook, invoking the book of Jeremiah.[100] Drogheda was a lump of clay, and God was the potter who could make or destroy as he wished. The exact number of dead soldiers is unknown; accounts are contradictory. The parliamentary officer Colonel John Hewson wrote that 'by any observation' there must have been three thousand bodies lying in the streets of Drogheda, of whom he thought about 150 were his comrades. This must be, he concluded, the hand of God.[101] In his letter home to Speaker Lenthall, written from his tent in a cold, damp field outside Dublin, Cromwell admitted to being 'in the heat of action'. 'I forbade them to spare any that were in Arms in the Town,' he said, before adding ruefully, 'I think that night they put to the sword about two thousand men.' He then justified his actions: 'I am persuaded that this is a righteous judgment of God upon these barbarous wretches . . . and that it will tend to prevent the effusion of blood for the future.'[102] But there is evidence of a conscience being pricked here. In a later letter, also to Lenthall, Cromwell included a list of the 'officers and soldiers slain at Drogheda'. At the end, following the final entry of 'two thousand Five hundred Foot Soldiers, besides Staff-Officers, Chyrurgeons, &c' is the terrible phrase: 'and many inhabitants'.[103] These civilians may have included unarmed men, possibly women too, and clergymen, both Catholic and Protestant, either shot at in error, or out of cruelty. Some time after the storming, Dean Nicholas Bernard, Royalist Protestant minister of St Peter's Church, told his parishioners how Cromwell's soldiers had deliberately fired through the windows of his own house.[104]

London heard of the fall of Drogheda on 29 September. It was a significant victory for the republic's army, and newsbooks continued to report on Drogheda well into October. Cromwell's letter to Speaker Lenthall describing the siege in detail was printed, and made available for people to buy.[105] Other accounts, rolling off Royalist presses, described sensationally how parliamentary soldiers killed with impunity, cutting off genitals and slices of flesh. Women and children were also said to have been among the slain. No evidence corroborates these claims.[106] Defeated soldiers were shipped off to Barbados; some managed to escape; others were spared initially, some later killed. Among the men with Aston on Mill Mount was Edmund Verney, son of Sir Edmund Verney, who had raised the royal standard alongside Charles I at Nottingham in 1642. The young Edmund was the brother of Sir Ralph Verney, who had fought on the other side, for Parliament, and whose family memoirs describe a family divided by war. In Drogheda, Edmund was spared and granted quarter. Three days later, however, he was supposedly walking along with Cromwell when a Mr Ropier took him aside 'in a pretence to speak with him', and stabbed him to death.[107]

With Drogheda fallen, the north of Ireland could be secured. News of the scale of the victory at Drogheda – the numbers of the dead – had spread quickly among Royalist troops, striking terror among them. Soldiers in Trim left in such haste that they abandoned their guns. Cromwell's summons to the chief officer in Dundalk to surrender threatened the devastation visited on Drogheda:

> I offered mercy to the Garrison of Treedah [Drogheda], in sending the Governor a Summons before I attempted the taking of it. Which being refused brought their evil upon them. If you, being warned thereby, shall surrender your

> Garrison to the use of the Parliament of England, which by this I summon you to do, you may thereby prevent effusion of blood. If, upon refusing this Offer, that which you like not befalls you, you will know whom to blame.

He then signed off, 'Your servant, Oliver Cromwell'.[108]

Cromwell marched his troops, many wounded and many sick, back to Dublin. After a week of replenishing supplies and appealing to Westminster for more food and men, the English army prepared to head south, through County Wicklow. They claimed Killingkerick and marched on through a bleak and desolated landscape towards the castle of Arklow, Ormond's family seat, and then on to Limerick. As the English approached, Irish soldiers bolted like birds from a disturbed nest. Sometimes soldiers had time to set fire to the castles they abandoned; at other times they were too rushed to gather up their guns, ammunition and food, so all was left behind for the English to take as their own. Cromwell installed some of his men in the castles while others marched steadily on. On Monday 1 October, about nine thousand troops reached Wexford, on the south-eastern coast.

Wexford was a famous 'seat of piracy'. It had been the base from which English ships had been attacked and plundered by Irish ships for years.[109] It was Catholic, and Royalist. On 3 October, Cromwell issued a summons to the town's commander-in-chief, Colonel David Sinnott. As in Drogheda, Cromwell's command to surrender was so that 'effusion of blood may bee prevented' and the town preserved from ruin. He delivered an open threat: 'By this offer, I hope itt will clearly appeare where the guilt will lye, if innocent persons should come to suffer with the nocent. I expect your speedye answare.'[110] Sinnott refused to surrender and instead requested time to confer with Wexford's mayor. Cromwell was annoyed by the delay: 'I consider that your houses are better than our Tents,' he snapped.[111] Indeed, for it was wet and stormy that October. He rejected Sinnott's offer to negotiate, seeing this as an appropriate option only if 'things stand upon a more equall Foot'.[112] Cromwell versus Wexford, with his nine thousand troops against Wexford's fifteen hundred, was anything but equal. As Cromwell and Sinnott corresponded, Royalists abandoned the fort of Rosslare, which stood at the harbour mouth. It was here that the artillery and supplies were landed from the English ships that had sailed down the coast from Dublin, and from here that Cromwell's cannon began to play against the earth-thickened walls of the castle. By noon on 11 October, three breaches had been made and the castle battlements beaten down. Sinnott asked to surrender, but Cromwell scoffed at his proposed terms, which included tolerance for Catholic clergy and permission for Royalist soldiers to march out with all their ammunition. He revised the terms. He would grant quarter to some soldiers, or let them go home, and take the officers as prisoners. The town would be preserved from plunder, and the townspeople protected. 'I shall ingage my Self That noe violence shall bee offred to their Goods,' he promised.[113] But then events took a different turn.

According to Cromwell, as the terms of surrender were being agreed, parliamentary soldiers occupied the castle and the enemy forces began to flee, scrambling over the high wall to the south and into the town. As the parliamentary soldiers saw this, they too scaled the walls of the town and, on meeting 'stiffe resistance' in the market square, put 'all to the sword that came in their way'.[114] This sent the townspeople into a panic, and they took flight by heading for the harbour walls: 'Men, women, Officers, and Souldiers endeavoured to betake themselvs to fly over the water in Boats, for the safety of their lives,' recorded an eyewitness.[115] Many drowned as they tried to cross the river or escape in boats that were so overladen they sank in the harbour. In less than an hour the town was empty. Cromwell's soldiers then ran amok through the deserted streets, taking what they could find, until Cromwell issued a proclamation ordering them to stop.

For the writer of *A Perfect and Particular Relation*, divine revenge had finally been wrought on Wexford for the wrong done to Protestants there in the rebellion of 1641: 'Here was a wonderfull providence seen in it. That when they were even on the brink to have conditions, it should be so marvellously denyed them. The hand of God was mightily in it; this town which was a seate of pyracy, and the ruine of many familyes in England, was thus justly met with.'[116] Once again, as at Drogheda, civilians had become caught up in a siege and had been killed. Cromwell's letter reported that not many fewer than two thousand Royalist soldiers died in all, of whom nearly three hundred drowned. This was compared to about twenty parliamentarian soldiers. We do not know how many ordinary men and women (even children?) also died. Writing to Lenthall, Cromwell admitted that the town was ruined and that the inhabitants had run away, but, like the author of *A Perfect and Particular Relation*, he attributed this to 'an unexpected providence'. In the end, he believed that God had 'brought a just judgement upon them'.[117]

By now winter was approaching, and the campaign would have to stop. As Cromwell turned further south, Cork and Kinsale dramatically switched allegiance and offered Cromwell and his troops quarter. From her house, Red Abbey, near Cork, the Royalist Lady Ann Fanshawe escaped in the middle of the night, having warned her husband, Richard, who was at Kinsale. She packed clothes, linen, £1,000 worth of gold and silver, as much household stuff as she could manage, and her husband's papers. She then fled, pregnant, on two horses shared between herself, her sister, her little daughter, three maids and two men. She was in a 'sad condition' and in 'perpetuall fear of being fetched back again'.[118] But the parliamentary troops were sick. Cromwell had fallen ill at Ross, and most of his men were, he said, 'fitter for an hospitall than the field'.[119] The 'country disease' was among them, caught from hours of marching in cold, wet weather and wading in foul water. They were feverish, and short of breath. They had 'loosness' in the stomach, aching limbs and a violent cough.[120] They made it to Youghal and set up camp there for the winter. In December, Cromwell's friend and right-hand man, Colonel Michael Jones, who was suffering with the fever, died.

With the new year came better weather, but unwelcome news from England. Parliament was urging Cromwell to return home, luring him with the promise of access to former royal palaces and gardens. Cromwell ignored his masters' summons, and pressed on. Kilkenny, the seat of the confederate supreme council, was still not captured. At the end of March, after two days of attack, Walter Butler, left in charge of Kilkenny Castle when Ormond fled, was forced to surrender. Clonmel, another confederate stronghold in the south of Ireland, fell in May after a difficult siege during which many soldiers on both sides died. Before he left Ireland in May, Cromwell handed over the nearly tamed kingdom to his son-in-law Henry Ireton, who became lord deputy. Cromwell set sail for England, in a new ship called the *President*. He never saw Ireland again. It was his successors who completed the conquest. Henry Ireton died in Limerick in 1651, but he was succeeded by his widow's new husband, the army officer Charles Fleetwood. By 1653, all of Ireland was conquered and the confederates surrendered. Ormond, meanwhile, made his way into exile and found Charles II in Paris. Charles II never did sail from Jersey to join those fighting in his name.

After a choppy, three-day crossing in late May, Cromwell docked at Bristol. He was greeted as a hero. Guns were fired three times to mark his safe return, and as he travelled east to London he was saluted by Members of Parliament, councillors of state, army officers and bystanders. His wife met him at Windsor on 1 June, as did Bulstrode Whitelocke, who asked Cromwell about his son, James, who had volunteered to serve in Ireland. Cromwell was able to reassure his friend of James's courage and 'sobriety' on the Irish battlefield.[121] At Hyde Park Corner, guns were shot before Cromwell turned down towards Whitehall which, so the newly launched newsbook *Mercurius Politicus* tells us, was thronging with crowds.[122] A grateful Parliament granted Cromwell and his family lodgings in the Cockpit opposite Whitehall, formerly used by Henry VIII for entertainments. Cromwell was also given the use of St James's House, Spring Gardens and St James's Park.[123]

Confronted by all the pomp, Cromwell is said to have put on a show of humility – such ostentatious display was not to his taste, but he would acknowledge it and not be ungrateful. He made sure, once again, to point out that the victories in Ireland were God's, and not his. There was no mention of Cromwell's ruthlessness, or of the civilian deaths in Drogheda and Wexford. Parliament, too, acknowledged the mysterious hand of God, while Royalists mocked their powerful providential logic, finding what the parliamentarians called 'necessities' 'specious'.[124] On 4 June, Cromwell's first day back in the Commons chamber, he was given 'hearty thanks' by Speaker Lenthall, on behalf of Parliament, for 'those great and strange Works, which God hath wrought by him, as the Instrument'.[125]

A portrait by Robert Walker from this year shows Cromwell as a formidable commander. His linen collar is white and crisp against his gleaming, silvery armour, a grey silk sash is tied carefully around his waist, his hand rests on a sword, his brow is furrowed. His mid-length, brown wavy hair has a hint of the cavalier.[126] As God's instrument, Cromwell was now central to consolidating the next phase of England's republic. He had crushed Ireland; Scotland was next.

Cromwell's behaviour in Ireland has never been forgotten or forgiven. Still, in parts of Ireland, people speak of the curse of Cromwell. There is often a sharp intake of breath when his name is mentioned. The towns of Drogheda and Wexford will be forever associated with the civilian blood spilt there. Colonial administrators under Elizabeth I behaved brutally when they crushed Ireland in the 1590s, but it is Cromwell who is loathed. The scale of the losses at Drogheda and Wexford was huge, and many ordinary people evidently died. But that Cromwell purposefully oversaw a massacre of civilians cannot be safely claimed. Appallingly, Cromwell's view of the Irish as barbaric bloodthirsty rebels, following their treatment of Protestants in 1641, and his firm belief that the English had a right to rule over them and a duty to spread the gospel, were shared by many back home. In February 1650, the chaplain John Owen preached before Members of Parliament as they observed a day of humiliation and thanks. He had just returned from the campaign and he urged the MPs to 'do your utmost for the preaching of the Gospel in Ireland', because 'they want it'. 'The land mourneth', he went on, and the Irish 'cry out of their darkness'.[127] In January

1650, Cromwell issued a long and scathing declaration to the Irish. It was the godly English against the popish Irish, and the heretics would be punished with blood:

> You are a part of Antichrist, whose Kingdome the Scripture so expresly speakes should be layed in blood, yea in the blood of the Saints; you have shed great store of it already; And ere it be long, you must all of you have blood to drinke; even the dreggs of the cup of the fury and wrath of God, which will be powred out unto you.[128]

With his characteristic repetitive flourish, Cromwell warned:

> We come to aske an account of the innocent blood hath bin shed, and to endeavour to bring them to an account (by the blessing & presence of the Almighty, in whom alone is our hope and strength) who by appearing in Armes seeke to justifie the same. We come to breake the power of a Company of lawlesse Rebells, who having cast off the authority of England, live as enemies to humaine societie . . . We come (by the assistance of God) to hold forth and maintain the lustre & glory of English liberty in a nation where we have an undoubted right to doe it.

This was, at the time, perceived to be a legitimate justification for war. It did not follow that killing with impunity and abandon was also considered legitimate (even if this did, regretfully, happen at Drogheda and Wexford). In the same declaration, Cromwell denied killing any unarmed Irishmen or women: 'Give us an instance of one man since my coming into Ireland, not in Armes, massacred, destroyed or banished,' he challenged.[129]

The deaths and losses in Ireland following the invasion of 1649 were catastrophic. Many more died in these wars than had died in the English civil wars of the 1640s – if not from the fighting, then from subsequent plague and starvation. During the 1650s, England's Parliament passed a series of acts that would utterly transform Ireland and entrench the view that prevailed: that Cromwell was to blame. These parliamentary acts set out how Catholic and Protestant Royalists would be punished – the original Ulster rebel from 1641, Phelim O'Neill, was hanged, drawn and quartered – and how their lands would be confiscated and redistributed among those who had fought for the Commonwealth, those who pledged loyalty to the Commonwealth, and those Englishmen and women keen to relocate to Ireland and own land (known as the 'adventurers'). The result was that Irish Catholics who once owned 60 per cent of the land were left with 20 per cent, and pushed out to the western counties. As Thomas Cobbes wrote, in his poem 'upon' Cromwell: 'Our land they've robbed, and turned churches to stables.'[130] But Cromwell, once he had left Ireland, was not solely responsible. There are instances of him intervening, and calling for more moderate treatment of both Royalist Protestants and Catholics in Ireland.[131] Henry Ireton, and then Charles Fleetwood, followed later still by Cromwell's son Henry, together with a host of commissioners in Dublin and committee members in Westminster, were all involved with the land and religious policies that decimated Ireland and its people, uprooting many, and scattering others overseas.[132] While Cromwell played a significant part, he did not act alone, and not always in the ways history has chosen to remember. At the end of this first eventful year of the republic, Cromwell's might and potential for brutality were clear. He was, as the poet Andrew Marvell foresaw, likely to prove 'climacteric'. But, at least for now, he was 'still in the Republic's hand'.[133]

1650

Conscience, that heaven-nursèd plant,
Which most our earthly gardens want.
A prickling leaf it bears, and such
As that which shrinks at every touch.

Andrew Marvell,
'Upon Appleton House'

The kingdom of Charles was transformed into a republic, and the so-called Council of State, which was then for the first time established by the authority of Parliament, summoned me, though I was expecting no such event.

John Milton,
A Second Defence of the English People

Some in the fledgling republic learned how to use words, not force. In the weeks leading up to Charles I's trial, an ambitious poet and fierce polemicist was watching events keenly. At speed, the forty-year-old John Milton wrote a powerful justification of why kings should be held to account. His sinewy *Tenure of Kings and Magistrates* was published on 13 February 1649 and it quickly attracted the attention and approval of the new council of state. Milton had already argued repeatedly against greedy bishops and the censoring of books, and, boldly, in favour of divorce (his own marriage was unhappy). At this stage, Milton did not believe kingship was in itself wrong, but that tyranny was. Milton could contemplate a single person holding power – a king or a chief magistrate – but argued that such a ruler should know the terms of their contract, their 'tenure', with the people. If a king breaches his contract, which he has sworn to uphold at his coronation, the people are free to exert their most supreme, God-given faculty, Reason, and depose that ruler. Radically, Milton argued that the people are always free to choose the kind of government they think best, and reject a ruler at will.[1]

By the end of March 1649, Milton had taken up a new appointment as the council's secretary for foreign languages – employed to compose letters in his perfect Latin and translate diplomatic correspondence for just under £300 a year. He became good friends with John Bradshaw, the council's president, and was given a suite of rooms in Whitehall at the Scotland Yard end of the rambling palace. His much younger wife, Mary, from whom he had been estranged for a while in the 1640s, joined him with their two toddler daughters, Anne and Mary. Milton served, and defended, the republic. He attended the council of state's meetings, met foreign visitors, penned propaganda for the state and kept an eye on what was being published. His domestic life continued to be strained: his wife's family was Royalist, as was his brother, Christopher.[2]

Royalists, too, could use words; their language was different: more sentimental, but no less powerful. Those mourning their dead king had sought solace in a little book that became a runaway bestseller as soon as the axe had fallen. In the days, possibly even hours, following Charles's death, *Eikon basilike*, the 'Royal Image', was available for grieving buyers to purchase as an authentic collection of Charles's personal reflections on the war years. It pretended it was written by their dead, martyred king but it was actually compiled by a loyal and well-connected vicar from Bocking, John Gauden. Thirty-five English editions and twenty-five foreign editions appeared in 1649 alone, before Parliament banned it. But copies were passed around and found their way to those in exile across the Channel. From the pages of this intimate book, a suffering Charles spoke simply to his bereft subjects and justified his actions: 'I did what I thought was best according to my reason and conscience.' And he guided and comforted his readers through the bewildering topsy-turviness of what was happening with his own prayers to God: 'Make me willing to go whither thou wilt lead Me by thy providence; and be thou ever with Me; that I may see thy constancy in the worlds variety and changes.'[3] *Eikon basilike* fast became a relic. Owners treasured their little copies, wrapped them in cloth and ribbons, lovingly inscribed them, used them to record family births and deaths, and handed them down to their children.[4] In some editions, a gorgeous frontispiece engraving of Charles I, exchanging his earthly crown for a heavenly one, did much to fix the idea of the martyr king in the nation's consciousness. In the absence of a head on a coin (although these still circulated, of course) or the glimpse of the monarch on progress, Royalists could contemplate this image, and remember.

Milton's first commission by the council of state was to shatter this image. With his eyesight already failing – he would soon become completely blind and depend on an amanuensis – Milton wrote *Eikonoklastes*: 'image breaker'. From a position of personal darkness, he cast a shadow over the dazzling light of royalty. He exposed the emotional and irrational pull of kingship and challenged the superstitious instinct and the custom that make men and women fall down before a king, as if he were a god. Even for a gifted writer such as Milton, the familiar image of a king – crowned, robed and hedged with divinity – was hard to blacken, and *Eikonoklastes* did not become a bestseller like *Eikon basilike*. But it remains a robust and searing exposition of why men and women like monarchy, and choose, in Milton's words, to become slaves, not citizens.[5]

The council of state also asked Milton – he who had defended a liberal, censor-free press – to investigate circulating newsbooks which satirised and mocked the councillors and Parliament.[6] *Mercurius Pragmaticus* was one such Royalist newsbook, set up by the sharp and entrepreneurial Marchamont Nedham. Described as 'hawk-nosed', with 'two earrings' and long black hair, and fond of an ornate wig (the latest fashion), Nedham was quick to change his mind.[7] Before he turned thirty, Nedham had launched the parliamentary newsbook *Mercurius Britannicus*, back in 1643. He spent time in jail for criticising Charles I, and then established *Mercurius Pragmaticus*, which meant he spent more time in jail, but this time for mocking the parliamentarians as 'mad sainted elves' and Oliver Cromwell as 'Copper-face'. Nedham switched his allegiances in exchange for his freedom and, in 1650, Milton helped him launch the parliamentarian newsbook *Mercurius Politicus*. Milton recognised in Nedham a fellow lover of words and the two became friends. Nedham was candid about his change of tack. 'Perhaps thou art of an Opinion contrary to what is here written,' he wrote in a defence of the Commonwealth. 'I confess that for a Time I myself was so too, till some Causes made me reflect with an impartial eye upon the Affairs of this new Government.'[8]

It would be easy to accuse Nedham of being a trimmer – a 'Jack of all sides', as Royalists scoffed.[9] But Nedham was one among many who needed to make sense of the new world, and who were compelled to both search their consciences and think about their survival. The king was dead, and the kingless government looked set to stay. Nedham began to argue that the Commonwealth was part of God's plan, and therefore legitimate – despite being born of the sword. So he reframed all that was novel as familiar: Athens and Rome were examples of republics in the past, as was Holland across the water, now. He defended what was happening in England as a return to what once was, like a tide on the turn. All things, he wrote, are 'in perpetuall *Flux*, and *Reflux*, like the *Tides* that follow her Motion; so that what hath been is that which shall be, and there is no new thing under the Sun'. Historical change was also not capricious, but directed by God, and God was punishing them for the ways of their old world: 'It was the weight of Sin which sunk the *old world* in a *Deluge*,' he wrote, 'and hath been the occasion (no doubt) of all succeeding alterations, by permission of Divine Providence.'[10] What seemed new and strange was not new; it was a kind of restoration.

Nedham's first issue of *Mercurius Politicus* appeared in June 1650. New issues then appeared weekly and, like the other newsbooks of the time, reported events chronologically, rather than by headline-grabbing importance. *Mercurius Politicus* was, Nedham joked, like a king's fool: loyal, witty and a voice of conscience: 'Why should not the Common-wealth have a Fool, as well as the King had?' he quipped on the paper's front page. Here, again, was the new masquerading as the old: a commonwealth is not so different from a court; the words of a newsbook not so different from those of a king's fool. Nedham then added, more seriously, that his paper could lead and persuade: 'You shall know that I have authority enough to create a fashion of my own, and make all the world to follow the humor.'[11]

This first edition told readers about Cromwell's victorious return from Ireland and about Charles Stuart, who was now on his way to Scotland. By the summer of 1650, the 'storm which threatened' from the north was serious.[12] As Ireland fell, the council of state knew that Charles, who had never sailed from Jersey to join Ormond and confront Cromwell's troops, would pursue the negotiations he had begun with Scotland and make a deal: an army with which to invade England, in exchange for Presbyterian promises. In February 1650 Charles had travelled to Beauvais, just north of Paris, to talk to his mother Henrietta Maria about the Scottish plan and, presumably, to ask for money. There, in Henrietta Maria's care, he left his mistress Lucy Walter and their baby son, James (who as the future duke of Monmouth would go on to challenge James II as king).[13] He made his way to Breda in Holland, and from there across the North Sea to Scotland. Royalists in England began to stir, sensing their opportunity.

Charles had been stalling on the punishing political and religious terms the Scottish Covenanters, led by Archibald Campbell, marquess of Argyll, were seeking in return for military support to reclaim the English throne. In his paper, Nedham mocked Charles for lingering en route to catch mackerel 'or some other odd fish' to fry, before he agreed to sit on the stool of repentance they were offering him. Charles had been brought up in the Anglican Church of his father and under the Catholic influence of his mother. While in exile, he had continued to sink to his knees to take communion (an abominable, idolatrous act according to Puritans) and to follow the liturgy of his beloved English prayer book, which Parliament had abolished long ago. If the Scottish Covenanters, so called because of the Covenant they had signed in rejection of this prayer book, were going to help Charles win back England, they had to ensure that he would recognise Scotland's Parliament and its Presbyterian Kirk. As well as being a limited king, he also had to commit to establishing a Presbyterian form of Church government in England and Ireland, and punish Catholicism.

The risk was ensuring that Charles would stick to these promises, and not go it alone by encouraging an uprising among Royalist Scots who were willing to compromise on strict Presbyterian conditions. Henrietta Maria had advised her eldest son that kings were absolutely allowed to renege on their promises – Milton's definition of a tyrant.[14] While negotiating with Argyll, Charles had also been corresponding with the loyal Scottish nobleman James Graham, marquess of Montrose. Once, a decade ago, Montrose was a Covenanter, and had fought to save Scotland's Kirk. But during the civil wars he had engaged with Charles I, and fought with him against the English Parliament. Such former Covenanters were known as the Engagers: they did not force the king to sign a Presbyterian covenant, and they broke the Solemn League and Covenant they had with England. This had bound the two kingdoms and their armies together in their common desire to preserve the king but limit his authority and, in England, establish Presbyterianism as Scotland had done.

Charles II rewarded Montrose for his loyalty to his father by making him lieutenant governor of Scotland. But Montrose, like Charles II, had a title without a country. Loathed by the Scottish Covenanters, he had fled into exile, and it was while wandering on the continent that he was commissioned by his king to scrabble together European soldiers and muster willing Royalist soldiers from the Highlands. The strategy, if it worked, would see Montrose lead an army to defeat the hard-line Scottish Covenanters, and go on to invade England. Charles II would then be installed as king in both of his kingdoms on his own terms, and without conceding to the Covenanters' humiliating demands.

Charles II, though, liked to keep everything in play. He had once pledged to support Montrose: 'I will never fail in the effects of that friendship I have promised,' he wrote, urging Montrose to 'proceed in your business with your usual courage and alacrity'.[15] But, while waiting at Breda before sailing to Scotland, Charles had been forced by the Scottish commissioners sent down to seal the deal to write to Montrose and instruct him to disband. Charles did so, and then changed his mind, before changing it back again. It was too late: in March Montrose crossed from Norway and landed in the north of Scotland with his clutch of northern European recruits. He had hoped that more local Scots would join him as he marched south, but few did. Most of his men were captured and slain by the stronger Covenanting troops. Montrose himself escaped, dressed as a peasant, before being betrayed and captured. He suffered a slow execution by hanging in the high street at Edinburgh, wearing his scarlet cloak trimmed with gold lace.[16] Despite being betrayed by Charles II, Montrose remained the devoted cavalier. The world should be 'Governed by no other sway / But purest monarchie', he wrote.[17]

On 23 June 1650, after a stormy crossing and a diversion up the coast of Scotland to beyond Aberdeen and round the corner to Elgin to avoid the patrolling ships of the republic, Charles II waited on his ship with some of his closest courtiers-in-exile: George Villiers, second duke of Buckingham, who had grown up with Charles and his siblings; Henry, Lord Wilmot (shortly to become earl of Rochester, and father of John, who would become the scurrilous Restoration poet); herald and Garter king-of-arms Sir Edward Walker; loyal Scots noblemen and friends John Maitland, earl (and future duke) of Lauderdale and William, second duke of Hamilton; and his chaplain Stephen Goffe (brother to the regicide army officer William Goffe). Just days before, English ships had been in the Moray Firth, looking for Charles. Before he could land on Scottish soil, Charles was forced to agree to fresh conditions and sign the latest version of the covenants. On a boat anchored off Garmouth, on the River Spey, a covenanted king was made. With the shores of one of his kingdoms now within sight, Charles could not turn back. Argyll, the most important man in Scotland at this time, greeted Charles and his entourage on bended knees, before demanding that those close to the king should be sent straight back to Holland, or safely removed from the ear and body of the king. Hamilton, for example, was banished to the island of Arran.[18]

As Charles travelled down through Scotland, church bells rang to welcome the returned king. The royal party was also greeted with reminders of what might happen if it attempted to uphold the 'sway of monarchy', without the help of the Covenanters. In Aberdeen, Stirling, Perth, Glasgow and Edinburgh, Montrose's body parts were nailed up on display. An arm was pinned to the gates of

Aberdeen, opposite the merchant's house in which Charles I had lodged. His head was impaled on a spike and displayed high on the Tolbooth in Edinburgh, where it stayed until 1661.[19]

In his makeshift Scottish court, Charles was watched like a hawk by solemn, glowering Scottish chaplains, who forced the king to pray alongside them and endure their bitter sermons, reprehending him 'sharply' if he smiled on Sundays or 'if his looks and gestures did not please them'. He would be taught to behave like the king they wanted. He was approached on 'bended knees and in the humblest postures', but he was not invited to council meetings or consulted about military plans or any aspect of Scottish politics.[20]

Back in Whitehall Parliament prepared for imminent conflict with Scotland. Cromwell had been brought back from Ireland, and Thomas Fairfax, lord general of the Commonwealth forces, was now called upon to lead a pre-emptive invasion of Scotland. But Fairfax was said to be 'melancholy mad'.[21] This popular, brilliant, ruthless leader of England's New Model Army, the genius behind many of the key civil war victories, such as at Naseby and Colchester, and who struck awe and fear, so John Milton claimed, into kings throughout Europe, was at odds with the republic.[22] Fairfax had claimed that he was fighting 'to maintain the rights of the crown and kingdom joyntly' and for a king who would heed the advice of his Parliament.[23] He did not attend the trial of Charles I but his wife, Anne, had been there, seated in one of the galleries in Westminster Hall and hidden behind a mask. When her husband's presence was called upon as one of the trial's judges, she supposedly shouted down, 'He had more wit than to be here.'[24] Fairfax had accepted a seat on the new council of state, but he rarely attended its meetings.

Fairfax was not the only one to be battling with his conscience. The MP Thomas Hoyle committed suicide on the anniversary of the execution.[25] In January, the Act for Subscribing the Engagement was passed, meaning that now all adult men, including those formerly loyal to the king, had to swear to be 'true and faithful to the Commonwealth of England, as it is now Established, without a King or House of Lords'.[26] Fairfax was allowed to subscribe an amended version, which did not compel him to approve of *all* past acts (the regicide, for example). The Act for the Engagement was read out in cities across the country, compelling men to come and sign. But not everyone did so. While some men came into London to pledge their loyalty, others were forced out, or silenced. The Act for the Removing of Papists expelled papists, delinquents and mercenary soldiers from London and its environs.

Across the country Anglican clergymen were rooted out and godly preachers planted. The Acts for the Propagating of the Gospel in Wales, Ireland and northern England authorised commissioners to eject clergymen in dark corners of the land who were too Anglican, too popish. The instruction to promote the gospel also extended across the Atlantic, to the Puritan settlers in New England, authorising them to preach the gospel of Christ to the indigenous peoples.[27] At home, ministers were encouraged to preach regularly in cities. Parliament also passed the Blasphemy Act, which sought to silence the more outrageous claims of religious fanatics who wanted to believe what their conscience told them. But Parliament also passed a Toleration Act which meant that, for the first time since the days of Elizabeth I, men and women were not required to attend church on Sundays, as long as they observed the sabbath in some way.[28] Here was the regime's attempt to commit to the liberty of conscience espoused by Independents such as Cromwell. For those of a more

Presbyterian bent like Fairfax, who favoured a state Church, such lack of religious uniformity was dangerous.

Imminent war with Scotland pushed Fairfax to announce his critical decision, on 25 June 1650, to resign his office as commander of the Commonwealth's forces. For Fairfax, who shared Scotland's Presbyterianism, along with many in England, a pre-emptive strike against Scotland would break the Solemn League and Covenant that Scotland and England had signed in 1643. 'I thinke it doubtfull . . . we have a just cause to make an invasion uppon Scotland, with whom we are joyned in the Nationall League & Covenant,' declared Fairfax.[29] Fairfax's fellow councillors of state – Cromwell, Whitelocke and the pious, 'silken' republican Sir Henry Vane the younger, who had negotiated the Solemn League and Covenant in Edinburgh – tried to persuade Fairfax to rethink. High-ranking officers who had fought alongside Fairfax and Cromwell on the civil war battlefield also tried: John Lambert and Thomas Harrison, veterans from Marston Moor. The men spent hours shut up in a room in Whitehall, arguing and praying. According to Whitelocke, who was at the time courting his third wife and keeping their forthcoming marriage a secret from his parliamentary colleagues, it was Fairfax's devout and Presbyterian wife, Anne, who was to blame for his turn against the Scottish design. 'The Lord Generall Fairfax, being advised with heerin, seemed att first to like well of it,' Whitelocke wrote, but was then 'perswaded to the contrary by the presbiterians & by his own Lady'.[30]

The less gossipy dilemma for Fairfax, and for others, was whether initiating such a war could be legitimate. The justification of war mattered then, as it continues to matter, and could push those at the top to resign their office rather than go against their conscience. 'It is probable there will be war between us, butt whither we should begin this war, & be on the offensive part, or only stand uppon our owne defence, is that which I scruple,' Fairfax told Cromwell, Whitelocke and the others sent to persuade him. 'I am to answer only for my own conscience,' he continued.[31] Many felt their consciences wracked during these years, and struggled to be consistent or sure.

Within two days, Cromwell had accepted his commission as Fairfax's successor: he was now the new captain general and commander-in-chief of all the Forces – and Fairfax his fool.[32] In the chapel of Somerset House, the preacher Henry Walker addressed the new lord general and his colonels and officers uneasy about invading their brethren and breaking a covenant. 'Stand to your Armes,' he said, 'for the Scots ambition might insult over all our consciences.' The Solemn League and Covenant did not matter now that Covenanting Scots were preparing to invade with the king and enforce their 'Kirk bondage' on English souls. Rather than acknowledge Fairfax's own prick of conscience, Walker told his listeners that Fairfax had resigned because he was weary and persuaded by his wife to 'take rest in her bosome'.[33] Milton publicly praised him as he set off north in search of 'that most delightful and glorious rest'.[34]

Though not yet forty, Fairfax suffered terribly from ill health, including disabling attacks of gout, and he had been wounded several times during the wars. He had, in effect, been at war since the age of seventeen, first serving Charles I, and then against him. On the death of his father in 1648 he had become the third Lord Fairfax of Cameron, and he had houses and country estates in Yorkshire to manage. As Oliver Cromwell stepped into the breach as the commander-in-chief, and prepared sixteen thousand men for a two-week-long march to Scotland, Thomas Fairfax made plans to return home to Nun Appleton Hall, in Yorkshire. He wanted to ensure that his only child – Mary, known affectionately as Moll – would inherit his estates, and he wanted to find her a tutor. He also wanted to build a new house, study history and write poetry (like many seventeenth-century public men), collect coins and reflect on honour. He was well provided for by Parliament, which granted him an annual revenue of £5,000 from seized houses formerly belonging to George Villiers, duke of Buckingham. This was the same Buckingham who was currently on the boat to Scotland with Charles II. Buckingham would marry Moll later in the decade – another example of the blurred lines of allegiance at this time. To tutor his twelve-year-old daughter, Fairfax chose a brown-haired, 'cherry cheek't' and hazel-eyed poet from Hull: Andrew Marvell. According to his contemporary John Aubrey, Marvell was an excellent poet, but a man 'of very few words'.[35]

It is hard to be certain about Marvell's allegiance at this time, or how relevant this was to his position in Fairfax's household. As a Yorkshire man, Marvell knew Fairfax's family and acquaintances. He was friends with the pro-Parliament and rather radical governor of Hull, Robert Overton. He was also friends with Buckingham. Marvell had not fought in the wars – he had been in Europe, touring Holland, France, Italy and Spain, mingling with Buckingham and his brother, Francis Villiers. When in London, Marvell moved in a largely Royalist literary circle, including the poets Thomas Stanley and Abraham Cowley. In the summer of 1650, on Cromwell's return from Ireland and on the eve of his departure for Scotland, Marvell forsook his cavalier friends and wrote 'An Horatian Ode upon Cromwell's Return from Ireland'. It is a poem that acknowledges the significance of this moment in the life of the republic, and a poem that Fairfax, and possibly Cromwell too, may have seen, even though it was not published until many years later. Marvell probably wrote it in the hope that it might secure him a job at Whitehall, but it is not straightforward praise. It mourns the ruin of the 'great work of time' even as it quivers with the excitement and might of the new state. Marvell could see that a restless, ambitious man like Cromwell, who had tamed the Irish in a year, would easily subdue the Scots. They 'no shelter now shall find', he wrote, as they lay hidden in the bracken, camouflaged in plaid.[36]

Up at Nun Appleton, Marvell tutored the young Mary, read French libertine verse with Fairfax and wrote more poems. He roamed through the beautifully laid-out gardens with their regimented flowerbeds of tulips, pinks and roses. He wandered into the deer park and the grassy meadows and among the ancient oaks that surrounded the house. He could see war everywhere. A mower to him looked like a military commander – such as Fairfax – surveying a battlefield. In the freshly scythed meadows down in the valley of the River Wharfe Marvell saw the scattered piles of hay as dead bodies. The women forking the hay were local pillagers looking for spoils after a battle. In 'Upon Appleton House', this entirely private poem, Marvell praised his patron Fairfax, who could now 'weed' ambition and 'till' his conscience on his estates, although he, and Fairfax too, still thought about public life and duties.[37] Soon Marvell would leave the Fairfaxes and Nun Appleton and make his way back south, to seek work at the heart of the republic.

Marvell may have prophesied a crushing victory in Scotland but Cromwell's chances there were not guaranteed. David Leslie, the lieutenant-general of the Covenanters' army, had nearly twenty-six thousand men, compared to Cromwell's sixteen thousand – although Cromwell's soldiers were certainly the more experienced in battle.[38] And while the Irish were considered barbarians, the Scots were brethren to the English. Even if their Kirk was not liked by all, they were not superstitious papists. Now, however, soldiers who had once fought alongside one other faced each other across the battlefield. In July, the English army issued a declaration to God's elect in Scotland: 'We undertake this business in the fear of God,' it said, 'with bowels full of love, yea, full of pity, to the inhabitants of the country'.[39]

On his way to Scotland, from Alnwick in Northumberland, Cromwell wrote, as usual, to his family. In a letter to his father-in-law, Richard Major, he asked after his new baby granddaughter, Elizabeth, born to his 'idle' son Richard and Dorothy (Doll) that March. He also asked for pity for the magnitude of the role he now had, and was keen that his father-in-law would not think him personally ambitious: 'I neede pittye. I knowe what I feele, great place and businesse in the world is not worth the lookinge after, I should have no comfort in mine, but that my hope is in the Lord's presence, I have not sought theise thinges, Truly I have beene called to them by the Lord.'[40]

The weather in Scotland was dreadful that summer. Cromwell and his soldiers were low on tents, food, hay for their horses. Their supply ships struggled to land in the winds. Scotland was, to many of these soldiers, a strange land. The terrain was boggy, rocky, often impassable. Steep glens and wide rivers slowed them down, or trapped them. One English soldier writing home described 'this earthly tabernacle', whose inhabitants seemed both pious and lascivious: the 'il favoured and durty women' who 'all look like witches', and the cursing men. In their quarters the soldiers slept in sheetless, flea-ridden beds and were forced to swallow drink that 'hath such a filthy tange, and so laxative' that it gave the soldiers the runs.[41] They were, according to another English soldier, Captain John Hodgson, a 'poor, shattered, hungry, discouraged army'.[42] Cromwell made his way to Dunbar, on the eastern coast, south of the Firth of Forth, where their ships from England could land safely in the sheltered bay. From there, hundreds of sick men were shipped home, and it was reported that perhaps the entire English army was preparing to retreat.

South of Dunbar, in a glen through which the Broxburn ran east towards the North Sea, the English army found itself trapped. On one side was water, where the Broxburn joined the sea; to the south, perched on top of Doon Hill looking down into the valley, were the Scottish Covenanter troops, led by Leslie. And all around rose the steep bluffs of the glen. 'Wee are upon an Engagement very difficult,' Cromwell wrote to Sir Arthur Hesilrige, governor of Newcastle, and they were 'sicke beyond imagination'.[43] More than ten thousand men were exhausted, starving, soaked to the skin and terrified. If the Scottish troops held their ground, they would lose. Leslie moved his troops down the slopes of Doon Hill to form a wide, threatening arc on the hillsides on the other side of the burn from where Cromwell and senior army officers John Lambert, Charles Fleetwood, George Monck and their men waited and watched.

The night of 2 September was 'a drakie nycht full of wind and weit'– typical of that summer.[44] The Scottish officers retired to warm lodgings; the English lay down to sleep in the damp summer corn. Cromwell, Lambert and Monck, guessing that the Scots would launch their attack the next day, decided that they could take them by surprise, at dawn. Cromwell rode through the night, up and down through his troops, 'biting his lips till the blood ran down his chin'.[45] At four o'clock in the morning of 3 September, the English trumpets sounded and the soldiers attacked, charging with their battle cry: 'The Lord of Hosts.' They crossed the river at the sea end to ambush the Scottish troops on the right-hand side of their self-made arc. This simple but inspired tactic meant that bolting Scottish soldiers and horses would have no choice but to stampede back through their own men, who flanked the steep slopes of the valley behind them. Captain Hodgson recorded the battle in his memoirs. The Scots were 'all in confusion', he wrote, and with 'the sun appearing upon the sea, I heard Nol say, "Now let God arise and his enemies shall be scattered" . . . I heard him say, "I profess they run!" and then was the Scots army all in disorder and running . . . The General made a halt, and sung the one hundred and seventeenth psalm.'[46] This psalm thanks God: 'For his merciful kindness is great toward us: and the truth of the Lord endureth for ever.'[47] John Aubrey recalls someone he knew who had fought at Dunbar, and who himself recalled Cromwell's extraordinary behaviour:

> One that I knew, and who was present, told me that Oliver was carried on as with a divine impulse. He did laugh so excessively as if he had been drunk, and his eyes sparkled with spirits. He obtained on that great occasion a great victory, though the action was said to be contrary to human prudence. The same fit of laughter seized him just before the battle of Naseby, as a kinsman of mine and a great favourite of his, Colonel J. P. then present, testified.[48]

Such bloodthirstiness could not be the reason for this miraculous victory. For Cromwell, their rout was a sign of God's mercy, and approval of the justness of their cause. Three thousand Scots died that day, 3 September 1650, and ten thousand were taken prisoner; a mere twenty English soldiers were lost.[49] Of the prisoners, four thousand were marched south to Durham. Many died on the way and many more died once imprisoned in Durham

Castle. They were buried, without ceremony, in the castle and cathedral grounds. Other prisoners were sent abroad, to Virginia and New England.[50]

The defeated Covenanters also looked to God to explain their defeat. 'It wes the visible hand of God,' the defeated Leslie wrote.[51] They had fought in the name of the Covenant, but they must have incurred the wrath of God through the sins of the royal family and the continued presence of malignants (non-Covenanting Royalists) in the land and, worse, among the troops. They would need to show more humiliation; they would need more days of fasting; they would need to purge their army of those not fully repentant. They must search hard within themselves and their (particularly carnal) behaviour to understand why 'God is angry'.[52]

Back at Westminster the news of Cromwell's victory was joyfully received by Parliament. The republic was buoyed up. The day after the battle Cromwell sat down to write several letters – to his wife, to Richard Major and of course to Parliament. With the latter he enclosed the list of prisoners taken and nearly two hundred colours. These flags were hung in Westminster Hall, and Thomas Simon – he who had engraved the new Great Seal of the Commonwealth – was sent up to Scotland to sketch Cromwell for the Dunbar medal that Parliament arranged to have struck in silver and gold. Cromwell tried to resist, protesting that a simple depiction of Parliament would suffice. In the end, a profile bust of Cromwell adorned the medals with, at Cromwell's request, the following words engraved around the edge: 'The word at Dunbar the Lord of Hosts'. For the first time, all soldiers of all ranks who had fought that day at Dunbar were given a medal.[53] It is battles and victories like this that nurtured these soldiers' belief in their cause and in their right to intervene in politics and put pressure on the Parliament in whose name they risked their lives. Fairfax, who had not yet left for Yorkshire, heard the news with the army officer Edmund Ludlow at Hampton Court, and rejoiced.[54] The victory, ultimately, was God's, as Cromwell and others so sincerely believed, and this meant that the English would need to make sure they were worthy of God's favour, and reform themselves, rooting out more sin. Cromwell urged Speaker Lenthall to 'give glory' to God and 'improve' his power, to use his authority to 'curb the proud & the insolent . . . releive the oppressed, heare the groanes of poore prisoners . . . reform the abuses of all professions'. Only then would England's republic truly shine.[55]

While the Covenanters were whipping themselves and wondering what on earth could have gone wrong, the earl of Clarendon speculated that the surprise loss would please Charles II, who was at Perth. Perhaps this was 'the greatest happiness that could befall him', Clarendon wrote.[56] It might give Charles the opportunity to build his own army, and force the Covenanters to compromise on their terms. A few days later, Charles received sad news. On 8 September, his younger sister, the fourteen-year-old Princess Elizabeth, who had worn black ever since the day of her father's execution, had died of consumption in Carisbrooke Castle, where she and her brother Henry, duke of Gloucester, were being held. From Wales, in marshy Newton by Usk, the deeply loyal and impoverished Royalist poet Henry Vaughan wrote in memory of the princess: 'Thou seem'st a rosebud born in snow, / A flower of purpose sprung to bow / To headless tempests, and the rage / Of an incensèd, stormy age.'[57] A couple of months later, in the palace in The Hague, Charles's other sister, Mary, gave birth to a baby boy: the future William III.

In the autumn of 1650, Charles attempted to assert his royal authority over the Covenanting Scots. He knew that they needed him and his 'malignants' among their army, which was weakened and shaken after Dunbar. They also needed the Engagers, whom they had evicted for being lapsed Covenanters. Argyll and his Covenanters were loyal to the king, but they were divided between a godly and a political course of action. Charles tried to persuade them to rethink, and to let him become involved with their military strategy. Scotland, despite the extreme and cooler shades of Puritanism among its people, began to unite as a country that needed to defend itself against the formidable and increasingly radical English army. The most extreme Covenanters withdrew and a new Scottish army emerged, made up now of Covenanters and repentant Engagers, as well as long-standing Royalists, prepared to create an alliance for Charles. And at last a date was set for Charles's much-desired, and oft-postponed, coronation. He now had a kingdom and an army – however miserable and divided he found the country, and however uncomfortable its religion made him.[58]

It was a chilly throne on which Charles finally sat. It was, as an account of his Scottish coronation described, a 'frozen Throne'.[59] Charles was crowned on 1 January 1651, in a small, plain chapel, high on Moot Hill in the grounds of the old abbey of Scone. There was no altar in this stripped-out chapel, just a table, and some benches for the nobility to sit on. Wearing 'a princely robe', the tall, 'niger haired' Charles processed under a canopy, held aloft by chosen Scottish noblemen. Argyll carried the crown; he and not a bishop would set it on Charles's dark head.[60] This was a ceremony the like of which had never been seen before, in any of the three 'distracted' nations of England, Scotland and Ireland.[61] Sir James Balfour, as Scotland's chief herald, was the mastermind behind the coronation, and what he devised was a warning shot across the bows of monarchy. It was a ceremony of terror and exhortation. Robert Dowglas delivered a thundering sermon, reminding Charles of his father's sins, and that crowns could fall: 'The Sins of former Kings, have made this a tottering Crown,' Dowglas warned, and Charles should be 'truly humbled for his own sins, and the sins of his Fathers house, which have been great'.[62] Charles was not daubed with oil like an English monarch, whereby the grace of God would enter into his bowels and turn him into the Lord's anointed. Instead of consecrated oil, 'the oyle of the Presbytery' was poured upon him.[63] The most important thing that Charles did was to swear to uphold the Kirk of Scotland, to observe its preaching, practices and ceremonies, to rule according to the laws of Scotland, and to endeavour to bring about thorough reformation in his other kingdoms – in Ireland and England – and establish Presbyterianism. He renewed the National Covenant and the Solemn League and Covenant, which he had already signed on the ship outside Garmouth. It was as a crowned, covenanted king that Charles was presented to the congregation in the church, and to the people waiting outside in the grounds of Scone, in the freezing cold.

Charles's devoutness and seriousness during the ceremony were commented on by Scottish ministers, but he probably felt wretched. Perhaps he comforted himself by thinking that he might not need to keep any of these promises anyway. There were still Royalists in England who he might be able to raise. Oaths, covenants, coronation promises mattered – one broke them at the risk of incurring the wrath of God. But, as it was, at the time of this coronation the Scots were not looking so strong. No one at this frosty, chiding ceremony was neglectful of the fact that, three months earlier, the Covenanting forces had suffered a spectacular, and unexpected, defeat at the hands of Cromwell. And, when deliberating over the terms at Breda, Charles had been mindful of the fact that he would not be able to impose the Covenant in his two other kingdoms without the consultation and consent of their Parliaments. 'It is not in my power', he had said rather primly to the Prince of Orange in April 1650, to impose Presbyterian government in England and Ireland, 'without the advice of my respective parliaments of those kingdoms, by whose advice and consent only laws are to be made or altered'.[64]

Others knew that ceremonies such as coronations matter because they inspire loyalty and obedience, and display a sense of order which looks natural, timeless: 'the coronation in it self be but a ceremony' but it would 'beget in the hearts of his People a more reverend and honourable esteem of his Majesty', commented a Dutchman.[65] The exiled Royalist Margaret Cavendish, married to the future duke of Newcastle, agreed. Ceremony 'heightens and glories the power of Kings, and States, it strikes such a reverence and respect in the beholders, as it begets fear and wonder . . . it becomes a kinde of a god,' she wrote.[66] Non-Royalists knew this too. Anticipating the effect that a crowned Charles II up in Scotland could have on the republic, press and satirical ballad-writers sought to tarnish the accoutrements of royalty. This 'Crown carrieth no luster', it was said: this new king is an 'Artificiall Meteor', a 'Scottish vapour'.[67]

1651

Behold, I present you with an History of Wonders; wonders so rare and great, that, as no former Age can parallel, succeeding Times will scarce believe them . . . Read on and wonder.

Thomas Blount,
Boscobel

Things back in London had been less dramatic than in Scotland. The MPs in Parliament sat on, when really they should have put themselves up for election. The republic, to survive, needed a legitimate constitutional basis and its Parliament was the purged remnant of the one summoned by Charles I back in 1640 – although many of the MPs who were once appalled by Pride's Purge had since returned. It was the reigning monarch who animated Parliament in early modern England: he or she called a Parliament, triggering an election, when one was wanted or needed, and then dismissed it. When a monarch died, Parliament (if one was sitting) was automatically dissolved.

The republic's MPs needed to manage all this themselves. But many in the House feared that fresh elections would return an unsympathetic Parliament. Royalist MPs might sneak in and strangle the fledgling republic. The House was also irreconcilably divided over religion. The Puritans who had once united against the king had split apart during the wars and the rift between the religiously moderate and the religiously radical was widening. Those in favour of some kind of national Church, albeit one without bishops running things, had tried to push through Presbyterianism. They battled with the smaller but powerful radical faction called the Independents – a group that included Oliver Cromwell, fiery Henry Marten and the godly Henry Vane. They wanted something less prescriptive, free from state control, a little more tolerant of those with differing religious beliefs (not extended to Catholics, of course). Beyond Westminster, there were even more extreme voices, particularly coming from the army, who wanted to further dismantle the Protestant Church. New sects arose with evocative names – Ranters, Muggletonians, Seekers – each with their own alarming, not always well-defined, ideas about God, salvation, sin and the Devil. They loosely shared the belief in the freedom to interpret the Bible as they liked and to worship (and sometimes live) how they liked. Ranters behaved as if they were exempt from any moral law and, believing in a divine spirit that was everywhere and in everyone, were accused of denying God. Muggletonians believed the tailor Lodowicke Muggleton was a prophet from the book of Revelation, and that there was no hell. Seekers were still looking for the true Church. These sects flourished, some of them only briefly, in a time of change that enabled wonder, possibility and some abandon. Other sects managed to survive: the Quakers and the Baptists.[1]

But most people living in England were not like this. Most wanted a vicar in their parish to lead their services, baptise their children, bury their dead and tell them what the Bible meant. Ordinary men and women were not particularly enthusiastic about the new order at Whitehall, but not all were despairing. While there are many voices impossible to recover, a good few kept diaries and journals, or wrote memoirs. In his diary, the Essex clergyman Ralph Josselin, fearing for the health of his family with a new smallpox outbreak in his parish, could move from the minutiae of his everyday life to the 'state of England' in a sentence. England was, he wrote, a divided and discontented nation, before describing his worries about a sore navel.[2] The scholarly Lucy Hutchinson (who wrote a biography of her republican husband, Colonel John Hutchinson, in the Restoration years) was keenly behind the republic.[3] The young Dutchman Lodewijck Huygens, who arrived in England with a party of Dutch ambassadors at the end of 1651, observed how London thronged with all kinds of people, of varying political and religious persuasions, going about their business, shopping for French niceties or Italian scarves in the New Exchange, riding in Hyde Park.[4] Men powdered their hair, and women wore ribbons, masks and beauty spots.[5] Across the country, men continued in their posts as county Justices of the Peace, sheriffs or constables, rubbing along with colleagues, only some of whom had been drafted in because they were of the right sort. In towns and villages, signs swinging outside some inns rang the changes: 'Here *was* the King's Head'; 'Here *was* ye King's Armes'. Other inns were still called 'The Crown', or 'The Garter', in Windsor.[6]

In his study in Whitehall, John Milton, when not busy writing letters for the council of state to be sent abroad, snatched moments to work on another book requested by the council: *A Defence of the People of England*. Europe had been shocked by England's behaviour and, in February 1651, Milton published his *Defence*. It had taken him a year to write, and it was a hefty tome, written in Latin. It was a counter-attack on the famous Frenchman Claude Saumaise – known by the Latinate name of Salmasius – who, in autumn 1649, had reprimanded the 'English rascals' for daring to kill their king.[7] Salmasius' *Defensio Regia, Pro Carolo I* ('A Royal Defence of Charles I') made him very popular with Charles and Europe's royalty; Queen Christina of Sweden invited him to her court. But to Milton, Salmasius was a foreign windbag meddling in England's affairs, writing for continental readers who knew nothing of his country's situation. Both used the Bible to justify their points. Milton emerges now as committed to a non-monarchical form of government which, according to the Bible, had God's approval: 'A republican form of government seemed to God more advantageous for his chosen people.'[8] God, Milton argued, did not endorse kings – although God would let a people decide who to raise over them – and kings are not made in the image of God. Kings are not a natural fact, but constructs, and can be pulled down. Milton used 'people' loosely: his people were a godly elite who could act, guided by God, as if representing all the people of England. But Salmasius – also a Protestant – read the Bible differently: kings were divinely appointed, sacred and accountable to God only. Salmasius was right that there was no precedent for setting up a high court without a king, and trying and then executing that king: the legitimacy of Charles I's trial was hard to defend. In 1651, those in England on the side of Salmasius and not of Milton had the opportunity to seek vengeance for Charles I's murder and fight, once again, for a king.

After his chilly coronation Charles was made commander-in-chief of Scotland's army, and he began to exert some authority over the squabbling Scottish factions: the Covenanters, the Engagers and stalwart Royalists. Any new-found confidence, however, was misguided. Oliver Cromwell was still in Scotland. He had been ill during the winter – there were even rumours that he had died – but he and his troops were fit by the summer campaign season. Led by Major-General John Lambert and Colonel George Monck, English soldiers secured the south-east of Scotland. Lambert had won a decisive victory at Inverkeithing and his wife, Frances, had joined him on his victorious campaign, ordering up French linen from London to wrap around her neck.[9] Edinburgh Castle had surrendered in December 1650 and, in August 1651, Stirling Castle would fall to Monck, full of great stores of guns, gunpowder, lances, pikes, claret wine, barrels of beef and even the records of Scotland, the chair of state and other shiny items of the Scottish regalia.[10] Next

Monck secured the city of Dundee. At the end of July, Charles made the understandable if risky decision to head to England – as fast as he could – with sixteen thousand troops and six thousand horses in the hope that Royalists would join him and swell his troops on the march down to reclaim the capital, London. He was joined by David Leslie, the lieutenant-general of the Scottish Covenanting army who had suffered the terrible defeat at Dunbar, and his loyal band: George Villiers, duke of Buckingham; John Maitland, earl of Lauderdale; Henry Lord Wilmot; and William, duke of Hamilton. Hamilton's rival, the staunch Covenanter Archibald Campbell, marquess of Argyll, refused to go.

Charles and his army moved quickly, and successfully at first. He was proclaimed king at Penrith in Cumbria, and at Rokeby near Durham on 6 August 1651, knighting men along the way.[11] Thomas Wentworth, who with his father the earl of Cleveland had sailed to Scotland with Charles, wrote from Penrith: 'By God's grace we are come as far as Penrith in Cumberland, with a good army . . . all absolutely at the king's command, as much as any army I ever saw under the command of his father . . . We have very good hopes that many others will follow.'[12] James Stanley, earl of Derby and lord of the Isle of Man, was encouraged by his wife to cross over from his island to join Charles's army in Lancashire.[13] Those who were unsure left the king's army, effecting a 'natural purge', while others defected from the enemy's side, so that the Royalists felt they 'shall prove best' in this next wave of civil war.[14] Copies of Charles's declaration, printed in Aberdeen and addressed 'to all His loving Subjects of His Kingdom of England and Dominion of Wales', were despatched all over the country, and overseas to Holland and elsewhere in Europe. In this he called on all men to assist him to bring 'justice upon Murtherers of our Royall Father' and restore his birthright, lawful government and the people's liberty. In exchange, he promised a 'full Act of Oblivion' to protect any who had once fought against his family – except the regicides.[15]

Parliament ordered that Charles's printed declarations should be recalled. They were rattled by how Charles had managed to slip past the English army in Scotland. Even 'stout-hearted' John Bradshaw, the council of state's president, could not, according to Lucy Hutchinson, conceal his fear; some even questioned whether Cromwell himself could have switched sides.[16] But, in fact, the 'natural purge' was weakening Charles. Many of the Scots army deserted and headed back to Scotland. Not every English city rushed to declare for the king: Carlisle, for example, refused. English Royalists, who shared Charles's distaste for Presbyterianism, were uneasy about joining an army packed with Scottish Presbyterians. As *Mercurius Politicus* pointed out, the odd marriage between the 'rough Cavalier' and the 'round Presbyterian', 'made to square together' in the Scottish army led by Charles, was not a happy one.[17] Former Royalist agents Isaac Birkenhead and Thomas Coke divulged plans about their planned risings.[18] Other men stayed away either because they were tired of war, or not sufficiently angry with the republic, despite the high taxes being levied to fund the war in Scotland, and the ongoing conquest in Ireland. And perhaps more supported, or tolerated, the republic than Charles had wanted to believe.

On 22 August, Charles and his men limped into Worcester, on the edge of the Royalist West Country. They had marched three hundred miles and had not amassed the support they had hoped for and needed. Charles was proclaimed king at Worcester Cross by the city's mayor, Thomas Lisens, but Lisens was not a Royalist.[19] Charles summoned the allegiance of the nobility, gentry and others, 'from sixteen to sixty', to gather at Pitchcroft on 26 August, armed and with their horses.[20] Cromwell, however, was hot on his heels, and his army was bigger. On 28 August, Cromwell and his leading officers John Lambert, Charles Fleetwood and Thomas Harrison arrived. They had twenty-eight thousand men with them. They sallied round to the south of Worcester, preventing Charles from moving further south towards London. Lambert won the pass over the Severn at Upton, a few miles outside Worcester, so the English army now had access to both sides of the river.

On the morning of 3 September, the anniversary of Cromwell's intoxicated dawn victory at Dunbar, Charles climbed up to the top of Worcester's cathedral tower, to survey the land and Cromwell's manoeuvres. He watched Cromwell's soldiers building a bridge of boats across the Severn, and could see firing at Powick Bridge, further south, where the River Teme met the Severn. Having secured two crossings, including Powick Bridge, the site of the very first engagement of the civil wars back in 1642, Cromwell then moved to the south-eastern outskirts of the city. He turned his attack to Fort Royal, the sconce perched on the little hill just outside the city walls of Worcester, rising above the Royalist base in the commandery. Charles, the duke of Buckingham and their troops surged out of the city through Sidbury Gate. Charles charged on his horse, leading his soldiers like a medieval king in battle, but they were pushed down the hill and back through the city gate. From conquered Fort Royal, a weary Cromwell described later that same night how they turned the king's 'owne Gunns upon him', and he 'had greate losse'.[21] The duke of Hamilton was shot in the leg, a wound from which he would not recover. He died, and was buried in Worcester Cathedral. Back inside the city, Charles's troops were beginning to quail. Charles is said to have told them: 'I had rather you would shoot me, then keep me alive to see the sad consequences of this fatal day.'[22] The fighting, often 'at push of pike', now happened in the streets of Worcester and around its glorious, and at that moment pillaged, cathedral. Charles turned to the north, and fled the city through St Martin's Gate. His army scattered. In the cloth-making town of Kidderminster, just eleven miles from Worcester, lived Richard Baxter, the famous Puritan minister and writer. He had preached before New Model Army soldiers and went on to publish forty books in the 1650s, selling thousands of copies. From his bed, Baxter heard the stampeding horses of the 'flying army', and the bullets fired after them. 'And till midnight,' Baxter would recall in his Restoration autobiography, 'the bullets flying towards my door and windows, and the sorrowful fugitives hasting by for their lives, did tell me the calamitousness of war.'[23] Charles was now on the run. He had to get to Royalist Wales as fast as he could, or to the south coast, across the Channel and back to exile.

It was evening by the time Charles, Buckingham, Lauderdale, Derby and Wilmot and some sixty other fleeing Royalists knew that the day was 'irrecoverably lost'.[24] Derby suggested that Charles seek refuge in Boscobel House in Shropshire, a hunting lodge owned by the Giffards. The Giffards were an important Catholic family who had protected Derby when he had landed from the Isle of Man and fought his way through Lancashire to join Charles II. Catholic recusants were experienced at hiding both themselves and others. For decades in England, since the last years of Elizabeth I's reign, Catholic families had escaped prosecution for refusing to acknowledge the Church of England and attend its services. Instead, they continued to hold mass in their houses and sheltered homeless Catholic priests.

Charles and his exhausted cavaliers rode north through the night. They were led by Charles Giffard who had fought with them at Worcester. Giffard took them not to Boscobel House but to another house owned by his family, White Ladies, a farmhouse set among the ruins of the former twelfth-century Augustinian priory just a mile from Boscobel. From White Ladies, tenant farmers John and George Penderel sent for their two brothers, Richard and William, who lived nearby: Richard at Hobbal Grange and William as caretaker at Boscobel House. Together these brothers, all Catholics, would help Charles hide and move between safe houses in the West Midlands, guiding him, scouting and gathering intelligence about the whereabouts of Cromwell and his troops. Richard agreed to chaperone Charles to Royalist Wales. He cut Charles's long, aristocratic hair and dressed him in green breeches and a leather doublet, like a woodman. Charles blackened his face with soot from the chimney.[25] They hid outside in the wood, Spring Coppice. Derby and Lauderdale left Charles, and made their way north, only to be caught up by parliamentary troops. Derby gave himself up and was executed for treason on 15 October, despite Cromwell supporting his plea for clemency.[26] Lauderdale was captured, and remained in prison for the next nine years. Buckingham managed to escape and made his way across the Channel.

After hiding in Spring Coppice all day in the pouring rain, Charles and Richard set off by foot, planning to cross the Severn into Wales. But the river was heavily guarded by Cromwell's men. They spent the night in the barn at Madeley, the home of another Catholic, Francis Wolfe, and then they retreated to Richard's home, Hobbal Grange, arriving early in the morning. On 6 September, they moved to Boscobel House and there, while parliamentary cavalry roamed beneath, Charles hid in an oak tree with another Worcester refugee, Colonel William Careless. The colonel offered Charles his lap to sleep on. Later, the poet Abraham

Cowley recalled the oak whose 'faithful boughs, in kind allegiance, spread / Their shelt'ring branches' around Charles's 'awful head'.[27] The 'Royal Oak', as it came to be known, no longer stands, but a descendant of it does, and saplings from that tree can be bought from Boscobel, now an English Heritage attraction.

After a day up in the tree, Charles moved into the house, hiding in the attic. The next day, he read in the garden. On the evening of 7 September, Charles rode with the Penderel brothers to Moseley Hall, an Elizabethan farmhouse. A fifth Penderel brother, Humphrey, had loaned Charles his mill horse, sturdy enough to carry the 'weight of three kingdoms on his back', Humphrey supposedly said.[28] At Moseley, Charles was hosted by Thomas Whitgreave and his Catholic chaplain John Huddleston, who hid him in the priest's hole. Henry, Lord Wilmot was also sheltering at this house. Charles had been disguised further – his hair was now shorn right off, 'according to the country mode'. Short hair, of course, was also what the Puritans preferred, so here was the king looking like a roundhead. In his Restoration account of this episode, Thomas Blount – another steadfast local Catholic – described in detail the king's rustic appearance on arrival at Moseley Hall:

> His Majesties Attire, as was before observ'd in part, was then a leather-doublet, a pair of green breeches and a Jump-coat (as the Country call's it) of the same green, a pair of his own stockens with the tops cut off, because embroider'd, and a pair of stirrop stockens, which were lent him at Madeley, a pair of old shoos, cut and slash'd to give ease to his feet, an old grey, greazy hat without a lyning, a noggen shirt, of the coursest linnen, His face and hands made of a reechy complexion, by the help of the Walnut-tree leaves.[29]

The royal party was nearly discovered when parliamentary soldiers arrived at Moseley and questioned Whitgreave, threatening to search his home. Father Huddleston, who was tutoring several young gentlemen at the Hall, had set them up as lookouts, positioned in several of the garret windows, little faces staring out. From Moseley Hall, the plan was to smuggle Charles west, towards Bristol. Jane Lane, the sister of the Royalist army officer Colonel Thomas Lane from nearby Bentley Hall, had been granted a pass by Parliament to visit a pregnant relative near Bristol. Charles would accompany Jane, disguised as her servant and mounted before her on a white horse – or so the portraitist Isaac Fuller's painting of the episode suggests.[30] On the journey, which began on 10 September, Wilmot followed the pair at a safe distance. Charles sometimes lodged with families who had no idea who their fugitive guest was. Others did recognise him, such as the butler of the manor at Abbots Leigh just outside Bristol. The self-publicising Royalist and highwayman James Hind, who had fought at Worcester, had supposedly accompanied Charles some of the way; Hind was later captured in a barber's shop on the Strand. 'Had I a thousand lives,' he supposedly said, 'I would adventure them all for King Charles.'[31]

After six weeks on the run, Charles finally arrived on the south coast of England. On 14 October, having found a skipper brave enough to carry him across the Channel, Charles sailed from Shoreham. Just after his ship had set sail, the republic's soldiers eventually caught up with the refugee, but they were too late. Charles arrived in Fécamp in Normandy two days later. All those who helped Charles during his flight would be remembered for their loyalty and courage. Jane Lane, who the council of state knew had travelled with Charles, also managed to get to France, where she was welcomed by Henrietta Maria at her exiled court in the

Louvre. At the Restoration, Charles II gave Jane £1,000 and a lock of his hair. There had been rumours that the pair became lovers while in exile.[32] Descendants of Richard – 'Trusty Dick' – Penderel's family are still paid an annual allowance by the Crown today.

Royalists interpreted Charles's lucky escape as nothing short of miraculous – particularly in the Restoration years, when it seemed certain that some divine plan must have been at work to preserve His Majesty. It is the stuff of romance, and the kind of story that shores up monarchy. 'Behold, I present you with an *History of Wonders*; wonders so rare and great, that, as no former Age can parallel, succeeding Times will scarce believe them . . . Read on and wonder,' wrote Blount in his account, published in 1660 once Charles II had been restored.[33] Isaac Fuller, also in the Restoration, produced a series of five paintings recounting and commemorating the king's adventures. Today you can visit Moseley Hall (now called Moseley Old Hall) and see the very bed that Charles briefly slept in, and the priest's hole in which he hid while Cromwell's soldiers lurked in the garden. The reliability of many of the sources, written and produced with the benefit of hindsight, is doubtful.[34] Blount's history supposedly pulled together eyewitness accounts from the time, but he was keen to emphasise the role that fellow Catholics played in protecting Charles.

Despite the luck of his post-Worcester flight and the miracle of his survival, Charles was, at the end of 1651, a broken man. He had begun the year as a crowned, if Covenanting, king; he ended it as a man on the run with a £1,000 reward on his head. The frozen throne in the north was left empty, and Charles II never trod on Scottish soil again. In fact, the next crowned monarch to visit Scotland was George IV in 1822, over a hundred years after the eventual union of the two kingdoms in 1707. For the

Royalist poet Katherine Philips, whose husband, James, had fought for Parliament, the sun that set over Worcester on 3 September, as Charles and his loyal nobles fled the city, was the sun of 'gasping' monarchy itself. 'Setting majesty' had, like the sun, 'quit the world', Philips wrote, 'depriving it of day'. Diadems were now 'cheap', and loyal heroes 'tumble in a common heap'. What kind of king was this, who could fizzle and fall, and who was unable, just like his father, to 'keep a throne'? Yet, even as Philips angrily reworked the familiar image of a king as a sun, she remained hopeful, because the thing about setting suns is that they rise again.[35]

On 12 September, nine days after the battle of Worcester, and with the whereabouts of Charles II unknown, Oliver Cromwell was given (again) a hero's welcome by the city of London. The day before, Bulstrode Whitelocke, and fellow MPs John Lisle, Gilbert Pickering and Oliver St John (Cromwell's cousin), had met Cromwell at Aylesbury, where they hawked, supped and 'had much discourse . . . about the passages in Scotland & at Worcester'.[36] Cromwell gave each of the MPs a horse and two prisoners to keep. Whitelocke kept the horse but granted the two prisoners passes to return home. In the fields of Acton, west London, the lord mayor, sheriffs, aldermen and recorder of the City, dressed in their scarlet robes, met the returning retinue. The procession numbered about three hundred coaches, plus the life guard, a London cavalry troop and 'a great number of commoners and gentlemen of quality'. At Hyde Park Corner, Cromwell was saluted by the 'blue regiment of volunteers lately raised' and at St James's, the great guns which had been wheeled out fired as he passed. The streets were lined with nobility, Members of Parliament, members of the council of state and 'thousands' of citizens. They took off their hats, a gesture of deference to authority.[37] Nedham reported on the 'innumerable Flocks of people' in his newsbook *Mercurius Politicus* but it is impossible to know how many cheering spectators were really in favour of the regime, or there for a glimpse of spectacle and power, or to gawp in disbelief.[38] Cromwell and Speaker Lenthall travelled together in a coach. An account notes how Cromwell did not wish to process on horseback, but preferred to be shielded from the crowds, 'desiring rather that the good he doth to this Common-wealth may be heard and felt then seen'.[39] Of Worcester, Cromwell said that it was 'for ought I know a Crowning mercy' – ironic use of 'crowning' here.[40] He would never go to the field again. The battle of Worcester had succeeded in stripping Charles of his prospects of an English crown, at least for now. The parliamentarian press shaped a powerful story about the victory at sunrise in Dunbar on 3 September 1650, followed a year later to the day, on 3 September 1651, with the decisive defeat of a young and barely crowned king, fleeing Worcester at sunset.[41]

Following Cromwell's triumphant welcome, almost four thousand Scottish prisoners, including Lauderdale, were paraded through the streets of London, from Aldgate in the east through the City to Westminster. Pity was shown, and white bread and money were distributed among them. Lauderdale was sent to the Tower. Less high-profile prisoners were either shipped abroad to colonies such as Barbados or sold into service in England; others were sent back to Scotland.[42]

Worcester marked the final battle on English soil of the civil wars that had begun in 1642. Many years later, in 1786, America's revolutionary and second president John Adams stood on Fort Royal Hill in Worcester and admonished the crowds who seemed to him so 'ignorant and careless': 'And do Englishmen so soon forget the ground where liberty was fought for? Tell your neighbors and your children that this is holy ground.'[43] Liberty was not simply political liberty, in the sense of shaking off the shackles of monarchy and asserting the sovereignty of the people. Liberty to many meant religious liberty, the freedom to follow one's conscience and serve God. Thomas Fairfax resigned his commission as commander-in-chief because he could not fight his Presbyterian brethren in Scotland; Cromwell and his soldiers fought at Dunbar in the name of God for their version of liberty. And the Royalists and Catholics who protected the fugitive Charles in their homes and orchestrated his escape served their king and followed their own consciences and principles. Some, such as Argyll and Charles II himself, were more pragmatic and prepared to compromise and swear troubling oaths. Charles agreed to sign the Covenant on board his ship off the coast of Scotland and some Royalists agreed to profess loyalty to the Commonwealth of England, without a king, in exchange for holding on to their property and leading a quiet life. What troubled many, and what undermined the legitimacy of the young republic, was the commonplace that a victory secured by the sword depends on the sword to maintain that victory. After the siege of Colchester back in 1648, Milton had asked, rhetorically, in relation to Fairfax: 'For what can War but Acts of War still breed?' After Ireland, Marvell similarly observed, ominously, in his ode about Cromwell that 'the same arts that did gain / A pow'r must it maintain'.[44]

During 1651, with Charles II in Scotland, on British soil, the threat from committed Royalists was high and the republic had to choose how to punish traitors. The administrators of the state had become adept at gathering information – capturing Royalists, seizing their papers, intercepting letters that revealed plots. On 29 March 1651, the Royalist agent Thomas Coke, son of Sir John Coke, Charles I's former secretary of state, was arrested in an upholsterer's on the Strand.[45] Thomas was forced to disclose the plans and the names of the leaders involved in an uprising planned in London, a collaboration between Royalist noblemen and Presbyterian ministers who were now willing to work with Royalists to restore monarchy. From the names divulged by Coke, Christopher Love, the Welsh-born minister of St Lawrence Jewry in London, was among the arrested, and he was singled out for trial as a ringleader. He was charged with treason against the free state of England, for attempting to 'crush the Commonwealth in its infancy', and he was sentenced to death.[46] This was a show of the republic's strength, of its attitude towards former Presbyterian allies and a redefinition of treason: against the state, not a king. Mary Love petitioned the council of state, and then Oliver Cromwell directly, who was up in Scotland, to show mercy to her condemned Presbyterian husband.[47] It did not work. On 22 August, the day that Charles arrived in Worcester, Love was executed on Tower Hill. On the scaffold, he declared that he died 'cleaving to all those oaths, vows, covenants' and would rather 'die a covenant-keeper, than live a covenant-breaker'. He addressed those Londoners who had gathered to watch him die directly, and asked them to think about the consequences of engaging in a war with their brethren in Scotland.[48] For men like Christopher Love, it was a time of choice. Those who condemned Love also had to decide how best to serve God and protect the republic: whether to punish or show clemency (to both their enemies and former allies); whether to continue to rule by the sword or not. Consolidating a legitimate, tolerant regime that was obeyed at home and recognised abroad was the huge task that Cromwell, the council of state and Parliament now faced.

1652

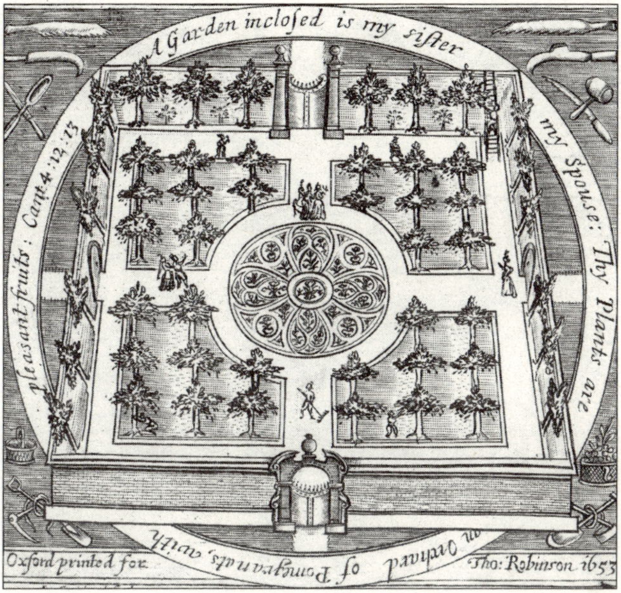
A Garden inclosed is my sister my Spouse: Thy Plants are an Orchard of Pomegranats, with pleasant fruits: Cant.4:12:13
Oxford printed for
Tho: Robinson 1653

I returned to my homeland, not quite sure of my safety. But in no other place could I have been safer.

Thomas Hobbes

Our Design is still to prove, That a Free-State Government is much more excellent than any other form.

Mercurius Politicus,
1–6 January 1652

On Monday 29 March 1652, at 9.56 a.m., a total eclipse plunged the country into darkness. Up in Yorkshire, a pregnant and frightened Alice Thornton ventured into her garden to witness the power of God. There was complete gloom for several minutes, the stars came out and a 'cold storme for a time did Posses the Earth'. The day became known as 'Black Monday'.[1] For the celebrated astrologer William Lilly, 1652 would be an 'annus tenebrosus': a dark year caused by multiple solar and lunar eclipses.

From his corner house on the Strand, Lilly foretold great changes, not just in England but throughout Europe. People were, he thought, 'very greedy of Novelties'. There would, he wrote, be 'great mutation in the Magistracy of Nations, in the change and alteration of Governours'. There would be war at sea (England did go to war with Holland in this year) and the beginning of a new, austere kind of sovereignty. 'Old things are departed', he mused, and monarchy 'generally disliked' and disturbed everywhere.[2] It was widely thought that other kings would fall: in 1649 John Owen had preached on how God would 'sooner or later shake all the Monarchies of the Earth'.[3] During 1651 Ralph Josselin scribbled repeatedly in his diary about how the thirteen-year-old Louis XIV of France was surely about to lose his crown. France's nobles were rebelling, at the time, against absolute monarchical authority, which Louis held dear. 'All authority belongs to us,' the French king pronounced in July 1652. 'We hold it of God alone.'[4]

Lilly's yearly almanacs – *Merlini Anglici Ephemeris* – sold in the tens of thousands, at home and abroad. His readings of the positions of stars had foretold, during the war years, parliamentarian victories. This secured him fame, and his predictions for the 1650s were followed closely by Parliament. But such was his reputed skill and respectability that Lilly was consulted and befriended by key republican figures, such as John Lambert and Bulstrode Whitelocke (who patronised Lilly's convivial Society of Astrologers), and by Royalists. Lilly's close friend and fellow astrologer was the Royalist antiquarian Elias Ashmole, founder of the Ashmolean Museum in Oxford, and future Windsor herald under Charles II.[5]

As Lilly also predicted from gazing at the skies, the year following Worcester was one of foreign embassies: ambassadors travelled from Europe to England to formally acknowledge the new regime. Initially, Charles had enjoyed an increase in status once he was safely back on the continent after Worcester, simply by virtue of the fact that he was a crowned king who at least had one kingdom (Scotland) to his name. Foreign courts and hosts recognised this. But, after Cromwell's decisive victory at Worcester, the English Parliament had set about absorbing Scotland into the English republic, and European powers were beginning to think differently about what was happening across the Channel.[6] A formidable navy, in which Parliament was investing, felling the country's trees to provide ships' hulls, meant that soon after Scotland, other Royalist satellites fell: Jersey, Guernsey, the Scillies, the Isle of Man. On the other side of the Atlantic, Barbados, whose governor Lord Francis Willoughby had declared for Charles II, finally surrendered to the naval forces led by Sir George Ayscue, the Commonwealth's general-at-sea. Virginia and the Bermudas quickly followed suit. 1652 was a year of recognition, and while such recognition was forced in some instances, it was a significant legitimacy boost for the regime.

In its first few years, the republic's diplomatic efforts had ended in tragedy. In 1649 Isaac Dorislaus, Parliament's resident at The Hague, was stabbed to death by Royalist exiles, and in Madrid in 1650, six English Royalists murdered the parliamentary diplomat Anthony Ascham in an inn. In the spring of 1651 councillors of state Oliver St John and Walter Strickland (formerly an ambassador in Holland) had a disastrous trip to The Hague, hoping to build an alliance – a 'league and amity' – with a fellow Protestant republic only to find that the United Provinces of the Netherlands were less keen to compromise their sovereignty and recent independence from Spain. The Dutch were also appalled by what the English had done to a crowned king. They shouted 'Regicides!' as the ambassadors and their retinue rode past them through the streets.[7] But it was not long before some European courts began to turn their support away from Charles Stuart, and to seek friendship with the new English regime because, quite simply, it looked likely to last. Alonso de Cárdenas, the Spanish ambassador, had been the first to visit England, towards the end of 1650, shopping for Philip IV of Spain at the sale of Charles I's goods. By the end of 1652 most major European powers had formally recognised the English republic.[8] Representatives from Portugal, Sweden, the Netherlands and Denmark sailed to England to pledge their friendship in order that they could negotiate and trade. Such recognition did not always mean approval but it was a concession to the republic's power. At the very end of the year France's ambassador, Antoine de Bordeaux-Neufville, grudgingly acknowledged the republic. Meanwhile Lorenzo Paulucci, secretary to the Venetian ambassador in Paris, had arrived in England in April, but he was not instructed by the supreme government of Venice to recognise a fellow republic. He snooped instead. He thought the new republic lacked pomp and grandeur, although he found its protagonists haughty, and he could see that in Parliament, General Cromwell 'is the one who has the first word, and the last also'.[9]

As long as they were formally addressed as 'the Parliament of the Republic of England' and by foreign ministers with real credentials, England's councillors of state welcomed ambassadors from kingdoms and republics alike with due protocol and ceremony, according to their rank. Sir Oliver Fleming, Cromwell's first cousin, was the assiduous master of ceremonies, having been in post since 1643. He knew Venice and Switzerland well, and he wrote a report for the council of state recommending some of the practices that other 'free states' (not monarchies) employed for greeting foreign visitors and conducting diplomacy.[10] When the Dutch arrived, in December 1651, the ambassadors lodged in finely furnished lodgings near Old Palace Yard. Lodewijck Huygens, who accompanied the ambassadors, reported that they were served fine food from silver dishes embossed with the republic's coat of arms, and slept in the king's old beds.[11] In September 1652, the high-ranking Portuguese ambassador Rodriguez de Sa e Menezes, count of Peneguiaõ, was welcomed with great ceremony.[12] He was later entertained with a comic, light-hearted masque about hospitality devised by the former court playwright James Shirley.[13] It was a curious echo of the kinds of expensive shows enjoyed by James I and his son, Charles I, in Whitehall's Banqueting House, when regaling nobility and ambassadors. There was not really money to spare – England's coffers were bare after years of war – but the performance of political authority mattered if the regime was to look legitimate and be taken seriously. Such rituals and formal entertainments constituted a common currency shared by European powers, and their appropriation by the republic was an attempt to show that things had not really changed as dramatically as they had. But it was, of course, novel. The ambassadors' English host was not a king or a queen, or a doge or an emperor, but a huge body of MPs and councillors of state, some of whom were high-ranking army officers. They met the ambassadors all crammed together in Westminster Hall, decked out with a Turkey carpet on the floor and velvet chairs.[14]

It was not just ambassadors and their entourages who sailed across the Channel this year. Many English men and women who had sought refuge on the continent during the wars began to think about going home, to recover their estates, settle affairs, be reunited with friends and family and grow old. Among the exiled English living in Paris was the ageing philosopher Thomas Hobbes. In February 1652, after eleven years abroad, he boarded a ship and sailed home. He was sixty-three years old. His hands shook, and he struggled to write. As a young man just out of Oxford, Hobbes had tutored Bess of Hardwick's grandson, William Cavendish, second earl of Devonshire, and he remained under the patronage and care of the Cavendish family for most of his life. Up in Derbyshire, in glassy Hardwick Hall and neighbouring Chatsworth House, Hobbes had made use of the extensive libraries. There he was surrounded by books and conversations about optics, mathematics, physics. He often crossed the county border into Nottinghamshire to visit the Cavendish cousins at Welbeck Abbey: William Cavendish, marquess of Newcastle, a keen equestrian, and his mathematician brother, Charles. As part of the Cavendish circle,

Hobbes came to know many of the great thinkers and writers of his day. He had spent time with James I's laureate and Shakespeare's rival, Ben Jonson, did some secretarial work for Francis Bacon and had befriended Galileo while in Florence in 1636.[15]

Hobbes began to develop his own philosophical and political ideas and, in 1640, he left for France, fearing war and the consequences of his *Elements of Law* which had secured him the reputation as a theorist of absolute sovereignty. In Paris he was no longer able to draw on an income from the Cavendishes, who had also fled to France, and he lived in poverty. He briefly taught the young Charles Stuart mathematics when he arrived in Paris in 1646; Charles thought he was 'the oddest fellow he ever met with'.[16] Hobbes also mingled with those who clustered around the exiled court at Saint-Germain, such as the exiled bishop John Bramhall and the poets Abraham Cowley, Edmund Waller and William Davenant. But Marin Mersenne, friar and scientist, was the intellectual star around which Hobbes orbited. For a while Hobbes had lodgings in Mersenne's convent and there he met and argued with the philosophers Pierre Gassendi and René Descartes. Events back home pulled Hobbes away from his primary interest in mathematics and physics, and towards politics. In response to the execution of Charles I, Hobbes began to write his most famous book, one of the most striking works of political philosophy ever written: *Leviathan: Or the Matter, Forme and Power of a Commonwealth Ecclesiasticall and Civil.*

Hobbes's *Leviathan* was an ambiguous beast. He had written it at great speed, breaking off from his longer-term project, *De Corpore*. He chose to write his new book in English, not Latin, and it was published in England first, before Hobbes's homecoming. In the reeling aftermath of Charles I's death, *Leviathan* was a powerful and urgent defence of absolute power that, ideally, should be invested in the body of a king, although it *could* reside in a body of people, such as a council of state. What mattered was deference to that sovereign power. 'So that it appeareth plainly, to my understanding,' Hobbes wrote, 'both from reason, and Scripture, that the sovereign power, whether placed in one man, as in monarchy, or in one assembly of men, as in popular, and aristocratical commonwealths, is as great, as possibly men can be imagined to make it.'[17] It is natural and rational to consent to sovereign authority, Hobbes argued, in exchange for protection and peace, whether that sovereignty is in a single man (a king, easy to imagine) or in an assembly of men (a kind of headless mass). Despite Hobbes's championing of monarchy (the book's famous frontispiece depicts a huge king who wields a sword and sceptre, and whose body is made up of obedient, thronging subjects), some read *Leviathan* as defending the sovereignty of England's republic, and thus as a plea to submit to its de facto authority. The means by which a regime came to power (hereditary kingship, or conquest by force, such as William the Conqueror) had to be put aside: 'There is scarce a commonwealth in the world, whose beginnings can in conscience be justified,' Hobbes wrote. To Hobbes, a safe, prosperous society, without the horrors of war, was a matter of a person's 'simple obedience' to a mighty power – the leviathan, the sea monster from the book of Job. He contended:

> That the condition of mere nature . . . is anarchy, and the condition of war: that the precepts, by which men are guided to avoid that condition, are the laws of nature: that a commonwealth, without sovereign power, is but a word without substance, and cannot stand: that subjects owe to sovereigns, simple obedience, in all things.[18]

Shortly before his departure for England in the freezing cold winter of 1651–2, Hobbes presented Charles II with a manuscript copy of *Leviathan*. It was this extraordinary book of political theory, this 'trifle' as Hobbes dismissively called it, that meant Hobbes was no longer safe in France, for it challenged monarchy as a natural fact. Any form of government was artificial, a construct, to which man consented. Edward Hyde, earl of Clarendon, who was otherwise fond of Hobbes, was appalled by his apparent justification of the new regime in England, and even Charles was displeased – although not for very long.[19] But Hobbes told Hyde that he wrote the book because 'he had a mind to go home'.[20] He could not be sure that he would be any safer in England. Later, Hobbes described his homecoming: 'I returned to my homeland, not quite sure of my safety. But in no other place could I have been safer. It was cold; there was deep snow; I was an old man; and the wind was bitter. My bucking horse and the rough road gave me trouble.'[21]

Hobbes had no family really, and no estates to come back to. He had grown up in Malmesbury in Wiltshire, a small town that teeters on the top of a lone hill, and dominated by its spireless twelfth-century abbey. He had lived in a modest stone house, and his alcoholic father had left the family when Hobbes was sixteen.[22] He owned some pastureland which had been left to him by an uncle who made gloves. Once back in England, Hobbes did not return to Malmesbury but set up home in London, in Fetter Lane, where he worked and wrote. According to his great friend and fellow Wiltshire man, the biographer John Aubrey, Hobbes was convivial and witty. He may have lost his trademark black hair with age (he was nicknamed 'Crow' at school), but he was still six feet tall with a twinkle in his eye and a penchant for singing the songs of Henry Lawes at bedtime, to exercise his lungs. He liked to wear fashionable French shirts, with a long dressing gown over the top, and Spanish black leather boots, all year round. He also liked to smoke a pipe of tobacco.[23] He was friends with prominent men and women from across the political divide, among them the eminent lawyer and historian John Selden (who had written about Britain's dominion over the sea) and the physician William Petty, who had nursed Oliver Cromwell when he was sick in Ireland, and who would soon produce the first ever map of Ireland, which made possible the devastating redistribution of seized Royalist and Catholic estates (about a third of the country).[24] He was also friends with the talented miniaturist Samuel Cooper from Covent Garden, who painted Cromwell and his family, and then Charles II after the Restoration.[25] Milton, although he admired Hobbes, did not like him and refused to meet him. Milton had rather different things to say about individual liberty and the right to resist power. Aubrey, however, believed that there was a curious alignment between Hobbes and Oliver Cromwell. Both men were born at the end of the sixteenth century under the same April stars (Hobbes on the eve of the Spanish Armada), meaning that both men, Aubrey thought, would be 'more eminent in . . . life than ordinary'.[26]

Hobbes's views about the Church were not ordinary. He seemed, like Cromwell and Milton, to favour Independency, the freedom to worship according to your conscience. For some, Hobbes's ideas about materialism and the physical world courted atheism, and the whiff of heresy lingered near him all his life. He seemed, dangerously, to believe that religion and God were of man's making, springing from ignorance, superstition and the anxious need to discover 'the causes of things'. 'Ignorance of natural causes disposeth a man to credulity,' he wrote, and in order to understand 'the visible things of this world . . . a man may conceive there is a cause of them, which men call God; and yet not have an idea or image of him in his mind'. The 'seed of religion', he wrote, is 'in man only'.[27]

Hobbes claimed that *Leviathan* encouraged others to return home and make peace with, or at least obey, the republic.[28] Certainly, the concluding chapter made it possible for those who had fought for the king in the 1640s to now consider submitting themselves to the victorious regime. *Leviathan* was, Hobbes concluded, a book 'occasioned by the disorders of the present time', and it was intended 'to set before men's eyes the mutual relation between protection and obedience'.[29] Later, in the early Restoration, Hobbes defended himself from charges that *Leviathan* was written to flatter the republic and its masters. By the early 1650s, Hobbes argued, men and women loyal to the Stuarts 'had done their utmost endeavour to performe their obligation to the king, had done all they could be obliged unto; and were consequently at liberty to seeke the safety of their lives and livelihood wheresoever, and without treachery'. And his book was written for them.[30]

Hobbes's patrons, the Cavendishes, went home. William Cavendish, third earl of Devonshire and the son of the William Cavendish whom Hobbes had tutored, had already gone home in 1645. In 1651, he paid £5,000 to Parliament in return for his sequestered estates, including the glorious Chatsworth.[31] He then lived quietly, away from politics. The Newcastle branch of the Cavendish family travelled back to England at the end of 1651. Margaret Cavendish, married to the marquess (and future duke) of Newcastle, and a former maid of honour to Henrietta Maria, left Antwerp. She was accompanied by her brother-in-law Charles. Margaret met with the republic's committee for compounding at Goldsmith's Hall to beg for income from her husband's estates, including Welbeck Abbey and Bolsover Castle, which were about to be sold to raise money for Parliament.[32] She was unsuccessful. Her husband, after all, had been a commander at Marston Moor and was, the committee clerks proclaimed, 'the greatest Traitor to the state'.[33] Her brother-in-law, however, was able to regain his estates, as long as he paid a fine. Here was the republic working out how, and whether, to forgive those 'malignants' who had fought for the king, and how it might both raise money and seek some kind of reconciliation with Royalists who wanted to come home and live in their houses.

While she was in England in 1652, Margaret – educated, intellectual, unconventional – caught up with a few friends, attended Henry Lawes's musical salons and began work on her first volume of poems, *Poems and Fancies*. The prolific letter-writer Dorothy Osborne sniped at Margaret's ambition and her outrageous writing – which she found 'ten times more extravagant than her dresse'. There were, she thought, 'soberer people in Bedlam'.[34] Margaret was William Cavendish's second wife, and they had no children. Margaret called her books her babies and she produced many. She presented herself as an 'authoress', and became England's first widely published female author. She wrote about herself, her childhood and her body. She wrote a biography of her beloved and supportive husband and an elegy for her brother, Charles, shot to death on Fairfax's orders after the siege of Colchester in 1648. She wrote poems, plays, essays and fiction. She wrote about utopian worlds, experimental science and atoms. Like her friend Hobbes, Margaret believed that the world was made up of matter in constant motion, and that this motion constituted an external, malign force. She pondered, for a while, whether the dancing and dusty motions of atoms could explain history, and violence and chaos – even account for the 'unnatural War' that 'came like a Whirlwind'.[35] Margaret wrote about everything that was happening and changing around her. She challenged the Baconian dream of certain knowledge, and although, like many women of her time, she believed that women were inferior to men, she also knew that 'women by Education may come to be far more knowing and learned' than men. She believed in absolute sovereignty, but imagined in her utopian fiction *The Blazing World* that this could be held by a woman.[36]

The diarist John Evelyn had also been in exile in Paris, and had met the Cavendishes and Thomas Hobbes. Evelyn, too, was tired of an unsettled life; he had travelled in Italy and 'run about the world' for nearly ten years, he said. By new year 1652, aged thirty-one, he was resolved to go home. He had been back to England for a couple of years, between 1647 and 1649, but now that there was 'so little appearance of any change for the better, all being intirely in the rebells hands', he decided that he might as well return to live there for good.[37] After all, France, too, was in the middle of its own bloody wars (called the Fronde), between the nobility and the court. Evelyn was no friend of the English republic. The execution of Charles I was, for him, a tragedy, and he loathed Oliver Cromwell and his fellow usurpers, whom he thought a 'head-lesse people'.[38] But he needed money: his sister Jane was about to have a baby, and he needed to rescue his father-in-law Richard Browne's house, Sayes Court, in the village of Deptford. He despatched his goods to England, took leave of his seventeen-year-old, pregnant wife Mary, who would join him in June, and left Paris behind in a hard frost.

When Evelyn sailed into Dover on the night of 6 February, it was cold but calm.[39] The England that he knew and missed had changed. It was in a vertiginous state. 'Independents and phanatics' replaced priests in pulpits; church services were 'new fangled'; buildings lay in heaps and forests had been felled. The royal elms in St James's Park were stumps.[40] Evelyn was saddened to find Worcester's great cathedral in ruins. St Paul's Cathedral was grubby after its wartime use as stables, and Inigo Jones's white 'Queen's House' in Greenwich had fallen into Bulstrode Whitelocke's hands.[41] One of the first of many public shows staged by the republic was the funeral of that 'stout rebell' Henry Ireton. Cromwell had left Ireton, his son-in-law, in charge of Ireland when he left in 1649. When Ireton died from fever, in December 1651, his body was brought back to England, 'carried in pomp' through the streets of London and buried in Westminster Abbey. Evelyn's hostility to this 'arch-Rebell', Cromwell and his 'Mock-Parliament men' is matched by evident admiration for the familiar solemnity and grandeur of the spectacle of horses cloaked in black velvet, the symbols of state and mourners marching to the beat of muffled drums. The headless English still knew how to put on a good show.[42]

Once at home, Evelyn was able to be reunited with family – his brother George – at the family home, Wotton, in Dorking. He was too late to see his sister, Jane, who had died in childbirth. He caught up with friends, Hobbes among them. He celebrated the birth of his first son, Richard, called on the law to recover jewellery that was stolen after a highway robbery, observed Christmas (in secret) and contrived a proper Anglican funeral service for his mother-in-law. He could, if he had wanted to, drink coffee in London's first coffee house, a simple shed in the churchyard of St Michael's in Cornhill. It opened in 1652, and was run by the Levant trader Daniel Edwards and his Greek servant Pasqua Rosee, a master coffee-brewer. But coffee was not to Evelyn's taste; he associated it with dirty rebels, gathering to talk about altered states. Instead, Evelyn began to design and plant his garden at Sayes Court, in the village of Deptford. Sayes Court was a rather run-down Elizabethan manor house with extensive grounds running north towards the Thames, near the noisy docks. At first the Evelyns shared the house with Mary's uncle, William Prettyman, and his family, but it eventually became their own. Living there marked the beginning of Evelyn's lifetime interest in botany and horticulture.[43] 'I might have one day hoped to have bin considerable in my Country,' he wrote, rather sadly, before his return to England. But now 'A Friend, a Booke, and a Garden shall for the future perfectly circumscribe my utmost designes'.[44]

Over the next forty years, Evelyn created several acres of flower gardens, orchards, espaliered fruit trees, groves, cypress-lined walks, carp ponds and farmland. He kept bees, whose hives reminded him of royal castles. Sayes Court became one of the most celebrated and innovative gardens in England, visited by Royalist friends and government men alike. It was a French- and Italian-inspired pattern of Eden and a source of food and good health: he grew fruits, vegetables, herbs, medicinal plants, and he built a laboratory where he, and Mary, could research and experiment.[45] Evelyn's garden is no longer there, and neither is the house, or villa as Evelyn liked to call it. Both are buried beneath Sayes Court Park. But the curious and virtuosic Evelyn did become someone 'considerable'. His diary, which he began when he was a small boy, is one of the period's most celebrated and valuable, and the new republican climate proved conducive to his intellect and work. Evelyn wrote prolifically during the 1650s. He translated Lucretius' *De rerum natura* – which he thought a 'stupendious . . . Theatre of Nature' – and he wrote about trees, air pollution and mechanics. He corresponded with fellow innovators and scientists including Robert Boyle, advised gardeners and planned his encyclopedic work on gardening, *Elysium Britannicum*.[46] His friend the poet Abraham Cowley had this to say about Evelyn: 'I know no body that possesses more private happiness than you do in your Garden; and yet no man who makes his happiness more publick, by a free communication of the Art and Knowledge of it to others.'[47]

From another carefully tended garden up in Yorkshire, Andrew Marvell was preparing to travel back to the South and enter public life. For nearly two years, Marvell had lived with the Fairfaxes at Nun Appleton. It had not all been easy retirement in cool glades. Neither Fairfax nor Marvell had been able to escape the political heat. In August 1651, Fairfax had agreed to the council of state's request that he defend Hull from the invading Scots army prior to the battle of Worcester.[48] Earlier that year, Marvell had possibly accompanied Walter Strickland and Oliver St John on their disastrous Dutch embassy.

By the summer of 1652, Marvell was in London. He knew Marchamont Nedham and the poet and polemicist John Hall, who worked with Nedham on *Mercurius Politicus* and was an apologist for the republic. Hall took on the role of promoting literary culture in general, and he defended writers with past and known Royalist sympathies. He was aware that Hobbes and his *Leviathan* could serve the republic well, and he enabled his Scottish friend Thomas Urquhart, who had fought for the king at Worcester, to publish the first English translation of François Rabelais' raucous *Gargantua and Pantagruel*. Marvell, with Hall and others, hoped that there could be a place for writers, thinkers, poets and painters in England's republic, regardless of their past loyalties or employment. In 1653, Milton wrote to John Bradshaw, president of the council, suggesting that the talented Marvell be employed as Milton's assistant. Although Marvell did not get this post until 1657, he and Milton became good friends.

Meanwhile, Marvell was employed in the Windsor home of John Oxenbridge, an Independent preacher, tutoring William Dutton, the nephew of a rich Royalist who, it was rumoured, might marry Oliver Cromwell's youngest child, Frances.[49]

Peace and stability required such reconciliation. In February 1652, the council of state passed the Act of General Pardon and Oblivion. John Evelyn recalled his brother George turning up at Sayes Court in March with a copy of what he called 'Cromwell's Act of Oblivion'. Parliament, so the act declared, was 'sensible of the miserable and sad Effects which the late unnatural War hath produced' and was resolved to find a 'quiet calm and comfortable Peace'. Worcester had reassured the council of the country's general 'affection to this present Government', rather than to the Stuarts, and they therefore agreed to pardon all 'Treasons Felonies, &c. committed before 3 Sept. 1651, and not hereafter excepted'.[50] A few months earlier the rich poet and politician Edmund Waller had had his sentence of banishment revoked. He had been imprisoned, fined heavily and sent off into exile in 1644 for 'Waller's plot', an attempt to secure London for Charles I while acting as a parliamentary commissioner. Now, in January 1652, like his friends-in-exile Hobbes and Evelyn, Waller too set sail for home. Soon he would be writing poems in praise of Cromwell.[51]

Parliament wanted peace, but it also needed money. Despite February's promise of pardon, later in the year Parliament passed an act that identified 678 Royalists – knights, gentlemen, yeomen – whose estates should be seized 'for their several Treasons against the Parliament and People of England'.[52] The government needed to boost the economy, collect taxes, rebuild and regulate trade, and invest in the scorched land. Trees needed to be planted to replace those felled in war, and to provide timber for new houses and ships. Fens in the east were drained to provide farmland that could be grazed by livestock or sown with crops. Cromwell and others on the council of state explored several regenerative schemes and ventures that could help rebuild England. Behind many of the innovative plans was Samuel Hartlib, a Polish entrepreneur and an all-round intelligencer. Hartlib was born into a Protestant family, the son of a successful merchant. He fled the Baltic town of Elbing and became a refugee of Europe's Thirty Years War. Since 1628 he had lived permanently in England, where he soon married an English woman, Mary. Everyone, it seemed, knew Hartlib (he was well connected through an English mother), and he had a finger in every pie. He flourished during the creative chaos of the 1650s when the country needed to heal, innovate and reform.[53]

Hartlib met and worked with all the principal characters from this time, and their political allegiances did not matter. John Milton dedicated his *Of Education* to him and Hartlib was in regular touch with the emerging scientist Robert Boyle, son of the Royalist earl of Cork. He was good friends with Boyle's sister, Lady Ranelagh, who was less Royalist and who had petitioned Parliament to pay Hartlib for his information gathering. Hartlib knew important councillors of state – Henry Vane, for example – and many MPs with influence who sat on the republic's new committees for trade and for excise. He had meetings with Oliver Cromwell and with the council of state's newly appointed (in March 1652) and brilliant secretary and spymaster, John Thurloe. Cromwell's cousin and councillor of state Oliver St John – he who had been part of the embassy to Holland and who also employed Thurloe – was once Hartlib's patron. Hartlib knew that Andrew Marvell was talented and he hosted John Evelyn, who came to visit him and his beehive in his Charing Cross home. Evelyn found him 'ingenious', while Hartlib noted how Evelyn 'is much for Perfumes', and they had a serious discussion about co-writing a History of all Mechanical Arts.[54] One day, Hartlib would have Samuel Pepys as his neighbour when they both lived in Axe Yard in Westminster. Hartlib's very closest friends included John Tradescant the younger, a botanist and Charles I's former head gardener at Oatlands Palace (demolished in 1650). Many flocked to the Tradescants' Lambeth home and paid sixpence to visit the exotic garden and marvel at 'the Ark', John and his father's collection of plants, animals and manmade curiosities gathered from around the world. It was the Royalist Elias Ashmole who helped Tradescant catalogue this collection in 1656, and who eventually came to own the collection, which became the Ashmolean Museum in Oxford. 'Artes cannot die' (a near anagram of John Tradescant) is the epigraph to this first ever museum catalogue.[55]

Hartlib was a consummate communicator: an 'intelligencer'. Fuelled by a Puritan zeal, he brought people together who shared his enthusiasm for progress, and sought new ways of thinking about the world. They exchanged ideas about agricultural methods, economic and educational reform, unemployment and poor relief, scientific knowledge. Through his Europe-wide network of virtuosi he heard as much about how someone could spin silk out of flax in Hamburg as he did about a local woman in Holborn who could cure the stone (from which he suffered terribly). He was committed to sharing and disseminating information as a way, following the famous early seventeenth-century thinker Francis Bacon, to advance learning, and to bind fellow Protestants. Hartlib was generous, idealistic and practical. His motivations were intellectual, religious and public-spirited. He saw himself as a 'conduit pipe' and others, like Milton, saw him as 'the incitement of great good to this iland'.[56] Hartlib wrote copious letters and he kept endless diaries full of jottings about people he had met or heard about, and things that piqued his interest, from brewing beer with Barbados ginger to the eighty-foot-long telescope being built at Oxford by Christopher Wren – big enough to 'see at once the whole Moone'.[57] Hartlib's surviving papers were bundled together and bought, at his death, by the scientific enthusiast William, Viscount Brereton. Rediscovered in the 1930s, these papers reveal the busy, creative, reforming and improving agenda of the 1650s, and the central role that Hartlib played in this.

Hartlib facilitated the publication of hundreds of tracts by members of his circle which presented genuinely revolutionary ideas about how to regenerate England, from the decimalisation of the currency to rethinking crop rotation. Some were outlandish dreams, such as a desire for a universal language or transforming lead into gold to solve the country's terrible coin shortage. Some proposals involved exploiting the land confiscated from Catholics in Ireland (the Act for the Settlement of Ireland was passed in 1652). Some were dismissed by government committees (free trade, for example), but some schemes were seriously considered. One of the circle was the merchant and trusted economist Henry Robinson, whose idea for a national bank, copying a Dutch model, was discussed around the meeting tables at Whitehall. Robinson also had progressive ideas about state schools and a national health service.[58] William Potter, another Hartlib associate, knew that there would simply never be enough gold or silver coins available, and he developed revolutionary ideas about paper money and credit, anticipating the first bank notes by forty years. He wrote: 'the case now stands with us, the only feasible means, whereby both to receive and multiply the decayed Trade of this Land, is by increasing amongst Tradesmen some firm and known Credit or

Security'.[59] Although Hartlib was involved in more than half of the new patents issued for inventions during the life of the republic, he did not himself accrue great wealth. Parliament agreed to grant him an annual pension, as an agent for the advancement of universal learning, but money was tight and payment irregular.[60]

Samuel Hartlib thought, and wrote, a lot about trees. His ideas about planting mulberry trees so that a silk industry could thrive in England caught the attention of Major-General John Lambert, who was a keen gardener.[61] Hartlib noted how fruit trees lined the roads throughout Normandy, and how Colonel Thomas Blount had planted thousands of ash trees (and vines) on his estate (formerly Crown lands) near Blackheath.[62] In his preface to his edition of a work on husbandry, Hartlib suggested that the Commonwealth create a surveyor of the woods, to preserve 'what is, and by all good improvement to procure and provide for what is wanting to the present age'.[63] During 1652 Hartlib was in regular contact with Ralph Austen, a celebrated cider maker in Oxford, and a cousin of Henry Ireton. Austen wanted to promote the planting of orchards as a way to heal England. In 1653, Austen published, with Hartlib's help, five hundred copies of *A Treatise of Fruit-trees*. This slim volume with an unpromising title proved to be hugely popular: two editions appeared in the 1650s, and a third in 1665. Austen's uplifting vision and simple prose inspired and comforted readers. The poor would be employed and wealth would be generated – he described ripe fruits hanging from branches as 'costly jewels or pearls' on gold cloth. People would eat lots of healthy fruit, have abundant wood for their fires and drink good English alcohol. The value of their land would increase and the production of fruit alcohols, such as cider and perry, would mean that fields could be sown with corn for bread instead of barley for beer. But planting fruit trees in England's blood-soaked soil was not only about making money, and thereby securing legitimacy for a shaky regime through economic success. Austen also promised spiritual rewards – and this is how he captured the imagination of readers – for planting orchards would replicate the Garden of Eden: 'God planted a fruit garden,' he said. There was profit and pleasure to be found in an orchard: the smell of almond blossom, the birdsong and the buzzing of bees, the cool shade offered on a hot summer's day. All of these delights are 'the Good of every thing, and a pattern of Heaven', Austen wrote.[64] Sowing a new Eden with cox apples and plum saplings would also prepare England for the second coming of Christ, something that Austen, along with Hartlib and many others at this time, believed was imminent. Back in 1642, Hartlib and his good friends the Scottish minister John Dury and the theologian and fellow exile Johannes Comenius – a reforming trio – had seen that the political upheaval in England might be the occasion for building a new Jerusalem.[65] 'For wee believe that his Kingdome will be set up,' wrote Hartlib. 'And because wee judge the time to be neere at hand, Wee prepare ourselves.'[66]

Not all of Hartlib and his circle's schemes could be realised in the Commonwealth; the political settlement of the nation got in the way, and it was this that needed tending first. Nevertheless, Hartlib and his men's ideas were scattered, and some would crop in fertile soil later. A national bank was realised with the opening of the Bank of England in 1694. William Petty's fresh and forensic interest in figures and statistics led him to become an innovative and respected economist under Charles II and James II.[67] Hartlib and his circle's yoking together of economic health and a nation's happiness – as with Austen's orchards – informed later thinking, such as Adam Smith's, about the 'pleasures of wealth' and the drive to invent.[68] The Hartlibeans encouraged improvement and ambition, and made both acceptable because they attended to the common good and to the country's spiritual health. Their political leanings meant that most of Hartlib and his circle thought in terms of a commonwealth, and not a kingdom. Contrary to Hobbes and his famous frontispiece to *Leviathan*, Hartlib and his fellow entrepreneurs did not imagine the state as a king's body, crammed with obedient subjects. Rather, they imagined a body of people where, in William Potter's words, 'no member can subsist by itself' and who nurtured each other.[69] When the Restoration came, many of Hartlib's circle went on to become founding members of the Royal Society. But their former association with the republican regime, and the fact that their creativity and industry were rooted in, and flourished during, the republican years were forgotten, or underplayed. John Evelyn, for example, distanced himself from his friendship with Hartlib (who died impoverished in 1662) and fellow Hartlibeans. British history, too, has often chosen to forget the ingenuity and inventiveness of its republican moment.

The inventor and alchemist Benjamin Worsley was a member of the Hartlib circle who may have inadvertently had a small hand in the republic's next war, which was with its Dutch republican neighbours. Worsley was an early imperialist, and his ideas about how to control Royalist Virginia and exploit its commodities – cotton, rice, fruits – had been welcomed by John Bradshaw, president of the council of state, and by London's merchants. To force Virginia, Barbados and Bermuda to switch allegiance to the Commonwealth, Worsley proposed that their trade be prohibited and regulated, and that no foreign ships without a licence could trade with English plantations in America; in 1650, this proposal became an act of Parliament.[70] Benjamin Worsley had spent time in the Netherlands, learning alchemy, observing the nation's economic success and reporting back to his friend Hartlib in London.[71] The following year, 1651, he claimed to have pushed through another act designed to increase British shipping and trade, the Navigation Act. This legislation also deliberately set out to challenge Dutch supremacy on the seas.

The Netherlands was England's biggest commercial rival. The Dutch dominated trading routes: their ships were stuffed with spices from the Far East and the West Indies and timber from the Baltic, and they brought those goods to England. William Petty had written to Samuel Hartlib in 1648 about England needing to improve its trade and manufacturing so that it could become 'potent and rich' like Holland.[72] England played dirty, raiding Dutch ships suspected of carrying English goods and maltreating crews. The Dutch, too, seized English ships, and London's newsbooks reported daily on skirmishes at sea and aggrieved seamen.[73] When Hartlib's patron and councillor of state Oliver St John returned from his failed embassy to The Hague with Walter Strickland, he was furious with the Dutch coolness towards plans for an intimate alliance between the two nations – a union that would, so St John claimed, advance Protestantism and protect the two countries' trade, even allowing the free movement of peoples.[74] How British attitudes have changed. To punish the Dutch, St John pushed through the Navigation Act. Benjamin Worsley, now secretary to the newly established council for the advancing of trade (for which Hartlib's son was the clerk), claimed that he had had a hand in this act right from the very beginning.[75] Certainly his 1651 pamphlet *The Advocate*, addressed to the council of state, fully endorsed the principles of the act. He showed how obstructing Dutch ships would help England, and also how attending to 'matters of trade' was linked to the 'breaking forth, very shortly' of the glory of God.[76] Religion was so often yoked to, and sometimes cloaked, material interests. The Navigation Act itself legislated that from Africa, Asia and America, only goods travelling in English ships (or ships belonging to English territories), manned with predominantly English crew, could land in English or Irish ports, or in any ports in territories belonging to the English Commonwealth. Goods from Europe and elsewhere, with some exceptions, could travel either in English ships, or in ships belonging to the nation from which the goods originated. Fish, however – so important to England – could only be imported and exported in English boats. The act was a bullying assertion of English nationalism, intent on economic gain (although not all merchants thought it was a good idea), and justified by the claim that England had the 'good Providence and Protection of God'. Charles II would renew this act when he was restored, aware of its benefits for English trade.

The Navigation Act was a clear challenge to the Dutch, preventing their ships from bringing profitable goods into England. The United Provinces sent over their ambassadors to England at the end of 1651 to dispute the act and smooth relations. They had some success, and the two nations seemed to be inching towards some kind of alliance. And then, on 19 May 1652, just off the coast of Kent, the Dutch admiral Maarten van Tromp failed to strike sail (a deferential lowering of the topsail) to the English admiral General Robert Blake. The Navigation Act enforced the salute, a ceremonial attestation of England's provocative, long-standing position that water could be owned.[77] But instead of tipping his topsail in England's supposedly sovereign waters, van Tromp fired a shot at Blake's ship. A battle ensued, and then war.

The First Anglo-Dutch war (two more were to come in the seventeenth century) was England's first full-scale war at sea and it lasted until 1654. Many in Parliament were unhappy about it. Cromwell, for example, still yearned for a union, and conflict with a Protestant nation troubled his conscience. 'I do not like the war,' he said, adding, 'I will do everything in my power to bring about peace.'[78] For some, such as the zealous Thomas Harrison, the war made religious sense. 'The Dutch must be destroyed; and we shall have an heaven upon earth,' Harrison reportedly said.[79] Fellow Protestants the Dutch may be, but these trading rivals had been corrupted by their wealth and desire for material luxuries and should be punished for their sins to prepare for the second coming. Back in 1640, an English traveller named Peter Mundy commented on the Dutch people's taste for nice things. Their costly homes were, he said, 'full of pleasure and home contentment, as Ritche Cupboards, Cabinetts, Imagery, porcelaine'.[80] Early in 1652, the astrologer William Lilly had predicted that 'the vengeance of Almighty God is ready to be poured forth upon the Dutch for their too, too much unthankfulness'.[81]

For some in Parliament the war could be justified because England was not fighting a fellow republic, but an aggressor. The Netherlands was really rather royal, harbouring English Royalists-in-exile and the Stuart family. The stadholder ('state-holder') was, nominally, an elected role, but it was held, before his death from smallpox in 1650, by William II of the House of Orange, who wielded significant power. William II was married to Charles I's daughter, Mary, and had been appalled by England's execution of its king. After William II's death, the House of Orange still had influence and support, for not all of the provinces that made up the country were committed republicans. While the rich, mercantile province of Holland was the most anti-monarchist, some provinces wanted to see the baby Prince of Orange (England's future William III) as stadholder. The Dutch and the English republics were not, then, as obvious bedfellows as some might have hoped. Not only was neither nation a settled republic, but the Dutch version of republicanism also differed from England's at this time. To the Dutch, England had become the 'Devil-Land'.[82] When Admiral van Tromp shot at, instead of saluting, Blake's ship in May, he was both enforcing the Dutch belief that the sea was free, and acting as an Orangist who refused to acknowledge England's regicide regime. In Blake, his opponent, van Tromp found a committed and zealous republican, leading the fleet of a vulnerable and tender state. As Andrew Marvell put it in 'The Character of Holland', 'they [the Dutch] invade by stealth / Our sore new circumcisèd Commonwealth'.[83]

The war arose from the republic's particular mix of patriotism, godliness and competitive mercantilism. Even though the conflict was partly motivated by economic need, it would cost the country dear. Such were the paradoxes of the time. On 9 July, Parliament printed a pamphlet justifying the war by announcing that the United Provinces had rejected all overtures of a friendly union, were hostile to the Commonwealth and were intent on undermining its trade and navy. All of this meant that they were not fellow Protestants after all.[84] There was plenty of Hollandophobia going around, and the regime could rely on this to keep some of the public on side. The merchant and poet Owen Felltham's *A Brief Character of the Low Countries* had been circulating for years in manuscript and in a pirated edition before it finally appeared in an authorised edition in 1652 – clearly it was thought to serve a useful purpose. Felltham delighted in insulting the Low Countries as 'the great Bog of Europe', and its people as muddy, watery amphibians who worshipped at the altar of trade: 'Their shipping is the Babel which they boast on for the glory of their Nation.' But criticism is often tinged with envy. ''Tis indeed a wonder,' Felltham admitted.[85]

Meanwhile, what kind of adult the sore, infant Commonwealth should become divided MPs and councillors of state. The settlement of the nation – the agreed form of its government beyond being declared a 'free state'– really needed to be curated by a full Parliament, with MPs freshly voted for by the people. But the Rump Parliament was still sitting, and the people had not been to the polls for over ten years. Any constitution the purged Parliament's MPs agreed upon would always be viewed as illegitimate and unrepresentative. On the other hand, fresh elections risked bringing in former, mostly Presbyterian, MPs (such as the noisy William Prynne) who would much prefer to invite back the king. The army officer John Jones was one of the many who warned of the risk that an entirely new Parliament posed to the republic. In a year when land, growth and husbandry occupied the minds of many, Jones reached for a horticultural image to argue for more time:

> Let there be patience used until burdens may be taken off, and the people enjoy some rest and opulency under the new change, let the old weeds that lie dead on the ground have time to rot, let the Commonwealth have some time to take root in the interests of men, before it be transplanted or grafted on another stock.[86]

In 1652, many men and women sought to put down roots and reconcile themselves to the new England. In 1653, Cromwell uprooted the very republic itself.

1653

Attentive be;
This, This is He.

Thomas Manley, 'To the Most Excellent,
The Lord Generall of Great Brittayne, Oliver Cromwel'

Everything changed in 1653. It was a year of high political drama, and by December the republic had morphed into a Protectorate, with Oliver Cromwell, lord general of the Commonwealth's forces, sworn in as its first Lord Protector. The rise of Cromwell as Protector was neither inevitable, nor entirely legitimate. In April, in an echo of Pride's Purge, the army kicked out the procrastinating MPs and forcibly dissolved Parliament. Eight months later, Cromwell was created (not elected) Protector, under Britain's first ever written constitution, which brought together England, Wales, Scotland and Ireland. The fifty-four-year-old Cromwell, who did not have an ounce of blue blood in him, became the first commoner to hold power in Britain.

Oliver Cromwell was a gentleman by birth, from Huntingdon in Cambridgeshire, distantly related to Thomas Cromwell, Henry VIII's chief minister, another man who rose high from humble beginnings. By profession, Oliver Cromwell was a farmer, politician and then, through force of circumstance, a soldier. He found his métier on the battlefield, and became admired, feared and powerful.[1] As commander of the army, he held enormous sway at Whitehall, and was lauded for his military successes in Ireland and Scotland, and at Worcester. He was prominent on the council of state, despite being absent on campaign for much of the time. After the miraculous victory at Worcester in 1651, Cromwell had been hailed by writers such as Payne Fisher and Thomas Manley as 'th'unwearied Atlas of our State', as an exceptional man upon whom the republic's survival depended.[2] '*This*, *This* is He', Manley wrote, believing Cromwell to be the 'patron and fort' of England's hard-won liberty. 'He, He, it is', Manley urged again. To Milton, who could no doubt observe Cromwell at work in Whitehall, he was 'our Chief of Men'.[3] And, as Marvell would later say of the 'indefatigable' and 'Angelic' Cromwell (though not without some ambivalence and reluctance): 'If these the Times, then this must be the Man.'[4]

Once back in Westminster after the battle of Worcester, Cromwell set about managing the MPs who made up the purged Parliament, urging them to put themselves up for re-election. He also pacified the new council of officers, who were frustrated with the slow-moving MPs who were not pushing through the changes they wished for. The previous August, high-ranking officers including Colonels William Goffe and Edward Whalley had presented Parliament with a petition, imploring the Members to reform law, religion and taxes, to pay the army's salaries, which were in arrears, and to decide who, at a future election, would be allowed to vote, and how MPs would be elected. How, for example, could it be ensured that only 'such as are pious and faithfull in the interest of the Commonwealth' be allowed to sit and serve?[5] At the same time as fielding petitions from his army colleagues, Cromwell was working on how to reduce the number of soldiers in the country and their financial burden on the tax-paying public, as well as trying to protect his – and Milton's and other Independents' – precious liberty of conscience from the Presbyterian MPs in the House. The House of Commons, which had begun to divide into factions during the wars in the 1640s, split further. Parties quarrelled about the precise form the government should take. The roots of party politics are here, with all the familiar overlaps, inconsistencies and defections. There were the commonwealthmen who clamoured for a thoroughly secular republican settlement, such as the army officer and councillor of state Arthur Hesilrige, and Algernon Sidney, the hot-tempered and fiercely anti-monarchical son of the earl of Leicester. In the 1660s, Sidney would press for rebellion against the restored Charles II: 'Monarchy is the worst evil that can befall a nation,' he wrote.[6] Then there were the godly republicans, such as the committed Henry Vane, who envisaged a state run by men with thoroughly vetted religious credentials: anti-Presbyterian, but generally tolerant of radical religious beliefs. This alarmed the more moderate Members of the House who feared the radical sects. Bulstrode Whitelocke favoured a more familiar solution for the three former kingdoms – a return to single-person rule. According to Whitelocke, even Cromwell himself suggested that something 'with somewhat of monarchical power in it would be very effectual'.[7] There was no single or obvious constitutional model for Britain without a hereditary king.

Back in December 1651, a few months after Worcester, Cromwell had summoned a group of politicians and army officers to meet at Speaker William Lenthall's house in Westminster. Now that there was, for the time being, no imminent Royalist threat, they needed to discuss what kind of settlement Parliament might accept. Bulstrode Whitelocke was there, along with Thomas Widdrington, Oliver St John, as lord chief justice, and high-ranking army officers Charles Fleetwood, John Desborough, Edward Whalley and Thomas Harrison. This select group agreed that God had shown England great mercy at Worcester, and that now it was incumbent on them to find a settlement 'such as may be to Gods honnor, & the good of this Commonwealth'. But they could not agree on what would be 'good'. Cromwell told them that 'we should consider, whither a republique, or a mixt Monarchicall government will be best to be settled, & if any thing Monarchicall, then in whome that power shall be placed?' The country's laws, Whitelocke agreed, were 'so interwoven with the power & practise of Monarchy' that it would be hard to settle the country without something like monarchy. Henry, duke of Gloucester and Charles I's third son, was young, and therefore supposedly 'uninfected with the principles of our enemies', suggested Colonel Whalley.[8] Henry was a serious contender for some kind of monarchical office, but it is possible that Cromwell was thinking of himself when he mooted a 'mixt Monarchicall government'. Royalists had long speculated about, and satirised, Cromwell's ambition. He was mocked as a brewer, hankering after a crown, a throne. In the 1648 play *Crafty Cromwell*, Henry Ireton and Henry Marten crowned Old Noll, with his copper-red 'Nose Dominicall'. 'Now Oliver Ascend the throne / Feare not to tumble downe', sang the chorus. Non-Royalists, too, became concerned. After Worcester, the writer and republican Lucy Hutchinson noted the 'reach of ambition in his breast' – not to be king, necessarily, but to have power.[9]

In November 1652, a year after the meeting at Speaker Lenthall's house, Bulstrode Whitelocke met Cromwell while both men were out walking in St James's Park one evening, taking the late autumn air among the roaming cattle and deer. Cromwell took Whitelocke aside, keen to hear his loyal friend's advice on how to handle the dawdling and bickering MPs. 'What if a man should take upon him to be king?' Cromwell suddenly asked. Whitelocke, assuming that Cromwell was referring to himself here, thought this would be a remedy worse than the disease, and he advised him against such an action. His Excellency, he said, already had, as lord general, 'the full kingly power', but if the free state were to become a monarchy, with Cromwell as king, then many would wonder why it was not a Stuart. And those who preferred a republic (which included many army officers) would 'desert' him, Whitelocke added, and he would be weakened. Pressed further, Whitelocke apparently ventured that perhaps it was time to make a deal with Charles Stuart. Since his defeat at Worcester, and with foreign powers turning to recognise the republic, Charles's fortunes were now so low that surely he would agree to being restored on whatever terms he could get. Cromwell, Whitelocke could tell, did not like this idea, but he was polite and promised further discussion on the matter. He joined other company, and walked on. After this, according to Whitelocke, relations between Cromwell and his confidant cooled.[10]

Most agreed that the republic needed a fresh and legitimate Parliament. The Rump Parliament was not popular. Many of its Members had held their seats unchallenged for over ten years, since the last election in 1640. If a Member died, a replacement was sent to Whitehall via a by-election. These were the MPs who had steered the army through the wars of the 1640s, created the New Model Army and negotiated with Charles I. Following Pride's Purge, when more than three hundred MPs either were excluded or stayed away from the House, it was the remaining MPs who had brought the king to trial, sentenced him to death and abolished monarchy. Since the purge, many MPs had returned, but some constituencies no longer had a Member representing them at Westminster. By 1651, most MPs had agreed to put themselves up for re-election, but added that they would not risk doing so until November 1654. Many feared, probably rightly, that they would lose their seats. And no one could agree on who should be allowed to stand for Parliament: even if known Royalists were excluded, along with Catholics, there was still the risk that 'Presbyterians and Neuters' could be voted in – people hostile to the new regime and its leaning towards religious tolerance. Henry Vane, a champion of liberty of conscience like Cromwell and Milton, favoured only holding elections to fill those constituencies with no representatives. Cromwell advocated a fresh Parliament, but one in which malignants and the ungodly could – somehow – be kept out. For elections to take place, Parliament would have to be dissolved – so even if it could be agreed on how new Members should be vetted, it was not clear who would supervise this vetting. If the Parliament was to adjourn, rather than dissolve itself, then that Parliament would control the elections, but this would lay current Members open to charges of rigging the votes. There was also the question of the franchise, and who would be eligible to vote. What about known Royalists? And would the franchise be extended, as the Levellers had pushed for, or not?[11]

Particular pressure for a new Parliament came from the army. Officers and junior soldiers were no longer occupied on campaigns (it was the navy that was engaged against the Dutch), and they were beginning to congregate in London, humming around radical preaching centres like Allhallows the Great, off Thames Street, and petitioning Cromwell as their lord general. Soldiers who had fought on the battlefields, watched their friends die and were still waiting to be paid felt that they deserved to have their demands listened to by Westminster. They wanted help for wounded soldiers and for widowed families. One such radical army officer was Major-General Thomas Harrison. He, like Cromwell, wanted a new Parliament, but he did not trust the electorate to return suitably godly Members to the House. As a Fifth Monarchist who believed that Christ would come again, Harrison believed the republic should be governed by a carefully chosen group of godly men, who would safely usher in Christ's second reign.

Many men and women of the time, of varying religious hues, shared these millenarian beliefs, including Cromwell for a while, but the so-called Fifth Monarchists did not come together as a specific movement until the aftermath of Worcester. They were pulled together by their disappointment with the worldly and slothful bunch that sat in Parliament, and an unshakeable conviction that England was about to witness the second coming. This reign of Christ's would be the fifth and everlasting monarchy, following the fall of the empires of Babylon, Persia, Greece and Rome and as prophesied in the Bible, in the books of Daniel and Revelation. But the ungodly Rumpers were in the way, refusing to reform England's unregenerate ways and relinquish their comfy seats in Parliament. So the Fifth Monarchists began to preach that it was legitimate to use force to overthrow the existing government to advance Christ's kingdom. From Allhallows the Great, where they first met in 1651, and later from St Anne's Church in Blackfriars, 'fifth kingdom men' bellowed about their glorious cause. Christopher Feake, one of the loudest and most notorious of the preachers, recorded their agenda: 'the Kingdom of our Lord Jesus Christ may be exalted speedily in these Nations, and also in all the earth; and that whatsoever stood in the way of it might be utterly pulled down, and brought to nothing'.[12]

In a revolutionary world, the opportunity to challenge and utterly reform institutions, as well as people and their behaviour, is exciting, terrifying and frustrating. This was the case in 1650s England. Multiple committees sat in Westminster dedicated to rethinking how to empty the prisons and help the poor, who should preach the gospel and how to vet (and pay) the clergy, how tolerant, or not, to be of unorthodox religious beliefs, how to punish swearing and adultery, and how to access the law. Ideas about all these areas of life were provocative and divisive, complicated by the army's enthusiasm for major, overturning reform, and many of the committees' proposals stalled. For those MPs tasked with designing the bill to settle when Parliament would dissolve itself, and when and how elections should take place, work dragged on. In January 1653, Thomas Harrison chaired this committee rather hopelessly, urging his Fifth Monarchist desire for a saintly parliamentary body. He was succeeded by councillor of state Arthur Hesilrige, who was loathed by the army because he wanted to reduce their numbers. Hesilrige was a fierce defender of the sovereignty of Parliament, and one of those accused by the army of holding on to his own power; certainly he had advanced himself in the north as governor of Newcastle, snapping up former bishops' lands and houses. But pious Thomas Harrison, too, had profited from confiscated lands. Believing in the imminent kingdom of Christ did not always mean eschewing worldly benefits.

By February 1653, Parliament was meeting every Wednesday to try to finalise the bill 'for the Dissolving of this present Parliament and for the calling and settling of future and successive parliaments'.[13] The House was slow and not entirely representative – only about forty MPs ever turned up to the sessions.[14] In March, a frustrated Cromwell stopped taking his seat in Parliament. That same month, Whitelocke perceived with alarm and dismay that the 'drift of Cromwell & his officers' – Thomas Harrison in particular – was to forcibly put an end to this procrastinating body. Although Cromwell was less intimate with Whitelocke than he used to be, Whitelocke claimed that he advised him strongly not to dissolve Parliament, considering it to be 'the most daungerous, & most ungratefull action that could be done'.[15]

We do not know for sure if Cromwell was indeed drifting towards expelling Parliament by force, but he was certainly angry, and many anticipated a sudden change. Lorenzo Paulucci, the gossipy Venetian secretary posted to England, speculated that Parliament would be dissolved in January, and in April he reported to Giovanni Sagredo, the Venetian ambassador based in France, that Cromwell 'has ceased to attend the House as usual, and that he is continually devising plans of personal aggrandisement out of doors with his own adherents'.[16] In early April, a newsbook reported that 'something extraordinary is speedily expected'.[17] There were concerns about whether Cromwell was unduly influenced by Harrison and other Fifth Monarchists. Unlike Harrison, however, Cromwell professed not to agree with the use of force to bring about Christ's kingdom.

On the night of 19 April, Cromwell called a meeting of about twenty army officers and politicians at his Cockpit lodgings, overlooking St James's Park. Hesilrige, who was not there, called it a 'junto'. The invited group included those who supported an immediate dissolution – Oliver St John and Thomas Harrison among them – and those who did not: Henry Vane, Bulstrode Whitelocke and Thomas Widdrington. They debated, long into the night, what to do with a Parliament whose time and credibility had run out. It was expected that the next day, Wednesday 20 April, the MPs would finally present their long-awaited bill – but how many new Members would be elected, and who they could be, were unknown, as was what would happen in the interregnum between dissolution and fresh elections. At this eleventh hour, Cromwell proposed to the men gathered in his home that Parliament should be dissolved but that it should appoint, prior to its dissolution, a small caretaker government of about forty men. This assembly of MPs and army officers could run the country until fresh elections could safely guarantee the survival of the Commonwealth. Whitelocke and Widdrington were vehemently against such an illegal action. Vane ended up promising that he would try to persuade his fellow MPs to pause debating the new bill until Cromwell's proposal had at least been considered. The conference broke up late, and planned to reconvene in the morning.[18]

Whitelocke arrived at Cromwell's house particularly early the next day, troubled by the discussions from the previous night. He found Cromwell dressed informally in a plain black coat and grey woollen stockings.[19] As he and the others resumed their discussions, they heard that Parliament was in session and that the eighty or so Members present were about to push through their bill for the new representative.[20] Clearly, the MPs were not going to consider Cromwell's proposal to elect a caretaker assembly, as Vane had promised he would encourage them to do. Whitelocke and Colonel Richard Ingoldsby were sent across the road to the House of Commons to find out more. Ingoldsby rushed back, reporting that it looked as if the Members were agreeing to prolong their power. They were, Cromwell was led to believe, going to cling on to their seats and only recruit new Members to the empty seats instead of calling a fresh election. Three separate messengers relayed what was happening in the chamber before Cromwell snapped. He grabbed his hat, summoned his soldiers and marched to St Stephen's Chapel where the MPs were sitting. By the clock in St James's Park, it was a quarter past eleven.

Cromwell took his seat in the chamber, and listened to the debate for a while, before whispering to Harrison that surely this was 'the time' to act. Harrison attempted to hold Cromwell back, but just as Speaker Lenthall was about to pose the final question pertaining to the bill, Cromwell suddenly cried out, 'This is the time I must do it.' He took off his hat and began to speak, in a controlled way at first, praising his fellow Members for their efforts and their care of the 'public good'. But he soon began to chide and insult them, accusing them of corruption, procrastination and self-interest. He spoke, according to lieutenant-general of the horse Edmund Ludlow, 'with so much passion and discomposure of mind, as if he had been distracted'. Peter Wentworth, a committed republican MP, reprimanded Cromwell for his 'horrid' language, so unbecoming in the parliamentary chamber. But Cromwell was now in a rage. With his hat tilted back on his head, he strode out into the middle of the chamber, where he paced up and down 'like a madman', kicking the ground like an impatient horse. 'You are no Parliament,' he shouted. 'I say you are no Parliament; I will put an end to your sitting; call them in, call them in.' The doors of the chamber opened, and two files of red-coated soldiers bearing muskets marched in. 'This is not honest, yea it is against morality and common honesty,' protested Henry Vane. Cromwell turned to his old friend. 'O Sir Henry Vane, Sir Henry Vane, the Lord deliver me from Sir Henry Vane,' he implored, before hurling abuse at certain Members ('whoremasters' to Peter Wentworth and Henry Marten; others were 'drunkards'). Harrison yanked at the gown of Speaker Lenthall, who was refusing to move, and plucked him down from his chair. Next to Lenthall was Algernon Sidney, astounded by such contempt for Parliament. Cromwell demanded that the gilt mace, the symbol of a legitimate sitting Parliament, remodelled for the republic back in 1649, be taken away. To Cromwell the mace was now a 'bauble', for this was no serious Parliament. 'It's you that have forced me to this, for I have sought the Lord night and day, that he would rather slay me than put me upon the doing of this work,' Cromwell railed at the stunned politicians. He then snatched the copy of the act of dissolution out of clerk Henry Scobell's hands, stowed it under his cloak and stormed out, ordering his soldiers to clear the chamber and lock the doors.[21]

Most of the MPs were shocked and humiliated. Whitelocke remembered that none of them, despite wearing swords, drew against Cromwell or the soldiers. Instead they 'tamely departed', like chastened sheep.[22] Speaker Lenthall was marched out between a file of two hundred men, without the mace preceding him as was customary, and bundled into his coach.[23] The city could see that he had been forcibly stripped of his power. Hesilrige and Sidney would never forget such a tyrannical swipe at the supremacy of Parliament; it fuelled their belief that Parliament was sovereign. But 'fierce' Fifth Monarchists rejoiced, sensing the opportunity at last for England to reform her unregenerate ways without a sluggish Parliament getting in the way.[24] Radical soldiers and 'the pulpitt men of Blackfriers' delighted in Cromwell's 'grubbing up of the wicked Parliament, not leaving a rotten roote thereof'.[25] When the news reached Wolverhampton, some locals took the opportunity to set up a Maypole to 'express our great joy'.[26] Maypoles, associated with pagan festivity and sexual wantonness, had been banned back in the 1640s. Now that this Parliament was turned out, some believed that all laws had been turned out with it. For different reasons, the 'Kings party' in exile 'rejoyced', Whitelocke recalled.[27] For Charles's adviser Edward Hyde, earl of Clarendon, this 'great alteration' could undermine the sway of Cromwell and usher in 'a speedy change of government to the King'.[28]

Most people seemed largely accepting of, even pleased with, the latest upheaval at Westminster. Paulucci wrote that 'What has been most remarked is the slight emotion or rather the indifference with which this action was viewed by the populace, who for the most part seem pleased and especially satisfied by a step which gives hopes of relief and better management in everything'.[29] And although extra troops filed into London to secure the city, prowling the streets on foot and horse by day, lodging with shopkeepers at night, Cromwell himself later recalled that 'there was not so much as the barking of a dog, or any general or visible repining'.[30] Ralph Josselin noted from his parish in Essex a week or so later that there was 'quiett every where notwithstanding this great change at hand, most serious men are silent under it'.[31] That week's issue of *Severall Proceedings in Parliament* underplayed the coup, describing simply how Cromwell asked the MPs to depart, while soldiers cleared the chapel and locked the door. Satirists got to work. The next day, the newsbook reported, 'there was a Paper by somebody, posted upon the Parliament house door, thus; *This House is to be Lett, now unfurnished.*'[32] A ballad quickly appeared with the same name, 'Here's a House to Be Let'. It mocked the Parliament men, turfed out for their empty words about liberty: 'The freedome of subject they much did pretend, / but since they held sway we never had any.' Poet and journalist John Birkenhead quipped, 'Whether ever since the House of Commons was locked up, the Speakers Chaire hath not been a Close-stoole?'[33]

Cromwell's violent dissolution of Parliament was fatal for the republic. It was a military coup and it was, as Cromwell knew and as others often reminded him, illegal. He had blown apart the notion of parliamentary independence which was what many had believed they were fighting for during the civil wars, and which was held dear by many MPs. On the afternoon of 20 April, the council of state was in the middle of electing a new president (the office had been re-elected every month, since John Lambert had stepped down in late 1651). Cromwell informed the councillors that Parliament had been dissolved, and with it the council of state. John Bradshaw, whose second term as the council's president was coming to an end, responded with defiance. He had heard the news, he told Cromwell, but Cromwell was 'mistaken to think that the Parliament is dissolved; for no power under heaven can dissolve them but themselves; therefore take you notice of that'.[34] Bradshaw was right. Back in 1641, Charles I had agreed to the passing of an act which stated that only Parliament could consent to its dissolution.[35]

Prior to its expulsion, this Parliament, purged by Colonel Pride in 1649, was already marred by illegitimacy. Now, in spring 1653, whatever Oliver Cromwell and the army were planning to erect in its place would also suffer for the violent and illegitimate manner of its conception. Whitelocke knew this, but he characteristically resolved to do what he could to ensure his own survival (as did many others). He looked to God to explain the capricious, topsy-turvy world, where things change suddenly, and servants overthrow their masters:

> Thus it pleased God, that this Councell, famous through the world for its undertakings, actions, & successes, having subdued all their ennemies, were themselves overthrowne by their own servants, & those whom they had raysed, now pulled down their raysers, an example not to be forgotten nor paralleld, instructing how uncertain & subject to change all humane affayres are, how apt to fall when they seem to be highest, how God makes use of strange means to bring his purposes to pass & how unsafe it is to joyne with such people as these.[36]

Cromwell's anger and frustration with Parliament had clearly been mounting. He had stayed away from parliamentary debates and council sittings, seeking God's direction in prayer with the army. But there is a missing element of this dramatic set-piece of the 1650s, related so vividly by Edmund Ludlow and others, the subject of engravings and paintings, rehearsed again and again in history books. We cannot know exactly why Cromwell expelled

Parliament on that day and in that way. We cannot be sure about the extent to which it was a rash or premeditated act. Cromwell's particular anger on that day seems to have come from the news that the politicians were pressing ahead with passing their bill for the new representative, and his rage was intensified by what he either thought or knew to be the contents of that bill once he got to the chamber.

But the legislation that Parliament was about to finally pass, and that Cromwell supposedly snatched from the clerk Henry Scobell, is lost. The piece of paper has never been seen again, and there is no record of its contents. In early 1660, Scobell's entry for the episode in the House of Commons journal was ordered to be expunged.[37] We cannot be sure what exactly the MPs were about to agree to, or why Cromwell behaved as impetuously and as unrestrainedly as the contemporary accounts suggest, and as Cromwell admitted immediately afterwards. 'When I went there,' he allegedly told the army officers waiting back at his house, 'I did not think to have done this. But perceiving the spirit of God so strong upon me, I would not consult flesh and blood.'[38] This does not sit well with Thomas Harrison's recollection of Cromwell's comment once in the House that the time was now 'ripe' to end this Parliament. Nor does it sit well with the fact that Cromwell took armed soldiers along with him to the House. It is possible, as has been argued, that Cromwell was mistaken about the contents of the act about to be passed, and that he genuinely believed that the MPs were conniving to prolong their power. This might explain the act's mysterious disappearance from the records: only when Cromwell was home, the theory goes, and able to read carefully the bill that he had snatched, did he perhaps realise he was mistaken, and destroyed the bill as evidence of his error.[39] Neither Algernon Sidney's nor Whitelocke's accounts say precisely what it was that was being discussed that angered Cromwell, or suggest that he was mistaken. Neither does Ludlow, and he surely would have seized on the chance to show Cromwell up. The newsbook *Severall Proceedings in Parliament* reported that Parliament was dissolved because the act the MPs were about to pass would give potential candidates and voters 'so much liberty that many disaffected persons might be chosen'. Perhaps the bill was not adequately providing for the exclusion of certain Members. A paper in Henry Marten's collection records that Cromwell said, 'The people shall not have their liberty, I say the people shall not have their liberty.'[40] In a speech a couple of months later, in July, Cromwell suggested that the act left out 'the things that did necessarily relate to due qualifications' and would therefore have 'thrown all the liberties of the Nation into the hands that never bled for it'.[41] But if the bill was unreliable in this way, then it is puzzling that Cromwell did not publish it to prove the point.

On 22 April, two days after the dramatic dissolution, Cromwell and his council of officers published a declaration justifying their 'grounds and reasons'. Cromwell appealed to the sad necessity of his action, recalling his duty to God and to the nation that God had protected – the nation which, he feared, Parliament was recklessly about to deliver back into the enemy's hands. The declaration mentioned nothing specific about the bill, only that Parliament's haste to push it through on the morning of 20 April confirmed his and the army's fears that Parliament only sought 'to perpetuate themselves', and hence the 'interests of all honest men and of this glorious cause' were about to be laid to dust. 'We have been necessitated,' Cromwell wrote, 'though with much reluctancy, to put an End to this Parliament.'[42]

England, Scotland and Ireland were now without a government. A council of officers was convened to decide what to do; this had been a sudden dissolution, an army coup led by Cromwell, and there was no ready-made plan in place. The Fifth Monarchist Thomas Harrison's proposal prevailed. At Cromwell's house the night before the dissolution a council of forty had been suggested, but Harrison favoured an executive council of seventy men, modelled on the ancient Jewish assembly of seventy-one men, the Sanhedrin. Major-General John Lambert suggested something smaller – a council of twelve. In the end, the officers decided on a larger assembly of 140 men. These men were nominated, and then voted for, by the council of officers. For the first time, Scotland and Ireland enjoyed some kind of representation – five of this Nominated Assembly's members were English soldiers in Scotland, and six were English soldiers in Ireland. Fairfax was invited to be one of the assembly, but he declined.

On 4 July, in the council chamber at Whitehall, Cromwell – as a nominated member of the assembly but primarily in his role as lord general of the army – addressed the chosen few. It was stiflingly hot, and Cromwell spoke for over two hours, weeping at frequent intervals.[43] The summer heat and Cromwell's troubled state were probably not the only reason the gathered men shifted and looked uneasy in their seats. They had been summoned by letter to attend, and they were conscious of the unprecedented and unknown nature of their office. They were not a Parliament, so were not allowed (yet) to sit in St Stephen's Chapel. No doubt they were aware too of the 'scantness' of the assembly.[44] Only eighteen among them were recalled MPs. There were a dozen or so Fifth Monarchists and about the same number of religious radicals. Others were drawn from the lesser gentry, and there was a clutch of noblemen: two peers, two future earls, four baronets, four knights.[45] Most men were unknown to each other. 'I am confident you are strangers,' Cromwell said, but he assured them that as men who 'knew the Lord', they had been chosen 'by way of necessity . . . by the way of the wise providence of God'. Their task was a godly one. 'Love all the sheep, love the lambs, love all, and tender all, and cherish all,' Cromwell told them, urging them to show mercy, pity and tolerance.[46] It was a speech of troubled conscience. As he sought to justify the 'last great change', Cromwell reached back to the wars of the 1640s and emphasised his belief in the strange but wonderful windings and turnings of providence which had brought them to this point. He wanted to persuade and inspire the assembled men that they had God's work to do, and had a godly nation to build, purged of vice and depravity. 'We are at the threshold, and therefore it becomes us to lift up our heads and to encourage ourselves in the Lord,' Cromwell said, before telling them: 'You are at the edge of the promises and prophecies . . . you should be sensible of your duty.'[47] He may not have seen himself as Moses leading his people away from bondage, but others did.[48] And this impassioned speech delivered on a scorching day was suffused with the language of the apocalypse, the dawning of a new light, another new beginning.

The practical, more sombre purpose of this meeting in the council chamber was the formal handing over of Cromwell's power to the assembly, and the relinquishing of the power of his sword. Throughout his speech he held in his hands the 'Instrument', the document that defined the office of these nominated men, and in whose own hands supreme authority now lay. Among them was a middle-aged leather merchant with the fashionably pious name of Praisegod Barbon, or Barebone. He ran a successful shop at the sign of the Lock and Key on Fleet Street, from where he also preached, attracting crowds of men and women, and the attention of the authorities.[49] He was an Independent, believing in a non-established church and in the 'great things' that would accompany Christ's second reign on earth.[50] Barebone had earned his place in the assembly either through recommendation by his congregation, or by army officers who approved of his godliness. He was one of seven Londoners chosen to represent the city, and he proved himself a prominent and active Member – as did the other Londoners. Perhaps Barebone felt particularly moved to the edge of prophecies as he listened to Cromwell, for it was his surname that was seized upon by critics of the assembly, wishing to denigrate its skeletal legitimacy and exaggerate its millenarian tendencies by misrepresenting it as a fanatical body of saints. To many hostile observers, the Nominated Assembly that ruled from July 1653 became known as 'Barebone's Parliament'. It is one of the many misconceptions of the age's Puritanism that it seems surprising, at first, to learn that Barebone's son, Nicholas, would go on to become one of Restoration London's most significant and notorious property developers, particularly after the Great Fire of 1666 which destroyed his father's shop. Well dressed, a bit of a rogue and a speculator, Nicholas was an economic rather than a religious radical. For him, free trade, spending, consumption and luxury would bring peace and plenty to England – not a Parliament of saints.[51]

In the week after 4 July, following Cromwell's clarion call, the assembly met to seek the Lord, ask for blessing and make decisions. The Fifth Monarchist lay preacher Arthur Squibb, nominated as MP for Middlesex, was among those who led the prayers at their first meeting. The assembly voted to call itself the Parliament of the Commonwealth of England and requested to sit in St Stephen's Chapel. They chose to keep the council of state, onto which they nominated Cromwell, John Lambert and Thomas Harrison. They reinstated Henry Scobell as the clerk and summoned back the banished mace. Edward Birkhead was restored as serjeant at arms to the House, an office first granted to him in 1646. It was agreed that he would carry the mace and attend on the new Speaker, Francis Rous. Rous, provost of Eton College, was in his seventies and a veteran politician from Cornwall. He had known the reigns of Elizabeth I and James I, and the fraught Parliaments of Charles I. He had opposed the king's trial, but had argued, Hobbes-style, for acquiescence and obedience to the new regime. He was a conservative choice for Speaker – this assembly was not as fanatical as its critics successfully argued, and the 'godliness' required of all persons who entered the House took in a wide range. And so this unprecedented group of moderate and radical men adopted the personnel and trappings of a legitimate Parliament, and began the business of governance. It is indicative of both the haste and the novelty underlying this assembly's coming together that one of its first tasks was to correct the 'Instrument', the document that Cromwell had signed and sealed authorising the appointment of the Members, but in which, unfortunately, several names had been misspelled, even by early modern standards.[52]

At sea, England was still at war with the Dutch. To men like Ralph Josselin and John Evelyn, the noise of the war was more real and more intrusive than the clamouring of the politicians at Westminster. Neither Josselin nor Evelyn dwelled on Cromwell's dismissal of the Rump Parliament in their diaries, but both men – Josselin from his village of Earls Colne and Evelyn from his garden at Sayes Court – noted hearing the guns from the hundreds of ships fighting in the English Channel in the summer of 1653. On 3 June, Evelyn recalled 'plainly' hearing the 'greate batall at sea, with the Hollanders'.[53] This was the battle of the Gabbard, named after the sandbank off the coast of Suffolk where the Dutch navy was overwhelmed by the superior gunpowder and novel tactics of the Commonwealth navy. They lost twenty ships, and England none, taking instead 1,360 Dutch prisoners. On 31 July, Josselin was woken up by 'the thumping, thundering Cannon, which filled into country houses, and our beds with the dreadfull noise, I have not ever heard the like shooting in my life'.[54] The cannon roared until evening, the sound carried high and far on the wind. Josselin prayed to God to protect his country. This battle, the battle of Scheveningen, proved to be decisive. The Dutch admiral van Tromp was killed and, in the end, both fleets retreated. Ships were badly damaged and the wounded sailors too numerous. Since both sides retired, both sides believed they were victorious.

To the Fifth Monarchists, the war with the Dutch was God's war. They railed against attempts to broker peace. The establishment of Barebone's Parliament gave the Fifth Monarchists their moment. William Aspinwall, believing that the saints were about to triumph in England, chose this year to leave his colonial life as a merchant and churchman in Massachusetts. He travelled home to England, where he published his *Brief Description of the Fifth Monarchy*. Aspinwall dared not determine the precise year for the beginning of this fifth kingdom, but, he claimed, it was near, and his little book laid out exactly how the saints would rule.[55] Women were particularly drawn to the Fifth Monarchist movement. Mary Cary, a gentlewoman who lived in London, had become a millenarian at the young age of fifteen. In the summer of 1653 she presented Barebone's Parliament with a set of reform proposals and a revised edition of her pamphlet, *The Resurrection*, in which she argued that England's war with the Dutch was in the name of

God, and the saints should continue to fight against this Protestant but ungodly and rather royal republic.[56]

Others turned away from the guns of war and cries of religious zealotry that tore through the country that summer. Izaak Walton was a linen draper from Stafford who had sold his cloth from his shop in the same London parish as Praisegod Barebone – St Dunstan-in-the-west – before moving east to Clerkenwell. As a younger man Walton had listened to John Donne's soaring sermons in St Paul's, and in his own parish church of St Dunstan's. They had become friends, and Walton wrote the first ever literary biography: his magisterial *Life of Donne* has left us with the little that we know about Donne's life.[57] In 1653 Walton was sixty, but his career as a writer was about to flourish. While learning his craft as a sempster he had written poetry and moved in circles that included the poet and playwright Ben Jonson, the antiquarian and biographer John Aubrey and the scholar and diplomat Henry Wotton. He had married twice, and had buried eight children. Walton was loyal to the dead king, and to the liturgy and light of the Anglican Church. In 1651, he had played an unexpected part in the fallout from the battle of Worcester. Before making his escape, Charles II had given his 'George' medal – the medal that signified his status as head of the Order of the Garter – to one of his officers, Colonel Thomas Blague, who had hidden it under a pile of dust and chippings at a Royalist safehouse near Stafford before going on the run himself. From here, it was rescued by the Royalist lawyer Robert Milward. Milward needed a trustworthy man to smuggle the medal out of Stafford, and he chose his old friend and client Izaak Walton. Walton safely carried the medal back to London, and delivered it into the hands of Colonel Blague, who was now imprisoned in the Tower of London. Blague later escaped and fled to France – and so gave back this insignia of the Order of the Garter to its rightful owner.[58]

But it was a small and quiet book about fishing, published in May 1653, that brought Walton great success in his lifetime, and beyond. *The Compleat Angler* is a conversation between two men about fish and fishing, 'not unworthy the perusal of most anglers'. It was prettily illustrated with engravings of trout, carp and pike. Available to buy for a few pence from the publisher and bookseller Richard Marriott's shop in St Dunstan's churchyard, it was advertised in the newsbooks in early May. By 20 May the eagle-eyed and insatiable book collector George Thomason, a friend of John Milton's, had secured his copy.[59]

The Compleat Angler was hugely popular. A second edition was published in 1655, and four further editions appeared in Walton's lifetime, with many others since. It has, in fact, never been out of print. But for all its tips on flies, bait and weather, this book is a great deal more than a manual. To read it is to move away from the heat of politics and the city (the summer of 1653 was said to be excruciatingly hot) and to breathe in the rain-filled air of the English countryside in the spring. As Piscator, the experienced fisherman, and Viator, the hunter, walk north from Tottenham along the River Lea towards Ware, talking about fishing, the book opens up like the green fields through which the two companions pass, to become a tale of friendship, and the past. As they walk and fish their conversation meanders, like the river, through a range of topics: small pleasures, favourite authors, sports. Piscator and Viator enjoy the quiet, patiently watching the water and berating the otters who get to the fish before they do (but whose hides make good gloves for London shops). They quote the Bible, the classics and the Elizabethan poets Christopher Marlowe and Walter Raleigh. They shelter under a sycamore when it showers, and in the evenings they drink ale at the inn where the sheets are white and smell of lavender and where the hostess fries the chub they have caught in butter, salt and thyme. Afterwards they express their loyalty to the king, to other cavalier poets and to England's past by singing ballads and declaiming verses in praise of simple country pastimes.

The anglers' delight in drinking and merry-making is pointedly non-Puritan (although it is wrong to assume that all Puritans were against such fun). In 1643, Parliament had ordered that all copies of James I's *Book of Sports* – his declaration in favour of rural pursuits which Charles I had reissued – should be burnt by the hangman.[60] 'Angling' in *The Compleat Angler* is almost synonymous with 'Anglican', and it is likely that the book appealed to many with enforced leisure time on their hands: Royalists lying low, sequestered bishops, ejected clergymen, secluded politicians. But many readers who shared Walton's love of fishing and bought his book did not share the author's loyalty to the dead king and the dismantled Anglican Church. Anyone looking for a book to buy in St Dunstan's churchyard that summer, or browsing the adverts in the newsbooks, might have been caught as much by Walton's *The Compleat Angler* as by *Waters for a Thirsty Soul*, a collection of sermons on the book of Revelation by a Presbyterian preacher from Derbyshire, William Bagshawe.[61]

As Barebone's got going, moderates at the helm of the new regime were keen to build bridges, even with the 'old malignants'. Cromwell, for example, granted the Royalist Sir Roger L'Estrange a pass to return to England to visit his dying father.[62] But he didn't grant such a pass to John Lilburne, ever the thorn in the Commonwealth's side, who had been banished from England two years earlier after a battle with Arthur Hesilrige over lands in Durham.[63] In the aftermath of the dissolution, Lilburne saw the opportunity to challenge his banishment and sailed back to England anyway. Now that the

Rump Parliament was no longer, and since it had never been a legitimate body anyway, Lilburne argued robustly, his banishment was not valid. Furthermore, he had been denied due process. He had not been tried by a jury in 1651, and this smacked of parliamentary tyranny. Parliaments, like kings, could become tyrants.[64] While in exile in the Netherlands, Lilburne had met a number of Royalist exiles, including George Villiers, the duke of Buckingham, and there were rumours that they and this former Leveller were hatching a plot to bring about a royal restoration.

Once in London, from his lodging in Little Moorfields, Lilburne sent a letter via his loyal, campaigning wife Elizabeth to Cromwell, pleading for His Excellency's protection. But Cromwell referred him to the council of state – there was, of course, no clear supreme authority in these early days following the dissolution – and the council threw him into Newgate prison to await trial for breaking his banishment, the sentence for which was a traitor's death. Lilburne had always had the ability to harness the sympathy of the people and petitions flooded in, from soldiers, apprentices and women, protesting against the severity of the act of banishment. 'You see the thing is so gross, that even Women perceive the evil of it,' petitioned a group of women whose hearts had melted 'in tendernesse towards so great and causelesse a sufferer'.[65] Bravely, the twelve-man jury in the Old Bailey did not convict him, but 'for the peace of this nation', the Barebone's Parliament sent him to the Tower. Lilburne was finally silenced, and he spent the rest of his days in prison or on parole, until his death in 1657.[66]

The trial and imprisonment of Lilburne, among the first tasks overseen by Barebone's Parliament, tested the legitimacy of this assembly as well as prodding at the problem of law. *An Hue and Cry* urged the 'saints' now calling themselves a Parliament to consider diligently 'the manner of the proceedings' against Lilburne, who was acquitted by a jury, but then marched to the Tower by soldiers on horseback.[67]

No doubt Barebone's Members were as divided over Lilburne's fate as they certainly were about one of the most toxic issues of the time: tithes. A staggering number of treatises published in 1653 argued either for or against the abolition of tithes. Tithes were a form of parish levy, paid by townsfolk and farm owners (calculated as the tenth part of their farm's annual produce) to pay for their local church and vicar. Those eligible for this tariff paid in cash or in kind and, when profitable Church lands had passed into lay hands in the sixteenth century, those new property owners continued to collect tithes from villagers who farmed their land.

Whether it was the Church's divine right to collect tithes, laid down in the Bible, or whether they were merely a levy enshrined in common law had been debated since the days of James I at the beginning of the century. For many, the payment of tithes represented stability and continuity. They kept the church and the vicar, and preserved the hierarchy in a community; many feared the consequences of questioning the status quo. Clergymen and lay landowners were, of course, keen to be able to continue to benefit from such a tax – 40 per cent of tithes were now paid to lay benefactors – and many wanted to keep these propertied men on side.[68] Those paying the money also feared for their souls. What would happen to the local vicar, his family and household if parishioners did not maintain him? Who would preach and pray for them, or bury their dead? The 'well affected' in Hampshire petitioned the House in September to maintain tithes, invoking their confirmation by Magna Carta.[69] But for farmers with modest lands, or those who suffered a bad harvest, the payment of a tenth of their produce could be crippling, and many resisted. Petitioners from Kent rounded up their complaints in a 1653 pamphlet addressed to Oliver Cromwell and Thomas Harrison, listing the names of impoverished men and women who had been imprisoned, whose families had been threatened and houses broken into at night, and who had had cattle, mares and money seized. For refusing to offer up the tithe milk of his one cow (the value of three pence), John Austin had had ten shillings stolen. To these and other men and women around England, tithes were greedy, oppressive and a despised remnant of the Catholic Church.[70]

In the vicarage at Earls Colne, Essex, Ralph Josselin worried much during these years about having enough money to support himself and his family, particularly around harvest time when his tithes would be collected. One night in August 1653, he dreamed that he was sent 'a bushel of wheate, and in the mouth of the sacke was a bundle of mony' which, like the porridge from the magic pot, kept increasing. Only the month before, Josselin had heard that the 'New Councell' had 'as their first businesse taken into consideration the matter of tithes'. And back in the autumn of 1648, following the wars, a wet summer and the unwillingness of some of his parishioners to pay tithes, Josselin had even contemplated leaving Earls Colne: 'I desire no great meanes to live richly in the world, but convenient food and rayment,' he wrote on 12 September 1648, but 'when the priests had not their tithes brought in . . . the priests leave the Temple'.[71]

The problem was agreeing on an alternative way of supporting the country's clergy. Radical sectaries did not want a single, national Church that the people had to finance.[72] And while Cromwell had sympathy with this, he was pragmatic enough to fear alienating the propertied men. But, in 1653, the din of millenarians such as John Spittlehouse warning the government in 'these Overturning, Overturning, Overturning dayes' to dash anti-Christian nations to pieces, tear down the law courts and throw out tithes and the entire Church system proved deafening over the summer and into autumn.[73] The 'radicals' within Barebone's were divided between themselves, with only twelve identifiable Fifth Monarchists holding as a (very noisy) group. Key figures began to withdraw, and to plot.[74] Cromwell had never taken up the seat given to him by the Barebone's Members, although he was voted unanimously onto the second council of state in November. John Lambert, too, had never taken his seat in the assembly and he was not re-elected to the second council. He preferred to watch events from his recently acquired home, Wimbledon Manor House, taking solace among his tulips and fruit trees in the beautifully laid-out gardens planted by Queen Henrietta Maria, the manor's former owner.[75] Both Cromwell and Lambert had distanced themselves from Thomas Harrison and his railing against peace with the Dutch. But Harrison also was retreating. Each Monday, Fifth Monarchists continued to meet for prayers at St Anne's in Blackfriars but there were rumours that the most radical of the Barebone's Members – who were meeting at millenarian Arthur Squibb's house – were planning to seize power for themselves.

On 2 December 1653, the committee for tithes presented its proposals for reform. The House debated them vigorously over the next week. The proposals were moderate, recommending that tithes should be retained, but with some wriggle room granted to those parishioners particularly unwilling to betray their consciences and pay tithes. Unsuitable ministers, considered 'not of good behaviour . . . or not apt, and able to teach, or hold not forth the faithful Word', would be ejected by a body of commissioners.[76] The proposal for the commissioners was rejected, by a small majority, and it was likely that the recommendation to retain tithes would be rejected too.[77]

The 'moderates' in Barebone's then acted before such a vote could be cast. On Monday 12 December, the radicals in the House were subjected to a barrage of criticism and cries for abdication. Sir Charles Wolseley spoke fervently in defence of tithes, as did several other Members. Speaker Francis Rous, instead of keeping order, was among the nearly fifty men who then walked out of the House and headed straight to Whitehall, where they formally resigned their power to Cromwell. Those left behind in St Stephen's Chapel were marched out, as had happened in April, by armed soldiers. Barebone's had imploded. For the second time in a year, Britain was without a government.[78]

It was at this point that John Lambert re-entered the scene. He was in his early thirties, a brilliant military commander and strategist, and constitutionally minded. He had been involved in drawing up the proposals offered to Charles I to broker peace. Unlike Cromwell's impetuous action in April, the events in the House on 12 December were carefully choreographed. Indeed, it is likely that the vote on the committee's tithes proposals was deliberately sabotaged so that 'moderates' could use their defeat to rage at the radicals and bring down Barebone's from the inside. Since at least October, Lambert had been hard at work drafting England's first ever written constitution. A few days before the House had heard the committee's proposals for tithes, Lambert had shown Cromwell his new plan for the government of England. He wanted to dissolve Barebone's and reinstate a monarchy. But this would be a limited monarchy (not unlike the kind Henry Ireton had proposed to Charles I back in 1648) and Cromwell would be its head. Cromwell balked at the title of king, and he refused (unlike in April) to use force to dissolve Parliament. So the railing speeches levelled at the radicals by the moderates in the House were orchestrated by Lambert. It looked as though the uncooperative radicals had forced

Barebone's to self-destruct. Cromwell may have been taken aback on the actual day by the resigning Members turning up at Whitehall, but he cannot have been surprised that the assembly had fallen apart. He accepted the Members' resignations and, by the end of the week, agreed to the tweaked terms of Lambert's constitution, known as the Instrument of Government. He would not be King Oliver, but he would agree to become Lord Protector.[79]

A few days later, in the early afternoon of Friday 16 December, a formal procession wound its way along Whitehall, to the court of Chancery, which sat in the south end of Westminster Hall. Cromwell, dressed in a black suit and cloak and wearing a hat with a gold band, travelled by coach. The road and palace yard were lined with soldiers, some standing, some on horseback.[80] Surrounding the coach was Cromwell's personal life guard, eighty or so high-ranking army men originally employed to protect Cromwell as commander of the army of the Commonwealth, mounted on horses and wearing shiny black and gold uniforms. Accompanying them, but on foot, were chief army officers, bearing hats and swords.[81] Ahead of Cromwell in the procession were the lord commissioners Bulstrode Whitelocke and John Lisle, robed judges and barons of the exchequer, the 'godly' and 'discreet' members of the quickly formed protectoral council, the scarlet-gowned lord mayor (the eminent goldsmith and banker Thomas Vyner), and sheriffs and aldermen of London. According to Edmund Ludlow, who was not there but waiting for news in Ireland, the mayor and aldermen were forced to participate in this ostentatious pageantry, having been summoned by letter.[82]

In Westminster Hall a chair of state had been set up, and Cromwell stood to its left. From the niches of the walls, the statues of England's past monarchs looked on.[83] For nearly the next hour, William Jessop, secretary to the council, read out Lambert's Instrument of Government. Lisle then read out the oath, and Cromwell signed and swore to take on the protection and government of England, Scotland and Ireland. His raised right hand was, apparently, shaking.[84] Cromwell's transformation into His Highness the Lord Protector was completed by sitting down in the chair of state, and putting his black hat on his head; the rest of the court remained bareheaded in recognition of his authority. The lord commissioners offered him the purse and seals, which he immediately gave back in recognition of the commissioners' authority. The lord mayor offered him his pearl-encrusted Elizabethan sword and the cap of maintenance, which Cromwell also immediately returned.[85] According to Ludlow, John Lambert played a key part in the ceremony, in Cromwell's exchange of a military for a civilian sword, which Ludlow found 'false':

> After the General had heard the Instrument of Government read, and taken the oath as directed in the close of the said Instrument, Major-General Lambert kneeling presented him with a sword in the scabbard, representing the civil sword; which Cromwell accepting, put off his own, intimating thereby that he would no longer rule by the military sword, tho like a false hypocrite he designed nothing more.[86]

Outside, when Cromwell left Westminster Hall, soldiers in the yard cheered and fired their muskets. Thomas Vyner, as lord mayor, processed before him carrying his sword. He also rode with Cromwell in his coach (the city sword safely stowed in the back) to Whitehall, to the Banqueting House to listen to a sermon by Cromwell's chaplain, Nicholas Lockyer. It was all over by four or five o'clock.

England – Britain – was now a Protectorate. The change was broadcast throughout the three nations by proclamations and in the newsbooks. It was proclaimed reluctantly in Ireland but apparently enthusiastically in Plymouth, to the sound of gunshots, ringing bells and cheering crowds. And, as had been traditional in England for years, bonfires were lit to mark the change. London's Inns of Court spent more on their bonfire for Cromwell than they had done for Charles I's coronation.[87] The Venetian diplomat Paulucci reported both apathy and admiration. For him, this solemn investiture conspicuously appropriated royal forms and the Instrument of Government 'practically makes him [Cromwell] king'.[88]

Power resided, once again, in a single man. Although the office was elective (but chosen by the council and not the people), the Protector's powers looked remarkably similar to those held by England's former kings and queens. Cromwell's authority, however, was limited, and agreed to, by a written constitution, and this was entirely new. As the Instrument declared, there would be a council, and a Parliament every three years. It may not have been the political solution that some desired. It was certainly a betrayal to the millenarian hopefuls; Cromwell's kingdom would only hinder Christ's. To Christopher Feake, Cromwell was now 'the man of sin, the old dragon'.[89] To Royalists, in his imitation of monarchy, Cromwell as Protector was a travesty of true monarchy and it was all too novel.[90]

Among all these competing voices, with the investiture of Cromwell as Lord Protector and the solemnisation of the Instrument of Government, England was doing something radical. It may have all looked somewhat royal, and it was easy for hostile Royalists and anti-Cromwellians to criticise it for being so, but this was royalty with a difference. There was no sacred blood, no transferral of divine grace, no sacramental transformation of the body into a semi-god, no bishops fussing around with consecrated oil and benedictory gestures. Cromwell was a godly man, and he believed God had been behind the downfall of the king and the victories at Dunbar and Worcester, but he was a commoner, and his transformation from Cambridgeshire gentleman, politician and soldier to 'His Highness' was secular. Like the oldest form of the English coronation, before the ceremony moved into the sacred space of a church, it was the oath that mattered. And, unlike in previous coronations, authority was circumscribed by a written constitution.

The title of Lord Protector was settled on in the few days before the ceremony. It signified a temporary position – someone who would, it was hoped, protect a country and its rightful but either absent or under-age monarch. History taught that the title was not associated with stability: England's former Lords Protector, Richard, duke of Gloucester (later Richard III) and Edward Seymour, duke of Somerset, had been killed. The title had precedent but 'protection', as defined in the Instrument, also chimed with Hobbesian ideas that authority should be obeyed if it protected the people – as long as you are being protected, then it does not matter how that authority came into power in the first place. Back in May 1650, a Royalist had predicted that Cromwell could soon become Lord Protector.[91] John Moore, in his 1655 book *Protection Proclaimed*, claimed that before they were called kings, the governors of Israel were 'protectors'. The form of address 'His Highness' was not as surprising, or as imitative of royalty, as Cromwell's critics liked to note. Rather, 'His Majesty' was the accepted form for a king.[92] Nevertheless, what exactly a Protector was, or would be, and what this heralded for England, Scotland and Ireland, was unclear. An anonymous satirist mocked the low-born Cromwell for playing at being a king, and for being a devil in a godly disguise:

> What's a Protector, 'tis a stately thing
> That Apes it in the non-age of a King
> A Tragique Actor, Cesar in the Clowne
> Hee is a brasse farthing stamped with a Crowne
> A fops proud Asse masked in a Lions skin
> An outside Saint with a white devil within.

A copy of this little libel was given to James Butler, marquess of Ormond, while the Leveller Richard Overton was sent to prison for possessing a copy.[93] For the veteran poet and writer George Wither, who had written verses for James I's son Prince Henry and was now a Hampshire Justice of the Peace and defender of Cromwell, Protector was the noblest of titles, and so much better than the vanity that attends those with the title of 'king'. It 'marks forth One, (as if from heav'n sent down) / Who seeks his Peoples weal, more then his own', Wither wrote in a long, grovelling poem.[94] Within four years England's republic, the free state, had morphed into a Protectorate. Whether this new constitutional body, with Cromwell at its head, would bring healing and settlement remained to be seen.

II : PROTECTORATE

If These the Times

1654

There is more in harmless Ceremonies of State than common and weak eyes discern.

Severall Proceedings of State Affaires in England, Ireland and Scotland, 20–27 April 1654

At the end of January 1654, Lorenzo Paulucci, the secretary to Sagredo, the Venetian ambassador in Paris, was finally granted an audience with England's new Protector at Whitehall. Paulucci had no official diplomatic status in England. His job was to report back to Sagredo who would, in turn, report to the doge and Senate in Venice. Since 1652, this astute Italian had been watching the political scene in London, angling for a formal reception by the council of state. For Paulucci, a representative of the hierarchical and ceremonial republic of Venice, it mattered how he was received by Cromwell, England's new Lord Protector. Appropriately, he was met and accompanied by Cromwell's master of ceremonies, Sir Oliver Fleming. Cromwell removed his hat when Paulucci entered, and bowed his head a little each time the Signory was mentioned – a sign of due respect to the most serene republic of Venice. Such etiquette, Paulucci wrote, indicates 'the forms observed under the new rule, as well as the tone of sovereign and supreme command assumed by the Protector'. Cromwell, Paulucci went on to say, looked a little careworn but 'may be said to assume additional state and majesty daily, and lacks nothing of royalty but the name, which he is generally expected to assume when he wants to'.[1]

Paulucci was not the only one spreading the rumour that, one day, the Lord Protector might actually become king. 1654 was a year of restored ceremony and forms, and of the rituals that attend and legitimise a single person in power. It was also a year in which Cromwell and the regime sought to broker peace and build bridges with former enemies. The oath of engagement to the Commonwealth was repealed, a number of Royalists were released from prison and politicians who could not brook the idea of a Protectorate, notably Arthur Hesilrige and Henry Vane, retreated for a while. Fifth Monarchists were deemed, by Cromwell, 'mistaken'.[2] The council of state was renamed the council of state to His Highness the Lord Protector, and its councillors began to turn Whitehall into a home for Oliver Cromwell and his family, and into a theatre of state.

In January, councillors Anthony Ashley Cooper (future earl of Shaftesbury), Walter Strickland and Colonels Philip Jones and William Sydenham set about recovering some of the goods and royal palaces that had been sold or leased to make money for the republic as part of the Sale of the Late King's Goods. They now needed them, they said, for the Protector's use. The sale, which opened in 1649, had been halted just days before Cromwell's investiture as Lord Protector.[3] Some men stood to make a great deal of money from the council's decision to retain certain palaces and parks. Hampton Court had originally been exempt from the sale but, in August 1653, it was put on the market, in an effort to raise money for the Dutch war. Now that the councillors wanted it back, Edward Backwell, a shrewd London goldsmith, demanded more money from the government than he had paid for the leases. Parliament had agreed that Anthony Ashley Cooper could offer the palace to Cromwell. Cromwell refused, and urged the council to press ahead with a sale. But Parliament resolved to keep it and, within four days of Cromwell's investiture as Lord Protector, it was clear that he would indeed use, and enjoy, Hampton Court. By the end of 1654, it was agreed that the palaces of 'Whitehall, St James' House and Park, the Mews, Somerset-House, Greenwich House and Park, Hampton-Court, and the Honour and Manor of Hampton-Court; with the Parks and Grounds thereunto now belonging, Windsore-Castle, the Little Park there, and other the Lands thereunto now belonging; and the House called the Manor, in or near the City of York' would all be 'vested in the present Lord Protector', to be passed on to all succeeding Lords Protector, and that this was in order to maintain 'his and their State and Dignity'.[4]

Since April 1653, John Embree had been in post as surveyor of works to the Commonwealth, replacing Edward Carter. Embree had previously served as the sergeant plumber under Charles I. His knowledge of the palaces was now put to use – as Inigo Jones's was when he had been surveyor of the king's works. Just days after Cromwell's investiture as Lord Protector, Embree set about restoring the privy lodgings, kitchens and butteries and clearing out the stables in the mews. Over the course of 1654, Embree spent £13,700 on maintenance and alterations, primarily to Hampton Court and Whitehall, both of which had suffered substantial neglect.[5] In February, Clement Kinnersley, keeper of the wardrobe, was instructed to source all furniture and furnishings from the various palace wardrobes, now belonging to the state, which could be used in the 'Protector's house'.[6] He spent nearly £13,000 in this first year fitting out the rooms at Whitehall with beds, carpets and curtains.[7] At the same time, Sir Gilbert Pickering, soon to become Cromwell's lord chamberlain, was among those ordered to buy back hangings and goods that had already been sold.[8] Tapestries, such as a set of six panels depicting the adulterous myth of Vulcan, Mars and Venus, were bought back from the merchant John Stone for £350. Turkey carpets were repurchased to keep the rooms warm as well as impressive. A tapestry depicting the tragic tale of Hero and Leander was bought back from the draper Ralph Grafton for £180. Goods taken from captured Stirling Castle were delivered to Kinnersley for 'his Highness': three chairs of state and 'divers silk curtains'.[9] Symbolic items were reclaimed too, whether or not they had fallen into private hands. In January, the council issued a warrant for the 'two great swords of the late King', which a Colonel Humphreys had bought. If he handed them over, Humphreys was promised the same price that he had paid for them.[10]

On 14 April, Oliver Cromwell and his loyal, beloved wife Elizabeth, and his eighty-nine-year-old mother, also Elizabeth, moved from their Cockpit lodgings overlooking St James's Park, into the privy lodgings that had been prepared for them inside Whitehall. They brought with them three of their four daughters: Elizabeth, the 'joy' of Cromwell's heart and married to John Claypole (who would become a prominent member of Cromwell's household at Whitehall), Mary (seventeen years old) and Frances (fifteen years old), both unmarried. Cromwell's 'dear Biddy', Bridget, was in Dublin, now married to the senior officer Charles Fleetwood, commander of the army in Ireland. Richard, Cromwell's eldest surviving son, was with his wife Dorothy and young family in Hursley Manor in Hampshire. Henry, the younger son, came back from Ireland in 1654, and lived between Chippenham and London. Elizabeth, the Protectress, was, according to Edmund Ludlow, not keen at first to move into Whitehall, but she soon, he sniped, 'became better satisfied with her grandeur'.[11]

The rooms the Cromwells lived in were those that Charles I had occupied before he fled in 1642: a series of interconnecting chambers running alongside the privy gallery, which ran east towards the Thames from Holbein Gate on King Street.[12] To the north were the Banqueting House and Pebble Court; to the south was the large privy garden. The great rambling palace that had served as government offices since 1649 became a home again. There the Cromwells dined and slept. Beds, bed hangings, counterpanes, curtains, chairs and stools reserved from the sale were put to use. A bed with black velvet curtains, fringed with gold and silver, was transferred from Somerset House, possibly for Cromwell himself to sleep in.[13] Another bed was moved from Wimbledon House, now owned by John Lambert. The skills of upholsterers, silkmen, braziers, turners and linen drapers were all employed. Plumes of feathers were added to the state bed at Hampton Court and two new services of plate were commissioned from the goldsmith Thomas Vyner – lord mayor of London and knighted in 1654 – for the Protector's table, and that of his staff.[14] Raphael's celebrated colour cartoon designs for tapestries depicting the Acts of the Apostles, acquired by Charles I in 1623, were hung at Whitehall, as were Henry VIII's large and valuable (listed as worth over £8,000) Abraham tapestries. These ten hangings, brightly coloured and glittering with gold thread, were moved from the Great Hall at Hampton Court to the Protector's centre of power at Whitehall.

As Protector, Cromwell did not travel around the country. He did not go on progress like Elizabeth I, a monarch whom Cromwell admired. But he did move regularly between Whitehall and Hampton Court, travelling out to Hampton, often by river, most Fridays for the weekend. There he lived in a suite of east-facing rooms overlooking Fountain Court, those that Henrietta Maria had lived in and which she had had laid out and furnished in the latest French style in 1641. The most important room in her suite of apartments was the state bedchamber, a corner room. Henrietta Maria used this room in the French style, meaning that it was a ceremonial room where important state business and receptions were conducted. The bed, raised on a dais and behind a rail, was an overt, silken symbol of power, not a place of private rest. Cromwell did not sleep in this room in the scarlet, gold and silver-lace trimmed four-poster bed with matching upholstered chairs, but it is not clear whether he also used this grand room for receiving high-profile guests.[15] In between the two windows a table was added, adorned with a pair of gilded candle-stands and an ebony-framed mirror – altar-like, and anticipating what would become the very epitome of mid-seventeenth-century interior decoration.[16]

Beyond this 'rich' bedchamber was Cromwell's study, furnished with an ebony table and a chair, and behind this was his 'little bedchamber', furnished with chairs and stools in a sky-coloured damask and matching carpet. Next door was his dressing room, furnished relatively simply with an old cupboard.[17] There were further private rooms which Cromwell shared with Elizabeth. Unlike former consorts, Elizabeth does not seem to have had her own designated suite of apartments at Hampton Court, although she did at Whitehall.[18]

As Cromwell moved from his study to his bedchamber, he would have walked past tapestries from the repurchased *Vulcan and Venus* set and, as he wandered through the Tudor long gallery, past the Paradise Room and Charles I's former bedroom, now bare apart from fire furniture, along the south front of the palace, he may have seen Andrea Mantegna's huge and expensive canvases depicting the Triumphs of Caesar, before they were removed, intended to be copied for a great set of tapestries.[19] In the privy garden Cromwell and his family could amble among classical statues – a brass Venus, a white marble Apollo – and pause at the huge black marble fountain. Beyond, new rivers and ponds were dredged and stocked with fish. Deer could be hunted in the parks. Cromwell liked to hunt game and hawk.[20]

Hampton Court was something of an antique piece, dating from Henry VIII's time and remaining relatively unchanged through the reigns of Edward VI, Mary I, Elizabeth I, James I and Charles I. Paulucci, the Venetian ambassador, described how Hampton Court was a 'relic of departed greatness'.[21] Monarchs and their consorts inevitably inherited furniture from their predecessors – not always happily. Henrietta Maria, for example, was not particularly pleased to find one of Elizabeth I's beds in her apartments at Somerset House.[22] Oliver Cromwell's appropriation of royal rooms, furniture and hangings follows this pattern – but Cromwell, of course, was not a king.

He had grown up in Cambridgeshire, in the small town of Huntingdon where he had attended the grammar school and spent time at his uncle Sir Oliver Cromwell's house, Hinchingbrooke. There was money there, until his uncle lost it. Cromwell was of South Welsh stock, a heritage he chose to reflect in the protectoral coat arms and in his personal seal. He was a Cromwell because his family had changed its name from Williams, choosing to make much of a connection, through marriage, to Thomas Cromwell's family back in the early sixteenth century.[23] There was a time when Oliver Cromwell was nobody. He was an MP in the late 1620s but felt compelled to leave Huntingdon following a humiliating dispute with the town's council. It was while living in obscurity, married to Elizabeth Bourchier and working as a tenant farmer in nearby St Ives on the River Ouse, that he had fallen in with a radical Puritan community and experienced a profound religious conversion. This may have been caused by an inheritance lawsuit he was caught up in, or by the frequent bouts of illness and depression from which he was said to suffer at this time; we cannot know. But Cromwell believed his disgrace and downfall were God's doing – he said he was 'a cheife, the cheife of sinners', and he became convinced that God had a purpose for him. His subsequent return to Parliament in 1640, as MP for Cambridge, and then his extraordinary success and popularity as a military commander, beginning on the civil war battlefields of East Anglia, were read as signs that God was indeed there, and that he would raise him up, this indefatigable and often ruthless son of war and fortune.[24] There is a famous, not wholly reliable, description of Cromwell by Sir Philip Warwick from the opening days of the Long Parliament in 1640. It is notable for Cromwell's scruffy appearance, and the details of blood on his shirt and a sword at his side:

> I came into the House well clad and perceived a gentleman speaking (whom I knew not) very ordinary apparrelled, for it was a plain cloth suit, which seemed to have been made by an ill country tailor. His linen was plain, and not very clean, and I remember a speck or two of blood upon his little band, which was not much larger than his collar. His hat was without a hatband, his stature was of a good size, his sword stuck close to his side, his countenance swollen and reddish, his voice sharp and untuneable, and his eloquence full of fervour.[25]

As Protector, Cromwell did not wield unchecked power. His power was shared with Parliament and with a protectoral council. Cromwell and Parliament made the laws – which needed Cromwell's assent – and Cromwell and his council governed. The council would elect a new Protector, but Parliament (when it was sitting) controlled the army and agreed taxes. Parliament, council and Protector all had a hand in who sat on the council. The council could vet candidates who put themselves up for election to Parliament, and exclude any Members who seemed either too Royalist or anti-Cromwell. Catholics could absolutely not stand for election, but could, mostly, practise their faith under the radar, as could those loyal to Charles I's Anglican Church, such as John Evelyn. The regime was pretty tolerant of the radical Protestants; no one, for example, was forced to attend state-decreed church services, but it seemed that some kind of national Church would indeed be preserved, with parish clergy vetted, or 'tried', for godliness.[26]

It is not clear how much the regal trappings of Cromwell's court were driven by him personally and how much they were pressed upon him as necessary, indeed inevitable, for a head of state. There was, of course, no other model but a royal one. Cromwell certainly intervened in the sale of royal goods, and contributed to the hike in reserved items. At the beginning of the sale, about £10,000 worth of former royal goods were kept back; by the end this had risen to over £50,000.[27] But we do not know for sure if Cromwell himself chose the black bed at Whitehall, or the Venus tapestries for his room at Hampton Court. He clearly liked music, and had the organ from Oxford's Magdalen College moved and installed in the Great Hall at Hampton Court, a companion to the pipe organ already there.[28] He appointed, as master of music in his household, the leading organist John Hingeston. Hingeston tutored the Cromwell daughters and his choirboys performed Latin motets at Whitehall. Elizabeth Cromwell was, apparently, involved with the furnishings.[29] While Royalists mocked her for being stingy, and for running a 'beggarly court', a poem printed in 1656 praised Cromwell's 'virgin' court for being 'so modest, and so regular', a place 'of business, not of pomp and pride'.[30]

John Embree's maintenance and repair work at the palaces may have been overseen by Cromwell, but his pay was authorised and scrutinised, and criticised, by the council. In November 1655, the council decided that Embree should be paid out of Cromwell's household allowance. In the first years of the Protectorate, the amount of money spent on the residences each year – approximately £14,000 – was similar to the Office of Works' annual budget under Charles I.[31] But the palaces had suffered a decade of neglect, abandonment and military occupation. Many of the costs were deemed necessary, to fund the restoration of a quasi-monarchical regime under which a palace is a home and a political theatre, and its head a chief magistrate, host and a curator of stuff.

To run the palaces, Cromwell assembled a team of loyal men who knew the houses. Many of them were also experienced in, and understood the importance of, protocol and ceremony, which was so important for foreign relations. Some men given household posts – adapted from those in a royal household – had already held office under Charles I; their knowledge was invaluable and trumped any former allegiances. Clement Kinnersley had been Charles I's yeoman of the removing wardrobe and, on the king's death, became keeper of the state's wardrobe. He was in charge of all the furniture, fabrics and art from the palaces. Shrewd and strategic, Kinnersley petitioned hard to keep his job and, with the establishment of the Protectorate, he became the keeper of the protectoral wardrobe. He knew the collection, and its worth, well. Kinnersley undoubtedly influenced how the palaces were dressed and furnished under Cromwell, and what Cromwell himself wore. Cromwell's tailor, shoemaker and hatter all worked under Kinnersley's direction.[32] In February 1654, when Cromwell had been entertained and feasted as Protector by London's lord mayor, the goldsmith Thomas Vyner, Cromwell had processed through the city decked out in a 'muske'-coloured suit and coat, embroidered with gold thread.[33] Cromwell, it seems, liked fine things, or at least he understood the legitimising power of being seen as a civilian and not a military leader, and of sometimes forgoing austere military dress and a glinting breastplate.

One of the most important members of the 'family' at Whitehall was Sir Gilbert Pickering, the son of a knight and married to Elizabeth Montagu, whose father had bought Hinchingbrooke House. (Her brother Edward Montagu would become Cromwell's general at sea and then, under Charles II, the first earl of Sandwich.) Pickering had led the parliamentary troops at the tough siege of John Paulet, marquess of Winchester's Basing House. He had acted as a judge at the trial of Charles I, but had not signed his death warrant. He was an MP and a competent administrator, and had sat on numerous committees from sequestration and law to foreign affairs and trade. He was 'honest Pickering' to Cromwell. A clergyman found him 'furious, fiery, implacable', and those hostile to the Protectorate saw him as 'finical, spruce and like an old courtier'.[34] In 1655, Pickering became Cromwell's lord chamberlain, the head of the household. He had worked with John Lambert on bringing Barebone's to an end and subsequently became prominent on the protectoral council. Pickering was a serious political man, and his role as lord chamberlain required overseeing the hosting of guests, particularly foreign visitors. He was no doubt helped by Cromwell's cousin, Sir Oliver Fleming, who had been in post as master of ceremonies since 1643.

Pickering also had an eye for culture and commerce. In 1649 he had been involved in drawing up the act for the Sale of the Late King's Goods and, in 1651, he took over the directorship of the famous, but now ailing, Mortlake tapestry factory. It had been established in 1619 and had flourished under the patronage and then ownership of Charles I and the directorship of Sir Francis Crane, together with the sought-after designer Francis Clein. Now Dutch prisoners of war were sent to join fellow Dutch weavers in the eighty-two-foot-long workroom that overlooked the Thames. A new series of tapestries depicting the story of Abraham was commissioned, overseen by Cromwell himself; this set now hangs at Blickling Hall, Norfolk.[35] In 1650, Pickering took out a ninety-year lease near the Old Tiltyard in Whitehall, and he built himself a home: Pickering House.[36] As lord chamberlain, Pickering secured employment for his young nephew, John Dryden, just out of Cambridge, as his clerk. (Dryden ended up as poet laureate and historiographer royal under Charles II, and a celebrated playwright.[37]) Later in the Protectorate, Pickering was selected to sit on a committee charged with considering 'the Advancement of Music'.[38] While cathedral and church choirs were dispersed, and their organs taken away, and while MPs debated the morality of singing, music – and culture more broadly – was being encouraged to find a place in the new regime.

The experienced diplomat and councillor Walter Strickland was another loyal friend to Cromwell. He became captain of the Protector's household guards. On account of the guards' striking livery of grey coats with velvet collars, edged with silver and black silk lace, they became known as Cromwell's 'magpie' guard.[39] Strickland had sat on the council of state since 1651 and had been a Member of Barebone's Parliament. He now had a seat on the well-paid protectoral council. Strickland, like many political men who held office at this time, benefited from the confiscating and selling of Royalist homes. In 1650 he had bought Flamborough Manor in Yorkshire, former home of Sir Henry Griffith who had fought for the king at Marston Moor.[40] The republican political elite lived in, and built, houses suited to their office.

Cromwell also had extended family around him. His fine-featured son-in-law, John Claypole, was one of the lords of the bedchamber, and in charge of the stables. He took care of the horses and coaches needed to move Cromwell and his household around London, and to shuttle between Whitehall and Hampton Court at weekends. Cromwell liked horses, and Claypole made sure to stock the stables with fine breeds. He was, in effect, Cromwell's master of the horse – an illustrious household office held, in the past, by Elizabeth's favourite, Robert Dudley, earl of Leicester, and, under James I, George Villiers, duke of Buckingham. Claypole had fought in the wars against the king but he was no military hero, which made his appointment as master of the horse surprising. He was, however, loyal. He was married to Cromwell's beloved daughter, Bettie, and he loved to hawk and stag with his father-in-law. At the Restoration, he gave a home to his mother-in-law, Elizabeth.[41]

Below stairs at Whitehall, two 'middling sort' held sway over the kitchens, cellars and coffers. John Maidstone, former sequestration commissioner in Essex and a future MP, and Nathaniel Waterhouse, a Welshman and a cousin of Cromwell's wife, shared the role of household steward.[42] From 1657, the powerful Welshman and councillor Colonel Philip Jones was appointed their superior as the 'comptroller' – as would have been found in a royal household. Jones was another loyal political ally of Cromwell's. He named his youngest son, born in 1654, Oliver. Since 1648, Jones had looked after the Gower lands that had been given to Cromwell in recognition of his military service. He became the governor of Swansea, a Member of Parliament, a chief and very strict commissioner for the 1650 propagation of the gospel in

Wales, a councillor of state and, following the downfall of Barebone's, a member of the protectoral council. He had overseen the seizing of Crown and Church estates in South Wales, and had taken advantage of his position and influence to become a landowner himself, snapping up manors and former bishops' lands in the Vale of Glamorgan. A young man from humble farming beginnings, Jones rapidly acquired power, status and wealth. He did not do so without facing serious charges of corruption and embezzlement: he was seemingly able to 'get an estate out of nothing'. And he was deemed responsible for how unhappy and oppressed the Welsh felt by England's republic.[43] By 1655, just before Cromwell made him Lord Jones, he had his portrait painted; this hangs in his home, Fonman Castle, which he bought in 1658 and which is still in his family. Although Jones was not yet forty, this conventional portrait depicts a forbidding man. Slightly portly, with an elaborate moustache and large white collar, Jones rests one gloved hand on his sword.

These men were Puritans, and promoters of the godly, but they were not averse to pleasure or culture. Many were already part of the ruling elite, but not all. It is of Cromwell's courtiers such as Philip Jones that the Welsh Fifth Monarchist preacher Vavasor Powell despaired, for these once 'precious and excellent men' were now 'choked up' with new houses, parks and 'gallant wives'.[44] For many, the Lord Protector and his creatures had become corrupted by wealth and greed, and were dragging the country back towards apostasy. For Royalists, Cromwell and his faux court were easy targets. 'Alas, alas!' cried a Cromwellian mock-courtier in a piece of Royalist satire, 'What will become of my dear Master, when his Kingdome is weighed in the Ballance and found too light? Who will have the fine Houses, the brave Parkes, the pleasant Fields and delightfull gardens, that we have possessed without any right?'[45]

Shortly after Cromwell became Protector, a self-styled prophet from Poplar, Anna Trapnel, fell into an eleven-day trance. As she lay in an inn near Whitehall, her prophesying prattle was witnessed by councillors. From her visions and hallucinations she predicted Cromwell's imminent downfall. He would be punished, she thought, for becoming Lord Protector and betraying the millenarians' dream of a godly regime in England which would usher in Christ's second reign. Anna's prophecies were recorded and published as *The Cry of a Stone*, and brought her fame.[46] She was arrested later in the year and imprisoned in Bridewell for 'aspersing' the government. Warnings about the protectoral office, and its temptations to sin, came from inside Whitehall, too. In his *Second Defence of the English People*, John Milton told the Protector that his role will 'try you most thoroughly; it will search you through and through'.[47]

Cromwell's 'first grand Action of State' was, in April, to bring the Dutch war to an end.[48] Walter Strickland, John Claypole and Oliver Fleming, in their household roles, managed an appropriately lavish reception for the Dutch ambassadors who had arrived in England the month before. Both the Dutch and the English now wanted peace, as long as the Dutch agreed to no longer give Charles II a home in their country. On 3 March, Lords Nieupoort, Beverning and Jongstall were escorted through London.[49] They were met by Fleming, the master of ceremonies, and Claypole, and escorted into Cromwell's coach. Following the Dutch ambassadors were their French and Portuguese counterparts, for this was a spectacle of the Protectorate's legitimacy and standing. It was now recognised by foreign powers, and would treat with them as an equal. A train of well over fifty coaches, led by beautifully furnished horses, wound its way through the streets of London to Westminster, where the procession was welcomed by a fanfare of trumpets.[50]

The next day the Dutch ambassadors were received by Cromwell in the Banqueting House at Whitehall, which had been suitably dressed and decorated for the occasion. Glorious tapestries adorned the walls and a sumptuous chair of state stood at one end of the room, centre stage on a railed dais which was covered in expensive carpets. This ambassadors' reception was public, and thousands of people, reportedly, crammed into the hall, overflowing into the galleries and surrounding rooms. Cromwell did not sit in the chair of state: he stood, surrounded by members of his council, and waited for the ambassadors to approach. Escorted by Fleming, Strickland and Philip Jones, they entered at the opposite end of the room, and processed towards Cromwell through a lane among the people, tipping their hats every now and again, as did Cromwell. As they got nearer to the Lord Protector, they offered a low salute, a gesture of recognition and respect, which Cromwell reciprocated.[51] Each side assured the other of their commitment to peace and restored friendship. Milton had told Cromwell in a sonnet that 'peace hath her victories / No less renown'd than war'. This performance was to broadcast one such victory.[52]

At this time, another prophet, Elinor Channel, was hanging around Whitehall, hoping for an audience with Cromwell. Elinor's message for Cromwell was rather different to Anna Trapnel's. She hoped that he might bring about the restoration of Charles II, and that a fresh Parliament might be able to do this. Elections for

Cromwell's first Protectorate Parliament – the first elections the country had seen since 1640 – were about to take place.[53]

As decreed in the *Instrument of Government*, the date for the opening of the first Protectorate Parliament was an auspicious one: Sunday 3 September, the anniversary of Cromwell's victories at Dunbar and at Worcester. It was an attempt at myth-making. This Parliament, however, did not buy into the myth. It was not going to restore Charles, as Elinor Channel imagined, but neither was it keen to commit the Instrument of Government to law and confirm Cromwell as Protector. In his first speech, which apparently lasted for three hours, Cromwell told his Parliament that they met 'on the greatest Occasion that . . . England ever saw', for they bore on their shoulders 'the Interest of three great Nations' and 'the interest of all the Christian People in the world'. He hoped that MPs would, after all the turnings and tossings, agree to heal and settle the three nations according to the Instrument of Government: to 'go forward, and not backward, and bring 'this Ship of the Common-wealth . . . into a safe harbour'.[54]

The republican Sir Arthur Hesilrige, however, was back, and he had never forgiven Cromwell for striking at the sovereignty of Parliament when he had dismissed the Rump so violently in 1653. He immediately started to undermine the Instrument of Government, picking provocatively at the constitution's toleration of religious sects. Soon the entire frame of government, as defined in the Instrument, was being rattled and MPs were asserting their fundamental right to alter their state. This right was one that had been voiced so powerfully in the opening years of the republic and, despite the Rump's failure to agree on a constitution, the right of Parliament to change the very form of government – be it a monarchy or republic or anything else – was held fast by many.[55] Cromwell countered this by asking all MPs to sign a recognition and promise 'to be true and faithful to the Lord Protector and the Commonwealth of England, Scotland and Ireland' and to not propose or consent to 'alter the government, as it is settled in one single person and a parliament'.[56] Hesilrige, and fellow republicans Thomas Scot, an intelligence-gatherer for the republic, and John Bradshaw, he who had presided over Charles I's trial, refused to sign.

Even those who did sign could not stop meddling with the Instrument and the powers of the Protector, particularly his control over the army. Just before Christmas, one MP even suggested that Cromwell should be offered the title of king. Cromwell's son, Henry, spoke in support, but then the idea was batted away. As it became clear that the MPs were about to present him with a revised constitution, Cromwell dissolved his Parliament. It was 22 January 1655 and this first Parliament had sat for a little over four months. The 'door of hope' which Cromwell had invited the Members to step through in his speech of 4 September was now, disappointingly, shut. And, Cromwell told them, while they had been bickering over government weeds, nettles, briars and thorns had 'thriven under your shadow'.[57] Enemies, he said, were plotting, and the country potentially faced war again. Cromwell, however, had already embarked on his own design, and his soldiers and sailors would soon be needed far from home – in the Caribbean.

1655

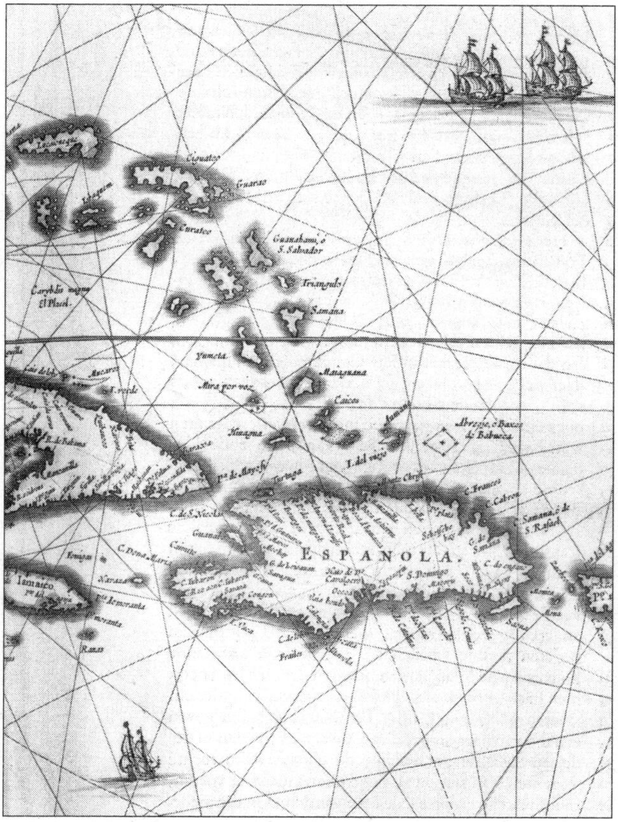
ESPANOLA.
Ciguateo
Guarao
Curateo
Guanahami, o
S. Salvador
Triangulo
Samana
Yumeta
Maiaguana
Mira por voz
Caicos
Hinagua
Tortuga
Abreojo, o Baxos
de Babueca
C. Frances
C. Cabron
Samana, ó de
S. Rafael
C. de S. Nicolas
S. Domingo
Jamaica
El Placel
Frailes
Ranas

I was shew'd a Table Clock whose balance was onely a Chrystall ball, sliding on parallel Wyers, without being at all fixed, but rolling from stage to stage, till falling on a Spring conceald from sight, it was throwne up to the upmost chanell againe made with an imperceptible declivity, in this continual vicissitude of motion . . .

John Evelyn,
February 1655

On 25 December 1654, while some, such as John Evelyn, were secretly celebrating Christmas in private homes and chapels, a fleet of English ships set sail from Portsmouth. They were on their way to Barbados, governed by English settlers since 1625. Sir William Penn, Cromwell's general-at-sea and commander-in-chief of the naval forces, sailed on the flagship, *Swiftsure*. A fresh gale was blowing, and it was raining. On the dockside, wives and sweethearts wept, and handed over seasickness cordials. For Henry Whistler, an ordinary soldier on board the *Paragon*, it was 'a sad day'.[1] Men were reluctant to leave their families and their homes; many had no knowledge of the full extent of the expedition's intentions as their ships eased out into the Solent; many never saw England again.

Once at Barbados, Cromwell's ships, built from felled trees from royal parks, would take on more men and sail on to attack, and conquer, parts of the Spanish Caribbean – Hispaniola, Puerto Rico, Cuba and Cartagena on the South American mainland. The order in which the Spanish territories would be seized was not yet decided. The purpose of the expedition, led by Penn, along with General Robert Venables who was in charge of the land forces, was 'to assault the Spaniard in the West Indies'.[2] It was known as Cromwell's 'Western Design'. It was inspired by anti-Catholic venom, imperial ambition and money. It was a Protestant crusade.

It was in the spring of 1654 that Cromwell's councillors had begun discussing an 'advantageous' design.[3] Spain dominated the Caribbean, and denied the English any right to trade. An attack on Spain's Caribbean possessions would be profitable – the territories were valuable, promising sugar and spices, even silver and gold. The Catholic Spanish were also the principal enemies of the Protestant cause; Cromwell's God would surely be behind such an expedition. A conquest also seemed realistic, to Cromwell. He had ships – 160 bobbing about at anchor now they were no longer engaged against the Dutch – and a big army to keep busy. The Spanish islands were believed to be neither fully fortified nor inhabited, and generally low on manpower.

Not everyone in Cromwell's council agreed that any design would be advantageous, and their discussions were fraught. Edward Montagu, the future earl of Sandwich but for now Cromwell's fellow Huntingdonshire man, member of the protectoral council and treasury commissioner, wrote notes. As they argued about whether, how and what to attack (France was the other option), Hispaniola was suggested. It was a large, well-positioned island 'beyond compare' according to Captains Hatsell and Lymerye, who knew Hispaniola well. Major-General John Lambert disagreed. To him, the whole design was foolish. The Caribbean was too far away, disease was known to be a problem from previous adventurers and the Protectorate had other concerns, and territories, closer to home: the settling of Ireland, for example, should surely be a priority. Neither did Lambert believe that such an expedition would successfully or significantly advance the Protestant cause. But Cromwell disagreed. He argued that God would want him to venture beyond England's shores: 'God has not brought us hither to where wee are but to consider the work that wee may doe in the world . . . Providence seemed to lead us hither, haveinge

160 ships swimminge,' he said.[4] There is no better example of entangled, self-fulfilling providential thinking. Idle warships at sea served as a reminder of God's approval so far, and as a prompt for further battles. Idleness was problematic. The Spanish in the Caribbean were considered lazy for not fully exploiting the land that they had conquered, or the people they had subdued. The 'idle loose persons' milling around the City of London could usefully be sent off to the Caribbean, to work the land there.[5] So too could rebellious Scots. The 'West India Design' could export Protestantism, purge the nation of troublemakers and make money.

Colonel Thomas Modyford was a politically influential landowner and sugar planter in Barbados. Initially shocked by the execution of Charles I, and fearful of what a new regime in England might mean for Barbados's autonomy and independence as a settlement, Modyford supported Lord Francis Willoughby, the governor of Barbados, who had declared for Charles II. But Modyford soon buckled and switched sides when the republic sent its ships and cannons there in 1651, under the command of Sir George Ayscue. Barbados surrendered, and agreed to recognise the Commonwealth and its Parliament.

Among Secretary John Thurloe's state papers, logged in December 1654, is a report Modyford wrote for the protectoral council about the Spanish Caribbean. Conquest in the Spanish Caribbean would be easy, Modyford suggested to Cromwell. The Spanish were lazy and weak, he wrote, and the indigenous people willing. But he advised that the English should not attempt to settle the islands, but the Spanish-held mainland, beginning at the Orinoco River, for not only would this cut Spain off from South America but there the English would also have 'Indians to practise on, who, without dispute, will by politic and rational means be as so many hands gained to the commonwealth'.[6] Modyford warned Cromwell that whoever was in charge of the expedition must be able to persuade the Englishmen already settled in the Caribbean to join the Protectorate's campaign, for they would certainly need more than the three thousand soldiers sailing over from England. Settlers' loyalty to Cromwell or even to England could not be assumed. Many had left England years ago, or had fled during the wars in the 1640s, and they had their own interests to protect – land, crops, slaves – and families. It would be a challenge to persuade them to offer themselves or their workers to accompany an expansionist plan hatched far away in Whitehall, ordered by a Lord Protector whom they did not know.

Cromwell's ambition was also fuelled by Thomas Gage, a seasoned traveller who had recently returned from living in the West Indies. His 1648 book, *A New Survey of the West Indias*, was a best-seller. Gage had dedicated it to Thomas Fairfax, offering him the promise of 'a New World'.[7] He devoted an entire chapter to the health benefits of cacao, particularly of drinking chocolate to comfort and strengthen the stomach – and which would do wonders for the financial well-being of the nation too. Gage was drinking five cups a day. In 1650 Mary Verney, the Royalist Ralph Verney's beloved and dying wife, was prescribed chocolate to drink as a final, futile cure.[8]

In 1654 Gage presented Cromwell with an advisory paper about a Caribbean conquest. Cromwell was struck by Gage's religious zeal. Since his return from the West Indies, Gage – once a Catholic – had been preaching the gospel loudly in Kent. For Gage, victory in the Spanish Caribbean would bring about the fall of 'Romish Babylon', and the conversion of the 'poore and simple Indians'. Gage, like Modyford, believed that such an undertaking would not be 'so hard and difficult as is by some apprehended', and, like Modyford, he stressed the sloth and sinfulness of the

Spanish, who fed 'like beasts upon their lusts' and were unfit for combat. Gage also believed that others living on the islands, who he referred to as 'the Mulattos, Negros and Indians', would not pose any threat – they were unarmed and they were willing, he said, to be converted to the light of the Gospel and fall under the 'protection' of a Protestant regime based thousands of miles away on the other side of the Atlantic. Counter to Modyford's advice, which was to attack the mainland first, Gage suggested that the ships should seize Hispaniola, the 'chiefest of all the islands'.[9] Hispaniola was a large but thinly populated island, fertile and temperate, and treasured by the Spanish as their first plantation. It had ginger, sugar, amber and exceptionally pure gold to offer.[10] Gage appealed to Cromwell's godliness and ambition, and flattered him as a 'protector', coupling together spiritual and economic profit as he signed off his four pages of advice:

> The Lord grant, that your faith may yett bee active abroad, as well as at home. The Lord grant, that yett you may ride on prosperously, conquering and to conquer. The Lord make your highnesse, as our protector, so also a protector of those poore Indians, which want protection from the cruelties of the Spaniards. The Lord make your highnesse yett his instrument, for the enriching of this poore island.[11]

Against the wishes of some on his council, Cromwell pressed ahead with planning an ambitious military expedition which promised 'a great present returne of profit'.[12] Bulstrode Whitelocke claimed that Cromwell was influenced, one might say misled, by Thomas Gage and his report.[13] The autumn of 1654 was spent making practical, hurried preparations: reluctant soldiers were recruited; the ships were stocked with arms, ammunition, beer, salted beef, biscuits and other victuals. As Thomas Modyford advised: 'Let them be well victualled, the beef well salted, and the beer well boil'd; for we have found it by experience, that it is the corrupt victuals, not the climate, that causeth sickness.'[14] Muskets, pikes, shovels and wheelbarrows, tents, spare rigging, sails and hammocks were ordered. Engineers, carpenters and horses were counted. Modyford warned that there would be no supplies at Barbados to supplement provisions. He also advised that the fleet should plan to land in Barbados in November, so that the fighting could be over by May, before the rains and the hurricanes arrived. But things were not ready in time. The eagerness to set off meant that the ships sailed before they were properly stocked, with the promise that supply ships would follow soon behind. In the rush, Major-General John Desborough forced soldiers aboard and made them leave their belongings behind. Lieutenant-Colonel Francis Barrington, a relation of Cromwell's, had to borrow shirts from his captain to wear on the crossing.[15]

When the thirty-eight ships and nearly three thousand men sailed west in December 1654 they did so in the name of the republic. This differed significantly from previous settlement attempts, those undertaken during the reigns of Elizabeth I or James I, when adventurers set off to make their own fortunes. In his instructions to the Caribbean expedition's military commissioners (Generals Penn and Venables) and the civilian commissioners who accompanied them and would govern the conquered territories (Edward Winslow, experienced former governor of New Plymouth, and the unknown Gregory Butler), Cromwell made it clear that all money, plate and possessions seized as part of the campaign should be reserved for the Protector and the state, not for themselves. All those on board knew the rules. As Henry Whistler noted in his journal: 'If any shall kepe ether goods or plat or mony in their hands above 3 dayes, and not bring it in to the publike stor hous for the yous of my lord protector, they should be proseded against as felons.'[16]

On the boats, sailors and soldiers travelled together, with soldiers dispersed across the fleet to preserve as many as possible from infections that would inevitably break out during the crossing. Chaplains sailed with them, including Thomas Gage. He preached to the crews on Sundays about the godliness of their trip, attended to those who fell sick and administered the rites to those who died. General Venables's new wife, Elizabeth, accompanied him on board his ship. Women did not usually go on campaign, but Cromwell had approved Venables's request because he and his wife did not intend to return to England, but to settle in the Caribbean. Elizabeth Venables was also not the only wife on board; many others expected that they too would soon start a new life on the other side of the Atlantic, following a swift victory. During the crossing and subsequent fighting these women worked as nurses.[17] Children, too, were on board, including perhaps the youngest of the Venables's children from their previous marriages. The shirtless Francis Barrington travelled with his family of six.[18] Along with the pikes and salted beef the ships carried seeds and crops to plant in the soon-to-be-conquered islands: beans and chickpeas.

In just over a month, on 29 January, early in the morning, the fleet sighted Barbados, 'one of the Riches Spotes of ground'.[19] It must have been a welcome sight. As the ships arrived, they regrouped and dropped anchor in Carlisle Bay. They had, Venables wrote back to Cromwell, been preserved from storms and diseases by God, with not twenty of their men lost en route.[20] Thomas Modyford greeted William Penn off the *Swiftsure* but the overall reception in Barbados was not quite what the troops from England hoped for. There was not enough food on the island to feed the weary, starving crews, and neither did locals rush to join their campaign, as had been anticipated. The expedition needed between three and four thousand more men, and horses, before it could attack. But those English merchants established in Barbados were, understandably, reluctant to hand over the men who managed their large estates. So the commissioners seized them. This, according to Francis Barrington, was cruel, and incurred the wrath of God.[21] The commissioners also seized some freemen who still owed money to those who had enabled them originally to travel to Barbados. Meanwhile, the supply ships promised from England, carrying extra food and arms, did not arrive. Venables's soldiers were short of weapons and they resorted to making their own pikes. Due to the wood available, these pikes were shorter, disparagingly called 'cabbage stalks'.[22] On 17 March, Penn wrote back to Cromwell to ask for food supplies from 'Old' England – they now needed to feed their extra recruits, and the provisions shipped in from the settlements in New England were not adequate. There were not enough bakeries in New England to supply both the islanders and thousands of 'Old' English soldiers and seamen.[23] The godly ambitions of the design were secondary to these day-to-day concerns about food and well-being – checking stocks of salt, ordering barrels of bacon or mutton from other ships in the fleet, delivering beef to another ship, going on shore for much-needed exercise, worrying about the sick. Those who kept journals or wrote letters home occasionally, and only briefly, mentioned listening to sermons on board and observing the Sabbath.

In March, Penn and Venables wrote a letter home to John Desborough, informing him, and the rest of the protectoral council, that they had finally settled on attacking the island of Hispaniola first. They would leave Barbados without their full supplies. Expedition commissioner Edward Winslow wrote back to Secretary John Thurloe, warning that setting off from

Barbados without all their supplies could cause friction between the land and sea forces, between Generals Venables and Penn.[24] Penn, too, despaired of leaving without proper provisions but chose, erringly, to trust in providence. On 31 March, at four in the afternoon, the fleet weighed anchor and set off north-eastwards, in a calm wind, to war. The fleet now numbered sixty ships and five thousand men. To the Spanish, who were well aware that the English had arrived in the Caribbean, the fleet was the largest ever to cross 'to these western seas'.[25]

Commanding one of the ships, the *Hound*, was Richard Rooth. Rooth, like Henry Whistler on the *Paragon*, kept a journal of the West Indies expedition, logging his ship's journey and his own hopes and worries. As the fleet prepared to set off from Barbados, Rooth asked for God's blessing on its undertaking, which, he hoped, would tend to the 'propagation of the Gospel'.[26] He still did not know where the fighting would begin. His fear of what lay ahead is palpable, pulsing underneath the meticulous recording of dates, wind speeds and the route which took them through balmy waters and past mountainous islands which rose up before them in the hazy heat. The fleet was becalmed in shallow waters just off Dominica. It anchored in St Lucia, and the men took on fresh drinking water and caught fish. At St Kitts, where a small colony of English men and women lived on the west coast, sharing the island peacefully with the French, they picked up a thousand more recruits and ate what Henry Whistler remembers as the best oranges of all. It was there that Rooth was able to open a sealed letter, which contained the instructions that Hispaniola was their target, and it was at about this point that the soldiers were informed by their superiors that, unlike in previous conflicts, they were not allowed to plunder. This was unwelcome and demotivating news.[27]

In mid-April, the ships arrived off the coast of Hispaniola. The island was low, but the shore on the south-western coast was rocky and steep, battered by surf. Rooth brought his ship to stay off the capital town of Santo Domingo, which lay in a wide bay. Others in the fleet plied backwards and forwards. From the shore, the Spanish fired. The English crews dodged the shots and waited, watching through the haze for Venables and the rest of the land soldiers who had, they thought, been dropped further down the coast to begin their attack on the town. But Venables and his troops did not arrive.

Due to the high surf, Venables and his ships of soldiers had been unable, as planned, to land a few miles to the west of Santo Domingo, at the River Haina. Instead Vice-Admiral William Goodson, who knew the Caribbean seas well, had sailed the *Paragon* and other ships much further along the coast, on to the sandy bay at Punto de Nizao which was over thirty miles from Santo Domingo. Thick woods, wide grassy plains, orange groves, cocoa trees, sugar plantations and the River Haina now lay between them and Santo Domingo.

Some 7,500 soldiers scrambled off the boats with their horses. They were neither prepared nor equipped for such a long march. They had three days' worth of provisions, and not nearly enough water.[28] The sun was scorching. It was late in the season and the land was white and bone dry. The rivers and streams were bare trickles. The soldiers began their advance along the coast, but they were hot and thirsty, and suffering from diarrhoea. To alleviate their thirst, the men sucked on the oranges they found, and ate sugar from the plantations they came across, worsening their upset stomachs.[29] 'We march'd in a most sad and miserable manner in an unknown Country tormented with Heat, hunger, and thirst,' wrote Venables.[30] Not forgetting who their enemies were, the soldiers vandalised and ransacked the Catholic chapels they stumbled across. Henry Whistler described how soldiers hauled an image of a Virgin and Child out of an abandoned monastery and pelted it with oranges. At another time, a statue of St Anne was decapitated.[31]

Venables and his men never anticipated that the Spanish would attack them with any effect; they had believed they would cow them. 'Jack Spaniard would not stand' was their mantra. After all, Francis Drake had looted (but not conquered) Santo Domingo easily in 1585. The Spanish, by their own admission, were few in number, but the English were unwell – dying – and they were terrified. Francis Barrington remembered how 'in that island we had not the common spirit of children, so metamorphosed we were'.[32] According to Henry Whistler, General Venables hid behind a tree when they were ambushed by the Spanish just outside San Jerónimo fort.[33] The soldiers retreated to the banks of the Haina, where they lay for five days, exposed in the sand, shitting in the already polluted river. And then the rain came.

On 19 April, Venables came on board Penn's ship, *Swiftsure*. He vomited. Whistler reported, scathingly, that Venables was not unwell but came to see his wife, Elizabeth, and lie with her. He had, Whistler believed, abandoned his men, who lay wet and starving in the sand on the banks of the Haina.[34] These men were so delirious they believed the fireflies swarming at night were Spanish soldiers or local inhabitants, approaching them with matches. Many of them were dying, their death rattles echoed by the thousands of giant crabs that scuttled out of their holes at night and fled towards the sea. The soldiers eventually made a final, bungled attempt to push beyond San Jerónimo to get to Santo Domingo. But the English soldiers had panicked, dropped their arms and bolted from the deadly lances of the Spanish troops, some of whom were women disguised as men. It is likely that about a thousand English soldiers died in that final skirmish, killed by only a few hundred Spanish.[35] Venables, still really unwell, ordered a retreat. A hastily called council of war decided to abandon Hispaniola. Back at the river, the retreating men slaughtered the horses that they could not take back on the boats, ate them, and waited to board their ships. Their dead were left behind, as were those who had been taken prisoner and others who had defected to save themselves. This was nearly two thousand men in all.

To retreat after two weeks was shameful and confusing, and the generals blamed their troops. 'We are ashamed of the cowardice of our men,' Penn wrote on 28 April.[36] A few days later, commissioner Edward Winslow died of a fever. Some said he died of grief and the ignominy of a failed expedition. His body was placed in a coffin and slowly, respectfully lowered into the sea and let go.

While the Spanish on Hispaniola, and beyond, thanked God for their miraculous and unexpected delivery from the king-killing heretics, the departing English took a day to seek their Lord, and ask for his guidance. The ships had to go somewhere, although they were not sufficiently provisioned to get far and the crews were ill and injured. Major Thomas White estimated that about five hundred men were suffering from untended and undressed wounds. The surgeons on board had not brought enough linen bandages with them. So the generals decided to make for Jamaica, the next island along, to the west of Hispaniola, and only a few days' sail. Attacking Jamaica had never been suggested as part of Cromwell's Western Design; there were no sugar works there and it was not one of Spain's prized possessions. But it was much smaller than Hispaniola, and supposedly poorly defended by the few thousand Spanish, Portuguese, indigenous people and African slaves who lived and farmed there. To the desperate English, stunned by defeat but still hoping God was on their side, it was worth a try.

Reports of quite how badly things had gone wrong in Hispaniola took a long time to reach Whitehall. On 9 June, well after the retreat from Hispaniola, the council had ordered that two thousand Bibles be shipped out to the West Indies.[37] The men over there urgently needed food and medicine, not the word of God. In England, rumours were circulating of a great victory, and of promised wealth. In April, a pamphlet had reported that 'the English are become Masters of no less than three and thirty gold and silver mines, which, if true, will doubtless make our English Continent the most flourishing Common-wealth under the Sun'.[38] In May, a new and bigger edition of Thomas Gage's book about the West Indies was published, embellished with maps, and promoted in the newsbook *Mercurius Politicus*.[39]

It was not until 24 July 1655 that the news of the army's defeat and rapid retreat from Hispaniola reached Cromwell.[40] It was a devastating blow, and he shut himself up alone in a room for an entire day.[41] God, who had previously delivered Cromwell and his army, granting them marvellous victories and showing them great mercies, had now rebuked him, and England. 'The Lord hath greatly humbled us, in that sad loss susteyned at Hispaniola,' Cromwell wrote to Vice-Admiral William Goodson. 'Noe doubt but Wee have provoaked the Lord,' he added.[42] God must be punishing the nation for its sinfulness; they must reform their ways.

The failure quickly became known. 'Or mouths ful of a great losse at Hispaniola,' Ralph Josselin jotted down in his diary on 3 August 1655. From the Caribbean, private letters arrived home, full of detailed and distressing news. John Daniell, the expedition's auditor-general, told his wife, mother and brother about seeing his major-general (James Heane) bored through with a lance, about the soldiers who were hanged if they tried to run away, and about being forced to eat their own horses. He was full of blame for Penn, who he believed had neglected the soldiers on the ground in Hispaniola.[43] Another member of the expedition published an account of his time, but remained anonymous, only providing his initials (I. S.) and describing himself as 'An Eye-witness'. In his *Brief and Perfect Journal*, I. S. blamed the sinfulness of many of the soldiers, and some of the cross-dressed English women who had apparently infiltrated the forces. He also blamed the cowardice of their commanders. God showed his hand by punishing them all: 'That an Army so numerous, strong and well provided, should be so cow'd out, beaten, and shamefully repulsed, by lesse then a handful of men . . . was certainly the work of God . . . O that men could be sensible of the guilt of sin, and humble themselves by repentance,' I. S. wrote.[44] At the end of November, Cromwell called for a day of national fasting and humiliation, asking the entire country to reflect on its sins, and why God had abandoned the expedition in the West Indies.[45] The failure could not be fathomed.

There were good reasons why the Western Design failed so spectacularly, and so quickly. About nine thousand men had made up the campaign, but by November, half of them were lost. Penn claimed that they were 'humbled for a wicked confidence in our numbers'.[46] By all accounts the expedition was not well enough prepared or adequately stocked for these numbers, or for the kind of expedition it was. The merchant, financier and political influencer Martin Noell was keen to make money from the Western Design and he had secured the contract for supplying the expedition. Noell had already made a fortune managing the saltpans up in Newcastle, and controlling the tax income from salt, coal, linen and silks. He had traded with Montserrat and Nevis, dealing in goods secured by piracy, was a member of the East India Company and had sat on the Trade Committee in 1655. His brother, Thomas, lived in Barbados, and he was also Secretary John Thurloe's brother-in-law. As the supplier, Noell was in charge of providing arms, tents, leather flasks to carry water (black jacks), brandy, bread, tools and shoes. But most of the 1,500 arms that Noell had shipped ahead to Barbados had been handed around among all the islanders before the English fleet even arrived. Only 190 guns remained. Of all the soldiers' needs, the leather flasks were the greatest, and there were not enough. Without a water flask, urged Venables in a letter back to Martin Noell, 'not one man can march in these torrid Regions'.[47] Thomas Noell wrote to his brother in early June, alerting him to the failure on Hispaniola, and hoping that more supplies were on their way.[48]

Venables lamented the lack of supplies, but he also chastised the ungodly recruits they had picked up in Barbados and en route to Hispaniola. They were, he thought, 'the most prophane, debauched persons that we ever saw, Scorners of Religion . . . cowardly'.[49] His wife, Elizabeth, agreed that these soldiers were unfit and 'wicked'. Unlike those veteran soldiers who had, with her husband, successfully stormed Ireland in 1649, many of the men were cast-offs. Poorly armed and under-fed they may have been, but they were also, apparently, a 'rascally rabble of raw and unexercised men'.[50] And while Venables seems to have understood his commission was to propagate the gospel, and was for the glory of God, Elizabeth, a staunch Puritan, thought the design was hypocritical. She blamed Cromwell and his council: 'They pretended the honour of God, and the propagating of the Gospel; But, alas! their intention was self honour and riches – and so the design prospered according to their hypocrisy.'[51] For his part, Venables was blamed by others for being cowardly, and for being distracted by Elizabeth. According to Henry Whistler, Venables 'could not part with his ladie'.[52] On the other hand, John Daniell was more loyal, and described Venables as 'noble and unwearied'.[53] After the defeat at Hispaniola, the expedition's chaplain Thomas Gage – he who had inspired Cromwell to attempt the conquest – preached on Joshua 7.7, which told of the Israelites' shocking defeat at Ai, and their punishment for the sin of greed. The next year, Henry Vane openly blamed Cromwell, and his selfish, covetous and ungodly occupation of the office of Protector.[54]

Meanwhile, across the Atlantic, a bedraggled fleet, perhaps some seven thousand in number, had landed in Jamaica in early May. The Spanish in Jamaica reacted differently to the Spanish in Hispaniola. They were seemingly not forewarned of the English ships' arrival in the Caribbean and they suspected they were raiders, not hopeful conquerors. They shot at the English, but then, when the army took its time marching on the small and only town of St Jago, men, women and children fled, up and away into Jamaica's woods and hills. When the English entered St Jago, they found it empty. The Spanish governor, Don Juan Ramirez, came to negotiate the terms of a surrender. Blinded and emaciated by syphilis, Ramirez lay in a hammock carried by black men.[55]

The English soldiers were still ill with the flux, and starving. The fleeing inhabitants had taken cattle with them, so the English ate sheep, dogs, cats and horses. 'We are in a sad condition,' wrote Francis Barrington; 'our people dying very thick'. The smell of death was everywhere – corpses lay unburied, or were hastily dug into shallow graves. The dogs that lurked in the towns soon dug them up and ate them. The English were still being punished, Barrington believed, and if they did not repent, 'the Lord will whip us with his third rod'.[56] Finally the long-delayed supply ships from

England caught up with them – and Barrington could wear his own shirts again. Although the Spanish governor had capitulated, and promised that the Spanish would be shipped off the island, the English had not yet conquered Jamaica. The inhabitants who had fled the town remained dispersed in the countryside, on their farms or hiding in the mountains. Some escaped by boat to Cuba, but many refused to leave Jamaica and resolved to ignore the terms of the treaty, and fight the English instead.

John Daniell saw the potential in Jamaica, or at least he tried to reassure those back home that Jamaica would prove a valuable prize. Henry Whistler, too, noted what Jamaica could become. The idle, Catholic Spanish, they believed, had not tended this garden of the Indies as well as they might, so here was an opportunity for the industrious and godly English to build, fortify and plant for profit. The Jamaican air was good, there was more water than on Hispaniola, and they found sugar, tobacco, cotton and chocolate. There were plenty of cattle, horses and pigs. They could mine copper and silver; there was possibly even gold (there was not).[57] Whistler would not be part of the conquest and settlement – what Venables called the 'fixing of a colony' – and he soon sailed home to England. Venables and Penn also left the partially conquered Jamaica. Venables was still unwell after Hispaniola, and Penn no longer believed that he and his ships were needed in the Caribbean. When these two expedition leaders arrived back in England at the end of August, they faced the wrath of Cromwell and his council for the disaster on Hispaniola, and for abandoning their troops in Jamaica. Cromwell sent both men to the Tower of London for a short spell: they were marched in via Traitors' Gate.

Many of those left behind in Jamaica would never again see England's shores. In July 1655, Francis Barrington, whose wife and six children had survived and landed with him in Jamaica, wrote a long letter home. Even when describing the terrible condition that the soldiers were in, Barrington was confident that, in a year or two, they would learn to manage the livestock, cultivate the wild land and plant crops. He and his family had been given a plot of land, and he anticipated making a bit of money. Jamaica is a 'gallant island', he wrote, and 'will produce as good a trade as any island in America'. This Puritan would turn from soldier to planter.[58]

Once Whitehall knew about Jamaica, Cromwell issued a proclamation encouraging families to sail out there and begin new lives.[59] Later in the year, Jamaica was being described as an extended limb of the Commonwealth body. In 1657, Edward Doyley, who had sailed from Portsmouth in December 1654 as a lieutenant-colonel, finally defeated the Spanish and became Jamaica's first English governor.[60] It was the first British colony to be seized by force from another European coloniser. Further expansion was expected, and Jamaica could finance this. The landing of the desperate troops in May 1655 marked the beginning of what the British Empire would become. The colonies shifted from being a collection of strung-out settlements and posts, such as Barbados, settled during the reigns of Elizabeth I and James I but with varying degrees of autonomy, to being a set of connected territories controlled more tightly from Whitehall. Charles II undid many things when he was restored in 1660, but he decided early on to keep Jamaica, as John Evelyn noted in his diary.[61] Britain's long and continuing relationship with Jamaica dates from the Western Design of 1655. Britain's current head of state, Charles III, is also king of Jamaica, although many Jamaicans would rather he was not.

Back in Wiltshire in 1655, Royalists were plotting. The young John Aubrey, the period's celebrated and well-connected biographer, knew and loved Wiltshire. He would go on to write a love letter to the county's chalky soil and gentle downs, about its churches, houses, families and customs, and about its ruins: Stonehenge, Avebury. Archaeology was born.[62] It was Aubrey's Wiltshire neighbour and friend, Colonel John Penruddock, who gave his name to the most significant Royalist rebellion of the 1650s, and one that seriously rattled Cromwell and the regime: Penruddock's Uprising.

John Penruddock lived with his wife, Arundel, and their children in Compton House in Compton Chamberlayne, a small village to the west of Salisbury, and just along from the village of Broad Chalke, where Aubrey lived. The West of England, the 'drooping West' as the wartime poet Robert Herrick once lamented, was widely Royalist, but with parliamentarian pockets, such as Dorchester, and the magnificent Wilton House, the home of the parliamentarian earl of Pembroke, Philip Herbert. The Penruddocks were a wealthy Anglican and political family – many were MPs. They owned most of the village they lived in, and had benefited for generations from the patronage of the earls of Pembroke. Their estates were confiscated during the civil wars; Penruddock eventually raised enough money to buy them back. He had lost two younger brothers in the wars and he remained loyal to the Stuart cause. He, like many other Royalists, hoped that, one day, they would stage a successful rebellion and restore Charles II. In 1655 Penruddock seized his chance.[63]

Since 1653, from his shifting places of exile on the continent, Charles II, urged on by Edward Hyde, earl of Clarendon (also a Wiltshire man) and James Butler, marquess of Ormond, had supported a particular nest of Royalist activity in England, led by six Englishmen who had fought for Charles and commanded troops at the battles of Edgehill, Naseby, Marston Moor and Colchester. They named themselves the Sealed Knot. In an intercepted, coded letter dated 2 February 1654, the name 'Sealed Knot' was first recorded. Colonel Edward Villiers told Clarendon that 'The sealed knott still meete, with an intention to designe somewhat in the interests of the king Mr Crosse [Charles Stuart] his servise; which when it comes to any maturity, a discreete chapman shall be sent over, as you apoint. We ar here very doubtful of the peace; and sanguine cavaliers will still have itt.'[64]

Five of the six members were sons of prominent county families, with significant estates: Colonel Edward Villiers, 'honest Ned', nephew of George Villiers, the first duke of Buckingham and cousin to the second duke; John, Lord Belasyse, son of a prominent Catholic family from Yorkshire; Henry Hastings, Lord Loughborough from Leicestershire; Colonel John Russell, younger son of the earl of Bedford; and Sir William Compton, from Northamptonshire and Warwickshire. The sixth member was Sir Richard Willys, an experienced soldier and, although knighted, the only non-aristocrat in the ring.[65] As was so common at the time, these men and their families' loyalties and politics were not entirely straightforward, and nor is excavating what being Royalist meant for each of them. Belasyse was related to both Thomas Fairfax and John Lambert; his nephew would go on to marry Oliver Cromwell's daughter, Mary. Edward Villiers's cousin, and John Russell's father, the earl of Bedford, had patronised the leading parliamentarian John Pym back in the early 1640s. And Russell's older brother William, now earl of Bedford of Woburn Abbey, was not a reliable Royalist. Oliver Cromwell knew the twenty-eight-year-old William Compton; he was a resolute but 'godly' cavalier. He was the brother-in-law of Elizabeth Murray, the countess of Dysart, who courted Cromwell at her lavish family home, Ham House, in Richmond during the

1650s.[66] Finally, the sixth member of the group, Sir Richard Willys, would later switch sides and act as an informer for Cromwell's spymaster, John Thurloe.

The Sealed Knot requested Charles II's exclusive support for their plans, and they demanded that they should be informed of all other plots planned by hopeful Royalists, so that they could advise on their feasibility, and co-ordinate them with their own risings. The Sealed Knot promised to serve Charles, to 'try the utmost that could be done, with the loss or hazard of their lives', but they were prepared to bide their time.[67] They had agents dotted throughout the country – the king's former surgeon, Richard Pile, was the agent in the West – and to their cause they recruited friends and old soldiers, but also Roman Catholics, Presbyterians and others uncertain about the Protectorate. It was even hoped that Thomas Fairfax might be persuaded to join the Knot. In October 1654 Charles wrote to Fairfax, but whether he ever received, read or considered the invitation is unknown.[68] Levellers, too, were approached, such as Richard Overton and John Wildman. Levellers and Royalists made strange bedfellows, but they were united by a common hostility to Cromwell. To Royalists, the Protector was the impostor king; to Levellers, he was far too king-like.

During late 1654 plans were developing for a general, co-ordinated rebellion that would sweep across the country. Arms and orders were secretly distributed in Yorkshire, the Midlands, North Wales and, in the South, from Hampshire to Cornwall. A splinter group of the Sealed Knot, largely made up of Royalist country gentlemen such as, in the West Country, Sir Hugh Pollard, Colonel Richard Arundell and the Cornishman Sir John Grenville, was intent on action.[69] Charles II, too, seemed impatient. He was frustrated in exile, and becoming increasingly unwelcome at foreign courts. He wrote how he could not 'bear this condition of life much longer'.[70] In July he had left Paris and moved to Cologne. In February 1655, he moved secretly to Middelburg on the Dutch coast, sheltered by a family connected to the household of his great-aunt Elizabeth of Bohemia, in readiness to sail to England. But Charles neither explicitly endorsed nor forbade action, and this confused and divided the plotting Royalists back home.[71] The Sealed Knot members advised caution. Nevertheless, in February, Henry Wilmot, earl of Rochester, Charles's hardened cavalier companion after the battle of Worcester, landed at Margate. He had been despatched as the appointed field-marshal general of the planned rising. Accompanying him was Sir Joseph Wagstaffe, who had been knighted for leading the army in the West Country in 1644 (after switching sides), and had lived in exile since 1648. At Margate, both Rochester and Wagstaffe managed to evade the port authorities, who had been told to be alert, and they safely made their way to London. Rochester then travelled north, in disguise, to lead an uprising in York, while Wagstaffe made his way west, to John Penruddock in Wiltshire.

The time was not right for such an ambitious revolt. When Cromwell had dismissed his first Parliament early, at the end of January 1655, he had spoken at length about 'that Cavalier party' that was determined to bring the Protectorate down. He blamed the MPs because, he said, the cavaliers had 'thriven under your shadow', and were now spreading like nettles and thorns while the politicians had argued among themselves about the Protectorate, the threat of radical religious sects and the expensive upkeep of the army. So distracted were the MPs by what was happening among them, Cromwell had said, that they were oblivious to what was happening around them (this is familiar).[72] But Cromwell's secretary of state John Thurloe and his network of spies were well aware. One such spy was Henry Manning, who had been with Rochester in exile. Royalist letters were intercepted and their codes and aliases cracked.[73] Known conspirators were arrested and examined. Extra soldiers were brought in and London was secured. As the various Royalist plotters witnessed the Protectorate's army rounding up and arresting their fellow conspirators, they became nervous. They suggested postponing the uprising to March, and then aborting it all together. Planned revolts in Newcastle, Chester, Hull and Nottingham and in the key coastal towns of Portsmouth and Plymouth fell apart. When Rochester arrived in Yorkshire full of conviction, he was met on Marston Moor by only 150 men, not the 1,500 he anticipated. To choose Marston Moor, the scene of Charles I's huge defeat in 1644, was a brilliant, if poignant and overconfident, choice of rendezvous. Rochester fled south, disguised as a grazier – not entirely convincingly. Along the way, he bribed the innkeepers with whom he lodged to keep his identity secret. By June he was back on the continent with Charles.[74]

In Wiltshire, however, Colonel John Penruddock pressed ahead with his assigned part in the co-ordinated rising, seemingly ignorant of the arrests that were taking place around him. The Leveller John Wildman had been seized in Wiltshire. Instead, Penruddock made his will, paid his debts and made sure that his house would pass to his wife and son, just in case he should not survive 'this great trouble'.[75] He well apprehended the gravity of the cause, the violence that it demanded and the danger he was about to lead himself and his men into. But he was, he told his wife, now 'used in the school of affliction'.[76]

In the very early spring of 1655, secret meetings, often hosted as fox hunts since these were not yet banned by the Protectorate, were held at Penruddock's home, and sometimes at Lady Agneta Phillips's Wiltshire home, or in the King's Arms in Salisbury. The conspirators planned to march into Winchester on 8 March, where the county assizes would be sitting for a few days. Commonwealth judges would be there, trying Hampshire's prisoners. Ambushing the assizes would enable the conspirators to capture prominent judges on the western circuit, and hopefully to recruit members of the public who had gathered in the city to watch the court proceedings. But Cromwell's soldiers got there first, and the rebels were forced to rethink. They chose instead to march into Salisbury, where the assizes would be moving next.

On the night of Sunday 11 March, Penruddock, Wagstaffe and a hundred men gathered in Clarendon Park. The crew included local gentlemen, ejected clergymen and their sons, soldiers, innkeepers, tradesmen and servants. Penruddock's gardener and four members of his household staff were among them.[77] They rode to Blandford to pick up eighty more recruits. There the rebels forced the town crier to proclaim for Charles II, but he refused.[78] They galloped on through the night, across Salisbury Plain, arriving in the sleeping cathedral city just before dawn.

Once in Salisbury, John Thorpe, publican and the keeper of Fisherton jail, unlocked the doors and released his prisoners to join the cause. At seven o'clock in the morning, the rebels stormed the lodgings of the two judges, Lord Chief Justice Henry Rolle and Baron Robert Nicholas (a Wiltshire man, and related to Charles II's secretary of state in exile, Sir Edward Nicholas). They also raided the home of Wiltshire's high sheriff Colonel John Dove, who had been one of the commissioners at Charles I's trial. Dove was dragged outside in his nightshirt. Penruddock loudly proclaimed Charles II as the rightful king – and he prevented Wagstaffe from murdering Rolle, Nicholas and Dove on the spot. Instead he took Dove hostage, and fled out of Salisbury on his horse. He expected to be met by thousands more recruits as they headed further west, into Dorset, Devon and Royalist

Cornwall. But few heeded their rallying cries. The elderly William Seymour, marquess of Hertford of nearby Wolf Hall, great-grandson of Edward Seymour (Jane Seymour's brother and Edward VI's uncle), had promised support, pledging men and horses. But on the night he kept his head down.[79] Neither did Sir John Strangways appear. Instead he wrote a poem in his commonplace book about keeping quiet, and private.[80] And neither did any of the six leaders of the Sealed Knot turn out to help Penruddock.

Accompanied by a motley crew of chained prisoners on stolen horses – thieves, debtors, sheep-stealers, a woman named Margaret Gingell accused of witchcraft – the Wiltshire rebels now numbered nearly four hundred. Among the resolved Royalists were some ordinary men and women, including butchers, innkeepers, cordwainers and tailors, who, they later claimed, were simply caught up in the great rising.[81] They soon began to drop out. Cromwell's soldiers were now on their heels, led by Major-General John Desborough. At Yeovil, Penruddock let Sheriff Dove go and pushed on further west.

By the late evening of Wednesday 14 March, Captain Unton Croke from Exeter had caught up with the exhausted rebels in the small town of South Molton in Devon, on the edge of Exmoor. Croke rooted them out of their lodgings; they had travelled over a hundred miles in under three days. Wagstaffe escaped, and secretly made his way to the coast, sheltering with sympathetic hosts in their homes along the way. He crossed the Channel and made his way back to Flanders.[82] Penruddock, however, was taken prisoner, along with fellow leaders Hugh Grove and Francis Jones, and more than 130 of the rebels. Some were let go; others pleaded for mercy. Edmond Mackes, an apothecary from Salisbury, was captured but readily confessed. Captain Croke wrote back to Cromwell very late on the night of the fourteenth: the cunning and evil fellows were fully 'broken and routed', he said, before adding 'Lord may have the glorie'.[83]

Penruddock was taken to Exeter prison. It was hot, and full. On 19 April, he was tried for treason by a jury in an elaborate but makeshift court set up in the hall of Exeter Castle. The most experienced and trusted judges had been called up to oversee the trials of the uprising's leaders. They included John Lisle, lord commissioner of the Great Seal; John Glynne, serjeant at law; William Steele, recorder of London; and Baron Nicholas and Lord Chief Justice Rolle, both of whom Penruddock had turfed out of bed in Salisbury on that first morning of the uprising. Penruddock's trial needed to be legitimate and high-profile, and a clear warning to future Royalist plotters. Devon's high sheriff Sir John Copplestone co-operated fully, hosting the judges and supping with them in his home. Presiding over all the proceedings was Edmund Prideaux, Oliver Cromwell's attorney-general, MP for Lyme Regis. Prideaux's career had taken off in the 1650s. In 1649, after having made a fortune as master of the posts, he had bought and restored the serene and cloistered Forde Abbey, a former Cistercian monastery nestled in the valley of the River Axe, near Chard. There he commissioned a grand new staircase, Italian windows, highly decorative ceiling wreaths and splendid Mortlake tapestries for the walls of the saloon.[84]

Despite the formality and ceremonialism observed by this temporary court – the careful gathering of evidence and the calling of witnesses, a jury consisting of local men and the judges and Prideaux all robed in scarlet – Penruddock robustly contested the charge of treason. For what, he argued, was treason in an age without a king, but with a Protector? He could not, Penruddock said, be charged with treason 'against a Protector who hath no power according to the law'. Indeed, 'neither is there any such in law as a Protector', he added. For Penruddock, there could be no charge of treason if there was no king: 'If I had seene a crowne upon the head of any person, I had known what had been treason: The law of England would have taken hold of mee, out of the respect it has to Monarchy; There was noe such land-mark before me,' he said. Do not be fooled, Penruddock told the jury directly, by the 'majesty' of the judges' looks, or the 'glory of their habits', for their sin was of a deeper hue than their scarlet robes, and that was 'the sinne of blood'.[85]

As it was, the trials of all the rebels held at Exeter, Salisbury and Chard were, it seems, correctly and fairly conducted. The treason ordinance of January 1654, which transferred the crime from being one against the state – the Parliament – to being one against Parliament and Protector had never been ratified. But secretary of state John Thurloe was reassured that, according to a statute from as far back as Edward III's reign, levying war against a 'king' extended to the chief officer of the country, and could therefore amount to high treason.[86] The title of king, then, did not matter; it was the supremacy of the office held that was important. When Penruddock demanded that Edward III's statute be read out in court, as proof that treason could be extended to a non-king, Prideaux became impatient: 'The court must not be dallyed with,' he stated. Prideaux's word prevailed: it was treason. Penruddock thought this arbitrary. What is treason today, might not be treason tomorrow, 'like ye winde in the Gospell, which bloweth wher it listeth', Penruddock wrote.[87]

On 16 May, Penruddock was beheaded for treason in Castle Yard, to the tolling of a single bell. He addressed the crowd that gathered to watch him die. 'The crime for which I am about to die', he said, 'is Loyalty.' He went on: 'Now Gentlemen, you may see what a condition you are in without a King.'[88] He was not a straightforward martyr, however. He had petitioned Cromwell for mercy, promising loyalty to him in exchange for his life.[89] His wife, Arundel, had also petitioned on behalf of her husband, writing directly to Judge John Glynne and Cromwell's son Richard. Arundel had even gone with her seven children to London to plead before Oliver Cromwell.[90] Penruddock's original sentence of hanging, drawing and quartering was commuted to the more honourable beheading, but that was all the mercy Cromwell would show Penruddock and his family. Compton House was seized, and the family's loyal chaplain John Martin gave Arundel and the children a home. Penruddock's head and body were transported back to Compton Chamberlayne, and he was buried with the French laced cap he wore on the scaffold.[91] Arundel continued, tirelessly, to petition Cromwell for money for her family. Eventually, she was granted a sum out of her husband's estate and her house was restored to her. It stayed in the Penruddock family until the twentieth century. Meanwhile, some of the judges who tried Penruddock and his fellow rebels would go on to serve the very king for whom the rebels had died. John Glynne, for example, worked well into Charles II's reign.

Not all of the twenty-six men found guilty alongside Penruddock on 23 April in Exeter were sentenced to death.[92] Some were banished to Barbados and, later, to Jamaica. Penruddock's cousin, Edward, was ordered to go to Barbados, but a successful petition meant he ended up in the more temperate colony of Virginia.[93] Those who were packed off to Barbados were managed by Martin Noell, who at this time was supposed to be chasing the delayed supplies for the desperate sailors and soldiers on the ill-fated Western Design expedition. Once in Barbados, the prisoners were sold as indentured servants. Marcellus Rivers, from Southampton, was one such prisoner. A few years later, in 1659, having made it back to England, Rivers and his fellow Salisbury man Oxenbridge Foyle petitioned the government for being wrongly condemned and sold as the 'goods and chattels of Martin Noel' in 1655. Rivers and Foyle sought reparation too, in their published petition, for their barbaric treatment on the scorching island, the 'Protestants' Purgatory'. The republican Arthur Hesilrige defended them in Parliament: 'The tenderness of liberty is great,' he said, and the Royalists' case today may be the roundheads' case tomorrow.[94]

Penruddock and his men failed in staging a full-blown revolt – for Hesilrige it was 'a little rebellion' – but they succeeded in shaking the regime.[95] During the summer of 1655 known Royalists, including Belasyse and Villiers of the Sealed Knot, were hunted down, rounded up and imprisoned; some surrendered. And then Cromwell pressed ahead with one of his – and John Lambert's – most novel, experimental and controversial political experiments. At the end of October, a declaration described the 'Insurrection in the West' as 'bold and dangerous', and it justified Cromwell's decision that the counties of England should be ruled by a team of major-generals, in the name of peace. Edmund Ludlow thought this a 'detestable project'.[96] Lists of Royalists were drawn up who, mostly, had fought on the side of the king: 'All that are peaceably-minded in the Nation are ready to say, These are the men of whom we go in danger.' Those Royalists who owned significant land and property would be taxed to pay for this surveillance team of major-generals and their soldiers. 'Certainly it is both just and necessary', the Declaration went on, 'that all those of whom the people have reason to be afraid . . . should pay for Securing the State against that Danger which they are the Authors of.' Major-General John Desborough, Cromwell's brother-in-law, was appointed in charge of the western counties. He became an ardent seeker of Royalists, and promoter of the decimation tax: a 10 per cent levy on the estates' income of eligible Royalists. The policy did not go through Parliament, and Royalists had to pay up, whether or not they were involved in plots against the Protector.[97]

The regime was rubbing on a sore that would prevent the healing of the nation. Royalists were taxed, and their freedom curtailed. Those Royalists, Thurloe said, who 'carry themselves with confidence and boldnes . . . and drinke and swagger' now found themselves temporarily banished from London and their travel restricted.[98] Meetings in private houses were banned, as were horse races, bear baitings and cockfights – any recreation that could mask a gathering of conspirators. Some resisted, some broke the rules undetected, some begged for exemption. Many, like Ralph Verney, paid up and lay low. The rule of the new major-generals, who were generally devout and devoted to Cromwell, was not just about suppressing Royalists and potential rebellions. They were instructed to root out sin, discipline the nation, reform its manners and provide for the poor. The appointed major-generals were to be examples of 'godliness and virtue' who should discourage 'all profaneness and ungodliness'.[99] Major-General Hezekiah Haynes, Ralph Josselin's friend, certainly believed that his work was approved by God, and that the decimation tax on Royalists was 'of the Lord'.[100]

Following Penruddock's rebellion, Cromwell's Puritan Protectorate sought to enforce what many had hoped for since Elizabeth I's time: a moral regeneration through the clamping down on blasphemy, swearing, drinking, adultery. Brothels and gaming houses were closed; well-affected ministers were installed in local parishes.

The censors became stricter. Secretary John Thurloe had become postmaster general in May 1655 and, by the autumn, the only newsbooks in circulation were *Mercurius Politicus* and *The Publick Intelligencer*. Both were edited by Marchamont Nedham. Some parts of the country responded enthusiastically. Dorchester, for example, was run by a committed Puritan elite. But the major-generals differed in character and temperament, and in their implementation of the law and interactions with the local corporations. For Lucy Hutchinson, writing her biography of her republican husband Colonel John Hutchinson, the major-generals were 'silly, mean fellows' who 'ruled according to their wills, by no law, but what seemed good in their own eyes'.[101]

The town of Bedford resisted the interference of their bullying Major-General William Boteler, and sought to allow citizens to elect their own mayor and aldermen. Boteler earned a reputation for cruelty and zeal, and was later reprimanded for his harsh treatment of Royalists as well as religious radicals. He is an example of the complicated Puritan. He had a vision of a godly, sin-free England and he sought to enforce this, but he was not averse to personal profit. When Margaret Cavendish's husband was eventually able to pay a fine in 1656 and recover their large estates, £2,000 went straight into Boteler's pocket as their region's major-general. In the town of Oundle, Boteler commissioned the beautiful Cobthorne House, an example of pared-down classicism in the mould of the Royalist Inigo Jones.[102]

One of the fanatics under Major-General Boteler's watch in Bedfordshire was the tinker John Bunyan. When Bunyan was young, the burden and temptations of sin had been great. He swore and cursed, and was chastised for doing so. He admired the ritual at Elstow Abbey, but he ignored God, and gambled and gamed on the Sabbath. He indulged in sinful pleasures with abandon; in his own words it was his 'delight to be taken captive by the Devil'.[103] In 1653, aged twenty-five, Bunyan arrived in Bedford, impoverished, with a new wife and a young family, including a blind daughter. He was experiencing an intense spiritual crisis and he found solace – and God's grace – in Bedford's Baptist church. He joined the Independent congregation led by John Gifford and, in 1655, Bunyan himself began to preach, in the church and out in the fields. He found he had a gift for talking about God's mercy. His language, stripped of the curses, was that of his listeners – colloquial, ordinary, vivid, but powerful and persuasive about misery and grace, and lifted by his attentiveness to the words of the Bible.

Later, in 1660, Bunyan was imprisoned for his non-conformity. He refused to promise to stop preaching, which he believed was his calling, and he remained in Bedford jail for twelve years.[104] It was there, as a prisoner, that Bunyan wrote the enduringly famous *The Pilgrim's Progress*. It has never been out of print since it was first published in 1678. Harbinger of the English novel, *The Pilgrim's Progress* has been read and loved by generations of readers seeking their way in the wilderness of the world. Gabriel Oak has a well-thumbed copy of the book in Thomas Hardy's *Far from the Madding Crowd*, and it frames the lives and behaviour of Louisa M. Alcott's little women. Such striving self-scrutiny and an unmediated relationship with the divine became embedded in the 1650s, facilitated by a godly regime that felt guided by providence and sought thorough reformation of the individual and of society. The Protectorate government, which did not establish a national Church, was unsure and divided over how tolerant to be of certain communities' religious practices that seemed too unstructured, too wild. After 1655, the republic's tolerance would be thoroughly tested by a new and rapidly growing sect from up in the North: the Quakers.

1656

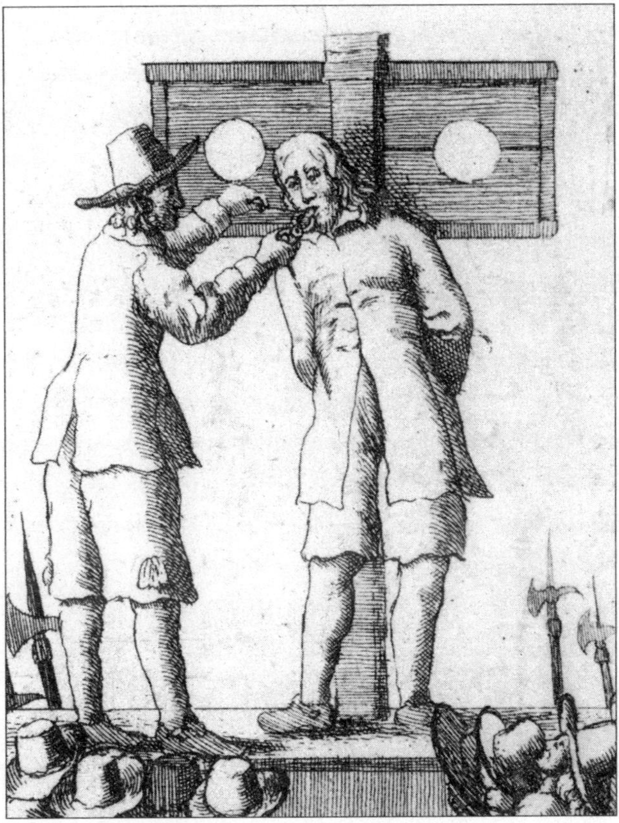

Many believe that the next year will bring with it a notable change in the world, yea; yea, many place the end of the world in that year.

Noah's Flood Returning (1655)

Some believed that the world would end in 1656, and that it would be the beginning of a new world. As Robert Gell expounded in his sermon, *Noah's Flood Returning*, preached before the lord mayor of London in August 1655, it was 1,656 years from Adam to Noah and the flood, and it was prophesied that 1,656 years from the birth of Christ would bring the end of time as it was then known. For those who believed Christ's second coming was imminent, 1656 was mooted as the year this could take place, and England needed to prepare to become a new kingdom. Ralph Josselin turned forty on 26 January and, as he did his annual accounts, he noted how 'some think their very world would end' in 1656.[1] Five years earlier Josselin had anticipated that 'our deare England in the farthest corner of the world' would be the new Jerusalem, the seat of the new kingdom of Christ.[2] Apocalyptic thinking – the belief that the visions John saw in his cave on the island of Patmos were soon to come true – dominated this third year of Cromwell's Protectorate. Diverse groups, from millenarians and Quakers and secret Jews to radical republicans and loyal Cromwellians, longed for, and imagined, new beginnings.

Antonio Fernandez Carvajal was a wealthy Portuguese merchant. He lived on Leadenhall Street in London with his wife Maria and their two boys, Alonso and Joseph. He owned land in the Canary Islands from which he derived great wealth. Next to Carvajal's home was his warehouse, where he stored the goods he shipped from overseas: bullion, gunpowder and cochineal, the brilliant red dye. Carvajal was a Jewish refugee. His family had fled Portugal, and then Spain, before settling in England in the 1630s. Jews were not allowed officially in England, and Carvajal pretended to be a Spanish Catholic, as did the rest of his small community of Spanish and Portuguese (Sephardi) Jews living in East London. He participated in mass at the Spanish ambassador's chapel, but observed Jewish rites secretly, in a private home. Carvajal was known as a successful merchant and supplier. In the 1640s Parliament had bought his gunpowder and granted him the contract to supply its soldiers with corn. The state profited from his lucrative trade in bullion in the early 1650s. Carvajal, connected to a wide network of merchants in the Americas, was also possibly a spy; he certainly enjoyed government protection. In August 1655, Cromwell formally recognised Carvajal and his two sons as English citizens, thereby granting them all the liberties and privileges of a naturally born subject. This citizenship nearly lost Carvajal his fortune a few months later when, following the declaration of war with Spain after England's invasion of Jamaica, his property in the Canary Islands risked being seized by the Spanish – since it now belonged to an Englishman. Boldly, Carvajal petitioned Cromwell on 9 November 1655 for help; Cromwell responded by ensuring that Carvajal's possessions and goods were smuggled safely back from the Canaries to England in a boat disguised as a Dutch vessel, thus avoiding the suspicion of the Spanish ships patrolling the seas.[3]

Cromwell almost certainly knew that Carvajal was Jewish. There were perhaps only twenty or so Jewish families living in London in the middle years of the seventeenth century. In 1290, Edward I had expelled the approximately two thousand Jews from England by royal edict. After 1492, to escape the Inquisition, some

Jews fled Spain and Portugal and a few made their way to England, where they settled, disguised as Catholics. In 1653, the Royalist spy James Howell wrote to a friend in Amsterdam, where Jews lived freely, and reported, with a cruel but common slur, that 'Touching Judaism, some corners of our city smell as rank of it as yours doth there'.[4] A couple of years later, the duke of Tuscany's envoy Francesco Salvetti described how the Jews in London 'organise their synagogues privately in some houses'.[5]

In spring 1656, this unofficially tolerated Jewish community was compelled to declare its true heritage. Carvajal, along with others, petitioned Cromwell directly to acknowledge them as Hebrews. After nearly four hundred years of living in secret, this was a risky admission, and one that would prove hugely significant for the history of Jews living in Britain.

Carvajal's decision was triggered, once again, by the ongoing war with the Spanish, which threatened goods and trade. Antonio Rodrigues Robles, a friend of Carvajal's and another wealthy member of London's Sephardi merchant community, was tipped off by a William Coxeter to the authorities as a Spaniard. Following this, two of Robles's ships that were moored on the Thames and loaded with cargo were seized, as were his books and papers. But Robles was Portuguese, not Spanish – and, moreover, he was Jewish, not Catholic. Robles appealed to Cromwell as 'the protector of afflicted strangers', assuring him that he was 'a Portuguese Jew'. His father, he said, had been killed and his mother tortured by the Inquisition. He had lived in England for many years. He had duly paid his taxes and deserved the privileges of a foreign merchant.[6]

At the same time as Robles exposed his identity to save his goods, Carvajal put his name to another petition, along with six others. This 'Humble Petition of the Hebrews' pleaded for formal state protection for all Jews living in England. They sought assurance that they could live peacefully and worship 'without fear of molestation'. And they asked for a small plot of land, out of the city, in which they could bury their dead.[7]

Both Robles's and Carvajal's petitions succeeded, and the lives of Jews in England changed. The authorities had examined Robles and called upon witnesses. He was not circumcised so they could not be sure he was a Jew, but his goods were returned to him and his Jewish heritage was accepted. Following his 'Petition of the Hebrews', Carvajal was able, in December 1656, to lease the first floor of a house on Creechurch Lane, just off Leadenhall, where he and his community could worship. This became England's first public synagogue. It no longer stands, but its oak benches still do, in the Bevis Marks synagogue built just around the corner, by a Quaker builder, in 1701. And, in February 1657, Carvajal and his friend Simon de Caceres leased (at a cheekily exorbitant cost) a plot of orchard land just off the Mile End Road. There, in 1659, Carvajal was buried. As his body was carried to its grave, Christian church bells rang out to commemorate the death of 'this Great Jew'. You can still visit this Jewish graveyard; it lies behind a door in a wall on Queen Mary's university campus.[8]

Carvajal and Robles shook off their disguise to protect their livelihoods, but they were also reading the times. Since September 1655, a high-profile and much-admired rabbi from Amsterdam had been staying in London, as a guest of the council of state, agitating for the readmission of Jews. Menasseh ben Israel was well known to Carvajal and his community, and he was one of the seven signatories on Carvajal's spring petition. But he was not hosted by his fellow Jews. Instead, he lodged in expensive rooms opposite the Exchange on the Strand, possibly at the state's expense. He had taken up an invitation first issued to him by the council of state in 1652, after he had met Oliver St John, John Thurloe and Walter Strickland when they had visited Amsterdam in 1651, as part of their official embassy to The Hague. At that time, before the war with the Dutch over the Navigation Act, England was hoping for a profitable alliance with a fellow republic. The English were 'a people in league and amity', Menasseh recalled. The English ambassadors were taken to visit the synagogue in Amsterdam, and they exchanged thoughts about the status of Jews in England.[9]

The war with the Dutch had delayed Menasseh cashing in his free pass to England straight away, but he was full of hope when he set sail across the North Sea in September 1655, with his son Samuel. He felt optimistic about approaching Cromwell, believing that England was now 'excellently affected to our nation'.[10] Jews in Europe were being persecuted, and needed new places of refuge. Menasseh hoped England would be such a haven. He knew much about the arguments for liberty of conscience that had been raging in England since the wars in the 1640s. From his English Royalist friends living in exile in Holland, from diplomat friends such as the religiously tolerant John Dury (Samuel Hartlib's great friend) and the political theorist and reformer John Sadler (who strongly supported the readmission of Jews), and from the merchants and travellers passing through his city, Menasseh was well aware of England's radical and expanding religious sects, of Baptists' talk of toleration and the views of one such as Roger Williams who argued that it was the will of God to welcome pagans, Turks and Jews.[11] He knew of Samuel Fisher's belief that a country's ruler should 'leave all men to worship God according to their several ways'.[12] He also knew that there were those in England pushing hard for the formal readmission of Jews, for religious and economic reasons. In 1646, the army chaplain and Cromwell's trusted friend Hugh Peter had suggested that 'strangers, even Jews' should be allowed to 'trade and live with us'.[13] Johanna Cartwright had petitioned Thomas Fairfax early in 1649, asking for their banishment to be repealed.[14] Soon before Charles I's trial, the Royalist newsbook *Mercurius Pragmaticus* had snidely responded to rumours about returning Jews: 'No marvell that those which intend to crucifie their King should shake hands with them that crucified their Saviour.'[15] In that same climacteric year John Sadler wrote that 'The more I think upon the Great Change, now coming on Them, and All the World; the More I would be Just and Mercifull to Them'.[16]

Suspected Jews were still being examined and imprisoned: in 1649, Anne Curtyn was thrown into the New Prison at Clerkenwell for denying Christ and adopting Jewish rituals, such as circumcision.[17] But the execution of Charles I presaged a revolution to Menasseh. He dedicated his book, *The Hope of Israel*, to the republic's council of state. 'The whole world stands amazed at these things, and the eyes of all are turned upon ye,' Menasseh told the council. All were keen to see 'whither all these things do tend'.[18] Now, in 1656, there was a Lord Protector, seemingly sympathetic to the Jews, and to whom Menasseh could appeal directly. Cromwell, Bulstrode Whitelocke wrote, 'was earnestly set upon' the readmission of Jews to England, and he invited Menasseh to dine with him.[19] Menasseh gave Cromwell and members of the protectoral council specially printed copies of his petition, *The Humble Addresses*, which his friend John Dury had helped him write. He appealed to Cromwell's leaning towards toleration, and he spoke about the economic prosperity Jews could bring England: their skill dealing in money, diamonds, wine and indigo. He proposed to Cromwell that Jews should live as citizens and trade freely, and that all laws against them be revoked.[20]

While waiting for the Protector and his council to respond to his proposals, Menasseh spent time meeting English friends and admirers. This affable, learned and enterprising man was known far beyond his Jewish neighbourhood of Vlooienberg, Amsterdam. Jews had lived and worked openly in Amsterdam since the beginning of the seventeenth century. In 1626, Menasseh had run his own publishing company from his home, printing Hebrew Bibles and works of Jewish history. His business thrived and his fame grew. Rembrandt provided etchings to illustrate the first edition of Menasseh's book *Piedra Gloriosa*, published in 1655. Menasseh had possibly taught Spinoza, the precocious young son of an Amsterdam Jewish merchant. He had met Henrietta Maria and he knew Queen Christina of Sweden from her time living in Antwerp, once she had abdicated her throne and was en route to Rome to become a Catholic. The scientist Robert Boyle saw Menasseh as one of the 'greatest rabbis of this age', and he and his sister Katherine, Viscountess Ranelagh, hosted him in their home while he was in London. Perhaps Menasseh also met John Milton there, since Milton was a close friend of Lady Ranelagh's. Milton, however, remained conspicuously quiet about Menasseh's visit and the matter of the Jews. This was surprising, given his sympathy for and intellectual interest in ancient Israel as an elect nation (as he believed England also was) and which was also, once upon a time, a republic. But this was before the Israelites pleaded with God to give them a king. 'It is a form of idolatry to ask for a king,' Milton had written in his first *Defence*. He also criticised the Jews for usury (although he himself was a successful usurer) and he did not like Jewish customs.[21]

While in London Menasseh probably also met Moses Wall, translator of *The Hope of Israel* and another old friend of Milton's.[22] The Welsh prophet Arise Evans also paid a visit, and tried to convince Menasseh that Christ would come again, but as Charles II.[23] Menasseh also surely met up with the London preacher Henry Jessey, with whom he had long corresponded about the plight of Jews. And of course he would have met the indefatigable networker and intelligencer Samuel Hartlib, with whom he shared mutual friends John Dury and Moses Wall. One of Hartlib and Dury's dreams had been to establish a college devoted to Hebrew studies in England. They wished to learn about and understand the Jews – and convert them to Christianity. As for Carvajal, he had kept himself apart from Menasseh's embassy, fearing exposure, but they are likely to have met, and perhaps saw in the Jewish new year together.

Menasseh's embassy to England was inspired by prophecy. He believed that the settlement of Jews in England, a country at the end of the earth, was the necessary prelude to the return of the dispersed Jews to their homeland, as promised by Moses in the book of Deuteronomy, and that this would be followed by the arrival of the Messiah. And he believed that this was imminent, that war, conflict, sedition – all seen in England – were proof that 'the day of the promised Messiah draws near to us'.[24] Further proof that the time was at hand came from a report by a Portuguese traveller in America, who described how he had met an Indian tribe high up in the mountains of the Andes, practising Jewish rites and claiming to be descendants of Reuben, one of the lost tribes of Israel. Finding one of the banished ten tribes was a sign that, as prophesied in Isaiah, the outcast Jews, scattered 'from the one end of the earth even unto the other', were being gathered again, and this heralded their forgiveness, their return to their homeland and the coming of their king.[25]

Not all Dutch Jews shared Menasseh's messianism or his enthusiasm for petitioning Oliver Cromwell, with whom they had recently been at war. But Menasseh's conviction chimed with the millenarianism shared by many English men and women, from prophets and Fifth Monarchists to more moderate Puritans. In 1649, Menasseh had written to John Dury, telling him the story about the Jewish Indians found in America. In his preface to Thomas Thorowgood's *Jewes in America*, Dury explained what this discovery in the New World meant for Christians: it was a sign that the conversion of the Jews could soon take place, and the conversion of the Jews was believed to precede the second coming of Christ.[26] Back in the late 1640s, Dury had assured Hartlib that he believed God would certainly 'bring to pass' the conversion of the Jews.[27] In 1651, Henry Jessey had written in his preface to Mary Cary's prophetic work, *The Little Horns Doom*, that since 'great changes' were now at hand, the conversion of the Jews would 'probably' have taken place by 1658. Previous millenarian writers had similarly predicted that this would happen in 1655 or 1656.

Readmitting the Jews, and converting them to Christianity, was a necessary condition for the second coming of Christ. For Moses Wall, the English should abandon their hatred of the Jews – after all, 'they have the same Humane nature with us', he pointed out – and move them towards Christ, make them 'reall Christians'. And, who better to convert Jews than the English: 'Happy is England, if it be instrumental in so blessed a work.'[28] To Dury, Wall, Hartlib and Jessey, England had become a republic in order to usher in the kingdom of Christ – and, in 1656, this was imminent, and therefore the conversion of the Jews was urgent. For Menasseh, England was the republic that, by welcoming and caring for his lost people, would eventually lead them back to the kingdom of Israel.

There were powerful economic reasons, too. Spiritual gain was not without material profit. The English republic, Menasseh noted in 1656, was 'most flourishing'.[29] It was still conquering Jamaica, and needed to expand its trade. The poet Andrew Marvell, ever alert to a country's cultural incongruities, mocked Holland's reputation for its broad tolerance of 'Turk-Christian-Pagan-Jew' since it was, really, economically driven. In his poem 'The Character of Holland', Amsterdam is a 'mint of schism' where one can trade at the 'bank of conscience'.[30] Satire this may be, but the idea that tolerance makes money was shared by many in England who were pushing for the readmission of Jews. Henry Robinson, a key figure on the council of trade advocating for credit and England's first national bank, enthusiastically campaigned for the return of Jews.

The council devolved its response to Menasseh's *Humble Addresses* to a small committee. Menasseh's proposals were complex in a Christian nation: a public synagogue would be a scandal; Jews might seduce and convert the Christians; they might harm trade. A larger committee of twenty-eight members was set up to consider a fuller response. It was populated by eminent lawyers, politicians, merchants, academics, diplomats and clergymen. Among them were faithful household staff such as Gilbert Pickering, judge John Glynne, fresh from the Penruddock trial, professor of Hebrew Ralph Cudworth, the minister Henry Jessey and the chaplain Hugh Peter. This committee debated whether or not there was any law forbidding the readmission of Jews – surely the royal whim of Edward I no longer held sway? – and what England stood to gain, and lose, by their return. The committee's deliberations over five days in December 1655 became known as the Whitehall Conference. The sympathetic Henry Jessey published their proceedings.[31]

The members of the Whitehall Conference were, predictably, divided. Jews, to many, remained largely unknown, existing only in the realm of imagination and rumour. Tales were told about their strange ritual practices and their trustworthiness. Many were also known to be successful and well-connected merchants. Mild and tolerant Major-General Edward Whalley – Charles I had once thanked him for his kindness when imprisoned under his guard at Hampton Court – argued that they would bring wealth, and they could be converted to Christianity. 'It seems to me', Whalley wrote to John Thurloe, 'that there are both politique and divine reasons, which strongly make for their admission into a cohabitation and civill commerce with us. Doubtlesse to say no more, they will bring in much wealth into this commonwealth; and where wee both pray for theyr conversion, and beleeve it shal be, I knowe not why wee should deny the meanes.'[32] John Lambert was also in favour, as was John Thurloe. Cromwell was present for some of the discussions, keen to know how the preachers interpreted the Bible on the issue. He was clearly sympathetic, but he held back from intervening directly. In many of the responses, money and millenarianism collapsed into each other. Profit was explained in both economic and spiritual ways; material gain could, indeed, be a sign of God's grace. Some voiced Christian hospitality: it was God's will to show kindness to strangers, and Jews were an afflicted people. Others feared that English merchants' business and trade would be threatened, and that instead of the Jews being converted, the English would 'turn Jew' themselves. The voices from the Whitehall Conference show the pragmatism, providentialism, pity and, to Thurloe, the peevishness of some of the Protectorate's most influential politicians, lawyers and religious men.[33]

Beyond the walls of Whitehall, public opinion was also divided, along familiar and stereotypical lines. There was panic that the

Jews would murder their children, turn St Paul's Cathedral into a synagogue and buy up the Bodleian Library. The veteran Puritan William Prynne was fiercely against 'this new distastefull pernicious project of bringing in the Jews' and he published a vitriolic attack. Jews were clippers, counterfeiters, cheaters and usurers and they would destroy English merchants.[34] The pernicious project, for Prynne, ever fearful of the passions being stirred, was 'worldly, carnal, sensual'; those in favour were simply seduced and misled by the smell of money. Far from being able to convert the Jews, he argued, the giddy, swayable English were more in danger of being taken in themselves by the hypnotic and sinful spectacle of Jewish ceremony. In January, Ralph Josselin had a dream, perhaps a nightmare: Thurloe had 'turned Jew'.[35] Merchants wavered between their own desire for wealth, and their fear of Jewish competition. Those who were most tolerant also had their concerns. Even Menasseh's sympathetic friend John Dury was wary of being too permissive. He told his friend Samuel Hartlib that the state would be wise to go carefully, since Menasseh's 'demands are great, & the use which they make of great priviledges is not much to their commendation here & elsewhere: they have wayes beyond all other men, to undermine a state, & to insinuate into those that are in offices'.[36]

The deliberations ended up nowhere. The lawyers agreed that there was no lawful impediment to readmitting the Jews in England, but the council chose not to publish a formal proclamation announcing this. Menasseh believed that his embassy and petitioning had failed. He and his son Samuel stayed on in London, but Menasseh was unwell and out of money, although he was supported by an erratically paid parliamentary pension. Just as Robles's and Carvajal's petitions were making their way through Parliament in the spring and summer of 1656, with Menasseh's name one of the signatories, Menasseh wrote his final work, which was a powerful, poignant defence of his people: *Vindiciae Judaeorum*. He did not go home until 1657 when, on 9 September, his son Samuel died. Menasseh travelled back to Holland with his body, but he only got as far as Middelburg, where he, too, died.

Menasseh's embassy was not a failure for the ground had shifted. There was no formal proclamation but John Evelyn was able to record in his diary, on 9 December 1655, just home from visiting Hobbes, that 'now were the Jewes admitted'.[37] The bookseller Humphrey Robinson, in a letter also dated in December, notes that the 'Jews, we hear, will be admitted by way of connivency, though the generality oppose'.[38] The matter was certainly not closed. Francesco Salvetti reported back to the duke of Tuscany on 28 January 1656 that 'the affair of the Jews continues' and that, meanwhile, 'they may meet privately in their houses, but they have not yet established a synagogue'.[39] It would be Carvajal's spring petition, which began by thanking the Protector for leave to worship privately, that secured their synagogue. History is not always made by grand gestures.

The story of Cromwell and the Jews has often been told to reveal his regime's revolutionary efforts to extend toleration and liberty of conscience, as well as to mark 1656 as the beginning of Jewish settlement in England.[40] Menasseh's embassy did not secure a formal proclamation, but the Whitehall Conference meant that sympathy and understanding of the Jews and their history were rigorously debated in the corridors of power, as well as in private homes and coffee houses, and circulated in pamphlets and private letters. After Menasseh's visit and Robles's and Carvajal's disclosure of their Jewish identities, England's Jewish community began, slowly, to grow. Jews were able to live, trade and worship 'unmolested'. When Charles II was restored in 1660, several London merchants took the opportunity to petition the new king to expel the Jews who were now living and flourishing in their city. The merchant Thomas Violet – he who had once named Carvajal as 'the Great Jew' and was well aware of his successful trade in bullion – complained how 'since this Toleration many people have bin seduced', with 'multitudes of men and women . . . turned absolute Jewes', and much damage done to the kingdom.[41] Charles II ignored these voices, and carried on with the readmission of the Jews that Cromwell had begun. John Dury rewrote his preface to a new edition of *Jewes in America* and foretold that it would be Charles II who would be credited with readmitting the Jews. In 1664, in response to another petition, this time by Menasseh's brother-in-law, the Jewish community finally received, in writing, a royal declaration that they could live at peace in Charles II's kingdom.

In May 1652, a twenty-eight-year-old man called George Fox climbed Pendle Hill in Lancashire. He was travelling from Yorkshire to Westmorland (now Cumbria), preaching along the way about an unorthodox knowledge of Christ. From the hill's plateaued top Fox looked down on the town of Pendle – home to the famous witches who were tried and executed there in 1612 – and out across the Lancashire countryside and towards the Irish Sea. He felt certain that the day of the Lord was near, and he saw a vision of the people that God wanted him to gather, and with whom he should share this knowledge. Fox – like so many of those debating the Jews – believed that the coming of Christ, prophesied by John, was about to take place. But he believed that Christ would appear within, privately. Fox was an early, and some said the original, Quaker.

Fox grew up in the Puritan parish of Drayton-in-the-Clay, Leicestershire. He was the eldest child of a devout and fairly well-off weaver; later in the 1650s he would inherit money from his father that freed him from financial worries. Fox himself was a trained cobbler, but as a nineteen-year-old young man, in the midst of the civil wars, he left and began to wander alone through the countryside, troubled and often in despair. He was particularly disillusioned with the Puritan ministers who, he said, did not possess 'what they professed', and drank and lied, and seemed vain and unkind. Like the distressed John Bunyan who eventually found comfort among the Baptists in Bedford, and like the many separatists and 'seekers' of these times who rejected the ministers and structure of the Church, Fox was in search of how to truly know God and Christ, how to be even purer than a Puritan.

Fox spent the late 1640s wandering through Derbyshire, the Peak District, Leicestershire and Nottinghamshire. He slept outside, or walked through the night. He fasted. And then, in 1647, when he was at his lowest and most alone, he heard a voice: 'There is one, even Christ Jesus, that can speak to thy condition.' Fox's heart leapt for joy: Christ revealed himself and Fox directly experienced his grace. He had, he said, received an opening, and gleaned the truth: Christ would appear within. 'All wait patiently upon the Lord,' he said, 'whatsoever condition you be in; wait in the grace and truth that comes by Jesus.' From now on he was moved to lead people from darkness to light, to help them receive Jesus and persuade them that the sinless state of Adam before he fell was achievable by all, to teach them to eschew the world's religions, 'which are vain', he said, and reject the appalling belief in predestination. The Lord would be known 'without the help of any man, book, or writing', without 'windy doctrines', he said, which blow a man's mind this way and that.[42]

Some of the men and women Fox met as he travelled through the Midlands and the North of England in the service of the Lord listened to his claims that all were open to Christ. Justices, sheriffs, soldiers, priests, mayors, jailers, prisoners, widows, wives and former Levellers, Seekers and Ranters became convinced that Christ would appear within them, too, and that this was imminent. They were comforted to learn that they were neither elect nor damned, and that purity and perfection were attainable. Many nodded and agreed when Fox railed against ministers, the payment of tithes and the made-up rituals of the Church – or 'steeplehouse' as he called it. A hillside, an orchard or a simple room in a friend's home would serve just as well as a place in which to stand and wait for Christ. Fox's rejection of social gestures and hierarchical niceties also appealed. You did not need to bow or scrape your knee to someone richer or more powerful than you, for deference should be shown to God only. You only needed to doff your cap when praying. Everyone was addressed as 'thee', since everyone was equal, and swearing oaths was simply unnecessary.[43]

Those who shared Fox's ideas became Friends and children of light. They chose not to speak if words felt superfluous or untrue, and they did not haggle over corn or wool prices at the market, preferring the fairness and integrity of a fixed price (drawing many to banking and commerce later). James Nayler, Richard Farnworth, William Dewsbury, Richard Hubberthorne, Francis Howgill, Edward Burrough – children of the wars of the 1640s – also became celebrated preachers, and spread the word.[44] You did not need an Oxford or Cambridge degree to teach about God, they said. Women, too, could preach, and a good number did, to the horror of many men. The 'tender' Elizabeth Hooton, wife and mother, was one of Fox's earliest converts and she went on to preach widely. These friends were not bound by the Bible or a congregation. They met while threshing, debating ideas or listening to a fellow Friend, or just waiting in silence, a practice they adopted from the Seekers. They wore their hair long and dressed in plain clothes. Some converts, like sixteen-year-old Elizabeth Fletcher, felt moved to appear naked in public, a testimony to her conversion and transformation, a pregnant sign of the dwelling of Christ inside her, and thus of her clean, sinless state.[45] Occasionally, during a meeting, someone might groan, or feel moved by God to say something; since all were spiritually equal, anyone, man or woman, was allowed to speak. Sometimes the experience of Christ and the moment of conversion would make the friends shake, or quake. Fox described this physical reaction in his famous journal, edited by his friend and fellow Quaker Thomas Ellwood, as 'the earth in people's hearts, which was to be shaken before the Seed of God was raised out of the earth. And it was so; for the Lord's power began to shake them, and great meetings we began to have.'[46] Those alarmed by the trembling, believing it to be some kind of satanic possession, disparagingly named Fox and those he convinced as Quakers.[47] Fox and his friends took the slur and made it their own. When Thomas Ellwood, newly converted, met his friends in Oxford he refused to tip his cap or bend his knee. A friend clapped him on the back and said, 'What, Tom, a Quaker!' To which Ellwood replied 'Yes, a Quaker . . . one of those despised people.'[48]

And they were despised. Many who met and heard Fox or Burrough or Nayler preach in their market towns, schoolhouses, churches and homes were concerned and enraged. Their beliefs were threatening because they rejected the Church and its services and mediating clergy. The idea of an indwelling Christ seemed blasphemous, and the notion that man could be without sin preposterous. These shaking Quakers were disruptive and irreverent. In Lichfield, Fox shouted barefoot in the streets, railing against the bloody city. He and fellow Friends frequently interrupted church services, moved to speak or to challenge a harmless minister. In early 1655, Cromwell had issued a proclamation prohibiting 'the disturbing of ministers' during their religious services.[49] When John Evelyn 'had the curiosity' to visit some Quakers in prison in Ipswich he branded them 'a new phanatic sect of dangerous principles'.[50] From his parish of Earls Colne, Ralph Josselin noted the 'great noise of people called Quakers', and their 'fits'. Such shaking was, he thought, a sign of devilish possession, and he begged the Lord to 'helpe us to stand fast against every evill'.[51]

Fox and his fellow Quaker preachers were frequently beaten or stoned in the streets and left for dead; many were imprisoned on charges of causing riots, disturbing the peace or blasphemy. The sufferers published their tales of persecution and maltreatment at the hands of incensed parishioners and local magistrates. In 1650, Fox was imprisoned in Derby for a year. After his release in 1651, he continued to travel and to preach, and to convert in the hundreds. Shortly after his vision on Pendle Hill in 1652, he addressed a thousand-strong crowd from a rock on top of Firbank Fell; this was one of the largest gatherings yet. The numbers of Quakers were swelling, and soon those in positions of influence and power would join, or support them. Sympathetic justices such as Luke Robinson began to protect Quakers who had been seized by the alarmed authorities, and ensured that the charge, often of blasphemy or disruption, was legitimate and the hearing fair.[52]

In Swarthmoor Hall in Ulverston, a small market town in the south of Cumbria, where the imposing hills slide into Morecambe Bay, Margaret Fell had heard about the charismatic George Fox.

His fame was spreading in her county and she was keen to meet him. Margaret's own parish church was an Independent congregation and she had an appetite for religious debate and unorthodox ideas. She had called for the readmission of Jews, writing herself to Menasseh ben Israel to offer support.[53] She often invited wandering preachers into her well-to-do Elizabethan manor home, where she lived with her husband Thomas Fell – judge and vice-chancellor of the Duchy of Lancaster – and their eight children. Fox arrived at their home in late June 1652, still full of the Pendle Hill vision. There he also met Ulverston's minister, William Lampitt, whom he found 'full of filth', and then he met and talked at length with Margaret. As Margaret listened to Fox she became convinced of his ideas, as did most of her children and household staff. It was the beginning of a close and enduring relationship.[54]

Margaret's husband Thomas did not openly become a follower, but he certainly supported his wife and her Quaker friends. As a judge he was able to help Fox, Nayler and others when they became entangled with the law. At the Lancaster assizes in October 1652, when Fox was in trouble for claiming 'that he had the divinity essentially in him', Thomas Fell successfully challenged his warrant.[55] We do not know if, secretly, Judge Fell was worried by his wife's relationship with the inspired and persuasive Fox. It was, after all, usual for Quakers to express their feelings for each other, regardless of their sex, in passionate terms. In any case, in 1669, some years after Thomas's death, Fox and Margaret married.

Margaret's patronage, and her wealth and connections, enabled the Quakers to grow, rapidly. She wrote countless letters, organising the Friends who passed through her home, Swarthmoor Hall, which became a Quaker hive. They began to convert in the hundreds, including the former Leveller John Lilburne. Margaret appealed directly to Cromwell for his protection, arguing for liberty of conscience. And she wrote, publishing nearly twenty books in the second half of the 1650s. She fiercely defended women preachers, of whom there were many. Ann Audland referred to Margaret as a mother: 'by thee I am nourished', she wrote.[56] Nearly half of all pamphlets written by women in the 1650s were by Quakers, and their work made up nearly 5 per cent of all Quaker books.

The Quakers' travels and writings were funded by collections gathered at their meetings in Swarthmoor Hall. Armed with books and pamphlets which they handed out wherever they went, the Quakers travelled two by two, in pairs of men or women. The bonds between them were strong, and erotically expressed: 'Thou art bound up in me sealed closed and enjoyed for evermore,' John Audland told Margaret.[57] They roamed the hills and trudged through muddy towns, staying in inns or barns or with anyone who would give them a bed. They never accepted payment for their preaching; the funds collected at Swarthmoor Hall paid for shoes and food while they were on the road. Many fell victim to the revived Elizabethan law against vagrants, and they spent days or even months in prison, pleading with local magistrates and appealing to the local major-general. They kept in touch with each other through Margaret, who oversaw their activities and whose home became a sorting house for their letters, which criss-crossed the country thanks to England's increasingly efficient postal service. Quaker pairs sailed the Atlantic to Barbados and the newly conquered Jamaica, and up America's East Coast to New England. Elizabeth Fletcher went to Ireland; Mary Fisher travelled to America via Barbados, arriving in Massachusetts in 1656, and then to Turkey.

In that summer of 1652, Margaret Fell was hosting another young man. This was the Yorkshire-born former soldier James Nayler. Nayler had fought hard for Parliament during the wars, at

Marston Moor and at Dunbar in 1650. He had served as quarter-master to John Lambert, whom he impressed. On the battlefields and in the soldiers' camps Nayler had heard the radical ideas that were being nurtured among the New Model Army soldiers who were risking their lives fighting the king, and who demanded a different and a better world in return. They argued about the Church, being punished by God, the general state of apostasy in England, the imminent coming of Christ and the work of God they believed they were undertaking. Like Fox, whom Nayler had met in 1651, Nayler claimed God had commanded him directly to go out and prophesy. While out ploughing on his farm in Wakefield, Yorkshire, to which he had returned after retiring from the army in 1651, Nayler heard God. As he recalled during his first trial for blasphemy:

> I was at the plow, meditating on the things of God, and suddenly I heard a voice, saying unto me, 'Get thee out from thy kindred, and from thy father's house,' and I had a promise given in with it. Whereupon I did exceedingly rejoice, that I had heard the voice of that God which I had professed from a child but had never known him.[58]

Obeying the divine command, Nayler left his wife and family. In 1652 he joined up with George Fox at Swarthmoor Hall. Nayler was fasting at the time and cut a rough but zealous figure. He was a gifted and melodic orator. He looked, so Thomas Ellwood claimed, like the simple husbandman he was, but he was equipped with a quick wit, a mastery of doctrine and a talent for robust debate. He became well known in London, where he arrived in summer 1655. He was also a prolific writer, and wrote ten pamphlets in 1656 alone. He became the movement's principal defender, and wrote most of his tracts in response to fierce opposition. The printer Giles Calvert, based at the Blackspread Eagle near St Paul's Cathedral, became the Quakers' main publisher. Quaker books were cheap, accessible and articulate. They advocated peace, not violence, and although they referred to themselves and each other as 'tender', their writing was often angry.

Although Fox saw himself, and was perceived by many, as the founder of the Quakers, it was Nayler who was adored. He was warned by fellow Quaker Richard Nelson of being idolised: 'Take good heed while thou forbears to have outward reverence of men, as capping and kneeling and the like, that thou steal not men's hearts away from God to thyself and so lord it on their conscience that they have neither God, nor Scripture, nor any privilege of their own experience, but take thee as a demi-god.'[59] Devoted to Nayler was Martha Simmonds, wife of the Quaker printer Thomas Simmonds, and sister to Giles Calvert. Martha also preached and wrote, sometimes with Nayler. She liked to exhibit her experience of the inner light, of the Spirit within her, through extravagant display. She walked barefoot through Colchester, in the freezing cold, dressed in sackcloth, with ashes scattered over her head and through her long hair. She implored England's fallen people, who she saw groping in the dark and wallowing in their filth, to repent, to look within and find a state of sinlessness there which, oddly, she likened to a king's crown: 'There is a Royall Diadem hid in thy uncleane heart, which never consented to the evill thereof; Oh that thou wouldst harken to it that thy inward eye might be opened, then wouldst thou see the beauty of it,' she wrote.[60]

Nayler's fame and his relationship with Martha pushed the Quakers, and Parliament, towards crisis in 1656. To the dismay of Fox, and his prominent fellow Quakers Burrough and Howgill, Martha claimed that Nayler was the Messiah. She began to disrupt their meetings, and they turned against her. She called on Nayler to help, and although he refused to chastise his fellow Friends, he did not rebuke Martha for claiming that he was the Messiah. His friends began to believe that Martha had bewitched Nayler. Others believed that it was Nayler who had seduced her, and that he was deluded and unstable.[61] Since early 1656 Fox had been in Launceston jail, apprehended while on a trip to convert Cornwall, that 'dark county'. On a visit to Bristol fair in July, Nayler agreed to go and see Fox, in the hope of a reconciliation between the two old friends. Nayler was arrested for vagrancy on the way, and thrown into Exeter jail; Fox met him there following his own release from Launceston. Nayler was, once again, fasting – he even spat out the water he was forced to drink. And he refused to acknowledge Fox as his superior. Margaret Fell reprimanded Nayler: 'I have heard that thou would not be subject to him to whom all nations shall bow; it hath grieved my spirit.'[62] Martha, meanwhile, railed at Fox, and bargained for Nayler's release. She had been employed nursing John Desborough's sick wife – and Cromwell's younger sister – Jane. Desborough, as major-general of the West, had visited Fox in Launceston jail. He had enjoyed a game of bowls on the castle green before turning back home, leaving Fox locked up. But Desborough agreed with Martha that her payment for caring for Mrs Desborough would be her Messiah's – Nayler's – freedom.[63]

Four days after walking out of Exeter prison, on 26 October 1656, James Nayler rode into Bristol on a horse. It was raining hard, and the streets were awash with mud. Martha led Nayler's horse, and another of his female disciples, Hannah Stranger, spread clothes before him in the muddy road. They sang 'Holy, holy, holy, Lord God of Israel' as they walked. Nayler's brown hair was long and bedraggled, and his beard was short, possibly forked. He was thin and frail. He looked, of course, like Jesus riding into

Jerusalem on Palm Sunday. Such blatant imitation was blasphemous and provocative. It was like a scene from a popular medieval mystery play, which had been banned long ago from England's towns and cities for dramatising the stories from the Bible and daring to impersonate the divine.[64]

The Bristol authorities were not happy. The city was home to a substantial Quaker community, but it had a Royalist past and the aldermen were increasingly fearful of the Quakers' growing presence. They were not the only ones to be afraid. By 1656, many cities, towns and villages across the country, and most of Whitehall, were alarmed by the Quakers, these subversive people from the North who were now rapidly spreading South. In 1655, Cromwell's son Henry had felt compelled to tell his father that the Quakers, and not former Royalists, were now the government's 'most considerable enemy'.[65] Cromwell had himself met George Fox in 1654, and he and his council were aware of John Nayler's fame in London. Some of Cromwell's men, chaplains and soldiers regularly attended Quaker meetings, as did wealthy merchants including Robert Rich, who owned profitable estates in Barbados, and who became a loyal and influential friend of Nayler's. Bristol's authorities knew that theatrical stunts such as Nayler's Jesus-like entry could move and persuade people and they promptly arrested Nayler, Martha, Hannah, her husband John Stranger and Dorcas Erbury, another female follower. After five days of interrogation in Bristol, the magistrates claimed that they did not know how to try and judge such an act, and they sent Nayler and the other four to London for further examination. The move to London escalated what *Mercurius Politicus* thought were simply 'strange and absurd pranks'.[66]

On 31 October, a committee of no fewer than fifty-five MPs was put together to debate the misdemeanours and blasphemies of James Nayler. The group, many of whom were lawyers, was asked to report on the case and prepare a bill that would take away 'such old laws made against tender consciences'. This, then, might present an opportunity to clarify the inadequate Blasphemy Act of 1650, and confirm the extent of the Protectorate's tolerance and how much freedom of conscience it was willing to grant to people. The committee began examining Nayler on 15 November, and Parliament started to debate the findings of the committee's report on 5 December, putting aside for the moment their discussion about the future of the Protectorate and who would succeed Cromwell, should he die. The committee had concluded that Nayler had 'assumed the gesture, words, names, and attributes of our Saviour Christ', and that this was blasphemy. Parliament now had to agree with this charge, be convinced of Nayler's guilt and settle on an appropriate punishment.[67]

Parliament's discussions lasted for ten days. Such a protracted debate puzzled some. John Beale confessed to his friend Samuel Hartlib that he was 'much troubled to heare that the Parliament spent 5 [sic] days about a simple Quaker'.[68] It is at this moment that the famous parliamentary diarist enters the scene. Thomas Burton had been returned as MP for Westmorland in the summer of 1656 and, on 3 December, he began to note down in painstaking detail who was saying what inside the House of Commons (they were discussing Ireland, and the union with Scotland, first declared back in 1651). The nineteenth-century historian Thomas Carlyle thought Burton dull and verbose, but his dense accounts of the Protectorate Parliaments bring the chamber and its characters to life.[69] His documenting of the MPs wrangling with the case of James Nayler reveals the profound fear, and cruelty, that potential toleration of this growing sect – and any radical sects – could instil. Many found the Quakers dangerous, infectious, seditious.

Some clearly hoped that a high-profile examination, and punishment, of the Quakers' chief polemicist would break them. The issue they confronted was blasphemy – what it was, how to punish it – and whether they, as Parliament, even had the authority to judge and sentence Nayler. His inflammatory piece of theatre stalled the MPs.

There had been other so-called impersonations of Jesus. The prophet Arise Evans, for example, had been arrested following a (false) rumour that he believed he was Christ. He was dealt with swiftly, and leniently.[70] But Nayler did not think he was Christ. Madman he was not. And neither was he impersonating Christ. Despite his long, straggly hair, beard, horse and female disciples, Nayler believed that he was neither himself on that horse, nor Christ. He believed he was a symbol of the truth of Christ's second coming: 'I am set up as a sign to this nation, to bear witness of his coming,' Nayler told the bewildered MPs when he was called before them.[71] He had once written that his body was 'a fit temple for the pure God to dwell in', and when he rode into Bristol on his horse that day, he believed that his body had become such a vessel, and that Christ was now lodged within him.[72] He knew that it might not end well. Nayler's wealthy merchant friend Robert Rich said later that Nayler went to Bristol 'to receive his crucifixion'.[73] But the distinction between believing you are Christ and believing that you are inhabited by Christ was hard to draw – for Quakers as much as for non-Quakers. As Hannah and John Stranger told Nayler: 'Thy name is no longer to be called James, but Jesus.' And when Dorcas Erbury told everyone that Nayler had raised her from the dead in Exeter jail, Nayler did not deny it.[74]

Nayler's Bristol prank did not fit the 1650 Blasphemy Act. Some of the MPs claimed he ungodded God. Others saw Nayler as an attention-seeking impostor and thought his crime one of 'gross, thick, dark idolatry' rather than blasphemy.[75] Those who agreed it was blasphemy disagreed about the punishment. Bulstrode Whitelocke, always close to the letter of the law, pointed out that, according to the 1650 Blasphemy Act, the punishment was six months in prison, maximum. Other MPs denounced the Quakers as 'pests from the north' and as 'infectious as the plague'. They called on Parliament to seize the opportunity to make an example out of Nayler, and destroy the spreading disease. Major-General Philip Skippon claimed that Nayler's crime was not just 'blasphemy' but 'horrid blasphemy', and worthy of a harsher punishment. The unforgiving Major-General William Boteler demanded that Nayler be 'stoned to death', as blasphemers would have been under Moses' law. 'The magistrate is to be a terror unto evil works,' he added.[76] But most MPs were not monsters, and Burton's record of their debates shows how difficult, new and serious the case was, and how thoughtful some of the men were about judging Nayler's crime. God, after all, was watching. John Desborough, who knew Martha and had released Nayler from Exeter prison, cautioned the House for this was a 'weighty matter':

> We may offend as well in proceeding and sudden stepping into judgments; especially in matters that concern life, which, when taken, we cannot restore . . . This is the first occasion that ever we had of this nature, here. I would have us to do things so as to justify us, before both the face of God and the nation too.[77]

The MPs' sessions over the next ten days were heated, and they often ran on well beyond their usual end time of noon. They called for candles so that they could continue to argue into the dark winter afternoons and evenings. And while many expected Cromwell to dissolve this Parliament as soon as the minimum term of three months was up on 9 December, he did not do so. Cromwell did not attend the debates. It is not until later, once Nayler's sentence had been delivered, that we hear his voice. Burton does tell us, however, that Cromwell's son, Richard, had said over dinner one night that Nayler deserved to be hanged.[78]

Eventually the crime of blasphemy was ascertained and consented to by the House, and his punishment was resolved. On 17 December, Nayler was called to the bar. He was sentenced not to death (which he escaped narrowly by ninety-six votes to eighty-two), but to corporal punishment followed by imprisonment. On 18 December, Nayler was whipped on his back as he walked slowly from Westminster, along the Strand and into the City of London. People watched, but many were shocked by such a cruel display. After being allowed a brief period of recovery, Nayler was then branded on his forehead with a searingly hot 'B' for blasphemy, and his tongue was bored through with a hot iron. Now he could no longer preach. Finally, he was forced to repeat his ride into Bristol, but sitting on his horse backwards – a traditional shaming ritual. He was then escorted back to London, to Bridewell prison.[79] When the political tide turned again in 1659, Nayler was released, but he died soon after.

James Nayler's case tipped the Protectorate into an existential crisis. It brought to a head the issue that Cromwell and his government struggled to resolve: how tolerant to be of these new and independent sects which included not only the Quakers but also the Baptists, who followed their own consciences and challenged Church, government and law, and whose charisma and powers of persuasion proved seductive and comforting. Such religious fragmentation had accelerated in the 1640s when the country was at war and when, with the collapse of print censorship, ideas could spread far and wide. But extreme versions of Puritanism had been fomenting for much longer than that. They were, in many ways, an unsurprising consequence of the Protestant Reformation which had begun in Britain over a hundred years earlier. This difficult, complicated and gradual shift away from the beliefs and doctrines of the Catholic Church spawned a myriad of differently shaded beliefs about an individual's relationship with the divine, about sin, repentance and forgiveness, and about who was damned and who might, or could, be saved.

Nayler's case also stoked the crisis of authority that threatened the very existence of the Protectorate. This concerned the extent of the power of the House of Commons, and the Lord Protector's power over that House. Did Cromwell have, according to Lambert's Instrument of Government from 1653, the right to veto, or not? Did he as Protector, like Charles I believed of himself as king, possess a negative voice? On Christmas Day 1656 Sir Thomas Widdrington, the Speaker of the Commons, read out a letter of Cromwell's addressed to the House that contested the legitimacy of Nayler's conviction. 'Although we detest & abhorr the giving or occasioning the least Countenance to Persons of such Opinions & Practises, or who are under the Guilt of such Crymes,' Widdrington read, 'we being intrusted in the present Government on behalfe of the People of these nations . . . doe desire that the house will let us knowe the Grounds and Reasons whereupon they have proceeded.' The MPs remained silent.[80]

During the fraught debates about the Jews and the Quakers that divided the House, and the country, in 1655–6, Cromwell seemed to be teetering on the edge of exerting control. He was clearly in favour of admitting the Jews, and he was troubled by the intolerance of some of the MPs in the Nayler case, and by their swelling powers. But he held back, for the moment. The next year, 1657, would see England's experimental constitution turned upside down all over again. The Commons stood in need, Cromwell said, of 'a check, or ballancing Power'. This should be in the form of a second chamber, not exactly a restored House of Lords, but an 'other' house, 'soe constituted' to restrain the House of Commons. As Cromwell defended this proposal to a large gathering of sceptical army officers he warned them that 'the Case of James Nayler might happen to be your owne Case', and that he, as Protector under the existing constitution, did not have the ability to 'control' such a powerful House.[81]

With James Nayler in prison, the Quakers united behind their martyr. Meetings became more frequent, and more formalised. Nayler begged George Fox's forgiveness. Edward Burrough wrote that Nayler's fall was not 'an occasion to destroy his people' but one 'to try them'.[82] By 1660, there were approximately sixty thousand Quakers. The Restoration Parliament was no friend to them, pushing through the punishing Quaker Act in 1662. Thousands of Quakers, including George Fox and Margaret Fell, were imprisoned under Charles II for not conforming with the reinstated Church of England. In 1669, Fox married Margaret Fell (in Bristol of all places) and, two years later, he sailed to Barbados, and on to Jamaica to convince more Friends and challenge slavery. 'All are God's free people who walk in the truth,' he said.[83] As Fox left England he was waved off by none other than his friend and fellow Quaker William Penn, whose father had led the disastrous 1655 expedition to Hispaniola. In 1681, this younger William Penn was granted a large tract of land west of New York. Here he founded the colony of Pennsylvania and ensured that one of its governing principles was that of religious toleration.[84]

The Royalist William Davenant had reconciled himself to the republic. In 1650, this former playwright, chief masque-writer for Charles I and self-claimed bastard son of Shakespeare, who had lost half of his nose to syphilis, had tried to escape across the Atlantic to Royalist Virginia. The council of state sent ships to catch up with him before he left the English Channel and he was imprisoned in Cowes Castle on the Isle of Wight. After his release in 1652, Davenant had set about reviving his literary and dramatic career without annoying the authorities. Indeed, he offered his services as a poet. In 1653, before Oliver Cromwell had become Protector, Davenant had presented the then council of state with a manifesto, entitled *A Proposition for Advancement of Moralitie, by a New Way of Entertainment of the People*. The people, Davenant argued, needed theatre for their conduct and well-being, and the state needed theatre, if it wanted peace and order and good citizens. The gentry, he thought, including those Royalists confined to their formerly sequestered country estates, should be called back to London, and encouraged to spend money and circulate in society. Entertainment was sociable and civilising, and therefore could be a moral influence. It was also, of course, profitable, and could generate business for musicians, actors, set designers, even the tailors who would be commissioned to supply the gentry with the appropriately fine clothes in which they could be seen out and about at the theatre.[85]

In early 1656, Davenant wrote to secretary John Thurloe requesting permission to stage a production. 'The People of England', he wrote, 'are observ'd by writers of other nations and by our owne to require continual divertisements, being otherwise naturally inclin'd to that melancholy that breeds sedition.'[86] Thurloe was persuaded, and granted him the licence. For ten nights, beginning on 23 May 1656, from his own home, Rutland

House near modern-day Barbican, Davenant put on a musical show to test the climate and reassure the authorities. It was called *The First Days Entertainment*. The protectoral council sent along an agent to secretly watch the ninety-minute performance; he reported back favourably. A few songs were even sung at the end in praise of Cromwell.[87]

The first scene was ancient Greece, and the characters Diogenes (a 'discontented cynick' and Puritan, à la William Prynne) and Aristophanes (a comic playwright à la Davenant) debated the point of drama and pleasure. Their speeches were punctuated by musical interludes and songs composed by the brilliant former court musician Henry Lawes. The audience paid five shillings a head and sat on benches in Davenant's back room. For the reclusive Diogenes, poetry and drama were idle and vain. For the outgoing Aristophanes, theatre was just plain good for you. Poetry makes you happy, and music 'unites and recollects a broken and scattered mind'.[88] The second half of Davenant's show was completely different. The scene shifted to the modern day, and to a comic exchange between a Londoner and a Parisian who swapped insults about each other's cities. It was a homage to 1650s London: its inns, its dirty streets, over-hanging smog, low-roofed houses, heavy bread and comforting turns of phrase. Davenant's move from classical Athens to contemporary London staked out a shared culture. This is who we are, Davenant seemed to be telling the gentry stuffed into his makeshift theatre, and this is what we want to do: go out, be seen, spend money and believe, sincerely, that a new kind of entertainment has a place in a kingless state. Indeed, it is necessary.

Davenant's show was printed and reprinted. Within a few months, he felt brave enough to put on something bolder, and strikingly novel. His *Siege of Rhodes* is Britain's first full-length 'opera'.[89] It brought together a glittering company of known and rising musical and theatrical stars to tell the story of the Ottoman Empire's conquest of Rhodes in 1522. Henry Purcell's father sang the part of Mustapha the Turk. For the first time on a London public stage, the leading female part of Ianthe was played not by a cross-dressed boy but by an actress: Catherine Coleman. She was the daughter of Alfonso Ferrabosco, who had composed music for James I's opulent masques. John Webb, Inigo Jones's protégé, designed the scenery. The recitative and lilting arias were composed by Henry Lawes, Henry Cook and Matthew Locke. The Ottomans were topical at this point in the 1650s. Just a few months before the first performance of *The Siege of Rhodes*, the Venetians had defeated the Turks in a major battle at sea in their ongoing war. That summer, the Venetian diplomat Francesco Giavarina wrote home after a meeting with Cromwell to report that the Lord Protector seemed keen to seek a Christian alliance with the Venetian republic against their weakened Muslim enemy. Davenant had run his opera past his friend Bulstrode Whitelocke, who had some experience vetting appropriate entertainments as master of the revels at Middle Temple in the late 1620s.

By 1658 the successful *Siege of Rhodes* had transferred to the newly refurbished Cockpit theatre on Drury Lane. The Cockpit had survived the closure of theatres by falling into private hands (the Beeston family), and spectators could pay a shilling per ticket. A sequel followed in 1659, along with two other operas spinning tales of Protestant triumph and imperial expansion: *The Cruelty of the Spaniards* (1658) and *The History of Francis Drake* (1659). Davenant's operas continued to be popular in the Restoration. The diarist Samuel Pepys saw *The Siege of Rhodes* several times, and enjoyed reading it aloud with his wife. Under Charles II, Davenant went on to become London's foremost theatre manager. In 1662 he opened his Duke's Theatre and put on Shakespeare.[90]

Since a parliamentary order against plays in 1642, the plays of Shakespeare, and his fellow playwrights Christopher Marlowe, Ben Jonson, John Webster, Thomas Middleton and many more had been driven underground. Theatrical performances or shows popped up every now and then, such as at the Red Bull theatre in Clerkenwell or in private homes around the country. New editions of popular Elizabethan and Jacobean plays continued to be printed in the 1650s, to be read and enjoyed at home. In this godly decade, with theatres mostly closed, opera – born in the Italian Renaissance court and the most sensual and stylised of all art forms – took root and flourished. Even when things were particularly unsettled, Davenant's shows went on. In May 1659, when the Protectorate was falling apart, John Evelyn went to see a performance of 'a new Opera, after the Italian way'. It was probably Davenant's *History of Francis Drake*. Evelyn noted how unusual it was that, 'in a time of such a publique Consternation, such a Vanity should be kept up or permitted'.[91] The 1650s enabled opera, tolerated Jews and feared the Quakers. Such a mixture is encapsulated in a surviving 1656 book in George Thomason's collection. Bound together with *The Siege of Rhodes* is Jonathan Clapham's *A full discovery and confutation of the wicked and damnable doctrines of the Quakers*.[92]

1657

Mr Speaker in ye name of ye Parlt presented Seuerall thinges to his Highnes Viz.: a Robe of Purple Veluet Lined wth Ermine: a Large Bible Richly Guilt & Bossed: Next a Sword & Lastly a Septer of Massie Gold: and then administred ye Oath to his Highnesse: June 26: an: 1657:

'Tis not names or words that governe the world, but things.

Henry Cromwell to Lord Broghill,
April 1657

Roger Boyle, Lord Broghill, son of the wealthy first earl of Cork, had been working away on his romance, *Parthenissa*. He published his huge work in instalments, each gathered into little quarto volumes and snapped up from the bookstalls by readers. Broghill had begun writing his tale of the adventures of the king of Parthia, and his lover Parthenissa, at the end of the 1640s. He continued it while pursuing a political career, first as an MP for Cork, and then at the heart of the regime, for Cromwell in London in 1654, before becoming president of the protectoral council up in Edinburgh, in 1655–6.

Romances were all the rage. They were advertised in the newsbooks and written, and devoured, by men and women alike.[1] The romances Broghill had read while in France as a young man, tales of classical and imaginary heroes and heroines, had cured him of his dislike of reading fiction, and inspired him to write his own. Indeed, Broghill thought, anyone literary should know about romances. 'He who was Ignorant of the Romances', Broghill wrote, 'was as fitt an Object for Wonder, as a Phylosopher would be, who had never heard of Aristotle.'[2] He was not alone in his pursuit of romance. William Fiennes, Viscount Saye and Sele wrote one, as did Edmund Waller, about the recent civil wars; both are lost. Hobbes wrote a long preface for William Davenant's romance *Gondibert*. The Royalist Dorothy Osborne, Broghill's friend, was an avid reader of romance, enclosing instalments of *Parthenissa* and Madame de Scudéry's *Grand Cyrus* with her letters to her fiancé William Temple, instructing him to pass on the copies to her friends when he was finished. She was not that taken by Broghill's *Parthenissa*. She found her friend's style rather affected, and she noted his fondness for the word 'Ambition'd'.[3]

Romances were about ambition – in politics and in love. In a letter to the scientist Robert Boyle (Broghill's brother), the lawyer John Mallet wrote that romances were all about 'the mysteries of love, of state, of glory'.[4] A romance was often a *roman-à-clef*. Percy Herbert's *Cloria and Narcissus* was a loosely veiled Royalist tale about the civil wars, in which a good king (Charles) is wronged and led astray by ambitious counsellors. A hero's wanderings, random encounters and changes of fortune were well suited to capricious times. In no other genre, Herbert wrote, could 'the multiplicity of strange Actions of the Times be exprest, that exceeded all belief'.[5] Tales about kings and princesses were not always clearly Royalist, however. The republican Henry Stubbe believed that *Parthenissa* 'excellently debated the case of a Republick'.[6]

In 1657, Broghill's stories about kings, soldiers, friends and lovers resonated. During this year, Cromwell and his Parliament fought about legitimacy and loyalty, and 'the charms of a crown'.[7] They were debates which required political ideals and necessities to be weighed against personal desires and one's conscience. Romance-writing was not an indulgent hobby, tinkered at by educated, retired men and women in their country houses, but a way to think and engage politically. When Broghill read his friend (and Royalist spy) Abraham Cowley's epic poem about King David, *Davideis*, he was struck by how Jonathan passed his crown to his beloved friend David. Jonathan, the son of Saul, king of Israel, was the rightful heir, but he yielded his kingship to David.[8] Broghill was a key protagonist in the overwhelming drama of 1657: the 'great business' of the offer of the crown to Cromwell.

For the first half of this year Parliament was preoccupied with whether or not Cromwell should be crowned King Oliver I. In February 1657, the MP Anthony Morgan wrote to Cromwell's son Henry: 'Wee are now at that crisis which was expected.'[9]

In December 1649, Robert Boyle, the scientist, wrote to his brother Roger, Lord Broghill. He was pleased to know that his older brother's military successes alongside Cromwell on the Irish battlefields matched his literary ones, and that Broghill could be as eloquent in war as in love. 'I am not a little satisfyd to find', he wrote, that 'You have now given Romances as well Creditt as Reputation. Nor am I moderately pleas'd to see You as good at reducing Townes in Munster as Assyria, & to find Your Eloquence as prevalent with Masters of Garrisons as Mistresses of harts.'[10] Robert, too, had tried his hand at romance-writing, before he became enamoured of chemistry.

The brothers were born in Ireland at Lismore Castle, a former bishop's palace and the seat of the wealthy and influential first earl of Cork, Richard Boyle. Cork was an early Protestant settler from England, and he was shrewd and ambitious. He travelled to Ireland with the Irish chancellor of the exchequer in 1588, the year of the Armada. He was twenty-two years old and he carried a gold bracelet and a diamond ring in his luggage. He bought up land, including Sir Walter Raleigh's extensive estates in Munster. On the day of James I's coronation, 25 July 1603, Richard Boyle was knighted, and made earl of Cork in 1620. He died in 1643, leaving eleven children to resist the rebelling Catholic Irish and navigate the burning political landscape of Ireland in the 1640s. When civil war in England broke out, the eldest son and heir,

Richard, remained loyal to Charles I, and Parliament seized his estates. Richard fled into exile in France.[11]

But Roger, one of his younger brothers, switched sides. In 1649, Broghill led forces in Munster for Cromwell, and persuaded his Anglo-Irish Protestant neighbours to support the parliamentarian victors. Cromwell and Broghill had marched through Munster together in a triumphal progress. In his reports back to Westminster Cromwell praised Broghill as 'eminently serviceable', although he did not reward him with the lord presidency of Munster. That went to Cromwell's son-in-law, Henry Ireton. During the harsh winter of 1649–50, Broghill had hosted an exhausted and unwell Cromwell at his family's home, the Old College, in Youghal. Once Cromwell had left Ireland, Broghill fought alongside Cromwell's son, Henry. The two became close, particularly when Henry was made chief administrator in Dublin. Broghill was rewarded with plenty of Irish land for his loyalty to the republic.[12]

Broghill's persuasiveness, his network of friends in Ireland, Scotland and England, which included Royalists, Presbyterians and Cromwellians, and his desire to effect reconciliation between men of differing beliefs, in the name of peace and settlement, would become his survival tactic during the 1650s. As president of the protectoral council in Scotland, in 1655–6, he worked with General George Monck – he who had once fought for Charles I, but then alongside Cromwell at Dunbar, in 1651. Together, Monck and Broghill sought to establish a civilian rather than a military regime in Scotland, building bridges with Royalists and Presbyterians in an effort to secure loyalty to the government in England. In her vivid memoirs, the Royalist Anne Murray, Lady Halkett from Fife, recalled, in between writing about her affairs of the heart, how Broghill and his wife (Margaret Howard, sister to the earl of Suffolk) always showed 'civility . . . to all the Royallists'. Many of them knew each other well from before the wars.[13]

Once reconciled with his Royalist elder brother, Richard, Broghill intervened to help him recover his confiscated Irish houses. He petitioned on behalf of other Irish friends and he pushed hard for a formal union between England and Ireland, believing this was in Ireland's best interests. Settlement, he believed, would come from uniting England, Ireland and Scotland, and from reducing the sway of the army in all three countries. He worked for what he thought was best for Ireland's old Protestants, and in his own best interests, and he always sought to preserve his family's fortunes. He believed in the hand of providence, and thought that Cromwell's office was part of God's plan. Broghill, too, was broadly tolerant, although hostile to Quakers and Baptists. He was against the punishing rule of the major-generals, whose continuation Parliament debated furiously in January 1657 – and eventually rejected. Broghill urged the MPs to think carefully. 'This is such a Bill as was never brought into a Parliament,' he said. And, of the Royalists: 'I believe that party are as bad as can be, but let us not be wicked also.'[14] He was not popular with senior army men like John Lambert, or with Ireland's lord deputy, Charles Fleetwood. Neither was he liked by those against the Protectorate and angling for a fully republican settlement, like Henry Vane. Otherwise, he was good friends with many at the heart of Cromwell's regime, men such as Bulstrode Whitelocke, who found him a man 'of great witt, learning & civillity'. And Cromwell liked and trusted Broghill, and his family.

One of Broghill's younger sisters was Katherine Jones, Lady Ranelagh. She was an intelligent, talented and much-admired character, later eulogised as 'the greatest Figure in all the Revolutions of these Kingdoms'.[15] Perhaps this was because she was so thoroughly connected to such a wide range of people and revolutionary concerns: to Irish, Scottish and Westminster personnel and politics; to social, cultural and religious reformation; to scientific progress. She seemed to move easily between royal circles, the Cromwellian court and radical republicans. During the wars she had found Charles I obstinate in his refusal to acknowledge Parliament, but she corresponded regularly with his younger sister, Elizabeth, the exiled queen of Bohemia. She was also friends with Edward Hyde, Charles II's close adviser and future earl of Clarendon. Another Boyle brother, Viscount Shannon, was, bizarrely, raising his wife's daughter by Charles II.[16] Meanwhile, John Milton believed Katherine to be 'exemplary'.[17]

At the age of fifteen Katherine had married Arthur Jones, a gambler and a drinker. Their marriage was not a happy one. In the early 1640s, after the Irish rebellion, Katherine left him and fled to England with her children, settling in London. She employed Milton to tutor her young son, Richard. She had access to Cromwell, and was able to petition him directly to recover her family's estates and secure a better salary for her brother, Lord Broghill. She was friends with the republican Henry Vane and was liked enormously by Samuel Hartlib, with whom she corresponded regularly, sharing many of the Hartlib circle's utopian ideas and innovative schemes. Hartlib thought her 'incomparable' and thoroughly committed to reformation.[18] Like Hartlib, Katherine was responsible for the ceaseless circulation of ideas about how to improve agricultural practices, reform children's education, rethink the economy or revolutionise law. She taught herself Hebrew and had hosted Menasseh ben Israel at her home in Chelsea when he was petitioning for the readmission of the Jews to England. She corresponded with French intellectuals and sheltered European Protestant refugees. Katherine was also hugely knowledgeable about medicine. Her letters detailed her own cures and recipes, sometimes enclosing a draft of some medicine that she had made up herself. She regularly asked her younger brother Robert to send her chemicals from his Dorset laboratory. The Boyles are an example of a tight-knit Anglo-Irish family who settled in England in the 1640s, maintained contacts among the elite and straddled the political and religious divisions of the 1650s. In what Robert Boyle called 'an Age so taken with Novelties as ours', the three siblings – Broghill, Robert Boyle and Lady Ranelagh – responded to the times by embracing innovation and experimentation of all kinds.[19]

By 1657, Robert, the youngest of the three, was living in Oxford. There he and a group of like-minded natural philosophers set modern science in motion, pursuing the empirical method that Francis Bacon had dreamed of earlier in the century. Every Thursday afternoon, the Experimental Philosophy Club met in John Wilkins's rooms at Wadham College. The hospitable and genial Dr Wilkins had gathered around him a group of young and talented scientists and thinkers. Wilkins had been warden of Wadham since 1648, a young Puritan chaplain appointed by the parliamentary committee tasked with purging the university of Royalists, or malignants. At the age of twenty-four, inspired by Galileo, Wilkins had published *The Discovery of a World in the Moone*, in which he speculated that there may be life on the moon, and that it may one day be reached by a chariot able to break free of the magnetic field of the Earth.[20]

Along with Robert Boyle, Wilkins's fellow experimental philosophers included a young and ambitious Christopher Wren and the ingenious mechanic Robert Hooke. John Locke, then a promising undergraduate at Christ Church (and a fan of French romances) was also acquainted with the club. Not all members were attached to the university: Boyle was not, and neither was the local cidermaker, Ralph Austen, whose alcohol and 1653 book on fruit trees and orchards were so popular. In 1656, Wilkins had married Robina Cromwell, Oliver Cromwell's widowed youngest sister. The couple enjoyed lodgings at Whitehall. Wilkins became close to Richard Cromwell, who had succeeded his father as chancellor of the university in 1657, but Wilkins was no sycophant and he resisted some of the government's more radical reforms for the university. In John Evelyn's words, Wilkins was 'most obliging & universaly Curious'. At Wadham he planted a botanical garden, installed beehives with a glass panel, so the bees could be observed, and exhibited a dizzying range of instruments and machines that he and Christopher Wren made: clocks, sundials, thermometers, magnifying glasses and telescopes, talking statues, a way-wiser (a pocket watch that could count your steps, like a seventeenth-century Fitbit). Evelyn, who counted Wilkins as his 'excellent & deare Friend', marvelled at his collection of 'magical curiosities', and was pleased to be given one of his beehives, which he took back to his own garden at Sayes Court.[21]

The philosophers' interests were wide – air, light, blood, astronomy, horticulture, mathematics and machines. Their aim was to understand all of nature, and to study it by induction and careful observation, rather than by abstract reasoning. As Seth Ward, Wadham's professor of astronomy and Wilkins's close friend, wrote, their club's aim was to 'make inquisitive experiments'. They hoped that 'out of a sufficient number of sure experiments, the way of nature in workeing may be discovered'.[22] Each member of the club paid a subscription, which enabled them to acquire chemicals, apparatus and instruments that they could all share. Experiments were agreed on and commissioned at their weekly meetings. They established a laboratory and, on top of Wadham College tower, they built an observatory. From there, Wilkins and Wren used the twenty-four-foot telescope they had made to observe Saturn, whose moon had only just been discovered by the Dutchman Christian Huygens in 1655.

The members' political and religious leanings were mixed, and, for this group, irrelevant. In 1644, Seth Ward had been ejected from his fellowship at Cambridge for refusing to consent to the Solemn League and Covenant, and Christopher Wren came from a Royalist, Anglican family who had been close to Charles I. Wren's father had been the dean of Windsor before being expelled by Parliament in 1643. His uncle, Matthew, former bishop of Ely, had been locked up in the Tower of London since 1642 for actively resisting Puritan forms of worship. Robert Hooke attended secret Anglican services in the physician Thomas Willis's rooms at Christ Church. But they were first and foremost a 'Knot of . . . Ingenious & free Philosophers'.[23] Of himself, Boyle told John Evelyn that he was 'addicted to experimentall learning'.[24]

Robert Boyle never disclosed his thoughts on Cromwell. Like his brother Lord Broghill, he favoured stability and settlement. He suggested that he believed a republic rather than a monarchy would better support the advancement of virtue (and therefore perhaps of science), because such a society would be less overshadowed by the glory of kings, and reward merit. 'Heroical Men ar more frequently (for the most part)', he wrote, 'in Commonwelths then in Monarchys: not that they ar more frequently born there; but partly because that in . . . Republickes the way to honour and preferment lys more open to desert, which is a quickning Spur and a great incitement.'[25] Boyle's addiction to 'reall

Learning', and his detailed, replicable and trustworthy documentation of his experiments, earned him the epithet the father of modern science. He was deeply pious, and his penetrating enquiry into the nature of things was inseparable from his religious faith. In the intense and bloody summer of 1649, when Cromwell was storming Ireland, Boyle had had an epiphany. To study the natural world was to study, and know, the divine. At the same time, scientific research was increasingly believed to be of immense social and economic value. Henry Oldenburg, to whom Boyle had been introduced by his devoted sister, Katherine, and who would go on to become secretary of the Royal Society, believed Boyle could be 'for the good of the learned Commonwealth'.[26] Not everyone agreed. The fiercely republican James Harrington quipped that the Oxford experimental scientists were 'good at two Things, at diminishing a Commonwealth and at Multiplying a Louse'.[27]

Boyle had moved to Oxford in 1655–6. Dr Wilkins lured Boyle from his home-made laboratory at Stalbridge Manor in Dorset to join what Oldenburg dubbed 'the Oxonian sparkles'. Boyle, six feet tall, temperate and frugal, according to John Aubrey, brought money as well as experience; he was able to practise science and support others to do so thanks to the substantial income of £3,000 per year from the rent on his estates in Dorset and Ireland, which his father the earl of Cork had given to him. Boyle also brought connections. He was part of a world of restless innovators that bound the Oxford club to the intelligence hubs of his sister Katherine and to those of Samuel Hartlib.

Once in Oxford, Boyle took lodgings with a well-known Oxford apothecary, John Crosse, on the High Street. He set up a chemistry laboratory – no doubt stocked with chemicals supplied by Crosse. He soon shared his rooms with a young student from the Isle of Wight, Robert Hooke. Hooke had been spotted and nurtured by John Wilkins. Hooke was a skilled draughtsman and dextrous instrument-maker, and he began to work closely with Boyle at this time, designing and making the sophisticated equipment needed for Boyle's experiments. With his friend Christopher Wren, Hooke made microscopes. He spent time carefully drawing what he saw underneath the glass, from urine particles to insects. Hooke coined the term 'cell', and his exquisite, detailed drawings of fleas and ants would be published in his *Micrographia*, the first ever book on microscopy. He went on to work with Wren on designing the streets of London after the Great Fire of 1666, and later he famously argued with Isaac Newton about the originality of his ideas about gravity.[28]

In the laboratory with Boyle in Oxford in the 1650s, Hooke worked on saltpetre, copper and air. They discussed Descartes, and when Boyle's illness affected his ability to see and write, Hooke helped. In these years, Hooke designed and made his celebrated air pump, which enabled Boyle to prove the existence of a vacuum and study, for the first time, the properties of air. Hooke's ingenuity was to make a glass dome, rather than a copper one, which meant that he and Boyle could place objects inside this dome, and then watch what happens when the air is sucked out. Candles flickered, a butterfly fell as though in a swoon, a lark collapsed. Boyle did not know that it was oxygen that was needed – this would not be discovered for another hundred years – but he knew that air was necessary, and that a vacuum was possible. In the 1660s, visitors would flock to watch his air-pump experiments at the Royal Society. Hobbes quibbled about vacuums, and questioned the integrity of Boyle's pump. Boyle also worked out that air could be compressed, and that it could expand. It had a 'spring', he said, like sheep's fleece scrunched up into a ball, and then released.[29] Perhaps he thought of sheep because hanging above him in his laboratory were rows of lamb bladders, which he would pump full of air in order to investigate pressure. And so Boyle also proved that the pressure of a gas is inversely proportionate to its volume, what we call 'Boyle's law'.

All this work, and writing, of Boyle and Hooke and the others began in Oxford in the 1650s in a climate of inclusive curiosity and commitment to experiment and to the social good of science. It was enabled by technological advances and by the work of generations of scientists beforehand, at home and in Europe. The disruption and displacement caused by the wars, or the republic, did not hinder such study. In many ways, the new political circumstances of the Commonwealth enabled these innovative and free philosophers. Without Wilkins's appointment, or 'intrusion', as warden of Wadham in 1648, these men would not have met and collaborated. Without the penalties imposed on those loyal to the Stuarts and hostile to Puritanism, some of these men from Royalist families, like the young Christopher Wren, might not have stayed in Oxford but pursued careers in the Church instead.[30] Finally, without these men's commitment to their scientific endeavour rather than to political ideals, some of them may not have survived the end of the republic.

In 1659, Wilkins was headhunted to become master of Trinity College, Cambridge. Two years earlier, Christopher Wren had been appointed, with Cromwell's approval, to the chair in astronomy at Gresham College in London, another hub of scientific activity connected to the Oxford group. The Experimental Philosophy Club's meetings moved to London, sometimes gathering in taverns, sometimes at Gresham College. It was in 1660, at a lecture of Wren's, that Wilkins suggested to his fellow philosophers that they should formalise their meetings and seek patronage for their work. Two years later, the Royal Society was formed. The scientific revolution of the seventeenth century has traditionally been associated with the restoration of Charles II and his patronage of the Royal Society. The Society's ties to Cromwellian Oxford and Wilkins's Experimental Club were suppressed, despite the fact that many members of this club went on to become the elected fellows of the Royal Society. Robert Boyle himself remained in Oxford well into the 1660s, working and publishing profusely. He travelled frequently to London, to perform public experiments at the Royal Society and defend his method and discoveries from attacks by Hobbes and other critics. He never married and, in 1668, he moved to live with his devoted sister Katherine in her house on Pall Mall, where he built a new laboratory. Visitors flocked to meet the chemist whom John Evelyn described as 'one of the most valuable Objects of our Nation'.[31]

Early in 1657, reeling from the James Nayler episode, it was time for Parliament to confront, once again, the constitution. The first Protectorate Parliament had never approved the Instrument of Government – and consequently Cromwell had dismissed his MPs in January 1655. A second Parliament was called in September 1656; those elected had to accept Cromwell as Protector before they could take their seats. Settlement, stability and survival were uppermost in MPs' minds. Disruptive Quakers, threats of conspiracies at home and Royalist plots from abroad, plus Cromwell's age – he was only in his late fifties but he was often unwell – made many fearful for the Protectorate's future. A new Treason Act in November dealt with would-be traitors, ensuring that attempts against the Lord Protector's life, or even imagining his death, would be punishable as high treason, as if Cromwell were a king.[32] But it was not clear what would happen should Cromwell die. The Instrument of Government from 1653 stated that it would be up to the council to elect a new 'fit person', but the reality of such an election would be fraught with difficulty and danger. Major-General John Lambert's own desire to succeed Cromwell as Lord Protector was widely, but unfairly, rumoured. For those hostile to the continued presence and influence of the army in the country's politics – Lord Broghill chief among them – Lambert's succession (as the army's darling) would be intolerable.[33]

In October 1656, the Irish MP and Broghill's friend Major-General William Jephson had unexpectedly raised a motion suggesting that the House should debate the succession again – and that perhaps it should be hereditary, rather than elective. This, Thurloe said, was batted away. But succession continued to be raised both in and outside the chamber that autumn – although the journal of the House of Commons remains silent about it.[34] It was gossiped about by ambassadors and railed against by army officers. In December, the Royalist agent Silius Titus told Hyde, earl of Clarendon, that 'there are great disputes about the Government, whether it shall be successive or elective, the soldiery part of the howse are for the latter, the Court partie (as they distinguish them) for the former'.[35] Some clearly thought that a hereditary Protectorate would mean making Cromwell a king. Francesco Giavarina, the Venetian ambassador, reported back to Venice in late September that Cromwell might soon be 'raised to the dignity of king'. Earlier in the summer the Swedish ambassador, Christer Bonde, had informed Charles X of Sweden that 'it seems likely that in the course of this parliament his highness will become king'.[36] Cromwell's stance against hereditary rule was well known, and he had had to argue against it before. In January 1655 he had quoted Ecclesiastes to his MPs to illustrate his absolute rejection of 'that Hereditary way', for 'who knoweth whether he may begat a Fool or Wise?'[37] But history had shown how much the English favoured hereditary succession, even when kings or councillors tried to bypass it, and even when the rightful heirs were female and Catholic, as was the case with Mary I.

In January 1657, the last-minute discovery of an assassination plot concentrated minds on Cromwell's mortality, and the Tudor problem of the succession. On 8 January, a group of anti-Protectorate conspirators attempted to burn Whitehall down – an echo of the Gunpowder Plot. Miles Sindercombe, a former soldier and Leveller, was the ringleader. He had been encouraged by a fellow Leveller, Colonel Edward Sexby, whom he had met in exile in Brussels. Sexby used Royalist connections (Levellers and cavaliers were uneasy bedfellows, but came together with Cromwell as a shared enemy), and he had Spanish money. He found the conspirators a house to rent in Westminster, and bought horses, harquebuses and pistols, which he hid in a violin case – a not uncommon item to be carrying around in 1650s London. To Sexby, and others, Cromwell was a tyrant, and his murder was justifiable.[38]

There were several assassination attempts before the January plot. A member of Cromwell's lifeguard, John Toope, had been recruited to disclose Cromwell's movements. Sindercombe had planned to shoot the Protector when he was on his way to Hampton Court one weekend, or when out riding in Hyde Park, or during the state opening of Parliament in September. They then decided to set fire to Whitehall. But Toope turned on his fellow conspirators and exposed their latest plot. In the chapel at Whitehall, underneath Cromwell's private apartments, a basket of brimstone, match and gunpowder was found. Sindercombe and his co-conspirator John Cecil were arrested. The third conspirator, William Boyes, escaped. Cecil confessed and was taken on by Thurloe as a double agent. Sindercombe remained resolute. He was found guilty of treason and sentenced to be hanged, drawn and quartered. Rather than face this public, brutal death, he killed himself in his cell in the Tower of London. He left a note that read: 'I would not have all the open shame of the world executed upon my Body.'[39] Poison had probably been laced into a handkerchief that was smuggled into his cell the night before his execution by three women, who claimed to be his two sisters and a 'sweetheart'. Sindercombe was given a suicide's burial on Tower Hill: an iron stake was driven through his naked body and down into the ground, a warning to potential traitors. The pamphlet that was soon published and told the whole story of Sindercombe's plot was another such warning.[40] A few days later, on 20 February, Cromwell held a celebratory and lavish feast in Whitehall's Banqueting House as a thanksgiving for his life. MPs ate, drank and were entertained with music and singing. For many of the guests, the Protector's survival was also their own.[41]

Sindercombe's plot highlighted how vulnerable Cromwell and his Protectorate were. Kings were mortals but kingship lived on. It was not certain that the office of Protector would live if Cromwell did not. The poet Andrew Marvell had, typically, foreseen this. After Cromwell survived a freak coaching accident in Hyde Park in 1654, Marvell (in a poem commemorating the anniversary of the Protectorate) imagined things should Cromwell have been trampled to death by his horses that day. Screams ricocheted through the corridors of Whitehall, 'the earth did from the centre tear' and the sun fell out of the sphere. The centre could not hold.[42] To many, it was Cromwell alone who bore the weight of the Protectorate on his shoulders, and kept the state in motion.

On 19 January 1657, John Thurloe told Parliament about Miles Sindercombe and the 'heinous' plot they had foiled. The issue of the succession immediately came up. John Ashe, MP for Somerset and a veteran parliamentarian, mooted a return to what he called 'the ancient constitution'. This was provocative. Surely you do not mean, Samuel Hyland warned, to make Cromwell 'the greatest hypocrite in the world', and to associate him with the idolatry and superstition that God himself had 'borne testimony against'? 'The old constitution is Charles Stuart's interest,' the republican (and sympathetic justice) Luke Robinson said. 'I hope we are not calling him in again.' George Downing, future reformer of the Treasury and the name behind Downing Street, thought the matter worth weighing seriously. The 'old and tried foundation', he said, might keep everyone safer. And then, the parliamentary diarist Thomas Burton reported with a rare use of an adjective, this 'hot' debate fell asleep. Nothing more was said for a whole month. It just vanished, like an 'ignis fatuus', a will-o'-the-wisp.[43] Instead, MPs turned to debating John Desborough's Militia Bill – should the reign of the major-generals continue, or not – and to raising desperately needed funds for the ongoing war with Spain. Jamaica, where the English had been since the summer of 1655, was still not fully secured as a colony. The MPs voted against the major-generals, but approved money for the war.

Behind the scenes, however, the issue of the succession was definitely not asleep. Lord Broghill and his friends, Bulstrode Whitelocke, Edward Montagu, John Glynne, John Thurloe, Nathaniel Fiennes and others, all dubbed 'Cromwell's creatures' by the republican army officer Edmund Ludlow, were hatching a plan.[44] A month later, in the afternoon of 23 February, the former lord mayor and the recently knighted Sir Christopher Packe presented Parliament, quite out of the blue, with a brand new constitutional proposal. This 'Remonstrance' had, Packe said somewhat disingenuously, 'somewhat come to His hand'. He had not, he whispered to his neighbour, even read it. It was widely rumoured to be the work of the romance-writer Roger Boyle, Lord Broghill.[45]

It was three o'clock and the weak February daylight was draining away when the MPs were asked whether they would stay to hear Packe's Remonstrance read out. Many clearly wanted to go home, knowing the contents of this petition would be difficult and divisive. But candles were called for and, as the evening drew in, the MPs heard, with some urgency, how Oliver Cromwell should now be pleased to 'assume the name, style, title, dignity and office of king of England, Scotland and Ireland'.[46]

There had been hopes and fears about crowning Cromwell before. John Lambert's Instrument of Government had originally suggested king as a title. Cromwell had refused what John Milton called a 'haughty' title but one that still seemed 'so great in the opinion of the mob'.[47] In 1655, the poet George Wither had also lamented the people's apparent desire for 'that Thing / Which, formerly, these Nations call'd a King'. The title, Wither argued, was irrelevant: 'It is the Man, that dignifies the Name,' he said.[48]

But in February 1657, amid rumours that Charles II was planning a new uprising, the title, the word – 'that Thing' – suddenly mattered a lot. Despite the fact that, in 1649, Parliament had abolished dangerous monarchy and the unnecessary House of Lords, Packe's Remonstrance now argued that the ancient constitution of king, Lords and Commons was best. Kingship suited the English temperament, the Remonstrance stated. It was what the English people knew, and liked. It was a title that would prevent further blood and confusion and could withstand 'the continual danger' to Cromwell's life. It would, therefore, guarantee security in the three nations. There was no chance that Charles II could claim the resurrected title of king as his own, for a bill passed in the autumn had ensured that the Stuarts were forever 'absolutely and utterly excluded and debarred from holding or enjoying the Crown of England, Scotland, and Ireland'.[49] Security, however, would not be guaranteed through the title passing automatically from Cromwell to his eldest son, Richard. After the previous autumn's debates about whether the Protectorate should be elective or hereditary, the Remonstrance nowhere mentioned that the title of king would remain in the house of Cromwell. And neither would this be an elective monarchy. Instead the Remonstrance proposed that the title would be perpetual through nomination; it would be up to King Oliver to nominate his successor at some point before he died.

This was a radical version of kingship. The architects of the Remonstrance – Broghill and the 'kinglings', as critics called them – had unyoked the word 'king' from its hereditary principle.[50] They framed this constitutional proposal as a return to the past, to the ancient constitution, but the kind of kings that Cromwell and his successors were being imagined as would lack the blood and divinity that had, since early medieval times, set kings and queens apart. The young Charles II, struggling in exile, believed that even though he was not an anointed king, he could still cure the sick on account of his royal blood. While the kinglings held that it was God who had preserved Cromwell's body during the wars, Cromwell would not be a sacred king. He would not be the Lord's anointed. The Remonstrance did not even mention a 'crown'. Broghill and his fellow kinglings were surely hoping to smuggle in hereditary succession by the back door. They were gambling on the chance that, once king, Cromwell would, in time, nominate his eldest son, Richard, as his successor, and hence the house of Cromwell, and a new kind of monarchy, would be established. But in February 1657, Cromwell – a commoner – stood to be inaugurated as something new.

The MPs' response to Packe's Remonstrance was, on that dark February afternoon, predictably heated. John Lambert, Thomas Burton records, was violently against this proposal, which undermined his Instrument of Government of 1653 and diluted the sway of the army. Some believed that it threatened Lambert's own chances of being made Protector. Cromwell's brother-in-law Major-General John Desborough and son-in-law Charles Fleetwood, lord deputy of Ireland, were also opposed, as were Cromwell's councillors, friends and household staff Gilbert Pickering and Walter Strickland. But there were many in favour. Judges and lawyers were mostly keen since 'king' was the title used in English law – not that this had bothered them before now. The split was broadly, but not wholly, between civilians such as Broghill, loyal to Cromwell but hostile to the army, and appalled senior army officers. It was not to reinstate a king that they and their men had fought on the battlefields. They talked openly about their dislike of the proposal.[51] There were those on the margins of Westminster politics who were as much against Cromwell as Protector, as king. For the republican Henry Vane, both a king and a Protector were ungodly, and jeopardised the spiritual health of the Commonwealth. Arthur Hesilrige, excluded from taking his seat in Parliament after the 1656 elections for challenging the Protectorate earlier in that year, was also outraged. So was the republican Lucy Hutchinson, who loathed what she called Cromwell's pocket Parliaments.[52] These commonwealthmen, and women, wished for a fully republican settlement, with no single person at its head.

For the whole of March 1657, Parliament debated and amended Packe's Remonstrance before presenting it to Cromwell. The

House was full and the sessions were long and demanding. Lord Broghill was considered 'prudent and dexterous' by MP John Bridges.[53] The Remonstrance was not just about the title of king – and the MPs could not face debating this clause until the very end. They also had to agree on the powers of Parliament, the extent of the regime's religious tolerance and the proposition of a new second House – Cromwell's wish for a 'check' on the power of the Commons following their judgement of the Quaker James Nayler's case. They agreed that the people's representatives in Parliament could not be Royalists or Catholics, but that no Members could be excluded from taking their seats without Parliament's approval. They agreed that Parliament, and not the Protector, made laws and set taxes, and that Parliament should approve those who sat on the Protector's council. The Protector would still be commander-in-chief, but the army could only be deployed with Parliament's consent. A Confession of Faith was agreed to, which opened the way to the establishment of a national Church. This appeased Presbyterian MPs. Laws against religious radicals, such as the Quakers, were to be tightened, meaning that the Protectorate would become a little less tolerant. MPs consented fairly easily to the restoration of a second House of Parliament – called simply the 'Other House' for want of a better name. They conceded that Cromwell would be allowed to nominate the Members of this Other House, who would hold their seats for life. But new Members, even if they already happened to be peers, could not pass on the privilege to their eldest sons. This would not be a hereditary chamber like the old House of Lords. Here was another new cloak for England's 'ancient' constitution.[54]

On the matter of the succession – the issue that had unsettled the House in the previous autumn – the Remonstrance's proposal that Cromwell should nominate his successor passed surprisingly easily. As William Jephson told Henry Cromwell, it met 'very little opposition' and this, Jephson added, boded well for an easy passage for the title of king.[55] But the House did not actually start debating the title of king for another three weeks. The agreed mode of succession did not, it turned out, have to be hinged to the title of king. On 24 March, the door of St Stephen's Chapel was firmly shut and no Member was allowed to leave without permission. Now the MPs would decide whether Cromwell should be called king, or not. It was, the Irish MP Sir John Reynolds relayed to Henry Cromwell, a 'pitcht battell' over a word. On the one side were Broghill and Whitelocke; on the other side, Lambert and Desborough.[56] After two days of fraught and 'bitter speeches', on 25 March the MPs agreed with a clear majority of 123 votes to 62 that Cromwell should indeed be named king.[57]

On 31 March, at eleven o'clock in the morning, Cromwell and the MPs gathered in the Banqueting House. There the agreed constitutional proposal, redrafted by Broghill and a committee, bound in vellum and named as the 'Humble Petition and Advice', was formally presented to Cromwell. Henry Scobell, the Commons' clerk, read it out, article by article. Speaker Thomas Widdrington spoke at length in its defence, and about the title of king. Quoting from Ovid's *Metamorphoses*, Widdrington presented Parliament's new constitution as a metamorphosed body: it was essentially the same, just in a slightly different form and with a new name. Parliament liked the body well – the Commons and the Other House – and they approved of the head. They just did not like the title 'Protector'. They wanted something that was familiar and known, and which had ancient biblical roots. They wanted a title that was known in law, and that was, importantly, understood to be *below* and not above the law. They wanted a king. This new frame of government was, Widdrington said, a 'medley or mixture of regality and liberty'. He then warned Cromwell that he had to accept the entire frame; he could not take it apart bit by bit for 'like a building well knit and cemented, if one stone be taken out, it loosens the whole'.[58] The head of this political body, therefore, had to be named king.

Cromwell – who had had sight of the Humble Petition a few days before this formal presentation – thanked Parliament, and asked to be given time to consult God and consider this 'thing . . . of weight, the greatest weight of any thing that was ever laid before a man'.[59] Cromwell was perhaps imagining the literal weight of a jewelled crown.

There was much that Cromwell praised in the Humble Petition. He was delighted with the Other House and his powers of nomination over its Members, and he welcomed its stance on religious toleration. In general, he considered Parliament's work a 'song of reconciliation'.[60] The title of king was, Cromwell had tried to reassure his army officers back in February, only a name, a mere 'feather in a Hatt'.[61] But it could not be both as light as a feather and a thing of weight. Cromwell took a few days to respond to Parliament, and when he did so, on 3 April, he told them that he could not be king. The title 'do stick with me', he said, before continuing: 'I have not ben able to finde in my duty to God & you, to undertake this Charge under that Tytle . . . it is my Conscience that Guides me.'[62]

Parliament fought back. It appointed a committee of ninety-nine and tasked them with persuading Cromwell to change his mind, and to report back on their meetings to the House. Broghill was a key spokesman on this committee, and he and his fellow members, who included Bulstrode Whitelocke (as chair), William Lenthall, Nathaniel Fiennes and John Glynne, urged Cromwell to reconsider. They met five times between 8 and 21 April and besieged him with lengthy speeches. To them, 'king' was not just a name or a feather in a cap. It 'carries more in it of weight than a meer title', Lenthall told Cromwell. He went on: 'The whole body of the Law is carried upon this Wheel.' But Lenthall also struggled to fully express the power of the title, falling back on the inarticulate 'thing': 'It is not a thing that stands on the top meerly.'[63] Broghill's speeches before Cromwell at these meetings were focused on the power of Parliament and on the law. He reminded Cromwell that this was Parliament's advice, and that it carried 'very great force and authority'. This was kingship created by Parliament, and Parliament, Broghill told Cromwell, had 'pitched' upon the title of king because it was a title which 'the law takes notice of'.[64] It was a title of which Parliaments had approved for hundreds of years. It was a title, too, that had divine approbation, and, he argued, providence was guiding Parliament. 'King' was a title and an office that subjects recognised, and would obey, and which would therefore effectively subdue the Royalists. But 'king', according to Broghill and the kinglings' arguments, was not synonymous with unbounded powers and privileges. Recalling the fraught debates between Charles I and his MPs in the 1640s, a king according to England's 'ancient constitution' was, to parliamentarians at least, an office that was limited and bound by the law. A king was more manageable, more containable than a Protector, whose powers were nowhere written down and circumscribed, said Broghill.[65] It was a title which, Glynne said, was 'as bounded as any acre of land'.[66] This may have been exactly what Cromwell did not want to hear. There were those republican critics, like Henry Vane or Edmund Ludlow, who believed Cromwell to be ambitious and greedy, and who, they thought, enjoyed the rather blurry powers of a Protector – and would therefore reject the more bounded office of king.

Cromwell deliberated and bought himself time. Meetings were postponed with the excuse of a cold. Broghill and his fellow spokesmen turned up only to be sent away. Sometimes Cromwell appeared half-dressed, a scarf wound around his neck, clearly suffering. He called informal evening meetings, inviting Broghill, Whitelocke and Thurloe to his private rooms in Whitehall. There they would spend hours, late into the night, advising him, allaying his doubts and scruples, and when not doing this, smoking tobacco, or occasionally writing verses.[67] Cromwell's own councillors, and household, were divided. There was also clearly pressure from opposing army generals, including Cromwell's close adviser John Lambert. He asked his chaplains, John Owen among them, to pray with him to help him seek the answer. There were some 'dark speeches' in which Cromwell told Broghill and the others of the great grief and trouble he was under.[68] He invoked God and providence, the years of civil war and the final image of a crown blasted from the head of a king and tossed into the dust:

> God hath seemed providential, not only to strike at the family, but at the Names . . . God hath seemed so to deal with the persons, and with the family, but he hath blasted the title . . . I will not seek to set up that which Providence hath destroyed, and laid in the dust, and I would not build Jericho again.[69]

He reached for the book of Joshua, and the story of the children of Israel who, after destroying the city of Jericho, sinned because Achan 'took of the accursed thing', and angered God. Achan had stolen gold, silver and a robe. He was guilty of greed and ambition, and subsequently incurred the wrath of God. The blasted title, Charles's crown lying in the dust of the destroyed kingdom, might well be Cromwell's 'accursed thing'.[70]

Providence had always been Cromwell's guide, but it had become increasingly hard to see what God's purpose was for him and for Britain. The failure of the West Indies expedition in 1655 had rattled Cromwell, and continued to haunt him. The postponements and the prayers with his chaplains suggest, in this kingship crisis, a man searching his conscience for the right decision. Was 'king' only a name, or was it more than this? 'Signification goes to the thing, certainly it does, and not to the name,' Cromwell had told the committee of ninety-nine.[71] And yet he felt he could not accept it. When a London uprising, orchestrated by the Fifth Monarchist Thomas Venner, was foiled in April, Henry Cromwell tried to push his father to resolve the kingship issue quickly: 'Titles and names are of little moment,' he said.[72] Henry had also told Broghill that "Tis not names or words that governe the world, but things'.[73] But as the April meetings between the Protector and the committee confirmed, there really was a great deal of 'thing' in the name.

As with so many of this decade's critical moments, we do not know exactly what was going on in Cromwell's mind. Although he told his army officers that he had not known anything about the Remonstrance and the offer of the crown until it was first presented to Parliament by Christopher Packe in February, this is unlikely. It was convenient, if not plausible, for Cromwell to feign ignorance about such an important constitutional matter, especially one being finessed by those close to him: Broghill, Whitelocke. It is possible that he was considering accepting the title. But John Thurloe, secretary of state and close to Cromwell, was in the dark. 'Whether his highness, when all this is done, will accept of kingship, I am not able to say,' he wrote.[74] In one of his meetings with the kingship committee, Cromwell requested a few tweaks and clarifications to the rest of the Humble Petition, and referred rather off-handedly right at the end of his speech to the title: 'Let the title be what it will.'[75] On 27 April, Cromwell's friend and former comrade-in-arms Francis Russell wrote to Henry Cromwell (his son-in-law), prematurely celebrating Henry's inauguration as a new duke of York. 'Your father beginnes to come out of the cloudes,' he wrote, 'and it appears to us that he will take the kingly power upon him.'[76]

Richard Cromwell, Cromwell's eldest son and set to become a de facto prince of Wales, remained silent and absent during this whole episode. He had, he reported to his brother Henry in March, been shut out of Parliament's debates about the Remonstrance lest he gossip, and he was wary of committing his thoughts to paper. He noted, however, that the House was 'afraid of titles', which suggests that he himself was not afraid.[77] According to Lucy Hutchinson, Oliver Cromwell, although he had a certain 'greatness', had grown 'wanton' with power. And so had his family. Henry Cromwell and his brother-in-law John Claypole were, she thought, two 'debauched, ungodly cavaliers' and his sisters were setting up for principality.[78] John Evelyn agreed that Cromwell 'was affecting' kingship, but he believed that Cromwell would refuse the title of king due to pressure from the 'Phanatics' in his army.[79] However, during April, there were signs that even recalcitrant army officers were changing their minds.

Beyond Westminster, communities were split. In Exeter, a congregation of Independents wrote to Cromwell directly to persuade him to refuse the ungodly crown. Toby Allein, a successful clothier, and his wife refused to sign this petition, and were consequently expelled from their church.[80] In London, a group of Baptist ministers petitioned Cromwell to avoid temptation and discard 'the old demolished fabric of government'. To accept the crown, they urged, would be a sin.[81] Royalists sneered, as they always had done at the preposterous image of an impostor sovereign. Some hoped that the sight of the false King Oliver might encourage people to finally clamour for the 'true' sovereign, Charles II. But Edward Hyde, earl of Clarendon, faithful in exile with Charles, despaired. He believed that any residual love for monarchy in the three nations would transfer easily to King Oliver. People liked the title, not the family, he noted.[82] It was, as George Wither had feared and as John Milton knew, the 'thing . . . call'd a king', and not the man, that could foster fidelity and inspire idolatry.

There were many who ignored the intricacies of what was happening at Westminster. Ordinary men who had fought against Charles I sought comfort, not ideology. At the Caernarfonshire quarter sessions in 1657, William Griffith appealed to the Justice of the Peace for money for himself, his wife and their five small children. He had been unable to work since the wars, having been 'shott thorough the necke with 3 shotts, 3 pieces of his skull taken out being broken with a pole axe, runned thorough the throat with a tucke, runned thorough the left side & thigh, and left for dead in a feild'.[83] Griffith was one among hundreds of soldiers and widows who petitioned the courts around the country for money and relief. Others that year were more worried about the prospect of increased taxes to pay for the war with Spain, or about avoiding that season's grievous new fever which, Lady Ann Fanshawe tells us, took many.[84]

Finally, on 8 May, six weeks after the Humble Petition was first presented, Cromwell delivered his final answer. He called his MPs to the Banqueting House, and there, underneath Rubens's magnificent ceiling painting depicting James I and the divinity that hedged England's kings, Cromwell rejected, definitively, the title of king. He had not, he said, been 'convinced of the necessity of that thing'. He was therefore unable to 'undertake this government with the title of a king, and that is my answer to this great and weighty business'.[85]

Most of the MPs were shocked. We were 'amazed', William Jephson told Henry Cromwell.[86] Others were angry, and moved for more time to coax Cromwell. Some thought he might yet change his mind. George Downing told the House that 'his conscience may receive conviction'.[87] Francis Russell felt duped. 'Your father hath of late made more wise men fooles than ever,' he told Henry, going on to describe how Cromwell himself was visibly lightened now that this weighty business was over. He 'laughs and is merry', Russell said.[88] Cromwell's son-in-law, Charles Fleetwood, was similarly relieved. Henry Lawrence, president of the council, finally found time to visit, unannounced, John Evelyn's garden – an appreciation of fine planting cut across political lines.[89] But Broghill, suffering with the gout that would plague him all his life, and exhausted and deflated by the outcome, withdrew for a while. That summer he went home to Ireland, to see his family and survey his recovered estates. Perhaps he turned again to his romance, *Parthenissa*.

For Cromwell, the title of king, the feather in the hat, was not right. To refuse it was at least consistent with his claims that God had, for the most part, been on his side and that kings could be ungodly, and with his repeated (but not necessarily sincere) avowals that he had never sought the position he held. The kingship crisis of 1657 rekindled past toxic debates about the prerogative of a king – or any chief magistrate – and the supremacy and powers of Parliament. Was he compelled, as Broghill had argued, to accept what Parliament offered? Did Parliament have the right to alter the form of government? Was the office of king in England a circumscribed one, or could a king claim (like Charles I did) to be answerable to God alone? The crisis also widened divisions between those who believed they had gained freedom from monarchy, and those who believed that it was tyranny, but not the legitimacy of single-person rule, that was in contention. The crisis also met head-on the reach of republican ideas in England at this point in the decade, and the gradual, rising tide of republicanism. For some, such as the political theorist James Harrington, republics were constitutionally preferable, as he had argued in his book, *Oceana*, in 1656. For others, such as Henry Vane, republics were best because they were godly, and the form of government clearly approved of in the Bible. But Broghill and the kinglings were right that the title of king was more than a feather in a hat. It was known, and still liked, and it had legitimacy and weight – but a weight that Cromwell claimed, in the end, his conscience could not bear. William Jephson joshed that the letters 'k i n g' should now be taken out of the English language. Cromwell's rejection of the offer may have saved his conscience, but it risked the life of the Protectorate. Within a few months, the constitution that had been hammered out and wrapped up in vellum as the Humble Petition and Advice was being challenged again. If Cromwell had been named and crowned king, he may well have shut down those who persisted in contesting his legitimacy.

For the rest of the early summer, the MPs pressed on with debating bills that could be passed before Parliament would adjourn on 26 June. The tax assessment was of great concern, as was the bill for regulating the amount of new building happening around London, and taxing it appropriately. It was, then, rather late in the day when Major-General John Desborough reminded Parliament, on 23 June, that the finalised Humble Petition and Advice

– with Cromwell reconfirmed as Lord Protector, but now with the right to nominate his successor, and the establishment of the 'Other House' – needed formal consent. Cromwell should swear a revised oath, and the people, too, should swear an oath, 'otherwise his Highness is in a pretty dangerous case'. 'It is more than stepping from Protector to Protector,' Colonel Robert Shapcott agreed. 'I would have some solemnity . . . but not unction, and the like.'[90] Not everyone agreed that a new oath was necessary, let alone some kind of solemn ritual. William Lenthall was concerned that the constitution was not yet quite perfect; there were still some outstanding decisions to be made, such as about how future Parliaments would be elected. And the exact wording of the Protector's oath could be problematic. In the 1640s, the meaning of Charles I's coronation oath – whether he was above the law and could be put on trial, or not – had divided parliamentarians. Broghill's sister, Lady Ranelagh, had herself worried about the sanctity of Charles I's oath in a letter to Samuel Hartlib.[91] The memory of this haunted the MPs. 'I would not have us to think of an oath without trembling,' one said. John Lambert was utterly against it. To him all oaths were 'snares'.[92]

Finally they agreed to nominate a committee to thrash out the wording of the oath and devise a thrifty ceremony. They chose Westminster Hall because this site could be quickly prepared. A sword was called for, and a suitable robe of honour, for 'Ceremonies signify much of the substance in such cases, as a shell preserves the kernel, or a casket a jewel,' MP William Lister said.[93] A guest list was hurriedly drawn up and, on the morning of the investiture, the master of ceremonies Sir Oliver Fleming invited those foreign ambassadors already present in London. Word spread, and crowds gathered in London to catch a glimpse of the Lord Protector being sworn in for the second time in under four years.

At 2 p.m. on 26 June 1657, Cromwell arrived by boat at Westminster. Cromwell mounted the Parliament steps and disappeared into the Painted Chamber along with Members of Parliament and his council. He gave his assent to the finalised clauses of the Humble Petition and Advice, and a series of bills, including awarding some confiscated Irish estates to Broghill, which included Ballymaloe House in Cork. Cromwell rested a while before processing to Westminster Hall. There, at the south end, under the great window, was a stage covered in carpets, a chair of state, and a table, covered with a cloth of Italian pink velvet and fringed with gold. On the table were some familiar – and some more unusual – ceremonial props: an embossed Bible, a sword, a sceptre, a robe, but also pens, ink, paper, sand and wax. Before the table sat the Speaker of Parliament, Thomas Widdrington. On each side of the Hall, tiered seats on scaffolding had been erected for the judges, MPs and the aldermen of London.[94]

Cromwell processed into the hall, preceded by robed judges, heralds, including the Garter (Sir Edward Bysshe, since 1646) and Norroy (William Ryley, since 1646) kings-of-arms, four serjeants at arms bearing their maces, Henry Lawrence as lord president of the council, and the commissioners of the seal. Immediately before Cromwell was Robert Rich, second earl of Warwick, holding the Sword of the Commonwealth aloft and, on Rich's left, the regicide Sir Robert Tichborne, bearing the sword of the City of London as lord mayor. Right behind Cromwell was Thurloe, then the protectoral councillors and Cromwell's family: his eldest son, Richard, and his sons-in-law Charles Fleetwood and John Claypole. Those who had been intimately involved with the great business of the offer of the crown, such as Bulstrode Whitelocke, followed closely behind.

Cromwell stood on the stage, under a billowing cloth of state. The hall fell silent. Thomas Widdrington addressed Cromwell and explained to him what the ceremony was for: a confirmation of his old name. Widdrington delighted in drawing attention to how something apparently new was, actually, old. 'A name you had before,' Widdrington told Cromwell, 'but it is now setled by the full and unanimous consent of the People of these three Nations assembled in Parliament. You have no new name, but a new date added to the Old Name.'[95] He went on to explain the symbolism of the ritual props. Again, legitimacy derived from precedence, not novelty. The robe of purple velvet lined with ermine was, Widdrington said, just like those 'anciently used at the solemn investiture of Princes'. It was 'an Embleme of Magistracy', with the purple and ermine representing the blend of justice and mercy expected of any ruler. The Bible, ornamented with bosses and gilt clasps, was full of 'Precepts and Examples for good Government'. The solid gold sceptre, 'of antient use', was like a staff, the kind a shepherd would use to guide his flock. Finally, the sword lying on the table was a civil rather than a military sword; its purpose was to defend rather than attack. The earl of Warwick and Whitelocke helped Cromwell into his princely robe. Then, with his hand on the Bible, Cromwell swore the oath that the MPs had so recently agreed upon, and which bound him to uphold the Protestant faith, to preserve the 'Rights and Priviledges of the People' and to govern the English, Scots and Irish 'according to Law'. The Presbyterian minister Thomas Manton – one of the chaplains who had prayed with Cromwell during the crisis over the title of king – ended the ceremony with a prayer. Then, with a blast from a trumpet, Oliver Cromwell was proclaimed Protector of England, Scotland and Ireland. The trumpets sounded again and the spectators gathered in the Hall cried, 'God save the Lord Protector.' Cromwell sat in the chair of state, sceptre in hand, sword at his waist.[96]

According to Hyde, earl of Clarendon, who was not there, this was a coronation. All that was lacking, he scoffed, was 'a crown and an archbishop'.[97] Francesco Giavarina, who was also not there (miffed that he had only been invited that morning), agreed that the only thing missing was a crown, but predicted that this would not be for long. 'He lacked nothing', Giavarina reported back to Venice, 'but the crown to appear a veritable king, and no doubt, if he lives, it will be placed on his head.' According to Giavarina, there was little cheer among the crowds that had gathered around Westminster to witness the procession.[98] The Londoner Edmund Prestwich, who claimed to be an eyewitness, left a detailed account. According to him, the chair of state on which Cromwell sat was no ordinary chair, but the 'Chair of Scotland'. This was St Edward's Chair, which lived in Westminster Abbey and had been used by England's kings and queens for their coronations since the time of Edward I – and is still used at coronations today. Underneath the wooden seat, between the chair's legs, was the Stone of Scone, upon which Scottish kings were crowned, seized from Scotland by Edward I in 1296, and returned in 1996. If this four hundred-year-old chair, and the stone, had indeed been hauled over the road to Westminster Hall, it would have been a bold and brilliant act of appropriation by those hurriedly deciding the details of this impromptu ceremony. It is a detail that has been seized upon by historians ever since, to illustrate Cromwell's inexorable slide towards monarchy and all things royal. But it is unlikely. Only Prestwich named the chair as the coronation chair – it is odd that no one else comments on it – and his posthumously edited account cannot be wholly relied upon.[99]

Cromwell's midsummer investiture was not a mock coronation, and Cromwell was not a king in all but name. He was something else, something still emerging. There was regality, and this inevitably involved the recycling of the props of authority (sword, sceptre, robe), but there was novelty too. Widdrington had described the Humble Petition when it was presented to Cromwell at the end of March as 'a medley or mixture of regality and liberty'.[100] They were improvising, but the differences mattered. Clarendon and Giavarina noted the absence of a crown, but the most meaningful absences were sacred. There was no holy oil, no prayers beckoning the grace of God, no transformation of the body. Cromwell's legitimacy rested on his oath, and on a written constitution. For the traveller Reverend James Fraser, who had just arrived in London from Inverness, passing through on his way to the continent, Cromwell was a rising sun, but not kinglike. He described what was going on as a 'Translation of Kingly Government into a Commonwalth, & of Monarchy into a state'.[101]

After the investiture there was, at last, a degree of stability, although Richard Cromwell felt that the 'publique peace' had been 'tumbled and tossed'.[102] MPs swore to recognise the authority of the Lord Protector, and so did most of those who sat on the Protector's council. John Lambert had not attended the ceremony, and he refused to swear the revised councillors' oath. Since Parliament – and Cromwell – had turned against the rule of the major-generals (Lambert oversaw five counties in the north), Lambert's influence had waned. He, along with other senior army officers, was strongly against the Humble Petition, which he rightly read as wresting power away from the army. Lambert lost his seat on the council and his post as major-general. He spent the next two years tending his garden at Wimbledon House, waiting for the times to change again.

Former Speaker William Lenthall was right when he pointed out that the Humble Petition was not yet perfect. There were still constitutional gaps to plug. Cromwell would nominate his successor, but what would happen beyond Cromwell's successor was left open.[103] When and how Cromwell would nominate his successor was not known; there was no form or agreed ceremony for this procedure. Richard, the eldest son, had been visible at the investiture, standing behind Cromwell and travelling back to Whitehall with him in the coach. In December he was given his first post, as a privy councillor, and a seat in the new Other House. But nothing was ever said about him becoming Cromwell's 'heir'. The Humble Petition had promised a Confession of Faith, a set of religious beliefs and practices to which the nation would subscribe, to be decided at some future point; it never was. Neither had the Humble Petition settled, for future Parliaments, what the franchise would be, or how and whether Scotland and Ireland would continue to be represented. How British the Protectorate Parliaments would be was left uncertain, as was how Ireland and Scotland might be represented in the Other House, or what kind of union there would be between the three nations.

There were changes to Cromwell's household. Some royal terms were used. The council was renamed the privy council and a Board of Greencloth was reinstated, to oversee the household finances which would be managed by Cromwell's new comptroller of the household, Colonel Philip Jones, who would be made Lord Jones. A new household livery was introduced for the master of the barges and the watermen.

And there were two family weddings, both rather surprising. On 11 November, at Whitehall, eighteen-year-old Frances married Robert Rich, son of the former Royalist Lord Robert Rich, and grandson of the eminent parliamentarian and Providence Island adventurer, the second earl of Warwick. It was the elderly Warwick who had carried the sword of state at Cromwell's investiture, while his grandson had helped hold up Cromwell's train. Frances and the young Rich were in love with each other, but this was also an advantageous and politically conciliatory union that had been encouraged by Warwick, despite Cromwell's misgivings about the rather decadent Robert. His late mother was Anne Cavendish, sister to William, third earl of Devonshire. His grandmother was the grand dowager countess of Devonshire, who presided over Chatsworth House, corresponded with Charles II in exile and aroused suspicion for hosting Royalist plotters at her Roehampton home. But she approved of the match between her grandson and Frances Cromwell. Her wedding gift was £2,000 worth of gold plate.[104] Rich, however, was already unwell, and the young couple were only married for a few months. In February 1658 he died from scrofula – the unsightly disease that kings professed to cure by their royal touch.

Just a week after Frances's wedding, her sister Mary married, with Cromwell's blessing, Thomas Belasyse, second Viscount Fauconberg. Fauconberg came from a distinctly Royalist family with extensive Yorkshire estates and Catholics in the nest. Fauconberg's uncles Sir Henry Slingsby and John Belasyse had both been involved in the 1655 Yorkshire rising which was meant to coincide with Penruddock's Uprising. Slingsby was still in prison in Hull and would be executed for treason in 1658. Mary had possibly been going to marry George Villiers, duke of Buckingham, recently allowed back into England following his flight after Worcester back in 1651, and rumoured to have reconciled himself with the republic. Buckingham, however, had wooed Thomas Fairfax's daughter, Mary, instead. He clearly did so in order to win his confiscated estates back from Fairfax, but

Cromwell also feared that Fairfax might be joining with Royalists to plot against him.

In line with the 1653 Marriage Act, Cromwell's daughters' marriages were civil, conducted by a Justice of the Peace (although Hyde, earl of Clarendon later gossiped that they had 'second' weddings performed by a divine). In Mary's case, it seemed that Fauconberg had insisted that they be married by the Royalist and Anglican Dr John Hewett, who later was found guilty of treason. Civil weddings had never been popular – most doubted their legitimacy in God's eyes as well as the legitimacy of the Parliament (Barebone's) that had passed this act. Ministers such as Ralph Josselin had continued to perform secret church weddings for their parishioners, facing fines or worse. In the early months of 1657, when the debates about the offer of the crown and the Humble Petition and Advice necessitated rapid decisions about approving or rejecting existing Protectorate legislation, it had been agreed that people could marry in churches again. It was Lord Broghill who told MPs that the 1653 Marriage Act was 'never looked upon as a law'.[105]

The Cromwell family weddings were private, although bells were rung for Frances and Rich in London. Newsbooks kept their reports brief. *Mercurius Politicus* simply reported that the nuptials were carried out with 'much honor', in between items about France and Sweden.[106] *The Publick Intelligencer* was similarly brief, including it among other Whitehall business of the day, such as petitions about whale-fishing in Greenland and merchants in Russia.[107] At Whitehall and Hampton Court, however, the Cromwells celebrated. There was sack posset to drink, and music, dancing and poetry. Guests wore fashionable 1650s dress: French periwigs for the men, ribbons and beauty spots for the women. Cromwell reportedly larked about at

Frances's wedding, as did some clowns. Andrew Marvell, who had been working in Thurloe's office, with Milton, since September, wrote songs for a musical entertainment for Mary, and William Davenant wrote an epithalamium. Marvell imagined Mary as Cynthia – the moon goddess so frequently associated with Elizabeth I and her virginity. There were enough elderly noblemen and women at this wedding who would have noted this echo from the late 1590s. Marvell included witty jokes about Mary's imminent loss of virginity – ironic in retrospect, as there were no children and Fauconberg was rumoured to be impotent. Marvell also gently questioned whether it was Fauconberg or Mary who was doing the social climbing in this match. But he was also careful to praise Cromwell as serene, honest and wise. For Marvell, Cromwell only 'seemed a king'; really he was both 'something more', and a 'subject on the equal floor'.[108]

In 1657, the celebrated miniaturist Samuel Cooper produced a four-inch miniature painting of Oliver Cromwell.[109] Cooper had already painted Cromwell and members of his family earlier in the 1650s. He made exquisite, tiny, life-like faces on vellum, encased in miniature oval frames to be treasured or given away as gifts, working from his Henrietta Street studio in Covent Garden. He enjoyed a reputation as one of the best portraitists of the age. He was the 'prince of limners' according to John Aubrey, a Van Dyck 'in little'.[110] In the 1640s he had painted England's elite families, including the Belasyses, the Riches and the Howards. Now, in this pivotal year, Cooper presented Cromwell as a pensive, serious man. Two neat white collars of Cromwell's undershirt rest on top of his studded cuirassier armour. His greying hair is shoulder-length, wispy and receding, and above his right eyebrow is the famous wart that Cooper had first sketched, perhaps in 1653, and which other artists, notably Sir Peter Lely, copied (and mistakenly became famous for).[111] Cromwell, apparently, had asked to be painted 'warts and everything'. The 1657 miniature is a finished version of this 1653 sketch. Cromwell's head is turned: he looks off to the left and down a little, not out at the viewer. There are no symbols of office; his military dress would have been appropriate since this miniature may have been intended as a gift for General Robert Blake, commissioned by Cromwell to mark Blake's victory over the Spanish in 1657. Cooper's Cromwell, particularly the earlier sketch, epitomises new artistic concerns – Rembrandt's portraits from the same time are similarly shadowy and intense – as much as it illustrates a new politics. It is the most natural and the most moving image of a head of state of the time, remarkable for its sense of interiority and lack of outward show. The next year, Cromwell would be dead. His eldest son, Richard, bought Cooper's 1653 miniature version for £100 – nearly £20,000 today – and later gave it to his sister, Mary.[112]

Meanwhile, on the new coins circulating in 1657, Cromwell looked a bit more regal. His profile head was crowned with a laurel wreath. Charles II adopted this innovation at his Restoration; he too wore a laurel wreath on his coinage, but he chose to look in the opposite direction, turning his back on the republic, though not on its artists. Shortly after Charles arrived back in England he asked Samuel Cooper to sketch him for the new coinage, and he employed him as his official limner.[113] Perhaps he admired Cooper's willingness to paint the man, and not the king.

1658

Must I thus leave thee Paradise? Thus leave
Thee native soil, these happy walks and shades,
Fit haunt of gods?

John Milton,
Paradise Lost, Book XI

The winter that saw in the new year of 1658 was freezing, and not just in Britain. The sea off the coast of Holland was frozen, as was Massachusetts Bay across the Atlantic. The Viennese rode their horses on the Danube and Swedish soldiers marched across the Danish Sound. In London, the frozen Thames delayed the doctors who were on their way to John Evelyn's son, fatally ill with that season's fever. They arrived too late, and Evelyn's five-year-old boy, Richard, died. 'Here ends the joy of my life,' Evelyn wrote in his diary. He, and many others, would remember this as 'the severest winter that man alive had knowne'. Crows' feet were frozen to their prey, said Evelyn, and 'hands of ice' enclosed people out in their boats.[1]

While men and women battled with the cold and feared for the floods and the poor harvest that would surely follow, the country's MPs travelled to London to take their seats in Parliament. A parliamentary recess had followed Cromwell's investiture in June 1657, and he now needed to recall the MPs. On 20 January, they duly assembled in the frosty Outer Court at Westminster to take their oaths of fidelity to the Protector, along with the new Members of the Other House. Cromwell had selected and summoned these Members just before Christmas, and he styled them as 'lords', although only a handful were lords in the hereditary sense. Cromwell gathered the Members of both houses before him but, as he felt unwell, his opening address was uncharacteristically short. He took the opportunity, as he usually did in his rousing, urging speeches, to recall the terrible wars, to remind his Parliament of

God's blessing on them and their country, and of the precious liberties they now enjoyed. He then handed over to Nathaniel Fiennes, commissioner of the Great Seal, and the new Speaker of Cromwell's 'Other' House. Clothed in his lavish commissioner's robes, Fiennes warned his audience not to shake the new constitution that the Commons had forged – like order out of chaos – the previous summer. The three nations, England, Scotland and Ireland, now had a chief magistrate – distinct from a king – and two Houses of Parliament. The Other House was new, Fiennes urged; let it take root, and flourish. The new political landscape, which trod a middle ground between the old and the new, was, Fiennes said, like a second Eden.[2] But this paradise did not last the winter. The Parliament barely survived two weeks before Cromwell dissolved it, and cast all of its Members out, back into the cold.

Sir Arthur Hesilrige was late to the opening of Parliament. Cromwell had, surprisingly, offered his old republican antagonist a seat in the Other House, probably to keep him out of the Commons where he might stir up trouble. Perhaps Cromwell was gambling on the chance that Hesilrige would never turn up, but would choose to stay up in the North, in one of his many houses. From the 1630s Hesilrige, himself only a baronet but married to a baron's daughter, had vigorously defended the rights of Parliament against Charles I and attacked the bishops, voting with Cromwell for their abolition. He had fought at Edgehill, the first battle of the civil wars, and had led Parliament through much of the conflict. He had not, however, supported Pride's Purge of the House of Commons, which he saw as an illegitimate army coup, nor the subsequent execution of the king, but he did accept a place on the republic's first council of state. As governor of Newcastle he had accrued power, wealth and property. He also earned a reputation for bullying and the mocking soubriquet 'bishop of Durham', for all the Church lands he greedily snapped up. Another called him 'Nimrod of the North'. He was a champion of the sovereignty of Parliament and enemy of the unchecked power of the sword. He had been appalled by Cromwell's dissolution of the Rump in 1653, and by the Protectorate that followed, refusing to recognise Cromwell's office. In the summer of 1656, he had been elected MP for Leicestershire, but his name was on the list of MPs the protectoral council excluded from taking their seats, deemed too critical of the Protectorate. But now, in January 1658, because the Humble Petition and Advice of 1657 had decreed that only the House of Commons – and not the Protector's council – could expel one of its own, republican-leaning Members such as Hesilrige could retake their seats and start shaking, again, the Protectorate's sandy foundations.[3]

On 25 January Hesilrige arrived outside the Parliament house and demanded to take his oath as a Member of the Commons, shunning Cromwell's offer of a seat in the lords. He made a great show of swearing to be loyal to his Protector and proudly took his place alongside fellow commonwealthmen Thomas Scot and Luke Robinson.[4] The House of Commons was quite different to the House that had fought over the kingship and the Humble Petition and Advice during the previous year: not only were the once-expelled Members back, but those influential and experienced MPs who were loyal to Cromwell and to the settlement they had hammered out had moved on to occupy new seats in the Other House: Lord Broghill, Bulstrode Whitelocke (now Lord), William Lenthall (also now Lord). Cromwell's allies were now dissipated and diluted.

Neither were those installed in the Other House his unanimous supporters. Cromwell had not found it easy to recruit men to this second chamber. In the autumn of 1657 he had begun compiling his list. In December, he summoned sixty-three men, but only forty-two accepted. Cromwell's eldest son, Richard, was the first to receive a summons, as might be expected for the man widely assumed to be, but not yet publicly declared as, Cromwell's successor. Richard's younger brother Henry also accepted a seat, despite being in Ireland and unable to ever attend. Other loyal family members included Cromwell's sons-in-law, Charles Fleetwood (Bridget's husband) and John Claypole (married to Betty), and his two brothers-in-law, John Desborough and John Jones. Representing the army were Colonel Thomas Pride and General George Monck, although Monck was up in Scotland. Edward Montagu, Cromwell's Huntingdonshire neighbour and now general-at-sea, was offered, and accepted, a place. Cromwell had invited five peers who were, supposedly, his supporters – including the second earl of Manchester (another Edward Montagu), his old ally and son-in-law's grandfather the earl of Warwick, and Nathaniel Fiennes's father, William, Viscount Saye and Sele. But they all ignored the summons.[5] Saye, who believed in the stabilising role of hereditary peers, rather than nominated Members, confessed that he feared Cromwell wanted to overthrow all the nobility and fill the house with his own. This, he argued, would not be a check on the Commons but a restraining bridle.[6] But, according to Cromwell, the MPs, soldiers, family and existing nobility that made up the Other House were all men who loved England and religion.[7]

When Arthur Hesilrige took his seat in Parliament house on that icy day he found the Members of the Commons in the middle of a heated, protracted argument. On 22 January, the Other House had sent the Commons a message suggesting they share a day of prayers and thanksgiving together. This was, seemingly, harmless enough. But the Commons could not agree on how to reply, for the message had come from 'the Lords'. To many of the MPs the Other House was absolutely not the restored House of Lords, which had been abolished in 1649, and should not refer to itself as such.

The Other House was something quite different, although no one could agree on what to call it. This was no petty matter. As with the issue of kingship – as with every constitutional twist and turn of this decade – names and forms mattered, for whether something was new, old or old but with a new meaning had political consequences. Were things being restored, or revolutionised? As the Presbyterian MP and alderman William Gibbes pointed out astutely: 'The great difficulty of this debate is, because it does not appear whether it is from what is old, or from what is new.'[8] 'There is much in names,' Anthony Ashley Cooper warned a few days later, wholly against the Other House being styled a House of Lords, adding, 'The word King, they know, carries all.'[9] One day, Cooper would accept the title of the first earl of Shaftesbury and sit plumply as one of Charles II's lords. The worry was that, if it became known as the House of Lords, the old peers, 'though they be drunkards', would also return, and that that they would appropriate the control over the Commons that used to belong to the old House of Lords, namely the right to veto laws.[10] The Humble Petition and Advice had suggested, but only vaguely, that the role of the 'Other House' would be advisory, with its former judicatory and legislative powers curtailed. As Major-General William Boteler claimed: 'It is quite another thing. We know they are another House . . . You are under a settlement which does clearly distinguish this from that constitution of a House of Lords.'[11]

Hesilrige waded in eagerly to these debates. For him, it was the sovereignty of the Commons – the 'people's' representatives – that mattered most of all, for the people were the origin of power and no House should be able to exercise a negative voice over them. To Hesilrige the Other House should not be a House of Lords. He was adamant that such a deliberate monarchical drift should be halted, for this tide would carry England back to the times of Charles I, and to the bondage of kings:

> If his Highness will make you dukes, earls, he may do what he will. Grant once Lords, then you will find tenderness, of course, to maintain the privileges of that House as Lords. The Commons of England will quake to hear that they are returning to Egypt, to the garlick and onions of (he called by a slip) a kingdom.[12]

It was a dangerous (and peculiarly English) thing to question the constitution yet again. 'They are another House, and that is enough,' Hesilrige said. 'If you can, let it alone. Englishmen cannot bear when it is well.'[13]

On 4 February the MPs were still arguing. Just as Hesilrige's ally Thomas Scot was poised to speak, they were interrupted by the arrival of the Black Rod. Cromwell was waiting in the Lords chamber. No one was expecting him, not even his trusted Thurloe. He had got wind of a petition put together by Hesilrige and 'the republicans' (as the French ambassador Bordeaux called them) which was expected to be presented to Parliament that day. It called for a return to the free state established in 1649, when the Commons were the 'original of all power'.[14] Cromwell summoned the Commons to the Lords chamber, and he spoke to them, standing under a rich cloth of state, about shame, grief and sorrow. He did not seek the position he held, he began, as was his wont, but was invited, nay implored, by them, the Commons with their Humble Petition and Advice, to undertake this government and all its burdens. He would, he said, rather be living on a hill with a flock of sheep. 'Noe man, noe man', he said, 'would seeke such a place as I beare.'[15] He reminded them that he had accepted his office last summer for the safety of the nation, and on condition that there should be a second House. He reminded them of the oath that he had sworn in the ceremony in the summer, and of the oaths that they too had sworn. He railed against their plans to undermine the foundations on which their new settlement stood, and to invent 'a Commonwealth, a Commonwealth'. Cromwell warned his Parliament of the real danger of a rebellion led by Charles Stuart, ready with an army and eager to take advantage of a divided state. 'You not only have disquieted yourselves, but the whole Nation is disquieted,' he cried. Blood and confusion would surely follow. The MPs had to go. 'I doe dissolve this Parliament,' Cromwell declared. 'Let God judge between you & me.' The mace, the symbol of a sitting Parliament, was then 'clapped under a cloak' and, once again, '*exit Parliamentum*'.[16]

How many times had the republic been here? Not even the Humble Petition and Advice, the constitution fought over so intensely in the spring and early summer of 1657, could, it seems, bring legitimacy and settlement. And yet there was still some hope. The army was, on the whole, still loyal to the Protector. Scotland was, for the moment, cowed under General Monck. 'I never observed a greater calme than at this time,' Thurloe wrote to Sir William Lockhart, the ambassador in France.[17] Royalist plots feared by Cromwell were successfully thwarted. There were some successes abroad: the valuable port of Dunkirk was seized from the Spanish in May 1658, and there was also little resistance in Jamaica, where the sown crops were beginning to yield. Foreign ambassadors, Bordeaux among them, speculated yet again that Cromwell might become king after all.[18] Crimson caps of estate were reportedly commissioned by Cromwell's master of the wardrobe, 'making the people talk largely of kingship'.[19] In early summer it looked as though a new Parliament would be summoned. And then Cromwell became unwell again.

The third of September was an auspicious date for Cromwell. It was the anniversary of two of his most significant victories, at Dunbar and at Worcester. It was the date he had chosen for the opening of his first Parliament as Lord Protector, in 1654. In 1658, it was the day Cromwell died. He was fifty-nine. Such an extraordinary coincidence was not lost on those reporting his untimely death. The newsbook *Mercurius Politicus* saw the hand of providence. Instead of bestowing a crown of military victory, God now chose to give Cromwell the crown of everlasting life on this most significant of days.[20]

Cromwell had been ill with a fever, a kind of malaria. He had spent most of that rainy summer at Hampton Court to be close to his daughter, Betty. She was grieving the death of her baby son, Oliver, and was herself dying, probably from stomach cancer. Cromwell was particularly close to Betty, despite his concerns once upon a time about her propensity for worldly vanities and company.[21] She died on 6 August and Cromwell became distracted with grief. For the watchful poet Marvell, now working in Whitehall alongside his friend Milton, it was Betty's death that caused Cromwell's just a few weeks later. While George Wither mourned the 'main prop of this Government', and Edmund Waller commemorated the conqueror of the seas, Marvell described Cromwell as an ageing father who, Lear-like, died of a broken heart.[22]

Cromwell's death took his court by surprise. In between feverish seizures, there had been moments when Cromwell was thought to be rallying. At the end of August he had been persuaded to move back to Whitehall, in the belief that a change of air would surely hasten recovery. It did not. Afterwards, some looked back for signs that the Protector's end was near. A few months earlier, during an unseasonably chilly June, a fifty-eight-foot whale had swum up the Thames and beached at Greenwich. Cromwell, John Aubrey thought, had been troubled by it.[23] In early August, the Quaker George Fox had visited Cromwell at Hampton Court, hoping for a private audience. He later recorded in his journal that he 'saw and felt a wafte of death' around Cromwell.[24] In the days leading up to Cromwell's death, a late summer storm had raged outside Whitehall, and great oaks had fallen. This, some said, was God calling back the great Protector, his ruling instrument.[25] But it was only happenstance. The astrologer William Lilly had not foreseen Cromwell's death in his almanac for 1658. He had wrongly predicted that 1658 would bring stability following the safe passage of the Humble Petition and Advice through Parliament the year before.[26] But Lilly was prophesying what the government wanted to hear. He could have predicted that Cromwell's neglect, or refusal, to name his successor, as he was expected to do according to the Humble Petition and Advice, would derail the government. There were plenty of people around who knew their Tudor history, and who knew that, should Cromwell die without having nominated a successor, crisis might follow.

When it became clear that Oliver Cromwell was indeed about to die, those close to him, such as his trusted secretary Thurloe, began to fret. Many speculated, even assumed, that Cromwell's thirty-year-old son Richard would succeed and that this was being prepared for. Throughout the Protectorate Richard had been addressed as Prince Richard, and he had been centre stage at Cromwell's second investiture in June 1657. Richard had moved from his Hampshire home to St James's Palace, a suitable residence for an heir. His father nominated him to the Other House and, from 1658, he had a seat on the privy council too. And yet, despite all this, Cromwell had never formally named Richard as his successor. Without a formal nomination, England, Wales, Scotland and Ireland were all in a 'miserable posture'. As Henry Cromwell wrote to Thurloe, 'if no settlement bee made in his life-time, can wee be secure from the lust of ambitious men?'[27]

Cromwell had, apparently, once written down the name of his chosen successor on a piece of paper and sealed it up in an envelope, addressed to Thurloe. When Cromwell became ill, he sent one of his bedchamber men to fetch this letter from his study at Whitehall – but it was nowhere to be found. Even if the letter had once existed, Thurloe claimed never to have seen it. He maintained that Cromwell had not settled on a successor: 'Truely I beleeve he hath not,' he wrote to Henry Cromwell on 30 August.[28] The official story, released from Whitehall, was that on the day before Cromwell's death, Thurloe and four or five other councillors assembled around the Protector's bed to witness him declare that he wished his eldest son to succeed him as Lord Protector. The rest of the council then unanimously accepted or agreed to fabricate (unlikely) this deathbed declaration when they met in the afternoon of 3 September. Richard Cromwell was duly proclaimed Protector, and the text of the Proclamation stated that he had been nominated by his father before his death. Richard remained entirely silent about the circumstances of his succession and when, or whether, his father ever named him as his heir.[29]

As with so many of the critical turning points in this decade – the dissolution of the Rump in 1653, the offer of the crown in 1657

– we cannot be sure about what happened or what Cromwell really wanted. Rumours circulated that Cromwell had nominated both his younger son Henry and his army officer son-in-law Charles Fleetwood; both might have made plausible successors. Henry was competent in Ireland and Fleetwood could manage the army. There were certainly those who thought Henry fitter to rule than Richard. But 'that hereditary way', which Cromwell said he could not bear, held fast. Cromwell probably never made a formal written nomination because he could not publicly acquiesce to hereditary succession, and (like Elizabeth I) could not face the fallout if he chose someone else. Cromwell was also – as his closest councillors seemed to be – in denial of his mortality. He was a soldier who had survived terrifying battles, and who believed he still had God's work to do. A few months after he had died, someone purporting to be a groom of Cromwell's bedchamber – perhaps Charles Harvey or Henry Walker – published an account of Cromwell's death. 'It is a fearful thing to fall into the hands of the Living God,' Cromwell supposedly said, three times, as he lay dying, quoting from the Bible which he had asked to be brought to him.[30]

Despite the fear in Whitehall and the storm raging outside, Richard Cromwell's succession was smoother than expected, and strangely quiet. On 4 September, Thomas Fairfax, who was probably in London at the time, wrote to his friend and governor of the Isle of Man James Chaloner: 'Yesterday and this day hath seen great changes on the one the Lord Protector died on the other his son the Lord Richard proclaimed Prot. but all things so quiet as if neither were happened.'[31] Even Thurloe, who had been so fretful, reported to Henry Cromwell on 7 September that 'it hath pleased God hitherto to give his highnes your brother a very easie and peaceable entrance upon his government. There is not a dogge that waggs his tongue, soe great a calme are wee in.'[32] The army officers seemed happy. 'It was pleasant to behold', *Mercurius Politicus* reported, 'with how much content and satisfaction they received the notice of it, and unanimously concurred thereunto, being resolved to their utmost to maintain the Succession.'[33]

Richard was not a military man. He had been too young to fight much in the civil wars, and many feared the restless army's reaction to a man they did not know, but his public proclamation was greeted by senior army officers, and applauded by the large crowd of people who had gathered around Whitehall and throughout the city to listen to the formal proclamation being read aloud.[34] While Oliver's body was being disembowelled, stuffed with spices and prepared for embalming (apparently it had already started to decompose; his physician George Bate recalled that the spleen was full of oily matter), Richard was presented with the City sword by London's lord mayor in a room in Whitehall.[35] Nathaniel Fiennes handed him the wording of the oath. He swore, as his father had done just over a year before, to rule 'as chief Magistrate of these Nations', according to law.

Once he had been proclaimed in London, Richard was then declared as Protector in market squares – in the places where kings were proclaimed – throughout Britain. Bonfires were lit, guns fired and church bells rang – traditional accompaniments to a regime change. County administrators printed welcoming and praising addresses and sent them to the new Protector.[36] Wine ran through the fountains in Southampton; beer was laid on in Kilkenny; a great banquet was held in Shrewsbury; Newcastle expressed sorrow for Oliver's death but great joy on the succession of Richard. There was, of course, the opportunity for less reverential behaviour. When Richard was proclaimed in Oxford, some young students lobbed carrots and turnip tops at the assembled civic leaders and military officers.[37] Otherwise, foreign ambassadors and European princes sent in their condolences, and their congratulations, recognising Richard as Lord Protector. Poets reworked conventional images. If Nature herself took note of Cromwell's death by whipping up a storm, Richard's succession was the sun that chased those clouds away. 'Methinks I see a Rising Sun,' wrote Samuel Fuller.[38] For many writers composing their elegies, Richard was praised as a worthy successor, a princely son of a father who was king-like, but not a king, and Oliver would continue to rule through Richard.[39] Richard was Joshua to Cromwell's Moses. His father had made England a 'Paradice', and Richard would continue to tend this garden.[40]

Royalists at home and in exile despaired. Their dream of restoring Charles II had never felt so hopeless.[41] Royalist pamphleteers pressed on with denigrating Cromwell as an impostor and a fake, predicting, one day, the restoration of the true king. England is 'wholly addicted to kingly government', the ghost of Charles I warned the ghost of Cromwell in one fanciful pamphlet.[42] But the seemingly smooth accession of Richard made a Stuart restoration look unlikely. For some, such as the Presbyterian minister Richard Baxter, the calm was eerie: 'All men wondered to see all so quiet in so dangerous a time,' he wrote.[43] The week before his father's death, however, Richard (who left no private papers and gave little away in his letters) seemed fearful. From Hampton Court, he wrote to his brother Henry: 'When the axe is layed to the roote, then there is noe hopes remaining.'[44]

Richard spent most of the 1650s away from Whitehall. He lived in the Hampshire village of Hursley, in the grand Hursley Manor (now the property of IBM), his wife's family home. Cromwell had arranged his marriage to Dorothy, the daughter of a wealthy and godly Hampshire Parliament man, Richard Major. In the summer of 1650, Cromwell, while on his way to Scotland, had asked Major to watch and 'counsel' his 'idle' son for he believed he was 'in the dangerous time of his age, and it's a very vaine world'.[45] Cromwell often worried that his children would be tempted by the vanity of the world and stray from the godly path. Richard was Cromwell's third son. His two older brothers had both died; the eldest, Robert, aged seventeen or eighteen in 1639, and Oliver in 1644, aged twenty-one, from smallpox. Richard was educated but he had not, unlike his late brother Oliver, gone to university. He knew Thurloe, from a time learning the law at Lincoln's Inn. Towards the end of the wars he had served Fairfax for a short while, but he did not go on campaign with his father to Ireland, or to Scotland. He had a new wife and a growing family. Richard and Dorothy had nine children during the 1650s; they buried five of them.[46]

Richard was not, as his critics claimed, living a retired country life hunting and hawking – although he did enjoy these things.[47] He may not have been, unlike his younger brother Henry, called to the Barebone's Parliament in 1653, but he had a busy public life in Hampshire, and exercised some influence. He was a Justice of the Peace and warden of the New Forest, overseeing the supply of timber for the navy's growing fleet of ships. Right at the beginning of the republic, in 1649, Richard had been involved with the grand project of draining the Fens to create more farmland. He was elected MP for Hampshire in 1654, and for Cambridge University in 1656. He attended Parliament, listened to his father's speeches and sat on numerous committees. In 1655 he became chair of the new committee for trade. He claimed to have been shut out of Parliament's kingship debates in February and March 1657 (lest he stray), but he was always careful never to express his personal views in any of his letters, even to his brother Henry.[48] He occasionally expressed frustration with those in Parliament who seemed intent on sabotaging a settlement 'where it might occasion difficulty to their getting into the saddle'.[49] He was devout, and believed intensely in God's providence, but did not seem to share the extent of his father's religious toleration. Some thought he rather leaned towards Presbyterianism.[50] He backed the rule of the major-generals and had the support of Colonel William Goffe, the major-general for his county, Hampshire. After Penruddock's Uprising, Richard had petitioned on behalf of John Penruddock's destitute family but he apparently told the diarist Thomas Burton that the Quaker James Nayler should be hanged.[51] From July 1657, he succeeded his father as chancellor of Oxford University, a prominent position that he fulfilled with commitment. He was close to his uncle-by-marriage John Wilkins, of Wadham, and no doubt mingled with Robert Boyle, Christopher Wren and other members of the Experimental Club. He counted Samuel Hartlib as a friend. He was twice considered as commander-in-chief in Scotland, which would have seen General George Monck relegated to his deputy, but a serious riding accident in August 1657 seems to have put paid to this plan.

Richard was more prepared for the role as Protector than some of his contemporaries expected or historians have judged since.[52] Lucy Hutchinson, who was never generous about the Cromwells, considered Richard 'a peasant in his nature, yet gentle and virtuous', who 'became not greatness'.[53] The loyal Bulstrode Whitelocke was surprisingly impressed by Richard at his accession, remarking in his *Diary* in October 1658 that at a meeting between Richard and Bordeaux, the French ambassador, Richard 'did carry himself discreetly & better then was expected'. A month later, Whitelocke was similarly struck by how Richard handled potentially rebellious army officers: 'He courted them att a high rate,' Whitelocke recalled, and the officers 'made large professions to him of their obedience & faithfullness'.[54] Richard's early speeches are eloquent and confident, even as they confess inexperience – an astute tactic perhaps. 'I must say I am not moulded to make speaches, I have infirmity, I want experience, and I want understanding,' he began, when speaking to an assembly of clergymen about establishing a national Church.[55] He confronted head-on the army's murmurings about his fitness for the post, for many of them were angling for Charles Fleetwood as their commander-in-chief. 'It is my disadvantage, that I have beene soe little amongst you, and am noe better knowne to you,' he said. 'It might have pleased God, and the nation too, to have chosen out a person more fitt and able for this worke then I am,' he admitted, before reminding them that, in the end, God's providence had prevailed: 'God hath done herein as it pleased him; and the nation, by his providence, hath put things this way.'[56]

Richard's transformation into Protector was not marked with an investiture. There do not seem to have been any plans to have one before Parliament could formally recognise him; he was not a king, after all. Meanwhile, Oliver Cromwell's death was being marked as if he had actually been a king, and at the state's expense. There was no other precedent. From 18 October until his elaborate state funeral on 23 November, Cromwell's wood and wax effigy lay in state in a candlelit room in Somerset House. Mourners, curious citizens and travellers to London came to see and pay their respects. Others threw dirt. The government's engraver,

Thomas Simon, carved the wax face from Cromwell's death mask. The eyes could open and shut. The robed effigy rested on a bed draped in a cloth of state, clasping a sceptre in one hand and an orb in the other. And resting on a velvet cushion on a nearby chair was a crown – reported as an emblem of honour in *Mercurius Politicus*, rather than a royal symbol.[57] After a while, the effigy was raised to a standing position – once Cromwell's soul had reached heaven (a curious Catholic hangover) – and the crown, it was reported, was then placed on the effigy's head, as a heavenly rather than an earthly crown. Two weeks before the public funeral Cromwell's body was buried late at night in secret in the Henry VII chapel in Westminster Abbey. After this, Cromwell's effigy rested on top of an empty coffin.[58]

On 23 November Cromwell was given a state funeral full of pomp and pageantry. His master of the wardrobe, Clement Kinnersley, turned to the past, to James I's funeral in 1625, but sought to outdo it. It was entirely fitting, the newsbook *Mercurius Politicus* reported, that his death should be marked 'with all honour and magnificence . . . as becomes the dignity and renown of so great a Prince'.[59] But for Edmund Ludlow the lying-in-state was 'folly and profusion' enough; he could not bring himself in his memoirs to linger on the unnecessary magnificence and 'vast expence' of the actual funeral.[60] Thomas Hobbes, on the other hand, thought it splendid.[61]

Richard did not walk in the funeral procession that took seven hours to wind its way from Somerset House to Westminster Abbey. Instead, Charles Fleetwood played the part of chief mourner, processing immediately behind the coffin, on top of which lay Cromwell's crowned effigy. Richard's brother Henry was not there either; he stayed in Ireland. As was traditional, there were no women. Cromwell's widow and daughters stayed in Whitehall; Mary was said to be inconsolable. Cromwell's household was represented – musicians, tailors, doctors, cooks accompanied the hearse – as well as those who had faithfully served the republic. Marchamont Nedham, Andrew Marvell, John Milton and Samuel Hartlib, friends who had all served the regime with their words, were among them, dressed in black mourning clothes. It was dark when the procession arrived at the Abbey. There were no candles available so the procession simply stopped, and there was no further ceremony. Cromwell's body, after all, was already there, lying next to that of his daughter Betty, and not far from the tombs of England's former kings and queens. For a while longer his effigy remained on show, enclosed in an elaborate wood and ironwork catafalque. The eighteen-year-old Francis Throckmorton, up in London from the country, paid two shillings and sixpence to see the Protector's monument before going on to the opera.[62]

1658 had already been a year of grief and loss for John Milton. On 3 February 1658, he lost Katherine, his second wife. Six weeks later, their five-month-old daughter, named Katherine after her mother, died. Milton was now living in a house in Petty France, overlooking St James's Park, with his three other daughters, Deborah, Anne and Mary. Completely blind, he relied on a team of amanuenses to write while he dictated his diplomatic letters for Cromwell. His house was busy and full of family, friends and visitors: his nephew Edward Phillips and his former student and amanuensis Cyriack Skinner, his wife's cousin the goldsmith Thomas Vyner, Samuel Hartlib, Marchamont Nedham, his colleague and friend Andrew Marvell, the republican and godly

Henry Vane. There was often music, and always conversation. Not everyone shared Milton's views about godly republics or liberty of conscience, particularly his anti-Puritan nephew John Phillips, whose scurrilous poems had been burned in 1656.

Milton had mostly kept quiet during Cromwell's Protectorate – getting on with his work as Latin secretary and only speaking out in defence of the Protestants massacred at Piedmont in 1655. He had initially welcomed Cromwell as Lord Protector in 1653. Cromwell, he thought, was worthy of authority, and offered the hope of liberty of conscience, so precious to Milton. Milton could countenance single-person rule, if that person merited it, but after Cromwell's death he began to criticise his tyranny and 'usurped power', his kingly aspirations and the anointing of his son, Richard.[63] He referred to the Protectorate as a 'short but scandalous night of interruption', and harked back to the early 1650s.[64] Unlike his friends and poets Andrew Marvell and John Dryden, Milton did not write an elegy on Cromwell's death. Neither did he welcome Richard with a poem. Instead, he published a revised edition of his *Defence of the English People* that he had been working on, in praise of a republic with no single person at its head.[65] His journalist friend Marchamont Nedham advertised the new edition in *Mercurius Politicus.*

At some point in 1658, this sad year, in between composing official letters to Charles X of Sweden or Louis XIV of France, Milton returned to his long-planned work about the fall of man, and Adam and Eve's dismissal from the Garden of Eden. *Paradise Lost* would not be published until 1667, but this astonishing epic arose from the dying ashes of Oliver's Protectorate, and the uncertainty of the first months of Richard's reign. Milton sometimes composed his lines at night in his head, or lying in bed in the morning, and then dictated them during the day, to whomever was there to serve as his amanuensis. He could, an early biographer said, reel off about forty lines at a time, 'as it were in a breath, and then reduce them to half that number'.[66] He only wrote for six months of the year, during the winter. As he apparently told his nephew Edward Phillips, 'his Vein never happily flow'd, but from the Autumnal Equinoctial to the Vernal'.[67] From the night of his own blindness, 'shut up at home, as I am', beginning in the cold, dark winter of 1658, Milton composed an epic that would tell the story of Adam and Eve, of Satan's rebellion, of the eating of the forbidden fruit, of the banishment from Eden, and the bringing of death, misery and woe into our fallen world.[68] He believed, and had always believed, in his vocation as a poet, and in his prophet-like ability, even a divine calling, to 'assert eternal providence / And justify the ways of God to men'.[69] To tell his story he drew on the dark materials of the civil wars, the political language of his moment, and his own experience. It is a twelve-book poem forged in the imagination of a man who had hidden from soldiers, heard warfare, scrutinised tyranny, witnessed the execution of a king, defended republicanism, worked at the very heart of the regime and who had contemplated liberty more deeply than anyone.

Paradise Lost is a poem about freedom. Eve, and then Adam, were free to choose and free to obey, and they were therefore free to fall. Eve, in Milton's poem, was free to follow the serpent through the garden to the Tree of Knowledge, free to taste and pluck the apple; Adam was free to follow Eve, and to fall like her. Like the angels in heaven, God made man on Earth 'Sufficient to have stood, though free to fall'. 'I formed them free, and free they must remain,' said Milton's God.[70] Satan, once an angel in heaven, was free to disobey God, and to rebel, and so Satan too was free to fall. Freedom for Milton was not unabandoned individualism, but the exercise of will governed by reason. For Milton, reason reigned supreme: 'for what obeys / Reason, is free'.[71] It is not, of course, easy to choose or reason well, in either religion or politics. Fallen man finds it particularly hard. But spiritual freedom – being free to choose God – could only be enabled by political freedom. Republics, not monarchies, allowed such freedom.

After Cromwell's death Milton turned again to prose and argued vigorously for a free Commonwealth, where 'reason' would hold sway, with a single parliamentary chamber allowed to sit in perpetuity (no unbridled democracy for Milton), and certainly without any single person at the helm. This would be a flourishing nation, worthy of God. *Paradise Lost* is full of echoes of Milton's most powerful, anti-monarchical prose, whether it is Satan – the fallen angel – who is puffed up with 'monarchal' pride, enthroned in the kingdom of Hell, before whom his fellow fallen angels 'bend / With awful reverence', or whether it is the arch-fiend railing against the hierarchy of heaven, and the required bowing and scraping before Christ, unfairly chosen and anointed by God as his Son, named 'king' and placed at his right hand.[72] Milton, despite William Blake's famous assertion, was certainly not 'of the Devil's party'. It is clear in *Paradise Lost* that Satan should never have rebelled against God – God is God, not a seventeenth-century English king who waged war on his subjects. And Adam and Eve should not have disobeyed God by eating the apple, for God should always be obeyed. Yet both Charles I and Oliver Cromwell often lurk awkwardly behind some of the poem's descriptions of an overbearing, king-like God. The poem's cries for liberty and warnings against the 'easy yoke / Of servile pomp', unreasoned obedience and unthinking subservience resonate so powerfully because they are also the cries of Milton about his own time.[73] Soon Milton would be imploring the English not to 'run their necks again into the yoke which they have broken', to not prostrate themselves before a king and become enslaved by custom.[74]

In the following year, 1659, the entire scaffolding of the Protectorate would come crashing down. The paradise lost in Milton's poem is the Garden of Eden from which Adam and Eve were expelled. It is also the idea of a paradise that Milton, and others in all their different ways, hoped England might have become during the 1650s, before Cromwell disappointed him, and before the dream of the perfect republic that Milton thought the English had a chance of creating melted away.

III : REPUBLIC

Another Scene Withdraws

1659

RICHARD Lord Protector of England Scotland & Ireland; and the Dominions & Territoryes therevnto belonging;

After ages may learne constancie from
these our inconstant revolutions.

Thomas Rugg,
Mercurius Redivivus, May 1659

1659 was a year of several revolutions – so much so that the barber Thomas Rugg chose to record it, in the hope that future generations 'may learne constancie' from such change. Many of the years in this decade were unsettled, but 1659 was particularly so. It was, in the words of William Prynne, driven by meddlers 'given to change'.[1]

The year began, as had 1658, with the opening of Parliament on a cold January day. It must have felt unhappily reminiscent of the year before, when Oliver Cromwell's last Parliament opened in the middle of a perishing winter, still with a constitution to settle. Old Members jostled with new to take their oaths at the door of the Parliament house. Richard Cromwell's first Parliament was an even larger and more mixed body than his father's last Parliament had been. The rules that had been agreed for the elections in December saw Members returned from boroughs as well as from counties, which meant that there were well over five hundred MPs eligible to sit. Many of these new MPs were young – barely weaned when Charles I died, said one report.[2] Such green politicians had little or no memory of the years of war, nor of the decade's earlier political dramas. Many were moderate; most wanted stability and more money, and simply to be able to get on with their lives. There were some old hands. Thomas Fairfax travelled down south from Nun Appleton to take his seat again. And there were a few more republicans whose voices had been silenced during the Protectorate years. Most notoriously, Henry Vane had managed to win the rotten borough of Whitchurch in Hampshire.

He came back after a spell in prison and a period in the political wilderness for expressing his hostility to Oliver's Protectorate.[3]

The great need, secretary John Thurloe said, was money. The country had crippling debts totalling about £2.5 million, and the troops were owed nearly £1 million in salaries.[4] As long as the army remained unpaid its loyalty could not be guaranteed. Richard had to call a Parliament, and he needed it to be willing to raise taxes and pay the soldiers. Thurloe was also aware that Richard's position really needed to be formally recognised and approved by Parliament, despite his being proclaimed Protector back in September. Calling on precedent from Elizabeth I and James I's reigns, Thurloe introduced an 'Act of Recognition of His Highness's Right and Title to be Protector and Chief Magistrate of the Commonwealth of England, Scotland, and Ireland, and the Dominions and Territories Thereunto Belonging'.[5] It was intended as a formality – to safely recognise, rather than rattle, Richard's position – but it was not a good idea. One Member pointed out that they had already recognised Richard's authority by swearing their oath before entering the Parliament house; others mentioned how much they liked Richard and trusted him. Deputy Major-General William Packer (who had bought the former royal home, Theobalds) was perturbed by the way the bill declared that Richard had become 'Protector by the death of his father'. 'This brings in hereditary government by a side wind,' he said.[6] Oliver's republican antagonist of old, Arthur Hesilrige, fortified by his allies Thomas Scot, Henry Neville (another enemy of Oliver's) and now Henry Vane, seized the opportunity to pick over the succession of Cromwell's son, questioning Richard's supposed 'nomination' by Cromwell, and undermining, yet again, the foundations of the Protectorate. 'If no successor was declared,' thundered Hesilrige, 'if God prevented it, do we think that it becomes us to set up one? It is a setting up what God has pulled down, and planting what God has plucked up.'[7]

In his long speeches, Hesilrige reached back to the terrible wars, urging his fellow MPs 'to consider what we have been; what we are, and what we shall be', reminding them how they had groaned under tyranny before shaking it all off back in 1649. He told them that they now constituted the decade's most free, full and clean Parliament, who knew more about their rights and liberties than ever before. For all his talk of Parliament representing the people, Hesilrige had little regard for 'the people' who 'care not what Government they live under, so as they may plough and go to market'.[8] The responsibility, he argued, lay with the MPs; they now had another chance to create a lasting settlement.

Like some other republicans, Hesilrige was not necessarily against Richard, or against any single person at the helm of the republic. It was the extent of that person's power that was the issue. The republican writer and MP for Reading Henry Neville also spoke in support of a 'Chief Magistrate', and he liked Richard. He believed him to be a pious man, fit for the post, but he wanted to see his office bound, with limited powers. MP John Bulkeley commented, favourably, on Richard's lack of ambition – he did not seem to 'grasp at greatness' – but he urged that they all 'look to the fitting the Government to this single person, making it neither too wide nor too narrow'.[9] Henry Vane told the MPs that the English people, like the Israelites, had been delivered from bondage and that God was now leading them to become a free state. They therefore needed to ensure the Protector was godly: 'Make him such an one as the Great One shall direct you,' he begged.[10] Thomas Scot, however, warned that 'a young lion's teeth and claws may grow'. And John Lambert, who had masterminded the Protectorate back in 1653, but had pulled back from the offer of the crown to Cromwell, and from Cromwell himself, feared 'the swelling of the power of the single person'.[11] Lambert had lost his commission as a major-general, but was now MP for Pontefract, which came with some land. He himself was accused of such swelling. Together these men constituted, loosely, a party of commonwealthmen. There were not that many of them, but they had a powerful way with words and they were hard to silence.

The debate over recognising, or not recognising, Richard occupied the MPs for far too long. The chaos was being watched and much discussed abroad. Writing from The Hague, George Downing told Thurloe that he hoped that sobriety would prevail and that MPs would let the constitution settle.[12] At 10 p.m. on 14 February, the House voted to acknowledge Richard as Lord Protector, but – in a deferral so typical of this period's Parliaments – the precise bounds and limits to his power would be agreed at a later point. This meant that one of the big sticking points was left hanging – whether or not Richard would, as Protector, also be commander-in-chief of the army or whether this control would be better placed in the lieutenant-general Charles Fleetwood's hands (which the army wanted) or should belong to the House of Commons (which Arthur Hesilrige and other commonwealthmen wanted).

While the MPs had been arguing, the army was agitating. On 6 April, Charles Fleetwood met Richard in Henry VIII's chamber in Whitehall. Fleetwood, caught between loyalty to the Protector as his brother-in-law and loyalty to his soldiers, presented Richard with a petition from the general council of officers. This petition was like 'Lightning before Thunder'.[13] The army wanted pay. The soldiers wanted Fleetwood as their general, not Richard, who lacked military experience and did not know them like his father did. They wanted to appoint, discipline and dismiss their own, rather than be at the whim and mercy of a Protector. They wanted, like Oliver had wanted, religious radicalism to be tolerated, and they rightly suspected that Richard was not as keen on the liberty of conscience as his father had been. He was rejecting petitions from Quakers who only shouted louder in retaliation. It was the junior officers who were particularly impatient. In the same way that Hesilrige harked back to the wars when addressing the MPs, these officers mourned the eclipsing of a cause for which they had risked their lives: freedom from the tyranny of monarchy and freedom to believe what their consciences dictated. 'We did ingage in Judgement and Conscience for the just Rights and Liberties, Civil and Religious of our Countreys, and not as a Mercenary Army' and 'we are now, as ever, equally indeared to our good old Cause', they warned. The phrase 'the good old cause' had first been used by Henry Vane a few years earlier, in his *A Healing Question Propounded and Resolved*, an inflammatory, anti-Cromwell pamphlet that had earned Vane a spell in prison on the Isle of Wight.[14] Now, in 1659, Vane, soldiers and fellow sympathisers united behind 'the good old cause', and a shared vision of a republic that would be free from the sins of greed and ambition which they saw could take hold of those in power.[15]

Richard accepted the petition graciously enough. It was read out in the Commons a couple of days later, but those Members sitting ignored it. This stoked the army's suspicion of Parliament's indifference, even hostility, to the soldiers who had fought for it. When they did respond, the MPs finally began to think about how to address the army's back pay.[16]

But then they voted provocatively to shut down the council of officers and its meetings, cutting off their right to petition and pressure Parliament any further. Richard, misguidedly, agreed to this – and he made the army angry. Fleetwood's loyalty to his brother-in-law was tested further when he heard that the Commons were now debating whether they should have control over the army, and how to slim down their numbers. Richard had promised Fleetwood and Major-General John Desborough that he would not let this happen. They felt betrayed. Fleetwood refused to respond to a messenger sent by Richard, summoning him to Whitehall. Instead he and Desborough called, rashly, for an immediate dissolution of Parliament. Richard refused.

This was the thunder that followed the lightning petition. Late that night, on 21 April, Fleetwood called on the regiments around London to meet at St James's Palace, now soldiers' quarters and a prison. Thousands of soldiers gathered in the fields around the palace, on foot and on fidgety horses. They funnelled their way along the narrow streets, advancing towards Whitehall. It was midnight. There was no beating of drums or blowing of trumpets. The men simply shouted, one sympathetic bystander described, for 'the good ould cause . . . A Comanwealth, and noe single person'.[17] A few loyal colonels, such as Edward Whalley and the former Hampshire major-general William Goffe, rallied to Richard's countercall, but they were not enough. Even Richard's own lifeguard defected. 'Thus here was a general without an army,' gloated Edmund Ludlow.[18]

At three o'clock in the morning Desborough demanded again that Richard dissolve Parliament. He assured him that his office as Protector would be safe. Richard now had no choice but to follow the order. When the MPs turned up to sit in Parliament the next morning (it was now 22 April), Nathaniel Fiennes sent them home. The doors to St Stephen's Chapel were padlocked and guarded by red-coated soldiers. Our parliamentary diarist Thomas Burton had written his last ever entry on Thursday 21 April: 'I went away at five, to Justice Lowther's funeral . . . What was done?'[19]

This was a family coup, as well as a military one. While Fleetwood and Desborough probably did not intend to overthrow their brother-in-law and nephew-by-marriage, let alone dismantle the Protectorate entirely, their actions were disloyal and destructive. They 'forsooke me', Richard told his brother Henry in the last letter we have between them.[20] A frustrated and fired-up army now had power, and there were plenty of radicals among them who were calling for the Protectorate to be overthrown entirely. With no Parliament in place, a council of officers was hastily convened. Fleetwood sat on this council along with Desborough and John Lambert, and he was named commander-in-chief of the army. Richard wrote to his brother Henry in Ireland for help, but no help came.[21] Henry Cromwell had long feared the army – and the ambition of Fleetwood and Desborough – and the country's changeability. He warned his brother:

> I doubt the flood is so strong, you can neither stem it, nor come to an anchor, but must be content to go adrift, and expect the ebb. I thought those, whom my father had raised from nothing, would not so soon have forgot him, and endeavour to destroy his family, before he is in his grave. Why do I say, I thought, when I know ambition and affectation to empire never had any bounds? I cannot think these men will ever rest, til they are in the saddle; and we have of late years been so used to changes that it will be but a 9 days wonder.[22]

Richard also appealed to the supposedly loyal General George Monck, commander of the forces up in Scotland. Monck did not stir. His soldiers did not want to fight fellow soldiers. He had already heard the news from Fleetwood, and from Thurloe, and he preferred to wait and see what would happen.[23] Richard failed, too, to raise Edward Montagu, the Protectorate's general-at-sea, and another ally of his father's. But Montagu was away with his ships in the Baltic, caught up in the ongoing dispute between Denmark and Sweden. Richard was stranded, and forsaken.[24]

Since the end of the previous year, leading republicans had been gathering at Henry Vane's Charing Cross home, next to Northumberland House, to talk politics.[25] Vane was close to Arthur Hesilrige – they and Cromwell had initiated the abolition of bishops in the 1640s – and to fellow republicans Thomas Scot, Henry Neville, Edmund Ludlow and John Lambert. He was hugely admired by Milton, who praised the young Vane for being wise and godly: 'on thy firm hand Religion leanes', Milton wrote, 'and reckons thee her eldest son'.[26] Vane had, briefly in the 1630s, been governor of Puritan Massachusetts. He was happily married to the equally pious Frances, Lady Vane, and they and their ten surviving children shared their time between London and their Durham home, the medieval moated Raby Castle (still in the Vane family today). In 1659, a new edition of his troublesome book appeared. *A Healing Question Propounded and Resolved* was a best-seller in 1656, and the printer Thomas Brewster saw another political and commercial opportunity. Customers at his St Paul's bookstall seemed to have an appetite for Vane's plan to cure England, and reignite the 'good old cause'.[27]

Vane's vision was for a godly republic, run by pious men. He believed that only 'faithful, honest and discerning' men should be entrusted to create a constitution and ensure, through the vetting of candidates, that the Parliament elected would be reliably godly. He wanted a government of like-minded saints who would not dictate men's consciences but whose infectious piety would free the entire country from sin and lead all willingly towards God. Vane believed his times were 'depraved'.[28] A ballad mocked Vane as an 'Anointed King of Saints', but his political ideas had traction and were seriously considered by other republicans and by the army.[29]

In the opening months of 1659, Vane had begun orchestrating a devastating publishing campaign. Pamphlet after pamphlet appeared that referred to Vane and bewailed the loss of the good old cause.[30] As the winter turned to spring, the bookstalls in Westminster Hall were overflowing with papers, pamphlets, petitions and revived army newsbooks that now called for the restoration of the purged Long Parliament, that 'fagge end' of Parliament brought in by Colonel Pride in 1649 and which Cromwell had so rashly turned out in 1653. A newsbook in early May reported that 'the govemement seemes now to bee naturally falling into a Commonwealth and free State, and the generall cry of the people is for the Longe Parliament to take possession againe'.[31] The army newsbook, *The Faithfull Scout*, welcomed such a return, 'after a long march from one Government to another', for a free state 'was the most purest Government under Heaven'.[32] Vane had had nothing to do with Pride's Purge, nor was he a regicide, but within days of the dissolution of Richard's Parliament, the restoration of the Rump Parliament was offered as the only way to save 'the good old cause', and establish a righteous government. On 25 April, the 'well-affected' people of Westminster petitioned Charles Fleetwood, imploring him to restore the 'Government as established without a King or House of Lords'. Only this would guarantee the death of monarchy, preserve their liberties and 'revive and strengthen the Good Old Cause'.[33] The years of the Protectorate were now being cast as an interruption, a falling away from God, a 'meer Chimera, and no way usefull'.[34]

At the end of March Fleetwood and Desborough had reached out to Henry Vane and the republicans through their fellow republican officer Edmund Ludlow.[35] Fleetwood and Desborough were dismayed by the extent to which Richard depended on his father's trusted civilian councillors and the 'kinglings' – Thurloe, Broghill, Whitelocke, Fiennes – more than on them as senior army grandees. They sought an alliance that would undermine Richard's authority, and preserve their own power and influence. Rumours were circulating that Richard, like his father, might be offered a crown and the title of king. There were genuine fears that the army might be disbanded altogether. And Fleetwood was managing an army fizzing with junior soldiers who were gathering behind Vane, and calling for a restoration of the Rump, and the free state it had established in 1649.

Fleetwood and Desborough probably did not think that, by talking to the republicans, they risked bringing the whole Protectorate tumbling down. On 2 May, Henry Vane, Arthur Hesilrige, John Lambert and Edmund Ludlow met Fleetwood and Desborough at Fleetwood's home, Wallingford House on Whitehall.[36] The republicans pushed for the restoration of the Rump. Would there still be a place for Richard in this settlement as Protector, Fleetwood asked. No, was the answer. He would be paid off, but he could keep Somerset House. The republican–military coalition met again on 4 May.[37] Fleetwood agreed that those MPs who had been turfed out in 1653 would be invited back, and there would be no Protector, and no Other House. Fleetwood, Desborough, Lambert, Vane, Hesilrige and Ludlow were given the unenviable task of forming a committee to decide how exactly that Commonwealth constitution would work. On Saturday 7 May, forty-two of the seventy-eight ex-Rumpers eligible took their seats. A few more filed in over the next few days. William Prynne, who had been excluded from the purged Parliament back in 1648 and had spent three years in prison for challenging the legality of the Commonwealth, tried to force his way in to reclaim his seat; once again he was kept out. The end of the decade found itself back at its beginning.[38]

Richard's position was now untenable. In its early May issue, *The Faithfull Scout* opened with a direct attack on the genesis of the Protectorate and the principle of single-person rule: 'Tyrants and Usurpers', it began, become, in time 'Tygers of Cruelty, cancelling the Laws and Liberties of a Nation, with the same Sword which first defended them'.[39] On 12 May, Richard wrote to his brother, Henry. 'It is better for me to throwe my selfe in the dust and crye before the Lord,' he said. 'This nation is full of raige and unquietnes,' he noted, but he also felt to blame: 'My sins hath brought what is come to pase upon us.'[40]

On 25 May, Richard abdicated as Lord Protector. 'I love and value the Peace of this Common-Wealth much above my own concernments,' he wrote in his letter of resignation to Parliament. He bowed to what he believed was God's providence. He was offered an annual pension (as was his mother, Elizabeth) and the promise that his debts would be paid.[41] He lingered on in Whitehall for a while, waiting for the money to appear, before retreating home to Hursley in Hampshire. The following year he fled to France, on the run from those to whom he owed money. His wife, Dorothy, was eight months pregnant when Richard left. He never saw her again. By the time he returned to England, in 1680,

Dorothy had died. Richard lived out his days in Cheshunt, Hertfordshire, in a house by the church owned by his landlady, Rachel Pengelly. He went by the name of John Clarke, but he had sometimes used other surnames, all rather poignantly beginning with 'C'. He died in 1712, aged 85.[42]

When Richard left Whitehall, so did the rest of his family. Mary Cromwell's husband, Thomas Belasyse, Lord Fauconberg, got in touch with Charles II, and sent him £1,000 before skulking off to the countryside. He was later arrested for conspiring against the Commonwealth and was sent to the Tower for a short spell.[43] Henry Cromwell resigned from his post in Ireland. John Thurloe lost his post as secretary of state. He still had Wisbech Castle in the Fens, Cambridgeshire – a former bishop's palace which he had bought in 1656, and which the architect Peter Mills had rebuilt for him as a handsome 1650s palazzo.[44] No celebrations marked the collapse of the Protectorate and the fall of the House of Cromwell. Two days before the purged Parliament had reconvened, John Evelyn found himself at the opera – at William Davenant's Cockpit theatre. Richard's abdication, for Evelyn, was 'wonderfull', although it was sudden, and the country was 'all Anarchy and confusion'.[45] Evelyn, long-term Royalist, and Davenant, less constant, had joined those conspiring for change. Davenant was arrested for planning a revolt, and Evelyn published his 'bold' *Apology for the King*, in between pressing on with his mammoth, but never completed, work on gardens and gardening, *Elysium Britannicum*.[46]

The Rump began to dismantle the monarchical trappings of the Protectorate before Richard had had a chance to pack his bags. On 16 May, Parliament decided to put Whitehall Palace and Somerset House up for sale. (No buyers came forward.) On 23 May, the MPs ordered that Whitehall be cleared of unnecessary stuff. The palace that had been the king and queen's, then the Commonwealth's, and latterly the Cromwells', was now back in the hands of 'the people', and should be for their use.[47] Furnishings and goods were sold to raise sorely needed money, not least to pay the army arrears. A few days earlier, on 14 May, the protectoral seal was ritually smashed in Parliament, and a new Commonwealth seal was ordered. The clock was rewound to 1649; time had run backwards.

Sir Archibald Johnston, Lord Wariston, a devout Scottish MP, was elected president of the restored republic's new council of state for a short term in the summer of 1659. He often found himself sitting in the Protector's old study in Whitehall, overlooking the Thames, and reflecting on the twists and turns of life and history: 'Whyl I am looking to the watter and seing it one tyme flowing and another tyme ebbing, I thought it the just figure of human things, tumbling and rolling, and so also my condition, tossed to and fro.'[48] Wariston was loyal to Richard, and he had tried to persuade Charles Fleetwood not to agree to the restoration of the Rump.[49] He felt uncomfortable, at first, about taking an oath to the restored Commonwealth, but he soon changed his mind. Henry Vane secured him a seat on the new council along with himself and fellow republicans such as Hesilrige and Neville, and army officers Ludlow, Desborough, Fleetwood and Lambert.[50] Thomas Fairfax had also been invited to sit on the council, in an attempt to create a body that blended radical with more moderate political players. Fairfax did not appear. Bulstrode Whitelocke survived, as he always managed to do, and took his seat. There too was Anthony Ashley Cooper, up from his Wimborne home. Much to Fleetwood's dismay, the council of state granted Parliament control over the army.

Fleetwood would be the commander-in-chief but Parliament, and not he, would appoint soldiers, and deal with rebel soldiers.

The restored Rump had a year – until May 1660 – to agree on what exactly the new republic would look like, and how exactly it would work. While there would be no single person at its head, the sticking point was whether to have a second chamber or not. The extent of the sovereign power of Parliament, and how properly representative this republic could and should be, and of whom, were matters that had dogged the Rump before its dismissal by Cromwell in 1653. Now they became live again, and animated further by new constitutional ideas that had been sown since. Even before Richard's abdication, Henry Vane, and the army, had been pushing for his dream of 'a select Senate', a body of 'able and faithful Persons, eminent for godliness'. These godly men would share power with Parliament and the council of state, encourage godliness and protect a degree of religious toleration. MPs and councillors of state would come and go, but the saintly senators would sit for life.[51] Vane would later be laughed at for his 'dainty project of a select senate' but, in the summer of 1659, it was a serious, if incendiary, political idea that accentuated divisions, created factions and eventually blew up.[52] Hesilrige and Vane fell out. Vane and Fleetwood disagreed. Fleetwood and Lambert argued. Hesilrige and Neville, and possibly Fleetwood, preferred another, more democratic model that was fast gaining traction.[53]

Henry Vane's home had not been the only place where republics were being designed. In a modest-sized house called Little Ambry, overlooking Dean's Yard in Westminster, lived James Harrington.

He was forty-eight, unmarried, had curly chestnut hair and an extraordinarily fine and arching moustache.[54] He had royally connected ancestors and came from an aristocratic family with Lincolnshire estates. He was well educated. He smoked tobacco and drank coffee, and had a wide circle of friends, including Henry Neville. He had attended on Charles I while a prisoner at Holmby House, moving with him to Hurst Castle. Harrington, apparently, was devoted to the king; perhaps he had discussed politics with him, not that Charles would have been happy with what might have been the beginnings of Harrington's republican ideas. In 1659, Harrington wrote prolifically. His genius, according to John Aubrey, lay chiefly, and radically, in 'Democraticall Government'.[55]

It was just after Cromwell's second Parliament had begun in the autumn of 1656 that Harrington brought out his great work: *The Commonwealth of Oceana*. He had begun writing it in 1654, that tricky first year of the Protectorate. *Oceana* is a portrait of an ideal republican state, modelled on the very best aspects of the Roman, Greek, Hebrew and Venetian republics, supported by debate, political participation and election. Oceana's past is a thinly disguised England which is now 'ripe' for republican government. Harrington dedicated his book to Oliver Cromwell, an offer of an urgent vision for England, and for Scotland and Ireland. It is no dry political tract, but rather a utopian fiction full of character and hope. He advocated the redistribution of wealth, and constraints on private property. He wanted to scrap primogeniture and limit dowries. Sovereign power, the affable founder of Oceana Lord Archon (a flattering version of Cromwell) tells the builders of his commonwealth, lies with a revolving senate and with the people; the senate debates laws, and the people vote on them. Harrington's 'people' did not include the very poor, or women, but he was inching towards what we would recognise as representative democracy. The principle was election, and rotation. The whole government, like the universe, should be in constant motion and revolution: 'for if it be not in rotation both as to persons and things, it will be very sick'.[56]

Harrington failed to persuade Cromwell in 1656. He brought out a second edition of *Oceana* in 1658, following Cromwell's second investiture as Protector. In 1659, when Richard was tumbling, Harrington saw another opportunity to persuade Whitehall to adopt his republican vision. Pamphlet after pamphlet appeared. He, like Milton, could see that many in England were still keen on kings.[57] He feared that pulling down the trappings of Richard's Protectorate and selling Whitehall Palace were not enough to prevent another person jumping 'into a throne'.[58] But, he believed, the country was 'an unnatural soyl for a Monarch'.[59] Too much had changed, and monarchy, Harrington argued, had been dying before the wars began.

Harrington's republican dream could not have been more different to Vane's, for he believed in wise laws, not godly men.[60] Unlike Vane's permanent senate of saints, Harrington's senate would comprise men (not necessarily godly), elected by the people, and the elected senators would debate and propose laws. An assembly, also elected by the people and which would sit constantly, would vote for these proposed laws. This would be a truly free Commonwealth, with people living under laws to which they had consented. Harrington's overriding belief in election, and his leaning towards broader participation, were phenomenal for his time. Harrington (and he shared this with Vane) did not particularly trust people – neither those in power nor those who voted for them – but he did trust laws. He believed that an elected assembly voting for laws proposed by an elected and rotating senate would ensure that good laws would get made, and these good laws would make men good.[61]

Hesilrige liked Harrington's proposal. So too did Charles Fleetwood. And soon the ideas were in the air. In taverns or in any of the country's new coffee houses (the Londoner Thomas Rugg notes there was hardly a street in London where you could not buy coffee), people were talking politics.[62] 'The palates of the English were as Fanatical as their Brains,' noted one scoffing observer.[63] Harrington and his friends regularly met at the Nonsuch tavern on Bow Street, and at the Turk's Head in New Palace Yard, round the corner from his home. By the autumn of 1659, they were meeting – and being listened to – nearly every night in an upstairs room at the Turk's Head. They became known as the Rota Club. They sat round a big oval table, from which a big slice had been cut out so that Miles, the owner of the Turk's Head, could move into the middle and keep the men's cups filled with hot coffee. John Aubrey recalls how the heady debates held in this stuffy, smoke-filled room were way beyond anything ever heard in St Stephen's Chapel where the Commons sat. The MPs' arguments, he wrote, were 'flatt' by comparison. Many of the decade's protagonists joined the club. It was a mixed crew, Aubrey tells us. Harrington's 'disciples' were there, along with other virtuosi.[64] There is no record of any women attending. John Milton's student Cyriack Skinner was the chairman of the club. He would pitch up after a day of writing down Milton's latest lines for *Paradise Lost*. William Petty, the mapper of Ireland and friend of Henry Cromwell's, was a member, as were former Levellers John Wildman and Maximilian Petty. Harrington's good friends Andrew Marvell and Henry Neville went along. Thomas Hobbes did too, as did John Evelyn, whose brother Arthur was married to Harrington's sister, Ann. Marchamont Nedham also turned up. He had lost his post as editor of *Mercurius Politicus* in May, but he changed tack (again) after the fall of the Protectorate. In August he had been recalled to write the news, and he endorsed the restored Rump in his pamphlet *Interest Will Not Lie*. 'It is the Interest of all to keep him out,' Nedham wrote, meaning Charles II.[65]

As the Rota Club became more and more popular, members of the public could pay eighteen pence to watch the Members at work. Samuel Pepys, now secretary to Edward Montagu, the general-at-sea, lived just around the corner in Axe Yard and went regularly to watch the debates.[66] The Rota Club was not a tight cabal of like-minded thinkers conspiring to institute a ready-made Commonwealth, although Harrington surely hoped his model would prevail. They were men brought together by ideas and the opportunity to think hard about government. The evenings were spent discussing different constitutional forms and principles, from classical Rome to current events in Westminster. Each member would then cast, secretly, a vote for his preferred idea. According to Anthony Wood, the antiquary from Oxford, it was the thrill of participating, and of voting, which made the club so popular and so fun. For Aubrey, the success of the Rota Club derived from the urgency of the time. Their debates were real and were necessary, for at this time, 'there was no possibility of the King's returne'.[67]

Things reached a crisis in autumn. Royalists, with encouragement from Charles II abroad, had been plotting a series of rebellions, with little chance of success. Whitehall may have been unsettled and squabbling about senates, but there was no will among the regime's antagonists for war. When Viscount John Mordaunt, a career Royalist rebel, declared for King Charles in Surrey, hoping to ignite a series of insurrections across the country, only thirty men turned up to echo his cries. Thomas Scot, the new Commonwealth's spymaster who had replaced John Thurloe, had also got wind of the plot, and was able to break 'the neck of this malignant design' before many rebels had a chance to stir. Would-be plotters were rounded up in Herefordshire, Bristol, Bath and Tonbridge.[68] Mary Cromwell's husband, Thomas Belasyse, Lord Fauconberg, was sent to the Tower. However, up in Cheshire, one rebellion did get under way which played a part in this year's bewildering sequence of events and exhausting pace of change.

Sir George Booth, once a parliamentarian, Member of Richard's Parliament, experienced soldier and popular local figure in Cheshire, had not received (or chose to ignore) the warning that the 1659 risings had been compromised. He managed to occupy Cheshire and parts of North Wales and Lancashire, which potentially provided a safe bit of coast on which Charles II or foreign allies could land. For nearly three weeks Booth held on, supported by about a thousand insurgents. John Lambert, however, restored to military office with the return of the Rump, was on his way with five regiments. On 19 August, Lambert and his experienced cavalry defeated Booth and the insurgents. Booth fled south, disguised as a woman and hoping to make it across the Channel. A suspicious innkeeper gave him away, noting 'Mrs Dorothy's' large feet and need for a razor. Booth was arrested and taken to the Tower, where Vane and Hesilrige interrogated him. He had, he asserted, been agitating for a 'full and free parliament', and not for the king.[69]

Whether or not Booth was telling the truth here, this cry for a full and free Parliament would get louder and louder over the coming months, and was spurred on by Lambert's provocative grab for power. Puffed up with success from his suppression of 'Booth's Uprising', and buoyed with the belief that God was on his side, Lambert and his officers turned on Parliament. With renewed vigour, the army – goaded by Lambert – badgered the procrastinating Parliament to not let its constitutional wishes from May be 'laid asleep', and to adopt Henry Vane's godly senate.[70] The army that had triumphantly restored the Rump in May was now in conflict with it, and Lambert was on the rise. An officers' petition demanded that Lambert be reinstated as a major-general, and that Desborough and Monck should be promoted. Charles Fleetwood shared these demands, known as the Derby petition, with Arthur Hesilrige, who was incensed. He assumed that Lambert was behind them and moved to throw him in the Tower. His officers were punished for petitioning.[71] On 5 October, the army responded with another very 'saucy' petition, according to Lucy Hutchinson. Desborough presented it to Parliament. It asserted the army's right to petition Parliament, but it also professed loyalty.[72] Parliament, fearing that sedition was spreading, came down too heavily. MPs voted to decommission Lambert and Desborough, and to strip Fleetwood of his office as commander-in-chief. Instead, military command should belong to a parliamentary committee, on which Arthur Hesilrige would sit. This was a red rag to an army that feared – as it had during Cromwell's Protectorate – being controlled by civilian politicians.[73] Lambert rallied his troops, and they marched on Westminster. When Speaker Lenthall and the MPs turned up for work on 13 October, they were sent home by the same army that had ushered them in the previous April. For the second time in less than six months, the republic had no Parliament. And, in a repeat of April 1653, the army had effected a coup that rendered the ship of state rudderless.[74]

From his home, Dalkeith Castle near Edinburgh, General George Monck, commander of the Scottish army, was monitoring events carefully. A pragmatic and strategic man, and a soldier all his life, Monck had, despite being loyal to both Oliver and Richard Cromwell, acknowledged the Rump when it was restored by the army in April. He had assured them of his and his soldiers' fidelity. 'Obedience is my greate principle,' he had said.[75] When Oliver Cromwell had first used his soldiers to dismiss Parliament, back in 1653, Monck had kept quiet, and accepted the offer of a seat in Barebone's Parliament. When this assembly was dissolved and Oliver Cromwell became Protector, Monck remained loyal. When Oliver died and Richard became Protector, Monck had welcomed him. In November he had thanked Richard for giving him custody of Holyrood House and other favours, and promised to serve him as best he could.[76] But he had not backed Richard when he faced the military coup in 1659. To do so had seemed futile and he remained loyal to his fellow soldiers. But John Lambert's and the army's behaviour in the autumn of 1659 alarmed him.

It was Oliver Cromwell who had advanced Monck's career. He had been a soldier since the age of sixteen, travelling to Cadiz, La Rochelle, the Netherlands, and to Ireland in 1641, leading his own regiment against Irish rebels. He had first fought for Charles I against Parliament, and spent over two years in the Tower of London for doing so, from 1644 until late 1646. There he wrote a book about strategy in war and fell in love with the laundress Anne Radford, who later became his wife. Monck could claim ancestry to Edward IV – a descendant of a bastard son – and was related to the earl of Leicester, but he was not from a wealthy or noble family. He had grown up in Devon, the son of the debt-prone Thomas and the better-off Elizabeth, the daughter of a successful Exeter merchant. George had had to work for his living, as a soldier. He was rather thickset and liked tobacco and a drink. He could joke but he also had a temper. He had shown courage and callousness on the field, and had been known to strike underhand deals with the enemy off the field, gambles that did not always pay off.

He was released from the Tower in order to fight in Ireland, for Parliament. In 1650 he had joined Cromwell on the campaign to Scotland, and had been granted his own regiment. He excelled at the battle of Dunbar, besieged Edinburgh Castle and brought Scotland under the Commonwealth's control, before taking to the sea and fighting against the Dutch in 1653. In 1654, Cromwell had made him commander-in-chief of the forces in Scotland: he was given money, power and soldiers whom he kept paid (unlike the troops in England) and well fed – and therefore loyal. He did not, however, share Cromwell's toleration of the sects. He abhorred religious fanatics – most of all the Quakers, who were sweeping through Scotland in the summer of 1659. He and his wife were in favour of a national Church, rather like Richard Cromwell. Monck was not on the side of liberty of conscience, but he did believe in the liberty of Parliament.[77]

In August, Charles II asked Monck's younger brother, Nicholas, a known Royalist, to deliver a letter to George. The letter enclosed an offer of a substantial annual sum of money (£100,000), in exchange for military support of his restoration. Monck had declined, but not immediately. It had been rumoured that he intended to join George Booth in his Cheshire rising and that he was, like Booth, in favour of a full and free Parliament – so not necessarily for the king, but not wedded to the current regime either. When Lambert turned his soldiers on Parliament in October, Monck was forced to show his hand. He demanded the restoration of the Rump. He had already offered support to Arthur Hesilrige, in a coded letter, and he immediately began to purge from within his own forces any soldiers who he suspected were in favour of Lambert's coup. He also began to prepare to march south, to London, should he need to.[78]

Meanwhile, in place of the council of state, a hastily established body of men called a 'committee of safety' – resurrected from the outbreak of war in 1642 – was entrusted with running the country. So at sea were its members – among them the political survivor Bulstrode Whitelocke, Henry Vane (for a while), Charles Fleetwood, John Desborough and John Lambert – that they even discussed recalling Richard from his place of exile and reinstating him as Lord Protector.[79] Aware that Monck was making moves to march down from Scotland, they sent John Lambert up to meet him. In early November, Lambert left London, to the awful and too familiar sound of soldiers beating drums, the soundtrack of war. The republic's army was now fighting itself. At the end of November, Arthur Hesilrige – who was not on the committee of safety – and a small group of fellow republicans similarly appalled by the expulsion of the Rump secretly made Monck commander-in-chief of the army in England, as he already was in Scotland. Hesilrige had also managed to muster senior officers such as the popular but rather radical Vice-Admiral John Lawson, who, like Monck, was for the restoration of the Rump. Lawson, who had been reinstated as vice-admiral when Richard's Protectorate fell, now commanded the Channel's warships. He sailed these vessels up the Thames and threatened to starve London through the winter unless the Rump Parliament was allowed to sit again. The committee of safety was forced to surrender, with Fleetwood ordered to retire to his country estate, as was Desborough. Henry Vane was also expelled, for conspiring with the army as a member of the committee of safety. He eventually withdrew to his home in Belleau, Lincolnshire. On Christmas Eve, Fleetwood handed over the keys to St Stephen's Chapel to Speaker Lenthall and, on Boxing Day, forty-two restored MPs took their seats. For Arthur Hesilrige, who saw himself as the guardian of parliamentary liberty, this was a triumph, and his very brief moment of glory.

The year ended, then, with the Rump Parliament restored for the second time. Everything had been turned upside down again. It was now that the bovine insult the 'Rump' stuck as the name of the unpopular, unfree Parliament, mocked and ridiculed in ballads and pamphlets. 'A Rump is the hinder part of the many-headed Beast, the Back-door of the Devils Arse, a Peake, Tyranny and Rebellion ending in a Stink . . . a Crab Commonwealth,' began *The Character of the Rump*.[80] As Thomas Rugg noted in his diurnal for December 1659: 'another jeering printed sheet that jeered the Parliment, and called it the rump and the Speaker the fart'.[81]

Richard Cromwell need not have fallen from power in quite the way he did. Perhaps a different personality may have better managed the unrest in the army and the wavering loyalty of a Fleetwood and a Desborough. Perhaps he could have reassured an unpaid army better, and disciplined the most zealous in the rank and file and those who were agitating for a return to the good old cause. He might have heeded George Monck's advice, offered at the beginning of his brief reign, to reduce the army and purge it of those whose religious ideas were so destabilising.[82] He might have reshuffled his council in a way that diluted the influence of his father's former allies – Thurloe and Broghill, for instance – whose hostility to the army was clear. He could, perhaps, have better handled what Lucy Hutchinson called 'such a perplexed government'. The republicans were vocal and verbose in

Parliament, but they were a minority and often outnumbered in votes, although as one commentator noted, 'standing pooles do corrupt'.[83] Perhaps he could have dissolved Parliament earlier, like his father might have done, and so silenced the voices of a Vane or a Hesilrige as well as stemmed the tide of the army's increasing mistrust of the sitting MPs.

Much blame has been laid at Richard's feet. He was the son who Cromwell worried was idle, who critics found under-prepared for his post and whose legitimacy was always in doubt as the 'pretended Protector'. Richard's perceived meekness and weakness, and the swiftness of his downfall, earned him the memorable and unkind epithets 'Queen Dick' and 'Tumble-down Dick'.[84] Consequently he has, for a long time, been unfairly and poorly represented by history.[85] There are only a few biographies, barely still in print, of this man who once had the top job. Not many would know that he ever did; even fewer would recognise his face from a portrait, his long, straight nose and wavy fair hair. Richard was not like his father, but the challenges he faced when he opened his first Parliament in January 1659 – an army that wanted money, a country with crippling debt, his legitimacy and the constitution in doubt – were similar to those faced by Oliver Cromwell during his Protectorate. As Edward Nicholas admitted even when deriding Richard as 'Tumble-down Dick', Oliver Cromwell also struggled to manage his Parliaments: 'And yet you remember that body was too hard for him.'[86] Oliver Cromwell, too, might not have been able to carry on keeping his politicised army in check. In 1659, the army was too great for Richard, and it brought him down. It is one of the many ironies of this endlessly revolutionary decade that, in 1660, it was the army that helped bring back Charles II.

1660

The last scean of some excellent play

Viscount Mordaunt to Henrietta Maria

In the early months of 1660, George Monck was like the falcon that Andrew Marvell had once imagined for Cromwell – seemingly at the Parliament's bidding, but not so tame that he might not break free and follow his own course. On 1 January 1660, Monck left Scotland without any orders and began to march south through the snow, his soldiers warmly dressed in thick woollen coats. This was in stark contrast to the unpaid, unshod and wavering English troops mustered by John Lambert. En route, Monck stayed with Thomas Fairfax in his newly built Nun Appleton just outside York. By the end of January, Monck arrived in London, accompanied by his wife, Anne, and their only son, Christopher.

On Friday 3 February, Monck made his way to Westminster with his formidable, disciplined army. He was plainly dressed but he rode on his horse in style, with trumpeters ahead of him, surrounded by his lifeguard, mounted and foot soldiers – nearly six thousand of them – following behind. The city was calm. On the Strand, outside Somerset House, the elderly, reinstated Speaker of Parliament, William Lenthall, greeted Monck. The two men embraced.[1] During his cold march south, while lodging and resting in England's towns and villages, Monck had heard the people's calls and received many a petition for a 'full and free Parliament', a Parliament that bore no stains of military meddling. This should be the Parliament that was sitting way back in December 1648, before Colonel Pride purged it, before Charles I was tried and executed. One of the first petitions Monck had received on his journey south had originated in the West, in his home county of Devon. Monck batted away the possibility of restoring the king: 'Monarchy cannot possibly be admitted for the future in these nations, because its support is taken away,' he said. The unhappy wars, Monck said, had given birth to several interests, 'both civil and spiritual'. He seemed to be echoing James Harrington in his invocation of how England was no longer suited to cultivating kings, for the political climate had changed. 'That Government then that is most able to comprehend and protect all Interests as aforesaid must needs be Republique,' Monck declared.[2] But he was inscrutable. Viscount Mordaunt, who had been behind the failed Royalist uprisings of the summer of 1659, wrote in a letter to Henrietta Maria, Charles I's widow, that 'Monck is so dark a man, no perspective can looke through him . . . it will be like the last scean of some excellent play, which the most judicious cannot positively say how it will end'.[3]

Londoners, too, had been calling for a full and free Parliament, and the restoration of those Members purged by force in 1648. They were weary, wrote Thomas Rugg in his diary, of the constant presence of soldiers, lodging in their homes and roaming their streets. And they were tired of rising prices and empty shops.[4] In December, after Lambert had kicked out the Rump, ordinary people had shut up their shops and taken to the streets, led by the city's apprentices – young men in their teens and their twenties who were learning a trade and looking to the future. These young shoemakers, grocers, apothecaries, tailors and haberdashers were motivated by money and stability, and not by political idealism. They called for a legitimate Parliament, and if such a Parliament voted back the king, then so be it. The young men massed in the streets to march towards the Guildhall to present their petition to

London's mayor. They proved an unpredictable crowd; a few were armed with pocket pistols, but some kicked a football about.[5] The committee of safety sent Colonel John Hewson and his red-coated foot soldiers to block the petition. The young men threw stones, rubbish, roof tiles and slippery shards of ice at the soldiers; some shots were fired. The riot lasted all day. One-eyed Hewson, himself once a cobbler, gave the orders to his men to shoot back. Apprentices pelted him with shoes and slippers. At least five apprentices were killed, according to Rugg; several more were wounded, including soldiers. Households were ordered to keep their sons at home and off the streets, but the apprentices continued to meet and to plot.[6]

On the day before Monck's arrival in London, on 2 February, more apprentices had gathered at Leadenhall, nearly seven hundred of them, beating drums and armed with swords, calling for a new Parliament.[7] London's common council, the body of men who governed the city with the Lord Mayor, had also declared in favour of a full and free Parliament, and was now angling to stop paying taxes. This common council was made up of men with little republican zeal, who did not share the affection of someone like Arthur Hesilrige for the restored Rump, and who did not all share memories of the wars. The Rump had declared that those Members who were refused entry in 1648 would not be readmitted, but that new elections would take place to fill the empty seats. They had still not declared, however, whether or how new candidates would be vetted. And it was still not really known whether Monck was an ally of the Rump, or whether he would force the Rump to heed the now deafening cries to restore the pre-purged Long Parliament. In response to London's rioters, the council of state ordered that the city's gates be burnt, preventing the city from defending itself if it came to an outright conflict between London and Parliament. It was not just in the capital that apprentices were rioting. The *Publick Intelligencer* reported tumult in Bristol, and a planned rising in Gloucester, too.[8]

On 6 February, Monck went to meet the Rump. He was welcomed and thanked by Lenthall. In return, Monck assured the MPs that their peaceful restoration was the work of God alone. But he also told them that, as he marched down from Scotland, he had encountered in each county cries for a free and full Parliament. The people yearned for settlement. Monck told the MPs that this would happen sooner if they did not force Members, as they were trying to do, to swear an oath abjuring the Stuarts (or any single person holding power) or a House of Lords, and if they readmitted those purged Members from 1648.[9] On 11 February, Monck demanded that the House clarify the terms for the election it had promised, and he urged Members to push ahead with an election for a fresh Parliament. He then told the city's common council what he had done.[10]

Samuel Pepys, who was just a schoolboy when Charles I was executed, began his famous diary on 1 January 1660. He began writing at a time of private grief. He and his wife Elizabeth had been married since 1655, but they had no children. Towards the end of 1659, Elizabeth had told Pepys that she thought she was pregnant, but then this hope was belied.[11] All of Pepys's private griefs and daily worries, his pleasures as well as the 'condition of the State', are recorded in his diary. His job in the exchequer office meant that he was worried about taxes not coming in, and about his own job and salary. He, like others, was unsure about Monck: 'All the world is at a loss to think what Monck will do,' he wrote.[12] However, on 11 February, once Monck had told the city that he was demanding a full and free Parliament, Pepys recorded joy and celebration. London believed that the Rump would soon be no longer. The church bells rang, bonfires were lit and rumps of meat were roasted on spits. The soldiers in the streets – representatives of an army that had brought the Rump into being, and then sacrificed it – were hailed and blessed by Londoners and given wine and money. It was a spectacle too great to ignore. Pepys rushed home to fetch his wife and show her the city on fire:

> But the common joy that was everywhere to be seen! The number of bonefires, there being fourteen between St Dunstan's and Temple-bar. And at Strand bridge I could at one view tell 31 fires. In King-streete, seven or eight; and all along burning and roasting and drinking for rumps – there being rumps tied upon sticks and carried up and down. The buchers at the maypole in the Strand rang a peal with their knifes when they were going to sacrifice their rump. On Ludgate-hill there was one turning of the spit, that had a rump tied upon it, and another basting of it. Indeed, it was past imagination, both the greatness and the suddenness of it.[13]

Addresses flooded in to Monck from all over the country, from Buckinghamshire, Hertfordshire, Norfolk, demanding the readmittance of the secluded Members of Parliament. From Nun Appleton in Yorkshire, Fairfax pleaded with Monck to listen to their cries, which he did.

On 21 February, seventy-three men, whose entry to St Stephen's Chapel had been blocked by Colonel Pride in December 1648, were allowed to take their seats in Parliament again. Monck and his soldiers shepherded them in. Among them was William Prynne. He arrived, Pepys tells us, with his grandfather's 'old basket-hilt sword' at his hip.[14] A great shout went up as he entered Westminster Hall. In the days leading up to this, Monck had been meeting and colluding with former Members. According to Bulstrode Whitelocke, who had retreated, waiting to see what would happen, 'Heer began the great turne, & the design of Moncke to take place.'[15] Some believed that Monck had always planned to reinstate the Long Parliament, and thereby restore the king. Edmund Ludlow thought Monck entirely unprincipled and ferociously ambitious. But Monck was keeping his options open. Soon he would begin to correspond secretly with Charles II in exile, after being approached by his Royalist cousin Sir John Grenville.[16] Near Westminster on the day that the restored Members took their seats in Parliament, Pepys sat drinking coffee with the composer Henry Purcell. They sang Italian and Spanish songs, and Matthew Locke's eight-part motet, 'Lord, Save the King'. They did not know whether or not a Stuart king would be saved; Richard Cromwell might come back, or perhaps Monck would wear the crown. 'Great is the talk of a single person, and that it would now be Charles, George, or Richard again,' wrote Pepys.[17]

On 16 March, the restored Long Parliament dissolved itself and elections for a fresh Parliament soon got under way. All eligible men could vote, regardless of their political or religious persuasion. Officially, no active Royalists were allowed to stand – but they did, and they won seats. Overall an unprecedented number of candidates stood for Parliament, many of whom had never done so before. Old Members departed. Arthur Hesilrige, who had believed Monck was at his bidding and loyal to the Rump, withdrew. (He died in 1661, before the Restoration regime could try him for treason.) Unlike the first fully British Parliaments of the 1650s, no Scottish or Irish MPs were eligible to sit. So, on 25 April, when the new Parliament, known as the Convention Parliament, met, it was an English Parliament. The House of Lords also reconvened: many young peers, with recently inherited titles, soon took their seats for the first time. A new generation had come of age. 'The times begines to change,' observed Thomas Rugg.[18]

In the Netherlands, Charles II and the exiled court were preparing to make overtures to the newly formed Convention Parliament. A declaration had been drafted and signed at Breda on 4 April, fully anticipating that this Parliament would soon invite Charles to come back as king. In the declaration, Charles pledged to respect the authority of Parliament, and to agree to however Parliament decided to protect liberty of conscience, and to however Parliament decided to deal with those who had fought for and served the Commonwealth, and profited from it with land and houses seized from Royalists. As it turned out, Charles's first Parliament would prove punishing on all these counts.[19]

On 1 May, the *Naseby*, so named after the crushing battle, with a bust of Oliver Cromwell at its bow, lay at anchor off the Kent coast. On board was Pepys, summoned by his patron Edward Montagu, general-at-sea. Monck was not the only one to have been communicating with Charles II in secret during the last few months. Montagu had been in touch with Charles since the summer. Suspecting him of moving towards the Royalist cause, Parliament had stripped Montagu of his naval command. But he could now re-emerge from a period of lying low at his home, Hinchingbrooke, to take his seat as a Member of Parliament, and resume being general-at-sea. In March he had told Pepys that he believed the king would now be restored, as long as Charles managed things carefully and soberly.[20] So Pepys and Montagu – soon to become the earl of Sandwich for his part in the imminent restoration – now waited in their ships until the instruction came to cross the Channel to collect Charles. People were already preparing to welcome back the monarchy. On the shore at Deal, a few maypoles had been set up, topped with flags, colourful ribbons streaming. In the streets of the town, some people were already drinking the king's health.[21]

That same day, 1 May, Charles II's declaration of Breda was read out before the House. The Commons and the Lords voted that the government of the country 'is and ought to be by King, Lords and Commons', according to the ancient constitution or, as John Evelyn called it, 'its antient and right basis'.[22] A few days later Charles was proclaimed king in London and throughout the three nations: England, Scotland and Ireland. The bells on Bow Church, Thomas Rugg noted, could not be heard above the shouts of joy.[23]

Pepys and Montagu set sail. The *Naseby*, soon to be renamed the *Charles*, crudely disguised its republican heritage. During the crossing, the ship's tailors cut a huge crown out of yellow cloth to stitch over the Commonwealth arms on the ship's ensign.[24] Once the fleet had collected the royal party – Charles and his brothers James and Henry, dukes of York and Gloucester – they sailed back to England. The weather was good, with a fresh wind. Charles II sat on the quarterdeck and moved Pepys to tears with the story of his miraculous escape from Worcester, back in 1651.[25]

On 25 May 1660, Charles II landed at Dover. As he set foot on English soil again, Monck was the first man he greeted; 'father', Charles called him. Charles then made his way to London, to claim his throne. On 29 May, his thirtieth birthday, Charles processed through the city in a blaze of colour and noise, surrounded by regiment after regiment, hundreds of men each wearing their colours, banging drums or blowing trumpets, or with swords drawn, in defence of the king. This was an extraordinary display of military might and unity by a new army: Monck had dismissed political and religious radicals, and promised the others their pay. Thomas Rugg watched the procession from a spot on the Strand. People shouted and cheered, and women threw springtime flowers onto the gravel-lined streets, churned up by the horses' hooves. Just a little further along, at Whitehall, lifelike puppets of Oliver Cromwell and his wife lay burning on top of a huge bonfire.[26] England's republic was no longer.

Epilogue: Restoration

'Tis not, what once it was, the world;
But a rude heap, together hurled.

Andrew Marvell,
'Upon Appleton House'

Charles II's coronation in Westminster Abbey on 23 April 1661 was pointedly splendid. It certainly made up for the miserable coronation he had endured in Scone ten years earlier. The day before his anointing and crowning in the Abbey, Charles processed through the streets of London, 'according to the custome', and yet also far outstripping it. Astride his horse Nun Appleton – the gift of Thomas Fairfax – he rode through four eighty-foot-tall triumphal arches erected for the purpose. They may only have been made of wood and canvas, but they were gorgeously decorated, and they towered over the streets. Hemmed in by the cheering crowds of his subjects – citizens no longer – Charles followed a richly dressed and bejewelled cavalcade of chaplains, judges, knights of the Bath, noblemen (including many who were freshly minted) and aldermen. Just ahead of the king was Edward Montagu, now the earl of Sandwich. Behind Charles was George Monck, now the duke of Albemarle. For the Garter king-of-arms, Sir Edward Walker, such magnificence had never been seen before; it surpassed all previous coronation processions. No cost was spared, noted the Venetian envoy, Francesco Giavarina. Pepys, for once, was lost for words: 'It is impossible to relate the glory of this day,' he wrote. He had mostly spent the day drinking with Sir William Penn in a house on Cornhill. (Perhaps they drank from one of the newly conceived coronation mugs – those made for Charles II were the first in what has become an unbroken tradition.[1])

This coronation was a muscular show of royal strength and magnificence. It needed to be, to overwrite the republic and its own ceremonies, which had worked hard to legitimise constitutional experimentation and novelty. Both Edward Walker, who as chief herald was in charge of the coronation ceremonies, and the classicist John Ogilby, mastermind of the procession, presented Charles as the legitimate, divinely ordained monarch, and the next in the long, uninterrupted line of English kings and queens. The ceremony was haunted, nonetheless, by the spectre of the republic. At the arch at Leadenhall, a woman dressed so as to represent Rebellion appeared, although she was dramatically shooed away by a woman denoting Monarchy. A painting on one of the giant processional arches depicted Charles II chasing away the – distinctively Cromwell-like – figure of Usurpation. One of the designers of the arches, Balthazar Gerbier, had been a spy for the republic; another, Peter Mills, had built elegant houses for the new republican elite, including for John Thurloe. There were other ironies and surprising continuities. Many of the horses in the impressive cavalcade came from Cromwell's stables, and Charles's own horse was a foal of the mare Thomas Fairfax had ridden at the battle of Naseby in 1645 – the battle that had crushed Charles I.[2]

Even the crown placed on Charles II's head in the ceremony bore painful traces of the recent past, and of the contingency of monarchy. In one sense, it represented a new start, as it replaced the medieval crown that had been so iconoclastically melted down in 1649. Yet it was made by Robert and Thomas Vyner, the goldsmiths who had served Cromwell – and made a great deal of money – in the 1650s. (It is this crown, known as St Edward's, that is still used today; the fact that it was in a sense forged in the dying fires of the republic is quietly forgotten, or at least obscured behind the myths of medieval continuity that surround the coronation ritual.) Clement Kinnersley, who had supplied Cromwell's palaces with furniture and tapestries, offered back the ancient and precious anointing spoon which he had bought at the Sale of the Late King's Goods back at the beginning of the decade, when monarchy had been abolished. (This, too, is still used to cradle the holy oil with which British monarchs are anointed, in imitation of biblical kings.) Towards the end of the ceremony, specially commissioned coronation medals were scattered and flung among the congregation. They depicted Charles II being crowned by peace, but the medals had been designed and cast by Thomas Simon, Oliver Cromwell's chief engraver.[3]

Many in Westminster Abbey that day must have shuffled uncomfortably in their seats during the coronation sermon. Bishop George Morley recalled the terrible wars, the destruction and lives lost. Edward Hyde, just made the earl of Clarendon, then read out the king's pardon, which asked everyone to forgive and to forget. Never before had there been a coronation pardon of such magnitude.[4] Pledging their loyalty to the new king were many who had fought his father at some of the most appalling battles of the civil wars, including Algernon Percy, earl of Northumberland, and Edward Montagu, earl of Manchester (a cousin of the other Edward Montagu, earl of Sandwich). As Charles stepped out of Westminster Hall, treading the traditional blue cloth that covered the route between the Hall and the Abbey, he needed only to look up to be reminded of what could happen to kings; there, on twenty-foot oak poles, at the southern end of Westminster Hall, were the severed, decomposing heads of Oliver Cromwell and his fellow regicides Henry Ireton and John Bradshaw. Forgiveness, for all Bishop Morley's words, only went so far: Parliament's 'Act of Free and General Pardon, Indemnity and Oblivion', passed in the summer of 1660, did not extend to those who had signed Charles I's death warrant, even if they were already dead. Oliver Cromwell had been dug up from his tomb inside Westminster Abbey only a few months earlier, in January 1661, his near-skeletal body hanged for treason at Tyburn, and his head hacked off. His body was thrown into the pit but his skull stared down at Westminster for over twenty more years, before it disappeared for a while. It is now buried at Sidney Sussex College, Cambridge.

Today, behind some railings in front of the House of Commons, there stands a confident bronze statue of Cromwell, sword and Bible in hand. It was erected at the end of the nineteenth century, a time when Cromwell – he who had railed against and turfed out his Parliaments – was revered as a champion of parliamentarian liberty. Cromwell's personal reputation continues to rise and fall, in tune with the times and changing political scenes. He is a hero to some – he was voted one of the top ten Greatest Britons in 2001 – and a tyrant to others. He remains widely loathed throughout Ireland, where the atrocities at Drogheda and Wexford will never be forgotten and where the subsequent treatment of Catholics and huge-scale redistribution of land are seen as Cromwell's personal legacy. But he is also seen as the godly revolutionary, fired up by religious fervour and intent on pushing further the Reformation that had begun over a hundred years earlier, under Henry VIII. At the same time, Cromwell's regime was more tolerant of radical sects and less punitive to Catholics than any before and after him, until the nineteenth century. Cromwell's revolutionary zeal was also offset by a political conservatism, and entangled with a ruthless personal ambition. For some, he betrayed the republic and the good old cause when he became Lord Protector. He is, for many, the man who would be king, although he was the man who would definitely not be king. He was a leader and his impact on England, Scotland and Ireland, and beyond, was, as the poet Andrew Marvell predicted early on, 'climacteric', but he did not want a crown, and his Protectorate was not a monarchy.[5] He believed in regular Parliaments and in the work that Parliaments could do and the taxes they could raise, and, for the first time, Scotland and Ireland were represented at Westminster. But Cromwell also found the MPs intensely frustrating and he did not trust them to carry out God's work. Such paradoxes are inevitable consequences of the period's complex and competing political and religious ideas, and of the difficulties inherent in bringing about and legitimising substantial political change. Forging a state and creating a constitution are fraught, and the casting of the experience of republican rule in the 1650s as either a failure or as quasi-monarchical remains a reason why Britain might prefer to keep the status quo.

The question of the legacy of England's republic is an even more unsettled one than that of Cromwell, although similarly polarising. Historians have long quarrelled over, and often underplayed, just how revolutionary – and republican – it all was.[6] After all, by the end of the decade, before Richard's fall, the regime looked pretty royal and, with the Restoration, some things swiftly went back to how they used to be. Certain political figures switched sides (Bulstrode Whitelocke, for example), others retreated, and the ground closed over. The beginning of Charles II's reign was backdated to 1649. Parliamentary acts since 1642 were declared null. Bishops were restored, a new Book of Common Prayer was published and Presbyterianism receded while Anglicanism reigned supreme. Quakers survived and continued to convert, but they were persecuted. Baptists, too, held on. Other sects – Fifth Monarchists, Levellers, Diggers, Seekers, Ranters – shrank back into the shadows. The Toleration

Act, granting freedom of worship to non-conformist Protestants, was not passed until 1689. Catholics would not be free for another hundred years after that. Above all, Charles II ruled with full prerogative; he did not return under any imposed conditions – or not any that limited his powers any more than his predecessors. The Bill of Rights restricting the prerogative of the British monarch was not passed until 1689, when William III and Mary II succeeded to the throne. Still, Charles I's catastrophic relationship with Parliament cast a long, long shadow. The 'cavalier' Parliament – the name given to the new Parliament elected after the Restoration – instituted a more punitive, less tolerant and less forgiving regime than Charles II might have led, had he felt able to meddle and assert his prerogative in the way that his father did.

Monarchy, however, had been transformed, and there were more revolutions to come. Parliaments continued to debate the constitution and poets (not least Andrew Marvell) picked at the king and his court. To foreign observers, the English were capricious seekers after novelty, forever tinkering and experimenting, quite unlike anyone else.[7] Within thirty years of the Restoration, England deposed Charles II's brother and heir James II for being Catholic (and suspected of absolutist ambition), and experienced another upheaval whose strangeness and wrinkles have been successfully smoothed over by an eighteenth-century label: the 'Glorious Revolution'. James's successor, William III, was Protestant and the Dutch stadholder: the experienced head of a republic, ironically. It was William's wife, Mary, who had the claim to England's and Scotland's thrones, as James II and VII's daughter. Religion trumped legitimacy, and the choreographers of William and Mary's accession as de facto sovereigns, and as equal partners in England's first ever joint monarchy, were quite prepared to recast (again) what a king could be. The troubled relationship between the head of state and Parliament that the republic, and the rest of the seventeenth century, tried variously to heal and remake, led eventually to the establishment of Britain's constitutional monarchy, which looked remarkably republican to others. In 1748, the French philosopher Charles-Louis de Secondat, baron de Montesquieu, memorably remarked that Britain's monarchy is really a republic in disguise: 'a nation where the republic hides under the form of a monarchy'.[8] It is revealing, and poignant, that Elizabeth II chose to name her first-born son and heir Charles, a nod to the century that abolished and then remade monarchy. It is an acknowledgement of fragility, and acceptance that the royals exist only as long as the people, and Parliament, want them to.

A non-monarchical settlement did not survive the republic, but a vitally important tradition of English republicanism was conceived. When James Harrington became aware that the tide had turned, in early 1660, his Rota Club broke up. 'Well, the King will come in,' he said. But he did not believe monarchy would last: 'Let him come in, and call a Parliament of the greatest Cavaliers in England, so they be men of Estates, and let them sett but 7 yeares, and they will all turn Common-wealthe's men.'[9] In the short term, Harrington was wrong – and he ended up in the Tower in 1661. He was eventually released from prison on account of poor health. Later generations would revisit Harrington's republican works in different contexts. His ideas were recalled by those Whigs attempting to exclude James II from the throne. His writings and prescient ideas about democracy were unearthed again, a hundred years later, by English republicans who were watching the dramatic events taking place across the Channel in France. Harrington's fictional realm of Oceana even influenced the constitution offered to the French National Assembly in 1793.[10] And, in America in 1779, when John Adams, the second president of the United States, was creating the constitution of the state of Massachusetts he wondered about renaming it Oceana.

Harrington is remembered now as one of England's great political theorists. So too is Thomas Hobbes, the defender of absolute sovereignty whose accommodation with the republican regime is often strangely forgotten. Henry Vane and his republican vision, which was so influential in the republic's last year, are less well known; Vane was considered too dangerous, and he was executed in 1662. But many of the lionised writers and thinkers of the second half of the seventeenth century were unequivocally shaped by the republic, regardless of their political leanings, and their work influenced the generations that succeeded them. The careers of Andrew Marvell, William Davenant, Margaret Cavendish, John Dryden, John Evelyn, John Bunyan, Robert Boyle, Robert Hooke, Christopher Wren, John Locke – among others – all first took form and took root in the 1650s.

And as for John Milton, the republic's greatest advocate, his epic *Paradise Lost*, now so entrenched in the canon of English literature, belongs firmly to England's republican past. When the Restoration came, Milton was forced into hiding with a friend. As a last gasp, he had brought out a second edition of his republican treatise: *A Readie and Easie Way to Establish a Free Commonwealth*. His last words of 'our expiring liberty' urged the English not to rush back into the yoke of monarchy. But rush back to the old bondage they did. Milton abandoned his political prose tracts, many of which were burned by the public executioner in the summer of 1660, and pressed on with *Paradise Lost*, while the decadent sounds of the restored regime jangled around him – what he called the 'barbarous dissonance / Of Bacchus and his revellers'.[11]

Paradise Lost, in the context, was a poignant title. Yet not everything *was* lost. If the enduring legacy, or character, of the republic can be represented by one person, it is perhaps not by one of the great statesmen or political theorists or poets – not Cromwell or Milton – but by one of the decade's lesser-known protagonists: Samuel Hartlib, a child of war. He was ceaselessly committed to improvement and reformation of all kinds, willingly embracing the new and looking askance at the familiar, and he straddled political divides while desiring both worldly and spiritual gains. In all this, he epitomises the revolutionary spirit of England's first and only republic.

List of Illustrations

Prologue: Execution
The execution of Charles I, engraving, from *Abscheulichste Unerhörte Execution . . .* (1649). This engraving copies the earliest known depiction of Charles I's execution, which was printed in a Dutch publication, *Tragicum Theatrum*. © British Library archive / Bridgeman Images

1649
Detail of the port of Drogheda, Ireland, engraving and etching attributed to Wenceslaus Hollar, originally produced for James Cranford, *The Teares of Ireland* (1642). © The Trustees of the British Museum

1650
Portrait bust of John Milton, engraving (1767), after a bust attributed to Edward Pearce (*c.*1660). © Penta Springs Limited / Alamy Stock Photo

1651
Charles II hiding in an oak tree at Boscobel after the Battle of Worcester in 1651, engraving (1660). © Bridgeman Images

1652
Engraving of an orchard by John Goddard, for the title page of Ralph Austen, *A Treatise of Fruit-Trees* (1653), taken from the copy held by Balliol College, Oxford. © Bodleian Libraries

1653
Oliver Cromwell dissolving the Rump Parliament in 1653, reproduced from a contemporary satirical Dutch print. © Lebrecht Music & Arts / Alamy Stock Photo

1654
Oliver Cromwell by Samuel Cooper, miniature on vellum (*c.*1653). © The Buccleuch Collections / Bridgeman Images

1655
Map of the Caribbean and Central America by Joan Blaeu, from his atlas *Toonneel des Aerdrycks*, Volume II (1650). © Royal Geographical Society / Bridgeman Images

1656
James Nayler standing on the pillory at the Exchange in London, where he had his tongue bored through with a hot iron, etching (1656). © Chronicle / Alamy Stock Photo

1657
The reinvestiture of Oliver Cromwell as Lord Protector, 26 June 1657, engraving, from *A Further Narrative of the Passages of these Times in the Commonwealth of England* (1658). © British Library archive / Bridgeman Images

1658
Oliver Cromwell's wood-and-wax effigy lying in state in Somerset House, etching, from *Some Farther Intelligence of the Affairs of England* (1659). © British Library archive / Bridgeman Images

1659
Richard Cromwell, engraving, from J. Granger, *A Biographical History of England* (1824). © Look and Learn / Bridgeman Images

1660
Roasting the rump, engraving, from Alexander Brome, *Rump: or, An Exact Collection of the Choycest Poems and Songs Relating to the Late Times* (1662), taken from the facsimile copy held by the National Library of Scotland, shelfmark Glen.119. © National Library of Scotland

Epilogue: Restoration
Detail from the coronation procession of Charles II through London in 1661, etching by Wenceslaus Hollar for John Ogilby, *The Entertainment of His Most Excellent Majestie Charles II . . .* (1662). © Penta Springs Limited / Alamy Stock Photo

List of Abbreviations

Abbott Wilbur Cortez Abbott, ed., *Writings and Speeches of Oliver Cromwell*, 3 vols (Cambridge, MA: Harvard University Press, 1939)

Acts and Ordinances *Acts and Ordinances of the Interregnum, 1642–1660*, 3 vols, ed. C. H. Firth and R. S. Rait (London, 1911), II

Aubrey, *Brief Lives* *Aubrey's Brief Lives, Edited from the Original Manuscripts*, ed. Oliver Lawson Dick (London: Secker and Warburg, 1949)

BL British Library, London

Burton, *Diary* *Diary of Thomas Burton Esq*, 4 vols, ed. John Towill Rutt (London, 1828), British History Online

Cary, *Memorials* *Memorials of the Great Civil War in England from 1646–52*, 2 vols, ed. Henry Cary, II (London, 1842)

Clarendon, *History* Edward Hyde, earl of Clarendon, *The History of the Rebellion and Civil Wars in England Begun in the Year 1641*, 6 vols, ed. W. Dunn Macray (Oxford: Clarendon Press, 1888)

Clarke Papers *The Clarke Papers: Selections from the Papers of William Clarke, Secretary to the Council of the Army, 1647–1649, and to General Monck and the Commanders of the Army in Scotland, 1651–1660*, 4 vols, ed. C. H. Firth (London: Camden Society, 1901)

CJ *Journal of the House of Commons* (London, 1802–3), British History Online

Correspondence of Henry Cromwell *The Correspondence of Henry Cromwell 1655–1659: From the British Library Lansdowne Manuscripts*, ed. Peter Gaunt (Cambridge: Cambridge University Press for the Royal Historical Society, 2007)

CSP: Domestic *Calendar of State Papers Domestic Series Preserved in the State Department [Commonwealth, 1649–60]*, 13 vols, ed. Mary Anne Everett Green (London, 1875–86)

CSP: Venice *Calendar of State Papers Relating to English Affairs in the Archives of Venice*, XXVIII–XXXII, ed. Allen B. Hinds (London, 1929), British History Online

Evelyn, Diary *The Diary of John Evelyn*, 6 vols, ed. E. S. de Beer (Oxford: Oxford University Press, 1955)

Gardiner, *History* S. R. Gardiner, *History of the Commonwealth and Protectorate, 1649–1656*, 4 vols (London: Longmans, Green, 1894–1901)

Hartlib Papers M. Greengrass, M. Leslie and M. Hannon, eds, *The Hartlib Papers*, published by the Digital Humanities Institute, University of Sheffield, 2013: http://www.dhi.ac.uk/hartlib

Josselin, *Diary* *The Diary of Ralph Josselin, 1616–1683*, ed. Alan Macfarlane (London: British Academy, 1976)

Letters, Writings, and Speeches *The Letters, Writings, and Speeches of Oliver Cromwell*, 3 vols, gen. ed. John Morrill (Oxford: Oxford University Press, 2022)

Lords Journal *Journal of the House of Lords*, 42 vols (London, 1767–1830), British History Online

Ludlow, *Memoirs* *The Memoirs of Edmund Ludlow, Lieutenant-General of the Horse in the Army of the Commonwealth of England, 1625–1672*, 2 vols, ed. C. H. Firth (Oxford: Clarendon Press, 1894)

Marvell *The Poems of Andrew Marvell*, ed. Nigel Smith (Harlow: Pearson, 2003; rev. edn, 2007)

Milton, *Complete Prose Works* *Complete Prose Works of John Milton*, 8 vols, ed. Don M. Wolfe et al. (New Haven, CT: Yale University Press, 1953–82)

NPG National Portrait Gallery, London

ODNB *Oxford Dictionary of National Biography* (https://www.oxforddnb.com)

Pepys, *Diary* *The Diary of Samuel Pepys*, 9 vols, ed. Robert Latham and William Matthews (London: HarperCollins, 1971)

State Papers Thurloe *A Collection of the State Papers of John Thurloe*, 7 vols, ed. Thomas Birch (London, 1742), British History Online

TNA The National Archives, London

Whitelocke, *Diary* *The Diary of Bulstrode Whitelocke, 1605–1675*, ed. Ruth Spalding (Oxford: Oxford University Press for the British Academy, 1990)

Whitelocke, *Memorials* Bulstrode Whitelocke, *Memorials of English Affairs from the Beginning of the Reign of Charles I to the Happy Restoration of King Charles II*, 4 vols (Oxford, 1853)

Whitelocke, *Memorials* (1682) Bulstrode Whitelocke, *Memorials of English Affairs from the Beginning of the Reign of Charles I to the Happy Restoration of King Charles II* (1682)

Notes

Prologue: Execution

1 *A Remonstrance of his Excellency Thomas Lord Fairfax, Lord Generall of the Parliaments Forces. And of the Generall Councell of Officers held at St. Albans the 16. of November, 1648* (1648), p. 62. It was 'wild' according to *Mercurius Pragmaticus* (5-12 December 1648), p. 4.

2 Andrew Hopper, *'Black Tom': Sir Thomas Fairfax and the English Revolution* (Manchester and New York: Manchester University Press, 2007), p. 97. On the purge see *The Memoirs of Edmund Ludlow Lieutenant-General of the Horse in the Army of the Commonwealth of England, 1625–1672*, ed. C. H. Firth, 2 vols (Oxford: Clarendon Press, 1894), I, pp. 210–12; *The Parliament under the Power of the Sword* (1648); Whitelocke, *Diary*, p. 225; William Prynne, *A True and ful Relation of the Officers and Armies forcible seising of divers Eminent Members Of the Commons House* (1648); *A Declaration Collected out of the Journalls of Both Houses of Parliament* (6–13 December 1648); *The Perfect Weekly Account Containing Certain Special and Remarkable Passages from Both Houses of Parliament* (6–13 December 1648); *The Kingdomes Weekly Intelligencer* (5–12 December 1648); *Mercurius Pragmaticus* (5–12 December 1648); *Mercurius Elencticus* (5–12 December 1648); *A Perfect Diurnall of Some Passages in Parliament* (4–11 December 1648). See also David Underdown, *Pride's Purge: Politics in the Puritan Revolution* (Oxford: Clarendon Press, 1971); and C. V. Wedgwood, *A King Condemned: The Trial and Execution of Charles I* (1964; repr. London: I. B. Tauris, 2011).

3 *The Parliamentary or Constitutional History of England, Being a Faithful Account of all the Most Remarkable Transactions in Parliament*, XIII (1755), p. 449.

4 'Rump' from Clement Walker, *Anarchia Anglicana, or the History of Independency. The second part* (1649), p. 32: 'This fagge end, this Rump of a Parliament with corrupt Maggots in it.'

5 *Mercurius Pragmaticus*, 5–12 December 1648, p. 6.

6 Michael Braddick, *God's Fury, England's Fire: A New History of the English Civil Wars* (London: Penguin, 2009).

7 *The Petition of the House of Commons, which accompanied the Remonstrance, of the State of the Kingdom, when it was presented to His Majesty at Hampton-Court, Decemb. 1st. 1641*, in *The Constitutional Documents of the Puritan Revolution, 1625–1660*, ed. S. R. Gardiner (Oxford: Clarendon Press, 1906), pp. 202–32. Ian Gentles, *The English Revolution and the Wars in the Three Kingdoms 1638–1652* (London and New York: Routledge, 2014), p. 82.

8 *ODNB*, 'Edward Littleton, Baron Littleton' (Lord Keeper of the Great Seal).

9 'His Majesty's Answer to the Nineteen Propositions of both Houses of Parliament, tending towards a Peace', in J. Rushworth, *Historical Collections of Private Passages of State*, 8 vols (1721), IV, p. 728.
10 Cited in Braddick, *God's Fury, England's Fire*, p. 209.
11 Ronald Hutton, *The Making of Oliver Cromwell* (New Haven, CT and London: Yale University Press, 2021), p. 255.
12 'Dancing barn' cited in Roy Booth, 'Caroline Theatre', in *A Companion to English Renaissance Literature and Culture*, ed. Michael Hattaway (Oxford: Blackwell, 2000), pp. 556–65 (p. 562).
13 *Mercurius Pragmaticus*, 5–12 December 1648.
14 *A Deep Sigh Breath'd Through the Lodgings at White-hall, Deploring the Absence of the Court, and the Miseries of the Pallace* (1642), A2.
15 *A deep sigh* . . . , A2.
16 Martin Parker, 'Upon Defacing of White-hall' (*c.* 1643), in *Poetry and Revolution: An Anthology of British and Irish Verse, 1625–1660*, ed. Peter Davidson (Oxford: Oxford University Press, 1998), pp. 320–2.
17 *A Remonstrance of his Excellency Thomas Lord Fairfax.*
18 *The Moderate* (16–23 January 1649). On the trial see *King Charls his Tryal: or A Perfect Narrative of the Whole Proceedings of the High Court of Justice in the Tryal of the King in Westminster Hall* (1649).
19 *King Charls his Tryal*, p. 5.
20 The Sentence of Charles I, TNA, SP 16/517, fol. 44v.
21 *King Charls his Tryal*, p. 39.
22 Death Warrant of King Charles I, Parliamentary Archives, HL/PO/JO/10/1/297A.
23 A shirt purported to be that worn by Charles on the day of his execution is in the Museum of London collection.
24 Fabian Philipps, *The Royall Martyr* (1660), appendix. On the execution see *A Perfect Diurnall* (30 January 1649); *King Charls his Speech made upon the Scaffold at Whitehall-gate* (1649). See also Wedgwood, *A King Condemned.*
25 'The Trials of Twenty-nine Regicides . . . 1660', in *A Complete Collection of State Trials and Proceedings for High Treason and Other Crimes and Misdemeanors*, 21 vols, ed. T. B. Howell et al. (1816), V, p. 1032.
26 *Diaries and Letters of Philip Henry*, ed. Matthew Henry Lee (London, 1882), p. 12.
27 Pepys, *Diary*, I, p. 280.
28 Marvell, 'An Horatian Ode upon Cromwell's Return from Ireland', l. 65; ll. 63–4.
29 Josselin, *Diary*, 2 February 1649.
30 This was apparently witnessed by Thomas Wriothesley, earl of Southampton and recorded in Joseph Spence, *Anecdotes* (London, 1820), p. 275. It is not wholly reliable, but it might have a ring of truth in it: see John Morrill and Philip Baker, 'Oliver Cromwell, the Regicide, and the Sons of Zeruiah', in *The Regicides and the Execution of Charles I*, ed. Jason Peacey (Basingstoke: Palgrave, 2001), pp. 14–35.

31 Oliver Cromwell to Colonel Hammond, 25 November 1648, in *Letters, Writings, and Speeches*, I, p. 628.
32 *A Perfect Diurnall*, 29 January–5 February 1649.
33 John Denham, *Coopers Hill a poem* (1643), p. 3.
34 Ephraim Pagitt, *Heresiography, or, a Description of the Heretickes and Sectaries Sprang up in these Latter Times* (1654), 'Of Quakers', p. 136.
35 Such histories began in the Restoration. The story of the period of the republic is often told as a coda to the civil wars – e.g. Blair Worden, *The English Civil Wars, 1640–1660* (London: Weidenfeld & Nicolson, 2009) – and the culture of the time is often best understood through biographies of Cromwell or other figures such as Milton. Gardiner, *History*, is still a majesterial narrative of the decade, completed by C. H. Firth, *The Last Years of the Protectorate* (1909). Political surveys of the 1650s include those by Toby Barnard, Barry Coward, Ronald Hutton and Austin Woolrych, together with a series of articles by Derek Hirst (see 'Bibliography'). The 1650s are now being looked at anew – see in particular the work of Jonathan Fitzgibbons – as well as being written about for a wider readership. See Anna Keay, *The Restless Republic: Britain without a Crown* (London: William Collins, 2022); Paul Lay, *Providence Lost: The Rise and Fall of Cromwell's Protectorate* (London: Head of Zeus, 2020); and, on the entire seventeenth century, Jonathan Healey, *The Blazing World: A New History of Revolutionary England* (London: Bloomsbury, 2023).
36 Walter Bagehot, *The English Constitution*, ed. Miles Taylor (Oxford and New York: Oxford University Press, 2001).
37 Robert Herrick, 'The Argument of his book', in *Hesperides, or The Works both Humane & Divine* (1648), p. 1; Katherine Philips, 'A Retired Friendship, to Ardelia, 23rd August 1651', in *Women Poets of the English Civil War*, ed. Sarah C. E. Ross and Elizabeth Scott-Baumann (Manchester: Manchester University Press, 2018), pp. 154–5, l. 29 ; 'Overturning dayes', echoing Ezekiel 21.27, in 'The Freemens Remonstrance to the New Representative', in *The Moderate Intelligencer*, 4–11 July 1653.

1649

1 David Norbrook, *Writing the English Republic: Poetry, Rhetoric and Politics, 1627–1660* (Cambridge: Cambridge University Press, 2000), p. 198. This is an English translation of the original inscription, which was in Latin.
2 *Fire from Heaven* (1649), title-page.
3 *The Rebels Looking-Glasse: or, The Traytors Doome* (1649), p. 2.
4 Elizabeth Poole, *A Vision: Wherein is Manifested the Disease and Cure of the Kingdome* (1649), p. 6.
5 Marvell, 'An Horatian Ode', l. 35.
6 *CJ*, VI, 7 February 1649. The act was passed on 17 March 1649. *The Clarendon Edition of the Works of Thomas Hobbes*, X: *Behemoth, or the Long Parliament*, ed. Paul Seaward (Oxford: Oxford University Press, 2009), p. 319.

7 *CJ*, VI, 6 February 1649. The act abolishing the House of Lords was passed on 19 March 1649.

8 *CJ*, VI, 1 February 1649.

9 Milton, *A Second Defence of the English People*, trans. Helen North, in *Complete Prose Works*, IV, p. 637; George Bate, *The Lives, Actions, and Execution of the Prime Actors, and Principall Contrivers of that Horrid Murder of our Late Pious and Sacred Soveraigne King Charles the First* (1661). See also Mark Noble, *The Lives of the English Regicides*, 2 vols (1798), I, pp. 47–66.

10 'An Act Declaring and Constituting the People of England to be a Commonwealth and Free-State', 19 May 1649, in *Acts and Ordinances*, p. 122.

11 *The Armies Vindication* (1649), p. 63.

12 *ODNB*, 'Philip Herbert'.

13 Thomas Fairfax, 'On the Fatal Day Jan. 30', Bodleian Library, Oxford, MS Fairfax 38.

14 Whitelocke, *Diary*, p. 229.

15 *ODNB*, 'Bulstrode Whitelocke'; Ruth Spalding, *The Improbable Puritan: A Life of Bulstrode Whitelocke, 1605–1675* (London: Faber and Faber, 1975).

16 Whitelocke, *Memorials*; Whitelocke, *Diary*. On the *Memorials*, the composition of Whitelocke's 'diary' and his collection of manuscripts and papers, see Blair Worden, 'The "Diary" of Bulstrode Whitelocke', *English Historical Review* 108 (1993), pp. 122–34, and Jonathan Fitzgibbons, '"To Settle a Government without Something of Monarchy in It": Bulstrode Whitelocke's Memoirs and the Reinvention of the Interregnum', *English Historical Review* 137 (2022), pp. 655–91.

17 Sir Simonds D'Ewes describing Marten, cited in *ODNB*, 'Henry Marten'.

18 Aubrey, *Brief Lives*, p. 193.

19 *ODNB*, 'Henry Marten'.

20 *A Perfect Diurnall*, 4–11 June 1649.

21 Cited in Blair Worden, *God's Instruments: Political Conduct in the England of Oliver Cromwell* (Oxford: Oxford University Press, 2012), p. 282.

22 Whitelocke, *Memorials*, II, p. 486.

23 *The Moderate Intelligencer*, 22 February–1 March 1649, quoted in Blair Worden, *The Rump Parliament 1648–1653* (Cambridge: Cambridge University Press, 1974), p. 187.

24 Whitelocke, *Diary*, 18 December 1648, p. 226. On these meetings also see the 'Annales', BL Add. MS 37344.

25 From the 'Annales', BL Add. MS 37344, and cited in Jonathan Fitzgibbons, 'Rethinking the English Revolution of 1649', *Historical Journal* (2017), pp. 889–914 (p. 893).

26 *The Armies Vindication* (1649), p. 63; and see Markku Peltonen, *The Political Thought of the English Free State, 1649–1653* (Cambridge: Cambridge University Press, 2023), p. 113.

27 *A Declaration of the Parliament of England, Expressing the Grounds of their Late*

Proceedings, and of Settling the Present Government in the Way of a Free State (1649). *CJ*, VI, 14 March 1649, pp. 163–5.

28 *CJ*, VI, 8 February 1649, pp. 133–5; Whitelocke, *Memorials* (1682), p. 372.

29 *CJ*, VI, 6 January 1649; 9 January 1649; 26 January 1649, pp. 112–13, 114–15, 123.

30 Whitelocke, *Diary*, p. 230.

31 Marvell, 'An Horatian Ode', ll. 35–6.

32 Oliver Millar, *The Inventories and Valuations of the King's Goods, 1649–1651, Volume of the Walpole Society* 43 (1970–2), p. xi. On the orders for Whitehall to be cleared, see *CJ*, VI, February 1649.

33 H. M. Colvin, D. R. Ransome and John Summerson, *The History of the King's Works*, IV: 1485–1660, Part 2 (London: HMSO, 1975).

34 'An Act for sale of the goods and personal Estate of the late King, Queen and Prince', 4 July 1649, in *Acts and Ordinances*, pp. 160–8; 'An Act for sale of the Goods belonging to the late King, Queen and Prince', 17 July 1651, in *Acts and Ordinances*, pp. 546–48. Also see Arthur MacGregor, 'The King's Goods and the Commonwealth Sale', in *The Late King's Goods: Collections, Possessions and Patronage of Charles I in the Light of the Commonewalth Sale Inventories*, ed. Arthur MacGregor (London and Oxford: Alistair McAlpine, 1989), pp. 13–52.

35 'An Act for sale of the Honours, Manors, Lands heretofore belonging to the late King, Queen and Prince', 16 July 1649, in *Acts and Ordinances*, pp. 168–91.

36 *Acts and Ordinances*, pp. 160–8.

37 Lodewijck Huygens, *The English Journal 1651–1652*, ed. and trans. A. G. H. Bachrach and R. G. Collmer (Leiden: Brill/Leiden University Press, 1982), p. 61.

38 Jerry Brotton, *The Sale of the Late King's Goods: Charles I and His Art Collection* (London: Macmillan, 2006), p. 257.

39 Brotton, *The Sale of the Late King's Goods*, p. 293; Valerie Cumming, '"Great Vanity and Excesse in Apparell": Some Clothing and Furs of Tudor and Stuart Royalty', in *The Late King's Goods*, ed. MacGregor, p. 344.

40 Brotton, *The Sale of the Late King's Goods*, pp. 300–1; Lucy Hutchinson, *Memoirs of the Life of Colonel Hutchinson*, ed. N. H. Keeble (London: Everyman, 1995), pp. 254–5.

41 Francis Haskell, 'Charles I's Collection of Pictures', in *The Late King's Goods*, ed. MacGregor, p. 227.

42 Cumming, '"Great Vanity and Excesse in Apparell"', p. 346.

43 Thomas Fuller, *The Church History of Britain* (1655), Book II, p. 141

44 Peter Heylyn, *Aerius Redivivus: or The History of the Presbyterians* (1672), p. 453.

45 *CJ*, VI, 9 August 1649.

46 Millar, *Inventories*, p. 50.

47 John Naylier, *The Foxes Craft Discovered* (1649).

48 Putney Debates, *Clarke Papers*, I, p. 301.

49 Putney Debates, *Clarke Papers*, I, pp. 302, 309.

50 *Foundations of Freedom; or An Agreement of the People: proposed as a rule for*

future government in the establishment of a firm and lasting peace (1648); John Lilburne, William Walwyn, Thomas Prince and Richard Overton, *The Agreement of the Free People of England, tendered as a Peace-Offering to this distressed Nation* (1649).

51 Cited in Worden, *Rump*, p. 198.

52 Lilburne, *Englands New Chains Discovered* (1649), n.p.

53 Lilburne, *The Hunting of the Foxes from Newmarket and Triploe Heaths to Whitehall* (1649), p. 9.

54 Marchamont Nedham, *The Case of the Common-wealth of England Stated* (1650), pp. 78, 77.

55 *The Picture of the Council of State Held forth to the Free people of England by Lieut. Col. John Lilburn, Mr Thomas Prince, and Mr Richard Overton, now Prisoners in the Tower of London* (1649), p. 15.

56 *A Perfect Diurnall*, 14–21 May 1649.

57 'An Act Declaring what Offences shall be adjudged Treason', 14 May 1649, *Acts and Ordinances*, pp. 120–1.

58 *A Perfect Diurnall*, 14–21 May 1649.

59 *To the Supream authority of this Nation, the Commons assembled in Parliament: The Humble Petition of divers wel-affected Women Inhabiting the Cities of London, Westminster, the Borough of Southwark, Hamblets, and Places adjacent* (1649), p. 4.

60 *Humble Petition*, p. 6.

61 John Rees, *The Leveller Revolution: Radical Political Organisation in England, 1640–1660* (London: Verso, 2016), p. 290; *Perfect Occurrences of Every Dayes Journall in Parliament*, 20–7 April 1649.

62 *Mercurius Pragmaticus*, 24 April–1 May 1649.

63 *The True Levellers Standard Advanced* (1649), p. 7; Gerard Winstanley, 'A Watch-word to the City of London, and the Army', in Winstanley, '*The Law of Freedom' and Other Writings*, ed. Christopher Hill (Cambridge: Cambridge University Press, 1973), p. 128.

64 John Owen, 'Human Power Defeated', Sermon XII, in *Complete Collection of the Sermons of the Reverend and Learned John Owen, D. D.* (1721), pp. 79–91.

65 *A Perfect Diurnall*, 4–11 June 1649.

66 Whitelocke, *Diary*, pp. 239–40.

67 'For my honoured and noble friends, the Lord Grey of Groby, Colonel Henry Martin, Col. Francis Russell, Capt. Fry', in John Lilburne, *A Preparative to an Hue and Cry* (1649), p. 39.

68 Agnes Strickland, *Lives of the Queens of England* (1865), IV, p. 276.

69 Jenny Uglow, *A Gambling Man: Charles II and the Restoration* (London: Faber and Faber, 2009), p. 21.

70 Micheál Ó Siochrú, *God's Executioner: Oliver Cromwell and the Conquest of Ireland* (London: Faber and Faber, 2008).

71 Cary, *Memorials*, p. 159.

72 Cary, *Memorials*, p. 151.

73 *Letters and Papers Illustrating the Relations between Charles II and Scotland in 1650*, ed. S. R. Gardiner (Edinburgh, 1894), p. xvi.

74 James Cranford, *The Teares of Ireland wherein is lively presented as in a map a list of the unheard off [sic] cruelties and perfidious treacheries of blood-thirsty Jesuits and the popish faction* (1642).

75 Cranford, *Teares of Ireland*, title page.

76 Ó Siochrú, *God's Executioner*; Toby Barnard, *Cromwellian Ireland: English Government and Reform in Ireland, 1649–1660* (Oxford: Clarendon Press, 1975; new ed. 2000); Toby Barnard, *Making the Grand Figure: Lives and Possessions in Ireland, 1641–1770* (New Haven, CT: Yale University Press, 2004); *The 1641 Depositions and the Irish Rebellion*, ed. E. Darcy, A. Margey and E. Murphy (London: Pickering & Chatto, 2012).

77 *Articles of Peace Made and Concluded with the Irish Rebels, and Papists by James Earle of Ormond, For and in behalfe of the late King* (1649), p. 3.

78 *The Marquesse of Ormonds Proclamation Concerning the Peace concluded with the Irish Rebells* (1649), p. 6.

79 'Observations upon the Articles of Peace with the Irish Rebels', in *Articles of Peace Made and Concluded*, p. 46.

80 Marvell, 'An Horatian Ode', ll. 74, 85–92.

81 'Speech by Oliver Cromwell to the General Council of the Army', 23 March 1649, in *Letters, Writings, and Speeches*, II, pp. 23–9 (p. 28).

82 Clarendon, *History*, V, pp. 610–12; *Letters, Writings, and Speeches*, II, pp. 54–5.

83 *A Perfect Diurnall*, 2–9 July 1649.

84 Whitelocke, *Diary*, p. 241.

85 Abbott, II, p. 103.

86 *Letters, Writings, and Speeches*, II, p. 72.

87 *Letters, Writings, and Speeches*, II, pp. 73–5.

88 George Wither, *Carmen Eucharisticon: a private thank-oblation, exhibited to the glory of the lord of hosts, for the timely and wonderfull deliverance, vouchsafed to this nation, in the routing of a numerous Army of Irish rebells before Dublin* (1649).

89 *Ormondes Breakfast or A True Relation of the Salley and Skirmish performed by Collonell Michaell Jones and his Party, against the Marques of Ormonde* (Dublin, 1649).

90 Abbott, II, p. 104.

91 Anon., *The Loyall Subjects Jubilee or Cromwels Farewell to England, being a poem on his advancing to Ireland* (1649).

92 *A Perfect Diurnall*, 20–7 August 1649.

93 *A Declaration by the Lord Lieutenant of Ireland Concerning his Resolutions for the Peace and Safety of Ireland* (Dublin, 1649).

94 *Two Great Fights in Ireland, on Sunday, Munday, Tuesday, & Wednesday last, between the Marq. of Ormonds forces, and the Lord Lieut. Cromwels, at the two strong garrisons of Tredah and Dundalke* (1649).

95 *The Last Great and Bloudy Fight in Ireland on Wednesday last, being the 29. of August, 1649. between the Marq. of Ormonds forces, and the Lord Governour Cromwels* (1649).
96 Cromwell to William Lenthall, 17 September 1649, in *Letters, Writings, and Speeches*, II, p. 96.
97 *Letters, Writings, and Speeches*, II, p. 97.
98 Gardiner, *History*, I, p. 131.
99 *Letters, Writings, and Speeches*, II, pp. 97, 98.
100 *Perfect Occurrences of Every Dayes Journall in Parliament*, 28 September–4 October 1649.
101 *Perfect Occurrences of Every Dayes Journall in Parliament*, 28 September–4 October 1649. And see *Two Letters one from Dublin in Ireland, and the other from Liverpoole* (1649) on 1,400 deserters from Ormond to Cromwell and 'near' 3,000 dead, and offering of quarter, which was refused.
102 *Letters, Writings, and Speeches*, II, p. 97.
103 Cromwell to William Lenthall, 27 September 1649, in *Letters, Writings, and Speeches*, II, p. 104.
104 *The Fare-well Sermons of Comfort and Concord preached at Drogheda in Ireland by Nicholas Bernard* (1651).
105 *Letters from Ireland Relating the several great Successes it hath pleased God to give unto the Parliaments Forces there* (1649).
106 Newsbooks that include women and children as slain at Drogheda are *Mercurius Elencticus*, 8–15 October 1649, and *The Man in the Moon*, 17–24 October 1649. Whether or not there was a large-scale civilian massacre at Drogheda remains disputed. The case for is made by Ó Siochrú, *God's Executioner*; the case against by Tom Reilly, *Cromwell: An Honourable Enemy* (London: Weidenfeld and Nicolson, 2001); Tom Reilly, *Cromwell Was Framed: Ireland 1649* (Alresford: John Hunt, 2014); also see *Cromwell and Ireland: New Perspectives*, ed. Martyn Bennett, Ray Gillespie and R. Scott Spurlock (Liverpool: Liverpool University Press, 2021). Ronald Hutton, *The British Republic, 1649–1660* (Basingstoke: Palgrave Macmillan, 2nd edn, 2000), argues that 'the fact that it has suited both nations to magnify the actions of Cromwell remains a glaring example of bad history' (p. 47).
107 Adrian Tinniswood, *The Verneys: A True Story of Love, War and Madness in Seventeenth-century England* (London: Vintage, 2008), p. 243.
108 Summons from Oliver Cromwell to governor of Dundalk, 12 September 1649, in *Letters, Writings, and Speeches*, II, p. 89.
109 *A Perfect and Particular Relation of the Severall Marches and Proceedings of the Armie in Ireland, from the taking of Drogheda, to this Present* (1649), p. 8.
110 Letter from Oliver Cromwell to David Sinnott, 3 October 1649, in *Letters, Writings, and Speeches*, II, p. 105.
111 *Letters, Writings, and Speeches*, II, p. 106.

112 Cromwell to Sinnott, 4 October 1649, in *Letters, Writings, and Speeches*, II, p. 107.
113 Cromwell to Sinnott, 11 October 1649, in *Letters, Writings, and Speeches*, II, p. 111; Cromwell to Lenthall, 14 October 1649, in *Letters, Writings, and Speeches*, II, p. 115.
114 Cromwell to Lenthall, 14 October 1649, in *Letters, Writings, and Speeches*, II, p. 115.
115 *A Perfect and Particular Relation*, p. 7.
116 *A Perfect and Particular Relation*, p. 8.
117 *Letters, Writings, and Speeches*, II, p. 116. See the petition that includes women and children: *The Taking of Wexford, a Letter from an Eminent Offcer in the Army, under the Command of the Lord Lieutenant of Ireland* (1649).
118 *The Memoirs of Anne, Lady Halkett and Ann, Lady Fanshawe*, ed. John Loftis (Oxford: Clarendon Press, 1979), p. 124.
119 Cromwell to Lenthall, [25?] November 1649, in *Letters, Writings, and Speeches*, II, p. 155.
120 Gerard Boate, *Irelands Naturall History being a True and Ample Description of its Situation* (1657; first published 1652), p. 182.
121 Whitelocke, *Diary*, p. 260.
122 *Mercurius Politicus*, 6 June 1650.
123 Gardiner, *History*, I, p. 286.
124 Royalist Joseph Beaumont quoted in Christopher Hill, *God's Englishman: Oliver Cromwell and the English Revolution* (London: Penguin, 1970; repr. 1990), p. 225.
125 *CJ*, VI, 4 June 1650, pp. 418–19.
126 Robert Walker, *Oliver Cromwell*, *c.* 1649, NPG.
127 *The Works of John Owen*, ed. Thomas Russell (London, 1826), I, pp. 91–2.
128 *A Declaration of the Lord Lieutenant of Ireland, For the Undeceiving of Deluded and Seduced People*, printed in *Letters, Writings, and Speeches*, II, p. 194.
129 *Letters, Writings, and Speeches*, II, pp. 201, 199.
130 Thomas Cobbes, 'A Poeme uppon Cromwell' (1650), in Andrew Carpenter, ed., *Verse in English from Tudor and Stuart Ireland* (Cork: Cork University Press, 2003).
131 John Cunningham, 'Oliver Cromwell and the "Cromwellian" Settlement of Ireland', *Historical Journal* 53 (2010), pp. 919–38; Sarah Covington, *The Devil from over the Sea: Remembering and Forgetting Oliver Cromwell in Ireland* (Oxford: Oxford University Press, 2022).
132 Ó Siochrú, *God's Executioner*; Cunningham, 'Oliver Cromwell and the "Cromwellian" Settlement of Ireland'.
133 Marvell, 'An Horatian Ode', l. 82.

1650

1 John Milton, *The Tenure of Kings and Magistrates* (1649).

2 Barbara Kiefer Lewalski, *The Life of John Milton: A Critical Biography* (Malden, MA and Oxford: Blackwell, 2000; rev. edn 2003).

3 *Eikón Basiliké the Pourtraicture of his Sacred Majestie in his Solitudes and Sufferings* (1648 [1649]), p. 229. See Robert Wilcher, '*Eikon Basilike*: The Printing, Composition, Strategy, and Impact of "The King's Book"', in Laura Lunger Knoppers, ed., *The Oxford Handbook of Literature and the English Revolution* (Oxford: Oxford University Press, 2012), pp. 289–308.

4 An example of one such treasured copy is in the Royal Collection.

5 John Milton, *Eikonoklastes, in Answer To a Book Intitl'd Eikon Basilike, the Portrature of his Sacred Majesty in his Solitudes and Sufferings* (1650). See edition in *The Complete Works of John Milton*, VI: *Vernacular Regicide and Republican Writings*, ed. N. H. Keeble and Nicholas McDowell (Oxford: Oxford University Press, 2013), pp. 279–424.

6 Lewalski, *Life of John Milton*, p. 245.

7 *ODNB*, 'Marchamont Nedham'.

8 Marchamont Nedham, *The Case of the Common-wealth of England Stated* (1650), A2.

9 Cited in Milton, *Complete Prose Works*, IV, Part I, p. 53.

10 Nedham, *The Case of the Common-wealth of England Stated*, pp. 2–3.

11 *Mercurius Politicus*, 6–13 June 1650.

12 Ludlow, *Memoirs*, I, p. 242.

13 Ronald Hutton, *Charles the Second: King of England, Scotland, and Ireland* (Oxford: Clarendon Press, 1989), p. 40.

14 *Letters and Papers Illustrating the Relations between Charles II and Scotland in 1650*, ed. S. R. Gardiner (Edinburgh, 1894), p. 26.

15 *The Letters, Speeches and Declarations of King Charles II*, ed. Arthur Bryant (London: Cassell, 1935), p. 14.

16 Gardiner, *History*, I, p. 253; Hutton, *Charles the Second*, p. 46.

17 James Graham, 'My Dear and Only Love', in *Memoirs of the Most Renowned James Graham, Marquis of Montrose. Translated from the Latin of the Rev. Dr George Wishart* (Edinburgh, 1819), p. 497.

18 Clarendon, *History*, V, p. 133; Gardiner, *History*, I, pp. 266–7.

19 Mark Napier, *Memoirs of the Marquis of Montrose* (Edinburgh, 1856), II, p. 767.

20 Clarendon, *History*, V, p. 134.

21 Cited in Worden, *The Rump Parliament*, p. 224.

22 John Milton, 'To my Lord Fairfax', *The Complete Works of John Milton*, III: *The Shorter Poems*, ed. Barbara Kiefer Lewalski and Estelle Haan (Oxford: Oxford University Press, 2012), p. 286.

23 *ODNB*, 'Thomas Fairfax, third Lord Fairfax of Cameron'.

24 Clarendon, *History*, IV, p. 486.

25 Worden, *The Rump Parliament*, p. 224.

26 'Act for Subscribing the Engagement', 2 January 1650, *Acts and Ordinances*, pp. 325–9.

27 'Act for removing all Papists, and all Officers and Soldiers of Fortune, and divers other Delinquents from London and Westminster, and confining them within five miles of their dwellings, and for encouragement of such as discover Priests and Jesuits, their Receivers and Abettors', 6 February 1650, *Acts and Ordinances*, pp. 349–54; 'Act for the better propagation and preaching of the Gospel in Wales, and for redress of some grievances', 22 February, 1650, *Acts and Ordinances*, pp. 342–8; 'Act for the promoting and propagating the Gospel of Jesus Christ in New England', 27 July 1649, *Acts and Ordinances*, pp. 197–200.

28 'Act for the better preventing of prophane swearing and cursing', 28 June 1650, *Acts and Ordinances*, pp. 393–6; 'Act for the better Observation of the Lords Day, Days of Thanksgiving and Humiliation', 19 April 1650, *Acts and Ordinances*, pp. 383–7.

29 'Conversation between Oliver Cromwell and Bulstrode Whitelocke, Thomas Fairfax, John Lambert, Thomas Harrison and Oliver St John', 25 June 1650, in *Letters, Writings, and Speeches*, II, p. 269.

30 Whitelocke, *Diary*, p. 260.

31 *Letters, Writings, and Speeches*, II, p. 271.

32 *The Man in the Moon*, 29 May–5 June 1650.

33 Henry Walker, *A Sermon Preached in the chappell at Sommerset-House in the Strand, on Thursday the 27 day of June 1650* (1650); quotations from 'Epistle'.

34 Hopper, '*Black Tom*', p. 203.

35 Aubrey, *Brief Lives*, p. 196.

36 Marvell, 'An Horatian Ode', ll. 105–8. On Marvell and his allegiance see Nigel Smith, *Andrew Marvell: The Chameleon* (New Haven, CT and London: Yale University Press, 2010); Derek Hirst and Steven Zwicker, *Andrew Marvell, Orphan of the Hurricane* (Oxford: Oxford University Press, 2012); Nicholas McDowell, 'Marvell Among the Cavaliers' and 'Marvell Among the Cromwellians', in *The Oxford Handbook of Literature and the English Revolution*, ed. Laura Lunger Knoppers (Oxford: Oxford University Press, 2012), pp. 253–71, 481–97.

37 Marvell, 'Upon Appleton House', l. 354.

38 Hutton, *Charles the Second*, p. 54. C. H. Firth, 'The Battle of Dunbar', *Transactions of the Royal Historical Society* 14 (1900), pp. 19–52.

39 *A Declaration of the Army of England upon their March into Scotland* (1650), p. 8.

40 *Letters, Writings, and Speeches*, II, pp. 289–90.

41 'Letter from an English Soldier in Scotland', *A Perfect Diurnall*, 16–23 September 1650; Gardiner, ed., *Letters and Papers Illustrating the Relations between Charles II and Scotland in 1650*, ed. S. R. Gardiner (Edinburgh, 1894), pp. 134–40.

42 *Memoirs of Captain John Hodgson*, in *Original Memoirs, Written during the Great Civil War: Being the Life of Sir Henry Slingsby, and Memoirs of Capt. Hodgson*, ed. Walter Scott (Edinburgh and London, 1806), pp. 83–198 (p. 143).

43 *Letters, Writings, and Speeches*, II, p. 319.

44 John Nicoll, *A Diary of Public Transactions and other Occurrences, chiefly in Scotland, from January 1650 to June 1667*, ed. D. Laing (Edinburgh, 1836), p. 27.

45 Abbott, II, p. 317, quoting a soldier's account.

46 *Memoirs of Captain John Hodgson*, pp. 147–8.

47 Psalm 117, King James Version.

48 John Aubrey, 'Impulses', in his *Miscellanies upon the following subjects* (1696), cited in Abbott, II, p. 319.

49 Cromwell to Lenthall, 4 September 1650, in *Letters, Writings, and Speeches*, II, pp. 322–9.

50 *Letters, Writings, and Speeches*, II, p. 337.

51 General David Leslie to the Marquess of Argyll, 5 September 1651, in *Correspondence of Sir Robert Kerr, First Earl of Ancram and his Son William, Third Earl of Lothian*, 2 vols, ed. David Laing (Edinburgh, 1875), II, p. 298.

52 *The Causes of a Publick Fast, and Humiliation, to be kept with all convenient diligence: by all the Members of this Kirk and Kingdom* (Aberdeen, 1650), p. 11.

53 Antonia Fraser, *Cromwell: Our Chief of Men* (London: Weidenfeld & Nicolson, 1973; repr. 2002), p. 466.

54 Ludlow, *Memoirs*, I, p. 254.

55 Cromwell to Lenthall, 4 September 1650, in *Letters, Writings, and Speeches*, II, p. 328.

56 Clarendon, *History*, V, p. 149. Hutton, *Charles the Second*, p. 54, notes how no personal reaction of Charles is recorded.

57 Henry Vaughan, 'An Epitaph upon the Lady Elizabeth, Second Daughter to his Late Majesty', in *Olor Iscanus* (1651); the title can be translated as 'the Swan of Usk'.

58 *The True Manner of the Crowning of Charles the Second King of Scotland* (1651). And see Gardiner, *History*, I, p. 389 on the 'stool of repentance'.

59 *The True Manner of the Crowning*.

60 *The True Manner of the Crowning*; *The Forme and Order of the Coronation of Charles the Second, King of Scotland, England, France, and Ireland* (Aberdeen, 1651). Later, the Scottish regalia was buried in the floor of a church in Dunnottar to keep it safe. Fraser, *Chief of Men*, p. 546.

61 John Shawe, *Britannia Rediviva: or the Proper and Soveraign Remedy for the Healing and Recovering of these three Distracted Nations* (1649).

62 *The Forme and Order of the Coronation of Charles the Second*, p. 4.

63 *The True Manner of the Crowning*.

64 *The Letters, Speeches and Declarations of King Charles II*, p. 15.

65 *A Letter from Holland Relating the Designes of the Scotch Presbyter* (Rotterdam, 1650), p. 4.

66 Margaret Cavendish, *The World's Olio* (1655), p. 51.

67 *The True Manner of the Crowning*.

1651

1 Important works on these sects, once dismissed by historians as the 'lunatic fringe', include Christopher Hill, *The World Turned Upside Down: Radical Ideas during the English Revolution* (London: Temple Smith, 1972, repr. 1991), quotation p. 16; Bernard Capp, *The Fifth Monarchy Men: A Study in Seventeenth-Century English Millenarianism* (London: Faber, 1972); A. L. Morton, *The World of the Ranters: Religious Radicalism in the English Revolution* (London: Lawrence and Wishart, 1970); Jonathan Scott, *England's Troubles: Seventeenth-Century English Political Instability in European Context* (Cambridge: Cambridge University Press, 2000).

2 Josselin, *Diary*, June 1651, pp. 247–8.

3 Hutchinson, *Memoirs*.

4 Huygens, *Journal*, p. 56.

5 Laurence Price, *Here's Jack in a Box* (1656); John Evelyn, *A Character of England as it was lately presented in a letter to a noble man of France* (1659).

6 Huygens, *Journal*, pp. 109, 69.

7 Claude Saumaise, *Defensio Regia, Pro Carolo I* (Leiden, 1649).

8 Milton, *A Defence of the People of England*, in *Complete Prose Works*, IV, Part I, pp. 325, 344.

9 *Letters from Roundhead Officers written from Scotland*, ed. J. Y. Akerman (1856), p. 36.

10 George Monck, *A letter of the Surrender of Sterling-Castle* (1651).

11 Cary, *Memorials*, p. 299.

12 Cary, *Memorials*, p. 304.

13 Gardiner, *History*, I, p. 436.

14 Cary, *Memorials*, pp. 309, 308.

15 *Charles Rex. His Majestyes Declaration, to all his Loving Subjects of his Kingdom of England and Dominion of Wales* (Aberdeen, 1651).

16 Hutchinson, *Memoirs*, pp. 248–9.

17 *Mercurius Politicus*, 4–11 September 1651.

18 Hutton, *Charles the Second*, p. 65; David Underdown, *Royalist Conspiracy in England, 1649–1660* (New Haven, CT: Yale University Press, 1960), pp. 46–7.

19 Hutton, *Charles the Second*, p. 64, fn 48.

20 Thomas Blount, *Boscobel: or, The History of His Sacred Majesties Most Miraculous Preservation After the Battle of Worcester, 3 Sept. 1651* (1660). Blount says that there were no more than twelve thousand men – ten thousand Scots and two thousand English – in Charles's army.

21 *Letters, Writings, and Speeches*, II, p. 488.

22 Blount, *Boscobel*, p. 11.

23 *The Autobiography of Richard Baxter*, abr. J. J. Lloyd Thomas and ed. N. H. Keeble (London: Everyman, 1974), p. 68.

24 Blount, *Boscobel*, p. 13.

25 Arthur Bryant, *King Charles II* (London: Longmans, Green & Co., 1932), p. 13.

26 *A Great Victory by the Blessing of God, obtained by the Parliaments Forces, against the Scots Force* (1651).

27 Abraham Cowley, 'Sylva', *The Third Part of the Works of Mr Abraham Cowley being his Six books of Plants* (1689), p. 131.

28 Blount, *Boscobel*, p. 39.

29 Blount, *Boscobel*, p. 41. *ODNB*, 'Thomas Blount'.

30 Isaac Fuller, *King Charles II and Jane Lane Riding to Bristol*, *c.* 1660s, NPG.

31 *The True and Perfect Relation of the Taking of Captain James Hind* (1651), p. 3.

32 *ODNB*, 'Jane Lane'.

33 Blount, *Boscobel*, 'To the Reader'.

34 A. M. Broadley (ed.), *The Royal Miracle: A Collection of Rare Tracts, Broadsides, Letters, Prints and Ballads Concerning the Wanderings of Charles II after the Battle of Worcester* (London: Stanley Paul & Co., 1912); A. Fea, *The Flight of the King after the Battle of Worcester* (London: J. Lane, 1897); *Charles II's Escape from Worcester: A Collection of Narratives Assembled by Samuel Pepys*, ed. W. Matthews (London: G. Bell, 1967); C. Penruddock, 'Mistress Jane Lane', *Wiltshire Archaeological and Natural History Magazine 26* (1892), pp. 1–38; Richard Ollard, *The Escape of Charles II after the Battle of Worcester* (London: Constable & Robinson, 2002).

35 Katherine Philips, 'On the Third of September, 1651', in *Women Poets of the English Civil War*, pp. 173–4.

36 Whitelocke, *Diary*, p. 271.

37 'A Perfect Relation of his Excellency the Lord Generall Cromwells Reception by the Nobility, Gent. and Citizens in and about the City of London', in *Another Victory in Lancashire* (1651), pp. 2–3.

38 *Mercurius Politicus*, 11–18 September 1651.

39 'A Perfect Relation of his Excellency the Lord Generall Cromwells Reception', p. 3.

40 Cromwell to Lenthall, 4 September 1651, in *Letters, Writings, and Speeches*, II, p. 491.

41 *A Perfect Diurnall*, 1–8 September 1651.

42 'A Perfect Relation of his Excellency the Lord Generall Cromwells Reception', pp. 3–4.

43 John Adams, *The Works of John Adams, Second President of the United States*, ed. Charles Francis Adams (1851; repr. Cambridge: Cambridge University Press, 2011), III, p. 394.

44 Milton, 'To my Lord Fairfax', in *The Complete Works of John Milton, III: The Shorter Poems*, p. 286; Marvell, 'An Horatian Ode', ll. 119–20.

45 Gardiner, *History*, I, p. 408.

46 *The Whole Triall of Mr Love, before the High Court of Justice in Westminster Hall* (1652), p. 17.

47 *ODNB*, 'Christopher Love'. Worden, *The Rump Parliament*, pp. 243–8.

48 *State Trials*, V, p. 259.

1652

1 Alice Thornton, *Book 2: The First Book of My Widowed Condition*, Durham Cathedral Library, GB_0033–CCOM 7, pp. 136–7, quoted in Joanne Edge, 'Black Monday: The Solar Eclipse of 1652', *Alice Thornton's Books*. Accessed 16 May 2024 (https://thornton.kdl.kcl.ac.uk/posts/blog/2022-10-25-black-monday-solar-eclipse-1652).

2 William Lilly, *Merlini Anglici Ephemeris: Astrological Predictions for 1652* (1651), A4; William Lilly, *Annus Tenebrosus, or The Dark Year or astrologicall judgements upon two lunar eclipses, and one admirable eclips of the sun, all visible in England* (1652), pp. 30, 40, 41.

3 John Owen, *The Shaking and Translating of Heaven and Earth* (1649).

4 Josselin, *Diary*. Louis XIV cited in Frank Furedi, *Authority: A Sociological History* (Cambridge: Cambridge University Press, 2013), p. 169.

5 *Mr William Lilly's History of his Life and Times: from the year 1602, to 1681*, 2nd edn (1715), as told to Elias Ashmole.

6 The Tender of Union was presented to Parliament in March 1652 and proclaimed in Edinburgh in April, but it was not passed by Parliament until 1657.

7 Huygens, *Journal*, 'Introduction', p. 1.

8 Sean Kelsey, *Inventing a Republic: The Political Culture of the English Commonwealth* (Manchester: Manchester University Press, 1997), p. 61.

9 *CSP: Venice*, XXVIII, 8 May 1652.

10 Kelsey, *Inventing a Republic*, p. 61. Report: TNA SP 18/1.73.

11 Huygens, *Journal*, pp. 40, 42.

12 *CSP: Venice*, XXVIII, 12 October 1652.

13 James Shirley, *Cupid and Death, A Masque, As it was Presented before his Excellencie, the Embassadour of Portugal* (1653).

14 Huygens, *Journal*, p. 41.

15 *ODNB*, 'Thomas Hobbes'.

16 Richard Tuck, *Hobbes: A Very Short Introduction* (Oxford: Oxford University Press, 2002), p. 33.

17 Hobbes, *Leviathan*, ed. J. C. A. Gaskin (Oxford: Oxford University Press, 1996), p. 138. Also see Hobbes, *Leviathan*, ed. Noel Malcolm (Oxford: Clarendon Press, 2012).

18 Hobbes, *Leviathan*, ed. Gaskin, 'A Review, and Conclusion', p. 470; Chapter 31, 'Of the Kingdom of God by Nature', p. 235.

19 Aubrey, *Brief Lives*, p. 152.

20 Edward Hyde, *A Brief View and Survey of the Dangerous and Pernicious Errors to Church and State in Mr Hobbes's Book Entitled Leviathan* (1676), p. 7.

21 Hobbes's autobiographical poem 'Vita Carmine Expressa', cited in A. P. Martinich, *Hobbes: A Biography* (Cambridge: Cambridge University Press, 1999), p. 216.

22 Sketch of Hobbes's house in Bodleian Library, Oxford, MS Aubrey 9, fol. 31v; Ruth Scurr, *John Aubrey: My Own Life* (London: Chatto & Windus, 2015), p. 116.

23 Aubrey, *Brief Lives*, pp. 147–59; Huygens, *Journal*, p. 74.

24 William Petty, *The History of the Survey of Ireland: Commonly Called the Down Survey 1655–6*, ed. T. A. Larcom (1851).

25 John Selden, *Mare Clausum and Of the Dominion of the Sea, or, Ownership of the Sea*, trans. Marchamont Nedham (1652); Samuel Cooper, *Portrait of Thomas Hobbes*, *c.* 1660, Cleveland Museum of Art.

26 John Aubrey, *Brief Lives*, 2 vols, ed. Andrew Clark (Oxford: Clarendon Press, 1898), I, p. 328.

27 Hobbes, *Leviathan*, ed. Gaskin, Chapter 11, 'Of the Difference of Manners' and Chapter 12 'Of Religion', pp. 70–1.

28 Martinich, *Hobbes*, p. 219.

29 Hobbes, *Leviathan*, ed. Gaskin, 'A Review, and Conclusion', p. 475.

30 Thomas Hobbes, *Mr Hobbes Considered In his Loyalty, Religion, Reputation, and Manners. By way of Letter to Dr Wallis* (1662), p. 20.

31 *Calendar of the Proceedings of the Committee for Compounding, 1643–1660*, 5 parts, ed. Mary Anne Everett Green (London, 1889–92), IV, pp. 289–30.

32 *ODNB*, 'Margaret Cavendish'.

33 Margaret Cavendish, *A True Relation of My Birth, Breeding and Life*, appended to *Natures Pictures drawn by Fancies Pencil to the Life* (1656).

34 *Letters from Dorothy Osborne to William Temple, 1652–54*, ed. Edward Abbott Parry (Cambridge: Cambridge University Press, 2013), p. 111. Margaret Cavendish, *Poems and Fancies* (1653).

35 Cavendish, *A True Relation*.

36 Cavendish, *The Worlds Olio*, 'To the Reader'. Also see her *The Philosophical and Physical Opinions* (1655); *The Description of a New World, Called The Blazing World* (1666); *The Life of the Thrice Noble, High and Puissant prince William Cavendishe, Duke, Marquess and Earl of Newcastle* (1667).

37 Evelyn, *Diary*, III, pp. 58–9.

38 'To my Unkle Pretyman', 2 December 1651, *The Letterbooks of John Evelyn*, ed. Douglas D. C. Chambers and David Galbraith (Toronto: Toronto University Press, 2014), p. 103.

39 Evelyn, *Diary*, III, pp. 56.

40 Evelyn, *Diary*, III, pp. 60, 67; Simon Schama, *Landscape and Memory* (London: Fontana, 1996), p. 159; John Evelyn, *Silva, or a Discourse of Forest-Trees* (1664).

41 Evelyn, *Diary*, III, p. 119; p. 64.

42 Evelyn, *Diary*, III, pp. 57–8.

43 *ODNB*, 'John Evelyn'; Gillian Darley, *John Evelyn: Living for Ingenuity* (New Haven, CT and London: Yale University Press, 2006).

44 'To my Unkle Pretyman', *Letterbooks of John Evelyn*, ed. Chambers and Galbraith, pp. 103–4.

45 Timothy Mowl and Brian Earnshaw, *Architecture without Kings: The Rise of Puritan Classicism under Cromwell* (Manchester and New York: Manchester University Press, 1995), p. 208.

46 John Evelyn, *An Essay on the First Book of T. Lucretius Carus De Rerum Natura* (1656).
47 Abraham Cowley, 'The Garden', dedicated to John Evelyn in *Abraham Cowley: The Essays and Other Prose Writings*, ed. Alfred B. Gough (Oxford: Oxford University Press, 1915), pp. 169–70.
48 Hopper, *'Black Tom'*, p. 116.
49 Smith, *Andrew Marvell*, p. 106; Nicholas McDowell, 'Urquhart's Rabelais: Translation, Patronage and Cultural Politics', *English Literary Renaissance* 35 (2005), pp. 273–303.
50 Evelyn, *Diary*, III, p. 61. 'Act of General Pardon and Oblivion', 24 February 1652, *Acts and Ordinances*, pp. 565–77.
51 *ODNB*, 'Edmund Waller'. Edmund Waller, *Panegyrick to my Lord Protector* (1655).
52 'An Additional Act for Sale of several Lands and Estates forfeited to the Commonwealth for Treason', 18 November 1652, *Acts and Ordinances*, pp. 623–52.
53 *ODNB*, 'Samuel Hartlib'. *Samuel Hartlib and Universal Reformation: Studies in Intellectual Communication*, ed. Mark Greengrass, Michael Leslie and Timothy Raylor (Cambridge: Cambridge University Press, 1994).
54 Evelyn, *Diary*, III, p. 162; Hartlib Papers, *Ephemerides*, 1655, Part 4: 29/5/54A.
55 John Tradescant, *Musaeum Tradescantianum: or A Collection of Rarities. Preserved at South-Lambeth neer London* (1656).
56 John Milton, *Of Education. To Master Samuel Hartlib* (1644), p. 1. Hartlib probably published *Of Education*.
57 Hartlib Papers, *Ephemerides*, 1655, Part 4: 29/5/46A.
58 Henry Robinson, *The Office of Addresses and Encounters* (1650); Henry Robinson, *Brief Considerations, Concerning the Advancement of Trade and Navigation* (1649); Henry Robinson, *Certain Proposalls in Order to the Peoples Freedome and Accommodation* (1652); *Samuel Hartlib his Legacie: Or An Enlargement of the Discourse of Husbandry used in Brabant and Flaunders* (1651); Thomas Jenner, *Londons Blame if not its Shame: Manifested by the Great Neglect of the Fishery* (1651); Anon., *Severall Proposals for the Generall Good of the Common-Wealth* (1651); Thomas Violet, *The Advancement of Merchandise* (1651). On the idea of credit see William Potter, *The Key of Wealth, Or a New Way of Improving Trade* (1650). On Ireland see Gerard Boate, *Irelands Naturall History*. On the place of the 1650s in the history of financial change see Carl Wennerlind, *Casualties of Credit: The English Financial Revolution, 1620–1720* (Cambridge, MA: Harvard University Press, 2011), and for an overview of the Hartlib circle see Charles Webster, *The Great Instauration: Science, Medicine, and Reform, 1626–1660* (London: Duckworth, 1975) and *Samuel Hartlib and Universal Reformation*, ed. Greengrass.
59 Potter, *The Key of Wealth*, p. 38.
60 *ODNB*, 'Samuel Hartlib'; *CJ*, V, 31 March 1647, grant of £300, and April 1649 granted an annual pension of £100 'for the Advancement of Arts and Learning'.

61 Hartlib Papers, *Ephemerides*, 1652: 28/2/36A. Samuel Hartlib, *A Rare and New Discovery of a Speedy Way, and Easie Means . . . For the Feeding of Silk-worms* (1652; reprinted 1655).
62 Hartlib Papers, *Ephemerides*, 1655, Part 4: 29/5/56A.
63 *Samuel Hartlib his*, 'To the Reader'.
64 Ralph Austen, *A Treatise of Fruit-trees* (1653), pp. 12, 35.
65 Samuel Hartlib, *Englands Thankfulnesse* (1642). On Hartlib's authorship see Charles Webster, ed., *Samuel Hartlib and the Advancement of Learning* (Cambridge: Cambridge University Press, 1970), p. 91.
66 Samuel Hartlib, *A Further Discoverie of the Office of Publick Addresse*, Hartlib Papers, 47/10/2B.
67 *ODNB*, 'William Petty'. Isaac Fuller, *Portrait of William Petty*, 1649–50, NPG.
68 Paul Slack, *The Invention of Improvement: Information and Material Progress in Seventeenth-Century England* (Cambridge: Cambridge University Press, 2014), p. 263.
69 Potter, *The Key of Wealth*, p. 2.
70 'Act for prohibiting Trade with the Barbadoes, Virginia, Bermuda and Antego', 3 October 1650, *Acts and Ordinances*, pp. 425–9.
71 Charles Webster, 'Benjamin Worsley: Engineering for Universal Reform', in *Samuel Hartlib and Universal Reformation*, ed. Greengrass, pp. 213–35.
72 William Petty, *The Advice of W. P. to Mr Samuel Hartlib for the Advancement of some particular Parts of Learning* (1648), p. 22.
73 Steven Pincus, *Protestantism and Patriotism: Ideologies and the Making of English Foreign Policy, 1650–1668* (Cambridge: Cambridge University Press, 1996), p. 60.
74 Ludlow, *Memoirs*, I, p. 267.
75 'An Act for increase of Shipping, and Encouragement of the Navigation of this Nation', 9 October 1651, *Acts and Ordinances*, pp. 559–62. It became better known as the Navigation Act.
76 Benjamin Worsley, *The Advocate* (1651), 'To the Right Honorable the Council of State'.
77 In 1652 Marchamont Nedham was paid £200 to translate John Selden's *Mare Clausum* (1635), which argued that the king owned the coastal seas. The council of state wished to transfer this concept of British sovereignty to Parliament.
78 C. H. Firth, *Oliver Cromwell and the Rule of the Puritans in England* (1900; repr. London: Putnam, 1947), p. 314.
79 *ODNB*, 'Thomas Harrison'.
80 *The Travels of Peter Mundy in Europe and Asia, 1608–1667*, ed. R. C. Temple, IV (1639–47) (Cambridge: Hakluyt Society, 1925), pp. 70–1.
81 Lilly, *Annus Tenebrosus*, pp. 18–19.
82 Pincus, *Protestantism and Patriotism*, p. 27, and see Helmer J. Helmers, *The Royalist Republic: Literature, Politics and Religion in the Anglo-Dutch Public Sphere, 1639–1660* (Cambridge: Cambridge University Press, 2015), p. 209.
83 Marvell, 'The Character of Holland', ll. 117–18.

84 *A Declaration of the Parliament, of the Commonwealth of England, Relating to the Affairs and Proceedings between this Commonwealth and the States General of the United Provinces* (1652).
85 Owen Felltham, *A Brief Character of the Low Countries* (1652), pp. 1, 36.
86 Worden, *The Rump Parliament*, p. 288.

1653

1 Hutton, *The Making of Oliver Cromwell*, is an excellent, and the most recent, account of Cromwell up to the end of the civil wars. A further volume is promised. Other notable biographies include John Morrill, *Oliver Cromwell* (Oxford: Oxford University Press, 2007); Peter Gaunt, *Oliver Cromwell* (Oxford: Blackwell, 1996); Barry Coward, *Oliver Cromwell* (London: Longman, 1991); J. C. Davis, *Oliver Cromwell* (London: Hodder, 2001; repr. London: Bloomsbury, 2010); Martyn Bennett, *Oliver Cromwell* (London: Routledge, 2006); Ian Gentles, *Oliver Cromwell: God's Warrior and the English Revolution* (Basingstoke: Palgrave Macmillan, 2011). Fraser, *Chief of Men* is, deservedly, still the best known among general readers, along with Hill, *God's Englishman*.
2 Thomas Manley, 'A Gratulatory Ode of Peace' and 'To the Most Excellent, The Lord Generall of Great Brittayne, Oliver Cromwel', in Payne Fisher, *Veni, Vidi, Vici. The Triumphs of the most Excellent & Illustrious, Oliver Cromwell* (1652). Most of the poem is a translation of Payne Fisher's 1652 panegyric 'Ad Illustrissimum Britanniarum Polimarchum, Oliverum Cromwellum', but '*This, This* is He' and 'th'unwearied Atlas of our State' are from the final section, which is Manley's alone.
3 John Milton, 'To Oliver Cromwell', in *The Complete Works of John Milton*, III: *The Shorter Poems*, p. 288.
4 Andrew Marvell, *The First Anniversary of the Government under H. H. the Lord Protector* (1655), p. 8.
5 *A Perfect Account of the Daily Intelligence from the Armies in England, Scotland, and Ireland*, 11–18 August 1652.
6 *ODNB*, 'Algernon Sidney'; *Sidney: Court Maxims*, ed. Hans W. Blom et al. (Cambridge: Cambridge University Press, 1996).
7 Whitelocke, *Diary*, p. 516. On the commonwealthmen and the divisions in the House see Worden, *The Rump Parliament*, and Austin Woolrych, *Britain in Revolution, 1625–1660* (Oxford. Oxford University Press, 2004).
8 *Letters, Writings, and Speeches*, II, pp. 516–19. The account of the meeting is based on Bulstrode Whitelocke's recollections.
9 Mercurius Melancholicus, *Craftie Cromwell, or Oliver Ordering our New State. A Tragi-Comedie* (1648); *The Second Part of Crafty Cromwell or Oliver in his Glory as King. A Trage Commedie* (1648), p. 32 [15]; Hutchinson, *Memoirs*, p. 252.
10 'Conversation between Oliver Cromwell and Bulstrode Whitelocke', in *Letters, Writings, and Speeches*, II, pp. 573–81; Whitelocke, *Diary*, p. 282.

11 On the franchise, see Keith Thomas, 'The Levellers and the Franchise', in *The Interregnum: The Quest for Settlement, 1646–1660*, ed. G. E. Aylmer (London and Basingstoke: Macmillan, 1972), pp. 57–78.

12 Christopher Feake, *A beam of Light, shining in the midst of much darkness and confusion* (1659), p. 41. On the Fifth Monarchists, see Bernard Capp, *The Fifth Monarchy Men.*

13 Worden, *The Rump Parliament*, p. 331.

14 Woolrych, *Britain in Revolution*, p. 527.

15 Whitelocke, *Diary*, p. 284.

16 *CSP: Venice*, XXIX, 29 April 1653.

17 Abbott, II, p. 631.

18 Whitelocke, *Diary*, p. 285.

19 *Sydney Papers, Consisting of a Journal of the Earl of Leicester, and Original Letters of Algernon Sydney*, ed. R. Blencowe (1825), p. 139. Algernon Sidney's account of this day is recorded by his father, the earl of Leicester, in his journal.

20 Ludlow, *Memoirs*, I, p. 354.

21 This account of the dissolution draws on the accounts of Whitelocke, *Diary*, pp. 285–7, and *Memorials*, IV (1853), pp. 4–7; Ludlow, *Memoirs*, I, pp. 351–5; *Journal of the Earl of Leicester*, pp. 139–41; and Hutchinson, *Memoirs*, pp. 252–3. Ludlow records later in his memoirs, in 1656, a conversation with Harrison about the dissolution during which he presumably passed on details to Ludlow. What became Ludlow's *Memoirs* was composed after 1660, when he was in exile. At the time of the dissolution, Ludlow was in Ireland, lieutenant-general of the horse and nominal commander-in-chief after Ireton's death, before Fleetwood's appointment and arrival in October 1652. On the sources, and the event, see C. H. Firth, 'The Expulsion of the Long Parliament', *History* 2 (1917), pp. 129–43; C. H. Firth, 'The Expulsion of the Long Parliament (continued)', *History* 2 (1918), pp. 193–206; Worden, *The Rump Parliament*, pp. 332–8.

22 Whitelocke, *Diary*, p. 286.

23 *CSP: Venice*, XXIX, 2 May 1653, Paulucci to Sagredo.

24 Whitelocke, *Diary*, p. 287.

25 Cited in Fraser, *Chief of Men*, p. 532. Also see John Spittlehouse, *The Army Vindicated, in their Late Dissolution of the Parliament* (1653).

26 *CSP: Domestic*, V, 7 May 1653, p. 313, and 2 June 1653, p. 371.

27 Whitelocke, *Diary*, p. 287.

28 Clarendon, *History*, V, p. 274.

29 *CSP: Venice*, XXIX, Paulucci to Sagredo, 22 April/2 May 1653, pp. 64–5. Also see Clarendon, *History*, V, p. 280 on the people being 'grateful' and *Clarke Papers*, III, p. 2 on the people being 'calm' and 'expecting great and good thinges'.

30 Cromwell's speech to the first Protectorate Parliament, 12 September 1654, in *Letters, Writings, and Speeches*, III, p. 86.

31 Josselin, *Diary*, 1 May 1653, p. 302.

32 *Severall Proceedings in Parliament*, 14–21 April 1653.
33 *Political Ballads Published in England During the Commonwealth*, ed. Thomas Wright (1841), p. 126; John Birkenhead, *Two Centuries of Pauls Church-yard* (1653), p. 61.
34 Ludlow, *Memoirs*, I, p. 357.
35 Blair Worden, '350 Years On: Cromwell and the Expulsion of the Long Parliament', in *Cromwell: Four Centuries On*, ed. Peter Gaunt (Huntingdon: Cromwell Association, 2013), pp. 74–84 (p. 74).
36 Whitelocke, *Diary*, p. 287.
37 *CJ*, VII, 7 January 1660, pp. 804–5.
38 Abbott, II, p. 644. Much, much later he refers to this whole episode, the dissolution and Barebone's Parliament, as 'a story of my owne weaknes & folly': *Letters, Writings, and Speeches*, III, p. 398.
39 Worden, 'Cromwell and the Expulsion of the Long Parliament', p. 77.
40 *Severall Proceedings in Parliament*, 14–21 April 1653; Blair Worden, *Literature and Politics in Cromwellian England: John Milton, Andrew Marvell, Marchamont Nedham* (Oxford: Oxford University Press, 2007), p. 113.
41 *The Lord General Cromwel's Speech Delivered in the Council-Chamber, upon the 4 of July, 1653* (1654), p. 17; *Letters, Writings, and Speeches*, II, p. 698.
42 *The Declaration of the Lord Generall, and his Councell of Officers, shewing the grounds and reasons for the dissolution of the Parliament, April 20. 1653* (1653), p. 3.
43 *Letters, Writings, and Speeches*, II, p. 664.
44 *The Lord General Cromwel's Speech Delivered in the Council-Chamber, upon the 4 of July, 1653*, p. 2.
45 Woolrych, *Britain in Revolution*, p. 540.
46 *The Lord General Cromwel's Speech Delivered in the Council-Chamber, upon the 4 of July, 1653*, pp. 17, 18, 21.
47 *The Lord General Cromwel's Speech Delivered in the Council-Chamber, upon the 4 of July, 1653*, p. 25.
48 John Spittlehouse, *A Warning-piece Discharged* (1653).
49 *ODNB*, 'Praisegod Barbon'.
50 Praisegod Barbon, *Good Things to Come, or, a Setting Forth some of the Great Things that will contemporize and take place when our Lord Christ shall come again* (1675).
51 In 1690 Nicholas Barbon wrote his *Discourse on Trade* on men being naturally desirous and consumerist. See *ODNB*, 'Nicholas Barbon'.
52 *CJ*, VII, 6 July 1653, pp. 281–2.
53 Evelyn, *Diary*, III, p. 84.
54 Josselin, *Diary*, p. 309. I. D., *Concordia rar Sonorum, Or a Poem Upon the Late Fight at Sea* (1653).
55 William Aspinwall, *A Brief Description of the Fifth Monarchy or Kingdome, that shortly is to come into the World* (1653).
56 Mary Cary, *The Resurrection of the Witnesses, and Englands fall from (the mystical Babylon) Rome* (1653).

57 Izaak Walton, *The Life and Death of Dr Donne* (1640).
58 *ODNB*, 'Izaak Walton'.
59 *A Perfect Diurnall*, 9–16 May 1653; Izaak Walton, *The Compleat Angler or the Contemplative Man's Recreation* (1653).
60 *Lords Journal*, VI, 5 May 1643, and printed as *It is this day ordered by the Lords and Commons in Parliament, that the booke concerning the enjoyning and tollerating of sports upon the Lords day, be forthwith burned* (1643).
61 William Bagshawe, *Living Water, or Waters for a Thirsty Soul Drawn out in Severall Sermons upon Revelation* (1653).
62 *ODNB*, 'Sir Roger L'Estrange'.
63 *ODNB*, 'John Lilburne'.
64 See the account of his 1653 trial in *State Trials*, V, pp. 407–60.
65 *To the Parliament of the Common-Wealth of England. The Humble Petition of Divers Afflicted Women, in behalf of M: Jo hn [sic] Lilburn Prisoner in Newgate* (1653).
66 Pauline Gregg, *Free-Born John: A Biography of John Lilburne* (London: Harrap, 1961). 'No mischief under Heaven that he'll not do', anon., *John Lilburne. Anagram. O! J Burn in Hell* (1653).
67 *An Hue and Cry after the Fundamental Lawes and Liberties of England* (1653).
68 C. John Sommerville, *The Secularization of Early Modern England* (Oxford: Oxford University Press, 1992).
69 Whitelocke, *Memorials*, IV, p. 38.
70 *No Age like unto this Age: or, Times Unparallel'd Oppression, Oppression, Oppression Being the Cries in Kent against the Great Oppression of Tythes* (1653); John Spittlehouse, *An Explanation of the Commission of Jesus Christ* (1653).
71 Josselin, *Diary*, pp. 309, 308, 136–7.
72 Mary Cary's suggestions in her proposals published in July 1653.
73 *The Moderate Intelligencer*, 4–11 July 1653, pp. 109–10.
74 Capp, *Fifth Monarchy Men*, p. 68.
75 *ODNB*, 'John Lambert'; Peter Thornton, *Seventeenth-Century Interior Decoration in England, France and Holland* (New Haven, CT: Yale University Press, 1978), p. 46. On Lambert's purchase in, or by, 1653 see *A History of the County of Surrey*, IV, ed. H. E. Malden (London: Victoria County History, 1912), pp. 120–5.
76 *CJ*, VII, p. 361; Whitelocke, *Memorials*, IV, p. 53.
77 *CJ*, VII, 10 December 1653, p. 363.
78 *CJ*, VII, 12 December 1653, p. 363. On Lambert's work on a new constitution and the dissolution of Barebone's Parliament see Woolrych, *Britain in Revolution*, pp. 556–9.
79 *The Government of the Common-Wealth of England, Scotland, and Ireland, And the Dominions thereto belonging; As it was publickly declared at Westminster, the 16. day of December 1653* (1654). On the Instrument see Barry Coward, *The Cromwellian Protectorate* (Manchester and New York: Manchester University Press, 2002), Chapter 2.
80 Contemporary accounts of the investiture include *Severall Proceedings of*

State Affaires, 15–22 December 1653; *Great Brittain's Post*, 14–21 December 1653; *A Perfect Diurnall*, 12–19 December 1653; *The Weekly Intelligencer*, 13–20 December 1653; *Mercurius Politicus*, 16–22 December 1653; Ludlow, *Memoirs*, I, pp. 372–3.

81 Mowl and Earnshaw, *Architecture without Kings*, p. 141. On this ceremony also see Roy Sherwood, *The Court of Oliver Cromwell* (London: Croom Helm, 1977); Laura Lunger Knoppers, *Constructing Cromwell: Ceremony, Portrait, and Print, 1645–1661* (Cambridge: Cambridge University Press, 2000).

82 *Mercurius Politicus*, 16–22 December 1653; Ludlow, *Memoirs*, I, p. 372.

83 Roy Sherwood, *Oliver Cromwell: King in All But Name, 1653–58* (Stroud: Sutton, 1997), p. 9.

84 Sherwood, *King in All But Name*, p. 9.

85 Sherwood, *King in All But Name*, p. 9.

86 Ludlow, *Memoirs*, I, p. 373.

87 Sherwood, *King in All But Name*, p. 12.

88 *CSP: Venice*, XXIX, 3 January 1654.

89 Capp, *Fifth Monarchy Men*, p. 73.

90 Clarendon, *History*, V, p. 287: 'new invented ceremony'.

91 Jeffrey R. Collins, *The Allegiance of Thomas Hobbes* (Oxford: Oxford University Press, 2005), p. 150.

92 John Moore, *Protection Proclaimed* (1655); Sherwood, *King in All But Name*, pp 3–4: 'Hitherto his Highness had been the style afforded Kings of England, his Majesty being adopted by Henry VIII and then used together with his Highness until the reign of James I, during which his Majesty became the fixed form of address.'

93 *The Character of a Protector* (1654); *Literature of the Stuart Successions: An Anthology*, ed. Andrew McRae and John West (Manchester: Manchester University Press, 2017), pp. 111–12.

94 George Wither, *The Protector. A Poem Briefly Illustrating the Supereminency of that Dignity* (1655), p. 14.

1654

1 *CSP: Venice*, XXIX, 31 January 1654.

2 *Letters, Writings, and Speeches*, III, p. 74.

3 Brotton, *Sale of the Late King's Goods*, p. 302.

4 *CJ*, VII, 19 December 1654, p. 404.

5 Paul Hunneyball, '"Cromwellian Style": The Architectural Trappings of the Protectorate Regime', in Patrick Little, ed., *The Cromwellian Protectorate*, (Woodbridge: Boydell Press, 2007), pp. 53–81 (p. 54).

6 *CSP: Domestic*, VI, 23 February 1654, p. 415.

7 Hunneyball, 'Cromwellian Style', p. 54.

8 *CSP: Domestic*, VI, 18 January 1654, p. 363.

9 *CSP: Domestic*, VII, 8 August 1654, p. 291. Also see Donald King, 'Textile Furnishings', in *The Late King's Goods*, ed. MacGregor.

10 *CSP: Domestic*, VI, 19 January 1654, p. 364. This may be the same Colonel John Humphreys who bore the sword of state before the lord president during the trial of Charles I, and which was placed in his custody: *State Trials*, IV, p. 1066.

11 Ludlow, *Memoirs*, I, p. 379.

12 *The Weekly Intelligencer*, 14–21 March 1654.

13 Hunneyball, 'Cromwellian Style', p. 68; King, 'Textile Furnishings', p. 319.

14 Hunneyball, 'Cromwellian Style', p. 70; Sherwood, *Court*, p. 30; Simon Thurley, 'Revolutionary State? Royal Palaces in Cromwell's England', Gresham College lecture, 11 March 2015.

15 Hunneyball, 'Cromwellian Style', p. 70.

16 Thornton, *Seventeenth-Century Interior Decoration*.

17 Hunneyball, 'Cromwellian Style', p. 70.

18 'Inventory of Goods Mostly Claimed as Belonging to Cromwell, at Hampton Court Palace in 1659', in E. Law, *The History of Hampton Court Palace, Stuart Times* (1885), Appendix C, pp. 277–308; transcription of TNA SP18/203, ff. 67–81.

19 'Inventory of Goods', pp. 280–1; Simon Thurley, *Hampton Court: A Social and Architectural History* (New Haven, CT: Yale University Press, 2003).

20 'Inventory of Goods', pp. 302, 308.

21 *CSP: Venice*, XXIX, 18 April 1654.

22 Thurley, *Hampton Court*, p. 113.

23 Lloyd Bowen, 'Oliver Cromwell (*alias* Williams) and Wales', in Patrick Little, ed., *Oliver Cromwell: New Perspectives* (Basingstoke: Palgrave Macmillan, 2009), pp. 169, 171.

24 Hutton, *The Making of Oliver Cromwell*, Chapter 1, and also see Simon Healy, '1636: The Unmaking of Oliver Cromwell?', in Little, ed., *Oliver Cromwell: New Perspectives*, pp. 20–37. 'War's and Fortune's son' from Marvell, 'An Horatian Ode', l. 113. Cromwell describes his conversion in a letter to his cousin's wife, Mrs St John, dated 13 October 1638: *Letters, Writings, and Speeches*, I, pp. 14–17.

25 Cited in Healy, '1636', p. 21.

26 Woolrych, *Britain in Revolution*, pp. 564–6; 'Instrument of Government', in *Constitutional Documents*, ed. Gardiner, pp. 405–17.

27 Sherwood, *Court*, p. 25.

28 'Inventory of Goods', p. 295; Sherwood, *Court*, p. 136.

29 Fraser, *Chief of Men*, p. 573.

30 *The Court and Kitchin of Elizabeth Commonly called Joan Cromwel, the Wife of the late Usurper* (1664), p. 35; 'A Panegyrick to his Highness my Lord Protector', in *The Unparalleld Monarch, or The Portraiture of a Matchless Prince* (1656), p. 74.

31 Hunneyball, 'Crowellian Style', p. 54.

32 On Clement Kinnersley, see Sherwood, *Court*. On Cromwell's household generally see Andrew Barclay, 'The Lord Protector and his Court', in Little, ed., *Oliver Cromwell: New Perspectives*, pp. 195–215.

33 *Severall Proceedings of State Affaires*, 2–9 February 1654.

34 *ODNB*, 'Sir Gilbert Pickering'.

35 *CSP: Domestic*, X, 26 May 1657, p. 385 (the cost to 'not exceed 150l').

36 *ODNB*, 'Sir Gilbert Pickering', and see Mowl and Earnshaw, *Architecture without Kings*, p. 22, for an account of Pickering's involvement with the elegant, rectangular Cobthorne House, Oundle, built in 1658 and an example of 'the architectural wave of the future'.

37 *ODNB*, 'John Dryden'; Mowl and Earnshaw, *Architecture without Kings*, p. 122.

38 Sherwood, *Court*, p. 137.

39 Sherwood, *Court*, p. 78.

40 *ODNB*, 'Walter Strickland'.

41 *ODNB*, 'John Claypole'; Barclay, 'The Lord Protector and his Court', pp. 201–2.

42 Barclay, 'The Lord Protector and his Court', pp. 202, 206–8.

43 Bowen, 'Oliver Cromwell (*alias* Williams) and Wales', p. 187. Also see Barclay, 'The Lord Protector and his Court' and *ODNB*, 'Philip Jones'.

44 *Strena Vavasoriensis* (1654), p. 19, cited in Austin Woolrych, *Commonwealth to Protectorate* (Oxford: Clarendon Press, 1982), p. 331.

45 *The Picture of a New Coutier drawn in a Conference, between, Mr. Timeserver, and Mr. Plain-heart* (1656).

46 *The Cry of a Stone or a relation of something spoken in Whitehall, by Anna Trapnel* (1654). And see Hilary Hinds's introduction in Anna Trapnel, *The Cry of a Stone*, ed. Hilary Hinds (Tempe: Arizona Center for Medieval and Renaissance Studies, 2000), pp. xiii–xlvii.

47 Milton, *A Second Defence of the English People*, cited in Worden, *Literature and Politics in Cromwellian England*, p. 258.

48 *The Perfect Politician Or, A Full View of the Life and Action (Military and Civil) of O. Cromwel* (1660), p. 254.

49 *A Perfect Diurnall*, 27 February–6 March 1654; *Severall Proceedings of State Affaires*, 2–9 March 1654.

50 *Mercurius Politicus*, 2–9 March 1654.

51 *Mercurius Politicus*, 2–9 March 1654; *Severall Proceedings of State Affaires*, 2–9 March 1654.

52 Milton, 'To Oliver Cromwell', *Complete Works of John Milton*, III: *The Shorter Poems*, p. 286.

53 *A Message from God [by a dumb woman] to his Highness the Lord Protector. Together with a word of advice to the Commons of England and Wales, for the electing of a parliament (recorded by Arise Evans)* (1654).

54 'His Highnesse the Lord Protector's Speech to the Parliament in the Painted Chamber, on Monday the 4th September. 1654', in *Letters, Writings, and Speeches*, III, p. 81.

55 On articulations of this right to alter the form of government see Markku Peltonen, *The Political Thought of the English Free*.

56 Woolrych, *Britain in Revolution*, p. 607.

57 'His Highnes Speech to the Parliament, in the Painted Chamber, at their Dissolution, Upon Monday January 22 1654[5]', in *Letters, Writings, and Speeches*, III, pp. 134–5.

1655

1 'Extracts from Henry Whistler's Journal of the West India Expedition', in *The Narrative of General Venables, with an Appendix of Papers Relating to the Expedition to the West Indies and the Conquest of Jamaica, 1654–1655*, ed. C. H. Firth (London: Longmans, Green & Co., 1900), Appendix E, pp. 144–69 (p. 144).

2 Secretary John Thurloe's 'Instructions' to Penn, reprinted in Granville Penn, *Memorials of the Professional Life and Times of Sir William Penn*, 2 vols (London, 1833), II, pp. 23–7 (p. 24). Penn's commission as commander-in-chief of the fleet dated 9 October 1654, in Penn, *Memorials*, II, pp. 21–2. Venables' 'Instructions', in Penn, *Memorials*, II, pp. 28–9. Also see 'Instructions unto Generall Penn, Collonel Venables' in *Narrative of Venables*, ed. Firth, Appendix A, pp. 107–15.

3 *Clarke Papers*, III, Appendix B: 'Edward Montagu's Notes on the Protector's Debates in the Council', p. 203. The veracity of these notes, dated 20 April and 20 July 1654, has been doubted although they are written in Montagu's hand.

4 'Edward Montagu's Notes', p. 207.

5 'Cromwell to the mayor, aldermen and common council of London', in *Letters, Writings, and Speeches*, III, p. 252.

6 'A paper of col. Muddiford concerning the West Indies', *State Papers Thurloe*, III, December 1654.

7 Thomas Gage, *The English-American his Travail by Sea and Land, or, A New Survey of the West Indias* (1648).

8 Gage, *The English-American*, p. 109; Tinniswood, *The Verneys*, p. 250.

9 Thomas Gage, 'Some briefe and true observations concerning the West-Indies, humbly presented to his highnesse, Oliver, lord protector of the commonwealth of England, Scotland, and Ireland, [by mr. Thomas Gage]', *State Papers Thurloe*, III, December 1654.

10 Gage, *The English-American*, p. 80.

11 Gage, 'Some briefe and true observations concerning the West-Indies'.

12 'Instructions unto Generall Robert Venables', *Narrative of Venables*, Appendix A, p. 113. The Swedish ambassador Peter Julius Coyet reported back to Charles X on the council's reluctance: Michael Roberts (trans. and ed.), *Swedish Diplomats at Cromwell's Court 1655–1656: The Missions of Peter Julius Coyet and Christer Bonde* (London: Camden Society, 1988), pp. 166–7.

13 Whitelocke, *Memorials*, IV, p. 189.

14 'A paper of col. Muddiford concerning the West Indies'.

15 Francis Barrington, letter from Jamaica, 14 July 1655, *Seventh Report of the Royal Commission on Historical Manuscripts*, Part 1: Report and Appendix (London, 1879), no. 949, p. 571. Francis's parents were Joan Cromwell, eldest daughter of Sir Henry Cromwell of Hinchingbroke and therefore Cromwell's aunt, and Sir Francis Barrington, MP.
16 'Henry Whistler's Journal', p. 150.
17 *Narrative of Venables*, pp. 102, 11.
18 Barrington, 14 July 1655, p. 571.
19 'Henry Whistler's Journal', p. 145.
20 *Narrative of Venables*, p. 7.
21 Barrington, 14 July 1655, p. 572.
22 *Narrative of Venables*, p. xxxvi.
23 Penn, *Memorials*, II, pp. 71–4.
24 Winslow's letter to Thurloe, *State Papers Thurloe*, III, 16 March 1655.
25 Carla Gardina Pestana, *The English Conquest of Jamaica: Oliver Cromwell's Bid for Empire* (Cambridge, MA: Belknap Press, 2017), p. 68.
26 'Richard Rooth's Sea Journal of the Western Design, 1654–55', ed. John F. Battick, *Jamaica Journal* 5.4 (1971), p. 8.
27 'Rooth's Sea Journal'.
28 The number of 7,500 is from an anonymous letter, 1 June 1655, in *Narrative of Venables*, Appendix D, pp. 127–39.
29 'Narrative of the Expedition to San Domingo', in *Clarke Papers*, III, pp. 54–60. Firth does not attribute this narrative to Thomas White but, in *Narrative of Venables*, he notes that the author is 'probably Major Thomas White', p. 118.
30 *Narrative of Venables*, p. 26.
31 'Henry Whistler's Journal', p. 152; St Anne's desecration in Pestana, *The English Conquest*, p. 111, citing a report of the governor of Hispaniola, Peñalva.
32 Barrington, 14 July 1655, p. 573.
33 'Henry Whistler's Journal', p. 154.
34 'Henry Whistler's Journal', p. 156.
35 Pestana, *The English Conquest*, p. 83.
36 *Narrative of Venables*, p. 31.
37 *CSP: Domestic*, VIII, 9 June 1655, p. 204.
38 *A Great and Wonderful Victory obtained by the English Forces, under the Command of General Pen and Gen. Venables* (1655), p. 6.
39 *Mercurius Politicus*, 24–31 May 1655.
40 Two official dispatches, one written by Venables and Butler dated 4 June, *State Papers Thurloe*, III, and another by Penn dated 6 June, Penn, *Memorials*, II, p.109, probably sent on the *Cardiff*, the first ship to sail back to England after the arrival in Jamaica.
41 Blair Worden, 'Cromwell and the Sin of Achan', in *God's Instruments: Political Conduct in the England of Oliver Cromwell* (Oxford: Oxford University Press, 2012), p. 22.

42 *Letters, Writings, and Speeches*, III, p. 230 (30 October 1655).

43 'A Letter from Jamaica', *State Papers Thurloe*, III, 3 June 1655: John Daniell to his brother Colonel William Daniell, in Scotland.

44 I. S., *A Brief and Perfect Journal of the late Preceedings and Successe of the English Army in the West-Indies, Continued until June the 24th. 1655* (1655), p. 7.

45 *A Declaration of a Day of Solemn Fasting and Humiliation* (1655). The date set was 1 December 1655.

46 Penn to Admiralty Commissioners, 6 June 1655, cited in Pestana, *The English Conquest*, p. 92.

47 Letter to Martin Noell, dated 13 June 1655, in *Narrative of Venables*, pp. 49–50.

48 Thomas Noell to Martin Noell, *State Papers Thurloe*, III, 5 June 1655. On the Noells see Richard B. Sheridan, *Sugar and Slavery: An Economic History of the British West Indies, 1623–1775* (Jamaica: Canoe Press, 1974; repr. 1994). Also see Stephen Saunders Webb, *The Governors General: The English Army and the Definition of Empire, 1569–1681* (Chapel Hill: University of North Carolina Press, 1979).

49 *Narrative of Venables*, p. 30.

50 *Narrative of Venables*, p. 100.

51 Lee Porcher Townshend, 'Some Account of General Robert Venables of Antrobus and Wincham, Cheshire . . . Together with the Autobiographical Memoir or Diary of his Widow, Elizabeth Venables', *Chetham Miscellanies*, Volume the Fourth (1872), pp. iii–28 (p. 28).

52 'Henry Whistler's Journal', p. 157.

53 Letter from Jamaica, *State Papers Thurloe*, III, 3 June 1655.

54 Henry Vane, *A Healing Question Propounded and Resolved* (1656). Pestana, *The English Conquest*, p. 105, notes Gage's sermon on Joshua.

55 On the arrival in Jamaica see Pestana, *The English Conquest*. On Ramirez, see Matthew Parker, *The Sugar Barons: Family, Corruption, Empire and War* (London: Hutchinson, 2011), p. 101.

56 Barrington, 14 July 1655, p. 572; on the dogs and the shallow graves: letter from Jamaica, 5 November 1655, *Narrative of Venables*, p. 142.

57 For description of Jamaica, letter, 1 June 1655, *Narrative of Venables*, pp. 138–9.

58 Barrington, 14 July 1655, p. 574.

59 *By the Protector. A Proclamation Giving Encouragement to such as shall transplant themselves to Jamaica* (1655); *A True Description of Jamaica, With the Fertility, Commodities, and Healthfulness of the Place* (1657).

60 Edward Doyley, *A Narrative of the Great Success God hath been Pleased to Give His Highness Forces in Jamaica against the King of Spains forces* (1658); *ODNB*, 'Edward Doyley'.

61 Evelyn, *Diary*, III, p. 257 (September 1660).

62 John Aubrey, *An Essay towards the Description of the North Division of Wiltshire*, ed. T. Phillipps (1838).

63 *ODNB*, 'John Penruddock'. Compton House was confiscated on Penruddock's

execution, but was soon back in the family, where it remained until the 1930s.

64 *State Papers Thurloe*, II, 2 February 1654; Underdown, *Royalist Conspiracy*, p. 75.

65 On the Sealed Knot and its leaders see Underdown, *Royalist Conspiracy*, pp. 73–87; Lloyd Bowen, 'David Underdown, Royalist Conspirators and the Character of English Politics', *History Compass* 2 (2013), pp. 341–51.

66 Nadine Akkerman, *Invisible Agents: Women and Espionage in Seventeenth-Century Britain* (Oxford: Oxford University Press, 2018).

67 Cited in Underdown, *Royalist Conspiracy*, p. 87; also see David Underdown, *Revel, Riot and Rebellion: Popular Politics and Culture in England, 1603–1660* (Oxford: Oxford University Press, 1985).

68 Underdown, *Royalist Conspiracy*, pp. 121–2.

69 Underdown, *Royalist Conspiracy*, p. 113.

70 Charles's letter, 3 December 1654: *Calendar of the Clarendon State Papers*, III (1655–7), ed. W. Dunn Macray (1876), pp. 3–4; *State Papers Thurloe*, III.

71 *Calendar of the Clarendon State Papers*, III, 'The King to Mr Roles', p. 16.

72 *Letters, Writings, and Speeches*, III, pp. 134–5.

73 *State Papers Thurloe*, III, 4 January 1655, 'An intercepted letter of King Charles II': 'Mr Westrope' to 'Mr Roles'; Underdown, *Royalist Conspiracy*, p. 162.

74 Fraser, *Chief of Men*, p. 648.

75 Austin Woolrych, *Penruddock's Rising, 1655* (London: G. Philip for the Historical Association, 1955), p. 12.

76 W. W. Ravenhill, 'Records of the Rising in the West, AD 1655', *Wiltshire Archaeological and Natural History Magazine* 13 (1872), p. 133.

77 List of prisoners in Ravenhill, 'Records of the Rising', *Wiltshire Archaeological and Natural History Magazine* 13, p. 139.

78 *Perfect Proceedings of State Affaires in England, Scotland and Ireland*, 29 March–6 April 1655.

79 *State Papers Thurloe*, III, 29 March 1655, 'Examination of mr. Saint Loe. [Taken by secretary Thurloe.]'.

80 *The Commonplace Book of Sir John Strangways, 1645–1666*, ed. Thomas G. Olsen (Tempe, AZ: Arizona Center for Medieval and Renaissance Studies, 2004).

81 *Englands Slavery, or Barbados Merchandize Represented In a Petition to the High and Honourable Court of Parliament, by Marcellus Rivers and Oxenbridge Foyle* (1659).

82 *ODNB*, 'Sir Joseph Wagstaffe'.

83 *Letter to His Highness the Lord Protector from Captain Unton Crook signifying the totall Defeat of the Cavaliers in the West under the command of Sir Joseph Wagstaffe* (1655), p. 4.

84 Earnshaw and Mowl, *Architecture without Kings*, p. 106.

85 Sources for the trials include John Penruddock, *The Triall of the Hon. Col. John Penruddock, of Compton, in Wiltshire, and his Speech* (1655); *The Speeches of Col. Penruddock, Col. Jones, Mr John Dean and Mr Lucas* (1655); *The True Speeches of Colonel John Penruddock and Mr Hugh Grove, delivered on the Scaffold at Exeter Castle* (1655); Ravenhill, 'Records of the Rising', *Wiltshire Archaeological and Natural History*

Magazine 13, pp. 119–88; pp. 252–74; 14 (1873), pp. 38–67; 15 (1875), pp. 1–42. Penruddock's account of his trial, reconstructed while awaiting execution in prison, in his family papers and in his handwriting: Ravenhill, 'Records of the Rising', *Wiltshire Archaeological and Natural History Magazine* 13, pp. 262–70.

86 Ravenhill, 'Records of the Rising', *Wiltshire Archaeological and Natural History Magazine* 13, p. 255.

87 Ravenhill, 'Records of the Rising', *Wiltshire Archaeological and Natural History Magazine* 13, pp. 262–70. On the legitimacy of the treason charge, see Jonathan Fitzgibbons, 'The Definition of Treason and the Offer of the Crown', in *Revolutionary England, c.1630–c.1660: Essays for Clive Holmes*, ed. Geoge Southcombe and Grant Tapsell (London: Routledge, 2017), p. 195.

88 *The Triall of Penruddock*, pp. 14, 15. Also see the MS version transcribed in Ravenhill, 'Records of the Rising', *Wiltshire Archaeological and Natural History Magazine* 15, pp. 6–10.

89 Ravenhill, 'Records of the Rising', *Wiltshire Archaeological and Natural History Magazine* 14, p. 65.

90 Petition, transcribed in Ravenhill, 'Records of the Rising', *Wiltshire Archaeological and Natural History Magazine* 14, p. 63.

91 'A List of Articles Exhibited in the Temporary Museum at the Council Chamber, Salisbury', *Wiltshire Archaeological and Natural History Magazine* 2 (1855), p. 30.

92 'Wiltshire Record Office list of prisoners with images next to names showing who was beheaded and who hanged,' *Wiltshire Archaeological and Natural History Magazine* 14, p. 65.

93 *Calendar of State Papers: Colonial, America and West Indies*, I, 18 January 1656.

94 *Englands Slavery, or Barbados Merchandize Represented In a Petition to the High and Honourable Court of Parliament, by Marcellus Rivers and Oxenbridge Foyle* (1659); Ravenhill, 'Records of the Rising', *Wiltshire Archaeological and Natural History Magazine* 15, p. 34.

95 Ravenhill, 'Records of the Rising', *Wiltshire Archaeological and Natural History Magazine* 15, p. 34.

96 Ludlow, *Memoirs*, II, p. 405.

97 *A Declaration of his Highnesse*, 31 October 1655. The document was probably co-written by Desborough, Lambert and Thurloe, overseen by Cromwell; Woolrych, *Britain in Revolution*, p. 627.

98 *State Papers Thurloe*, IV, 'Secretary Thurloe's memorandums of the plot in March 1654–5, and reasons for erecting a new standing militia in all the counties of England'.

99 'Instructions to the Major-Generals', Abbott, III, p. 845.

100 Christopher Durston, *Cromwell's Major-Generals: Godly Government during the English Revolution* (Manchester and New York: Manchester University Press, 2001), p. 53.

101 Hutchinson, *Memoirs*, p. 257.

102 See Durston, *Cromwell's Major-Generals*, on Boteler as a bullying and zealous Puritan, and Paul Hardacre, 'William Boteler: A Cromwellian Oligarch', *Huntington Library Quarterly* 11 (1947), pp. 1–11. On Cobthorne House (*c.* 1658) see Mowl and Earnshaw, *Architecture without Kings*, p. 118.
103 John Bunyan, *Grace Abounding to the Chief of Sinners* (1666).
104 On Bunyan's life see the editor's preface to John Bunyan, *The Pilgrim's Progress*, ed. Cynthia Wall (New York and London: W. W. Norton, 2009).

1656

1 Josselin, *Diary*, p. 360.
2 Josselin, *Diary*, p. 224.
3 *ODNB*, 'Antonio Fernandez Carvajal'; Lucien Wolf, 'The First English Jew', *Transactions of the Jewish Historical Society of England* 2 (1896), pp. 14–46.
4 Lucien Wolf, 'Crypto-Jews under the Commonwealth', *Transactions of the Jewish Historical Society of England* 1 (1893–4), p. 55; David S. Katz, *Philo-Semitism and the Readmission of the Jews to England, 1603–1655* (Oxford: Clarendon Press, 1982).
5 Steven Nadler, *Menasseh ben Israel: Rabbi of Amsterdam* (New Haven, CT and London: Yale University Press, 2018), p. 166.
6 *CSP: Domestic*, IX, 25 April 1656, p. 294.
7 *CSP: Domestic*, IX, 24 March 1656, p. 237; 'The Humble Petition of The Hebrews at Present Residing in this citty of London'.
8 David Katz, *The Jews in the History of England, 1485–1850* (Oxford: Oxford University Press, 1996), pp. 139–42.
9 Menasseh ben Israel, *Vindiciae Judaeorum* (1656), p. 5.
10 Nadler, *Menasseh*, p. 195, quoting from a letter addressed 'To All Persons of the Hebrew Nation', 2 September 1655.
11 Roger Williams, *The Bloudy Tenent of Persecution* (1644).
12 Samuel Fisher, *Christianismus Redivivus* (1655).
13 Hugh Peter, *A Word for the Army and Two Words for the Kingdom* (1646).
14 Johanna Cartwright, *The Petition of the Jews for the Repealing of the Act of Parliament for their Banishment out of England* (1649).
15 *Mercurius Pragmaticus*, 26 December 1648–9 January 1649; Katz, *Philo-Semitism*, p. 178.
16 John Sadler, *The Rights of Kingdom* (1649).
17 James Shapiro, *Shakespeare and the Jews* (New York: Columbia University Press, 1996), p. 25.
18 Menasseh ben Israel, *The Hope of Israel* (1650).
19 Cited in *Menasseh ben Israel's Mission to Oliver Cromwell: Being a Reprint of the Pamphlets Published by Menasseh ben Israel to Promote the Re-admission of the Jews to England, 1649–1656*, ed. Lucien Wolf (London: Macmillan, 1901), p. xl.
20 *To His Highnesse the Lord Protector of the Common-wealth of England, Scotland, and Ireland. The Humble Addresses of Menasseh ben Israel, a divine, and doctor of physick, in behalfe of the Jewish nation* (1655).

21 Milton, *A Defence of the People of England*, trans. Donald Mackenzie, in *Complete Prose Works*, IV, Part I, p. 369. See also *Milton and the Jews*, ed. Douglas Brooks (Cambridge: Cambridge University Press, 2008), especially the chapter by Nicholas von Maltzahn, 'Making Use of the Jews: Milton and Philo-Semitism', pp. 57–82.

22 Menasseh ben Israel, *The Hope of Israel . . . Whereunto are added, In this Second Edition, Some Discourses upon the point of the Conversion of the Jewes by Moses Wall* (1652).

23 Arise Evans, *Light for the Jews, or, The Means to Convert them in Answer to a Book of theirs called The Hope of Israel* (1656).

24 Ben Israel, *The Hope of Israel*.

25 Ben Israel, *Vindiciae Judaeorum*; Deuteronomy 30.1–5; Isaiah 11.11–12.

26 Thomas Thorowgood, *Jewes in America* (1650).

27 Hartlib Papers, 4/1/15A-B.

28 Moses Wall, 'Considerations Upon the Point of the Conversion of the Jewes', in ben Israel, *The Hope of Israel*, p. 48, and 'The Translator to the Reader' in the same; *A Narrative of the Late Proceeds at White-Hall Concerning the Jews* (1656), p. 4.

29 Nadler, *Menasseh*, p. 166.

30 Marvell, 'The Character of Holland', ll. 72–3.

31 *A Narrative of the Late Proceeds at White-hall*.

32 *State Papers Thurloe*, IV, 12 December 1655.

33 *A Narrative of the Late Proceeds at White-hall*.

34 William Prynne, *A Short Demurrer to the Jewes* (1656), p. 120.

35 Josselin, *Diary*, p. 337.

36 John Dury, *A Case of Conscience, Whether it Be Lawful to Admit Jews into a Christian Commonwealth. Written to Samuel Hartlib* (1656).

37 Evelyn, *Diary*, III, p. 163.

38 *CSP: Domestic*, IX, 31 December 1655, p. 82.

39 Cited in Wolf, *Menasseh ben Israel's Mission to Oliver Cromwell*, p. lix.

40 John Coffey, 'Puritanism and Liberty Revisited: The Case for Toleration in the English Revolution', *Historical Journal* 41 (1998), pp. 961–85.

41 Thomas Violet, *A Petition Against the Jews* (1661), p. 2.

42 *The Journal of George Fox: A Revised Edition*, ed. John L. Nickalls (Cambridge: Cambridge University Press, 2010; first published 1952), pp. 11, 35, 13.

43 On the Quakers see Pink Dandelion, *The Quakers: A Very Short Introduction* (Oxford: Oxford University Press, 2008); *Early Quakers and Their Theological Thought*, ed. Stephen W. Angell and Pink Dandelion (Cambridge: Cambridge University Press, 2015); Adrian Davies, *The Quakers in English Society, 1655–1725* (Oxford: Clarendon, 2000).

44 Fox, *Journal*, p. 73.

45 *ODNB*, 'Elizabeth Fletcher'. On Hooton and Fletcher and Quaker women in general see Phyllis Mack, *Visionary Women: Ecstatic Prophecy in Seventeenth-Century England* (Berkeley and Los Angeles, CA: University of California Press, 1992).

46 Fox, *Journal*, p. 22.

47 Francis Higgingson, *Brief Relation of the Irreligion of the Northern Quakers* (1653). Justice Bennet of Derby at Fox's 1650 trial first used the term Quaker: Fox, *Journal*, p. 58.
48 Pink Dandelion, *An Introduction to Quakerism* (Cambridge: Cambridge University Press, 2011), p. 27.
49 *A Proclamation of his Highness, Prohibiting the Disturbing of Ministers and other Christians in their Assemblies and Meetings* (1655).
50 Evelyn, *Diary*, III, p. 178.
51 Josselin, *Diary*, p. 362.
52 *ODNB*, 'Luke Robinson'.
53 Margaret Fell, *The Call of the Jewes out of Babylon* (1656).
54 Fox, *Journal*; Margaret Fox (formerly Fell), *A Brief Collection of Remarkable Passages and Occurrences Relating to the Birth, Education, Life, Conversion, Travels, Services, and Deep Sufferings of that Ancient, Eminent, and Faithful Servant of the Lord, Margaret Fell* (1712); Isabel Ross, *Margaret Fell: Mother of Quakerism*, 2nd edn (York: Ebor Press, 1984); Bonnelyn Young Kunze, *Margaret Fell and the Rise of Quakerism* (Basingstoke: Palgrave, 1993).
55 Fox, *Journal*, p. 134.
56 Mack, *Visionary Women*, p. 174.
57 Mack, *Visionary Women*, p. 154.
58 'The Examination of James Nayler, upon an Indictment of Blasphemy, at the Sessions at Appleby', in George Fox and James Nayler, *Saul's Errand to Damascus* (1653), p. 30. John Deacon, *Exact History of the Life of James Naylor with his parents, birth, education, profession, actions, & blaspheemies* (1657).
59 Cited in Leo Damrosch, *The Sorrows of the Quaker Jesus: James Nayler and the Puritan Crackdown on the Free Spirit* (Cambridge, MA: Harvard University Press, 1996), p. 119.
60 Martha Simmonds, *A Lamentation for the Lost Sheep of the House of Israel* (1655), p. 1; also see *When the Lord Jesus came to Jerusalem, he beheld the city, and wept over it* (1655); *O England, Thy Time is Come* (1656).
61 John Deacon, early biographer of Nayler, cited in Damrosch, *The Sorrows of the Quaker Jesus*, p. 116.
62 Cited in Carole Dale Spencer, 'The Man who "Set Himself as a Sign"', in Angell and Dandelion, ed., *Early Quakers and their Theological Thought*, p. 68.
63 *ODNB*, 'John Desborough'.
64 John Deacon, *The Grand Impostor Examined: Or, The Life, Tryal, and Examination of James Nayler, The Seduced and Seducing Quaker with The Manner of his Riding into Bristol* (1656).
65 Hill, *The World Turned Upside Down*, p. 246.
66 *Mercurius Politicus*, 29 October–6 November 1656.
67 Burton, *Diary*, I, 5–16 December 1656; *A True Narrative of The Examination, Tryall and Sufferings of James Nayler* (1657; authorship uncertain, although

Robert Rich may have been involved). See Kate Peters, *Print Culture and the Early Quakers* (Cambridge: Cambridge University Press, 2005), p. 241.

68 Hartlib Papers, HP 31/1/7A: John Beale to Hartlib, 23 December 1656.

69 *ODNB*, 'Thomas Burton'; Jonathan Fitzgibbons, 'Reconstructing the Debates of the Protectorate Parliaments: The Pitfalls of J. T. Rutt's Edition of "Thomas Burton's" Diary', *Parliamentary History* 35 (2016), pp. 221–41.

70 *ODNB*, 'Arise Evans'.

71 Burton, *Diary*, I, 6 December 1656.

72 Fox and Nayler, *Saul's Errand to Damascus*, p. 160.

73 Damrosch, *The Sorrows of the Quaker Jesus*, p. 144.

74 Deacon, *The Grand Imposter Examined*, pp. 11, 18.

75 Burton, *Diary*, I, 8 December 1656.

76 Burton, *Diary*, I, 5 December 1656.

77 Burton, *Diary*, I, 5 December 1656.

78 Burton, *Diary*, I, 12 December 1656.

79 *Mercurius Politicus*, 15–22 January 1657.

80 'Letter from Oliver Cromwell to Sir Thomas Widdrington', 25 December 1656, *Letters, Writings, and Speeches*, III, pp. 324–5.

81 'Passages betweene the Protector and the hundred officers of the Army', 7 March 1656, in *Letters, Writings, and Speeches*, III, pp. 340–2 (p. 341).

82 Preface to Richard Hubberthorne, *The Cause of Stumbling Removed* (1657).

83 *ODNB*, 'George Fox'.

84 *ODNB*, 'William Penn'; Mary Geiter, *William Penn* (Harlow: Longman, 2000); *William Penn: Political Writings*, ed. Andrew Murphy (Cambridge: Cambridge University Press, 2021).

85 William Davenant, *A Proposition for Advancement of Moralitie, by a New Way of Entertainment of the People* (1654).

86 'Some observations concerning the people of this nation', Davenant to Thurloe, transcribed in C. H. Firth, 'Sir William Davenant and the Revival of Drama during the Protectorate', *English Historical Review* 18 (1903), pp. 319–21.

87 *CSP: Domestic*, IX, June 1655–6, p. 396.

88 William Davenant, *The First Days Entertainment at Rutland-House* (1656), p. 36.

89 William Davenant, *The Siege of Rhodes* (1656).

90 Pepys, *Diary*, IX, 19 December 1668, p. 396. On Davenant see *Drama of the English Republic, 1649–1660*, ed. Janet Clare (Manchester: Manchester University Press, 2002) and Stephen Watkins, 'The Protectorate Playhouse: William Davenant's Cockpit in the 1650s', *Shakespeare Bulletin*, 37 (2019), pp. 89–109.

91 Evelyn, *Diary*, III, 5 May 1659.

92 Davenant, *The Siege of Rhodes*, after p. 41. The bibliographical number for this particular edition, part of George Thomason's collection, is Thomason / E.498[6].

1657

1 *Mercurius Politicus*, 19–26 January 1654, carries an advertisement for *Parthenissa*.
2 Roger Boyle, *Parthenissa, A Romance in Four Parts* (1655), 'Preface'.
3 Dorothy Osborne to William Temple, on *Parthenissa*, 18/19 February 1654, in Osborne, *Letters to Sir William Temple*, ed. Kenneth Parker (London: Penguin, 1987), p. 180.
4 John Mallet to Robert Boyle, 27 March 1657, in *The Works of the Honourable Robert Boyle*, ed. T. Birch, 6 vols (1772), VI, p. 634.
5 Percy Herbert, *The Princesse Cloria: or, the Royal Romance* (1665 edition containing all parts), 'To the Reader', A1v.
6 Henry Stubbe, *Malice Rebuked, or a Character of Mr Richard Baxters Abilities* (1659), p. 42.
7 Roger Boyle, *Parthenissa, That most Fam'd Romance. The Six Volumes Compleat* (1676), p. 657.
8 Abraham Cowley, *Davideis: A Sacred Poem of the Troubles of David* (1656); Broghill, 'To Mr Cowley on his Davideis', in Ted-Larry Pebworth, 'The Earl of Orrery and Cowley's "Davideis": Recovered Works and New Connections', *Modern Philology* 76 (1978), pp. 136–48. Charles II made Lord Broghill the first earl of Orrery in 1660.
9 *Correspondence of Henry Cromwell*, p. 204.
10 *The Correspondence of Robert Boyle, 1627–1691*, ed. Michael Hunter, Antonio Clericuzio and Lawrence M. Principe, 6 vols (London: Routledge, 2022), I, pp. 82–3.
11 *ODNB*, 'Richard Boyle, first earl of Cork'; 'Richard Boyle, second earl of Cork'.
12 On Broghill see Patrick Little, *Lord Broghill and the Cromwellian Union with Ireland and Scotland* (Woodbridge: Boydell Press, 2004) and *ODNB*, 'Roger Boyle, first earl of Orrery'. Little challenges the prevalent myth, following Thomas Morrice, 'Memoirs of the most remarkable passages in the life and death of the right honourable Roger, earl of Orrery', in Roger Boyle, *A Collection of the State Letters of the Rt Hon. Roger Boyle, the first earl of Orrery*, ed. Thomas Morrice (Dublin, 1743), that Broghill was forever a closet Royalist.
13 *The Memoirs of Anne, Lady Halkett and Ann, Lady Fanshawe*, p. 86.
14 Burton, *Diary*, I, 7 January 1657.
15 Gilbert Burnet, *A Sermon Preached at the Funeral of the Honourable Robert Boyle; at St Martins in the Fields, January 7, 1691/2. By the Right Reverend Father in God, Gilbert Lord Bishop of Sarum* (1692).
16 On Lady Ranelagh's political ideas being circulated among her circle see Michelle DiMeo, *Lady Ranelagh: The Incomparable Life of Robert Boyle's Sister* (Chicago: University of Chicago Press, 2021). On Shannon's daughter see Lisa Jardine, *The Curious Life of Robert Hooke: The Man Who Measured London* (London: HarperCollins, 2003), p. 346, n.12.
17 *ODNB*, 'Katherine Jones (née Boyle), Viscountess Ranelagh'.

18 Frequently referred to as such throughout the Hartlib Papers.
19 Robert Boyle, *New Experiments Physico-Mechanicall, Touching The Spring of the Air, and its Effects, (Made, for the most part, in a New Pneumatical Engine) Written by way of Letter To the Right Honorable Charles Lord Vicount of Dungarvan, Eldest Son to the Earl of Cork* (1660).
20 Aubrey, *Brief Lives*, pp. 319–20; John Wilkins, *The Discovery of a World in the Moone* (1638).
21 Evelyn, *Diary*, III, p. 110.
22 Cited in Webster, *The Great Instauration*, p. 162.
23 Webster, *The Great Instauration*, p. 162 – it was possibly Boyle who said this: letter to Hartlib, 14 September 1655.
24 *Correspondence of Boyle*, I, p. 214: Boyle to Evelyn, 23 May 1657.
25 Robert Boyle, *The Aretology or Ethicall Elements of Robert Boyle Begun at Stalbridge . . . 1654*, in *The Early Essays and Ethics of Robert Boyle*, ed. John T. Harwood (Carbondale, IL: Southern Illinois University Press, 1991), p. 132.
26 *Correspondence of Boyle*, I, p. 227: Oldenburg to Boyle, 30 August/8 September 1657.
27 From James Harrington, *The Prerogative of Popular Government*, cited in Webster, *The Great Instauration*, p. 170.
28 Robert Hooke, *Micrographia* (1665); Jardine, *The Curious Life of Robert Hooke*.
29 Robert Boyle's first book: *New Experiments Physico-Mechanicall, Touching the Spring of the Air, and its Effects*.
30 Jardine, *The Curious Life of Robert Hooke*.
31 *Robert Boyle by Himself and His Friends*, ed. Michael Hunter (London: Routledge, 2020).
32 'An Act for the Security of His Highness the Lord Protector His Person, And Continuance of the Nation in Peace and Safety', *Acts and Ordinances*, 27 November 1656, p. 1038.
33 On John Lambert see David Farr, *John Lambert, Parliamentary Soldier and Cromwellian Major-General, 1619–1684* (Woodbridge: Boydell & Brewer, 2003).
34 Secretary Thurloe writing to Henry Cromwell, 28 October 1656, *State Papers Thurloe*, V: 'There was a motion made this day by an Irish gentleman, to take into consideration the 31st article of the government.' See C. H. Firth, *The Last Years of the Protectorate*, I, p. 64.
35 Cited in Jonathan Fitzgibbons, 'Hereditary Succession and the Cromwellian Protectorate: The Offer of the Crown Reconsidered', *English Historical Review* 128 (2013), pp. 1095–1128 (p. 1102).
36 *CSP: Venice*, XXX, 6 October 1656; Roberts, trans. and ed., *Swedish Diplomats at Cromwell's Court*, p. 75.
37 'His Highnes Speech To the Parliament, in the Painted Chamber, at their Dissolution, Upon Monday January 22 1654[5]', in *Letters, Writings, and Speeches*, III, p. 144.
38 Edward Sexby, *Killing Noe Murder* (1657).

39 *Mercurius Politicus*, 12–19 February 1657.
40 *The Whole Business of Sindercome* (1657), p. 14.
41 *Mercurius Politicus*, 19–26 February 1657.
42 Marvell, *The First Anniversary*, ll. 205–6.
43 Burton, *Diary*, I, 19 January 1657, pp. 353–67.
44 Fitzgibbons, 'Hereditary Succession and the Cromwellian Protectorate'.
45 *CJ*, VII, 23 February 1657, pp. 204–6; MP Robert Beake to Leonard Piddock, 28 March 1657, cited in Little, *Lord Broghill*, p. 148.
46 'The Remonstrance of 23 February 1657', in Patrick Little and David Smith, *Parliaments and Politics during the Cromwellian Protectorate* (Cambridge: Cambridge University Press, 2007), Appendix 2, pp. 306–12.
47 Milton, *A Second Defence of the English People*, in Milton, *Complete Prose Works*, IV, p. 672.
48 George Wither, *The Protector. A Poem Briefly Illustrating the Supereminency of that Dignity* (1655), p. 4.
49 'The Remonstrance of 23 February 1657', p. 307. 'The pretended Title of Charles Stuart, &c, Renounced and Disannulled', *Acts and Ordinances*, 27 November 1656, p. 1037.
50 *A Narrative of the late Parliament, (so called) Their Election and Appearing* (1658), p. 22.
51 *Clarke Papers*, III, p. 91.
52 Hutchinson, *Memoirs*, p. 261.
53 *Correspondence of Henry Cromwell*, p. 221.
54 On the month of debates in Parliament see Burton, *Diary*, I, from 23 February to 31 March.
55 *Correspondence of Henry Cromwell*, p. 214. 'Soe little opposition' cited in newsletter in *Clarke Papers*, III, p. 94.
56 *Correspondence of Henry Cromwell*, pp. 236, 239.
57 *CJ*, VII, 25 March 1657, pp. 510–11. 'Bitter speeches' from Samuel Morland to John Pell: BL, Lansdowne MS 755, no. 62: 'Whitehall, 26 March 1657'.
58 Burton, *Diary*, I, 31 March 1657.
59 'The Lord Protectors Speech at the Presenting of the Peticon & humble Advise, on Tuesday the 31th of March. 1657', in *Letters, Writings, and Speeches*, III, pp. 345–9. An abbreviated form of Cromwell's speech also circulated in that week's newsbooks, *Mercurius Politicus* and *The Publick Intelligencer*. In a letter to Henry Cromwell dated 3 March, Anthony Morgan tells how army officers had got hold of a copy of the Remonstrance and shown it to Cromwell; *Correspondence of Henry Cromwell*, p. 215.
60 'Speech of Oliver Cromwell to the committee of Parliament in Whitehall', 21 April 1657, in *Letters, Writings, and Speeches*, III, p. 401.
61 'Passages betweene the Protector and the hundred officers of the Army, touching Kingshipp', 27 February 1657, Version A, in *Letters, Writings, and Speeches*, III, p. 341.

62 'Speech of Oliver Cromwell to the committee of Parliament in Whitehall', 3 April 1657, in *Letters, Writings, and Speeches*, III, pp. 353–4.
63 *Monarchy Asserted, to be the Best, most Ancient and Legall Form of Government, in a Conference had at Whitehall, with Oliver late Lord Protector and a Committee of Parliament* (1660), p. 11.
64 *Monarchy Asserted*, pp. 28, 26.
65 *Monarchy Asserted*, p. 68.
66 *Monarchy Asserted*, p. 18.
67 Whitelocke, *Memorials*, IV, p. 290.
68 Burton, *Diary*, 20 April 1657; 'Speech of Oliver Cromwell to the committee of Parliament in Whitehall', 20 April 1657, in *Letters, Writings, and Speeches*, III, pp. 383–90.
69 *Monarchy Asserted*, pp. 41–2.
70 Joshua 7.1. Blair Worden, 'Cromwell and the Sin of Achan', in *God's Instruments*, pp. 13–32.
71 *Monarchy Asserted*, p. 33.
72 Henry Cromwell to the Protector, 22 April 1657, *State Papers Thurloe*, VI, p. 222.
73 Cited in Little, *Lord Broghill*, p. 154.
74 *State Papers Thurloe*, VI, p. 243.
75 'Speech of Oliver Cromwell to the committee of Parliament in Whitehall', 20 April 1657, in *Letters, Writings, and Speeches*, III, p. 389.
76 *Correspondence of Henry Cromwell*, p. 264.
77 *Correspondence of Henry Cromwell*, p. 221. It was reported by the French ambassador in February that Richard had been seen with a copy of the draft 'act' about 'royalty' in his hands: Firth, *The Last Years of the Protectorate*, I, p. 129n.
78 Hutchinson, *Memoirs*, p. 256.
79 Evelyn, *Diary*, III, 22 March 1657, pp. 190–1.
80 Bernard Capp, *England's Culture Wars: Puritan Reformation and Its Enemies in the Interregnum, 1649–1660* (Oxford: Oxford University Press, 2012), p. 253; Toby Allein, *Truths Manifest* (1658).
81 Firth, *The Last Years of the Protectorate*, II, p. 154.
82 Clarendon, *History*, VI, p. 21.
83 Civil War Petitions. Accessed 16 May 2024 (https://www.civilwarpetitions.ac.uk/petition/the-petition-of-william-griffith-of-llangian-carnarvonshire-1657).
84 *Memoirs of Anne, Lady Halkett and Ann, Lady Fanshawe*, ed. Loftis, p. 137.
85 *Monarchy Asserted*, p. 112.
86 *Correspondence of Henry Cromwell*, p. 269.
87 Burton, *Diary*, II, p. 140.
88 *Correspondence of Henry Cromwell*, p. 273.
89 Evelyn, *Diary*, III, p. 193.
90 Burton, *Diary*, II, 23 June 1657.
91 Hartlib Papers, HP26/13/1A–2B.

92 Burton, *Diary*, II, 23 June 1657.

93 Burton, *Diary*, II, 24 June 1657. A ceremonial sword inscribed with Cromwell's name, held in the collection of the Cromwell Museum, Huntingdon, was possibly used during the investiture.

94 *CJ*, VII, pp. 545–6, 577. On the ceremony see *Mercurius Politicus*, 25 June–2 July 1657; 'An Exact Relation of the manner of the Solemn Investiture, or happy inauguration of his Highnesse the Lord Protector at Westminster', in *A Further Narrative of the Passages of these Times in the Common-Wealth of England* (1658); 'Procession, with ceremony of the investiture and installation of his Highness Oliver Cromwell, as by the Parliament appointed to be performed in Westminster-Hall . . . Written by me Edmund Prestwich, of the City of London, an eye and ear-witness to all that passed on this glorious occasion. Now set forth by me John Prestwich', in John Prestwich, *Prestwich's Respublica, or, A Display of the Honors, Ceremonies & Ensigns of the Common-wealth under the Protectorship of Oliver Cromwell* (1787), pp. 3–21.

95 *A Further Narrative of the Passages of these Times*, p. 31.

96 *A Further Narrative of the Passages of these Times*, pp. 30–4.

97 Clarendon, *History*, VI, p. 32.

98 *CSP: Venice*, XXXI, 13 July 1657, p. 82.

99 Prestwich, 'Procession, with ceremony of the investiture and installation of his Highness Oliver Cromwell'. The sketch in *A Further Narrative of the Passages of these Times* does not show St Edward's Chair, or any chair of state.

100 Burton, *Diary*, I, 31 March 1657.

101 James Fraser, 'Triennial Travels. Part First Containing a Succinct and Breefe Narration of the Journay and Voyage of Master James Fraser through Scotland, England, and France . . . from June 1657 to June 1658', Aberdeen University Library, MS 2538; Joad Raymond, 'An Eye-witness to King Cromwell', *History Today* 47 (July 1997), pp. 35–41.

102 *Correspondence of Henry Cromwell*, p. 287.

103 See Jason Peacey, 'The Protector Humbled: Richard Cromwell and the Constitution', in Little, ed., *The Cromwellian Protectorate*, and Patrick Little, 'Monarchy to Protectorate: Re-drafting the Humble Petition and Advice, March–June 1657', *Historical Journal* 79 (2006), pp. 144–9.

104 Sherwood, *King in All But Name*, p. 112.

105 Christopher Durston, *The Family in the English Revolution* (Oxford: Blackwell, 1989), p. 84.

106 *Mercurius Politicus*, 12–19 November 1657.

107 *The Publick Intelligencer*, 16–23 November 1657.

108 Marvell, 'Two Songs at the Marriage of the Lord Fauconberg and the Lady Mary Cromwell'; Marvell, *The First Anniversary of the Government under His Highness the Lord Protector*, ll. 387–90. On the weddings see Sherwood, *King in All but Name*, pp. 108–19.

109 The 1657 miniature is now at Compton Verney, Warwickshire.
110 Bainbrigg Buckeridge, *An Essay towards an English School of Painters* (1706).
111 The 1653 miniature is in the duke of Buccleuch's collection.
112 *Warts and All: The Portrait Miniatures of Samuel Cooper*, exhibition catalogue, ed. Emma Rutherford and Bendor Grosvenor (London: Philip Mould, 2013), pp. 71–7; David Piper, 'The Contemporary Portraits of Oliver Cromwell', *Volume of the Walpole Society* 34 (1958), pp. 27–41. Another version of the 1653 miniature is Samuel Cooper, *Portrait of Oliver Cromwell*, 1656, NPG. Also see Edward Mascall's 1657 unadorned portrait of Cromwell in the Cromwell Museum, Huntingdon.
113 Samuel Cooper, *Drawing of Charles II*, Royal Collection Trust, 1660/2. Also see Samuel Cooper, *Unfinished Portrait of Charles II*, Chiddingstone Castle, early 1660s.

1658

1 Evelyn, *Diary*, III, pp. 206, 211.
2 'His Highnes the Lord Protectors speach to both Houses of Parliament', in *Letters, Writings, and Speeches*, III, pp. 461–6; *The Speech of the Right Honourable the Lord Fiennes, Commissioner of the Great Seal* (1658), p. 5.
3 *ODNB*, 'Sir Arthur Hesilrige'.
4 Burton, *Diary*, II, 25 January 1658.
5 *State Papers Thurloe*, VI, January 1657, 'Mr. Marchamont Needham to mr. Swyst, secretary to Lockhart'.
6 C. H. Firth, 'A Letter from Lord Saye and Sele to Lord Wharton, 29 December 1657', *English Historical Review* 10 (1895), pp. 106–7; Firth, *The Last Years of the Protectorate*, II, p. 13.
7 *Letters, Writings, and Speeches*, III, p. 493.
8 Burton, *Diary*, II, 22 and 30 January 1658.
9 Burton, *Diary*, II, 3 February 1658.
10 Burton, *Diary*, II, 2 February 1658. Major-General Haines called the old peers 'drunkards'.
11 Burton, *Diary*, II, 2 February 1658.
12 Burton, *Diary*, II, 30 January 1658.
13 Burton, *Diary*, II, 30 January 1658.
14 *A True Copy of A Petition Signed by very many Peaceable and Well-affected People, Inhabiting about the City of London* (1658).
15 *Letters, Writings, and Speeches*, III, 4 February 1658, p. 492.
16 *Letters, Writings, and Speeches*, III, pp. 496, 495, 497. Burton, *Diary*, II, 4 February 1658.
17 Coward, *The Cromwellian Protectorate*, p. 100.
18 Firth, *Last Years of the Protectorate*, II, p. 273.
19 Sherwood, *Court*, p. 131.
20 *Mercurius Politicus*, 2–9 September 1658.
21 *Letters, Writings, and Speeches*, II, Cromwell to his wife, Elizabeth, p. 439.

22 Marvell, 'A Poem upon the Death of His Late Highness the Lord Protector'; Edmund Waller, 'Upon the Storme and Death of his Late Highnesse Ensuing the same', in *Three Poems Upon the Death of His Late Highnesse Oliver Lord Protector of England, Scotland and Ireland, written by Mr Edm. Waller, Mr Jo. Dryden, Mr Sprat* (1659); George Wither, *Salt upon Salt: Made out of Certain Ingenious Verses upon the Late Storm and the Death of His Higness Ensuing* (1659).

23 John Aubrey, 'Omens', in *Three Prose Works*, ed. John Buchanan-Brown (Fontwell: Centaur Press, 1972), p. 27. Evelyn saw the whale and drew it: Evelyn, *Diary*, III, p. 214.

24 *Letters, Writings, and Speeches*, III, p. 520.

25 Waller, 'Upon the Storme and Death of his Late Highnesse'; Wither, *Salt upon Salt* mocks such interpretation of the storm. See also Thomas Fuller, 'An Elegie upon Oliver, late Lord Protectour, And congratulation of the most Illustrious Richard in his Succession', in *Musarum Cantabrigiensium* (1658), pp. 33–4, and, in the same, Samuel Fuller, 'Don't ask me why the Court in black is clad', pp. 37–9; Samuel Slater, *A Rhetoricall Rapture As Composed into a Funeral Oration At the Mournfull Moving of His Highness Stately Effigies from Somerset-House* (1658); J. H., *An Elegie upon the Much Lamented Death of his Highnesse Oliver The Late Lord Protector* (1658).

26 William Lilly, *Merlini Anglici ephemeris; Astrological predictions for the year, 1658* (1658).

27 Firth, *Last Years of the Protectorate*, II, p. 301; Henry Cromwell to Thurloe in *State Papers Thurloe*, VII, 8 September 1658.

28 *State Papers Thurloe*, VII, 30 August 1658.

29 *Mercurius Politicus*, 2–9 September 1658. John A. Butler, *A Biography of Richard Cromwell, 1626–1712, The Second Protector* (Lampeter: Edwin Mellen Press, 1994).

30 *A Collection of Several Passages Concerning his late Highnesse Oliver Cromwell, In the Time of his Sickness; Wherein Is Related many of his Expressions upon his Death-Bed* (1659), p. 6. On the succession see Jonathan Fitzgibbons, '"Not in Any Doubtfull Dispute"? Reassessing the Nomination of Richard Cromwell', *Historical Research* 83 (2010), pp. 281–300.

31 Hopper, *'Black Tom'*, p. 118.

32 *State Papers Thurloe*, VII, 7 September 1658.

33 *Mercurius Politicus*, 2–9 September 1658.

34 *CSP: Venice*, XXXI, 20 September 1658; *Mercurius Politicus*, 2–9 September 1658.

35 George Bate, *Elenchus Motuum Nuperorum in Anglia, or, A Short Historical Account of the Rise and Progress of the Late Troubles in England* (1685). Bate had been Charles I's physician while the court was at Oxford, and then became Cromwell's chief physician in 1653 after treating him in Scotland in 1651. He became Charles II's royal physician at the Restoration.

36 *A True Catalogue, Or, An Account of the Several Places and Most Eminent Persons in the Three Nations, and Elsewhere, Where, and by Whom Richard Cromwell was Proclaimed Lord Protector of the Commonwealth of England, Scotland and Ireland* (1659).

37 Amy Calladine, 'Public Ritual and the Proclamation of Richard Cromwell as Lord Protector in English Towns, September 1658', *Historical Journal* 61 (2018), pp. 53–76 (p. 66).
38 Fuller, 'Don't ask me why the Court in black is clad', in *Musarum Cantabrigiensium*.
39 J. H., *An Elegie upon the Much Lamented Death*.
40 Slater, *A Rhetoricall Rapture*; Thomas Sprat, 'To the Happie Memory', in *Three Poems Upon the Death*.
41 Clarendon, *History*, VI, pp. 98–9.
42 *A Dialogue Betwixt the Ghosts of Charls the I, Late King of England: and Oliver the Late Usurping Protector* (1659).
43 *The Autobiography of Richard Baxter*, abr. Lloyd Thomas and ed. Keeble, p. 89.
44 *Correspondence of Henry Cromwell*, p. 400.
45 *Letters, Writings, and Speeches*, II, pp. 289–90.
46 Jason Peacey, '"Fit for Public Services": The Upbringing of Richard Cromwell', in Little, ed., *Oliver Cromwell: New Perspectives*, p. 243; *ODNB*, 'Richard Cromwell'.
47 George Wharton, *A Second Narrative of the late Parliament (so called)* (1658).
48 *Correspondence of Henry Cromwell*, p. 221.
49 *Correspondence of Henry Cromwell*, p. 287.
50 Richard Baxter, *Holy Commonwealth*, ed. William Lamont (Cambridge: Cambridge University Press, 1994), described by Lamont as a 'love poem to Richard Cromwell'.
51 Burton, *Diary*, I, 12 December 1656.
52 Coward, *The Cromwellian Protectorate*; Ronald Hutton, *The Restoration: A Political and Religious History of England and Wales, 1658–1667* (Oxford: Oxford University Press, 1993). For an alternative view, see Peacey, '"Fit for Public Services"'. Coward does not argue, however, that Richard's lack of preparation was the cause of the Protectorate's downfall.
53 Hutchinson, *Memoirs*, p. 256.
54 Whitelocke, *Memorials*, IV, pp. 337, 338.
55 C. H. Firth, 'A Speech by Richard Cromwell, 14 October 1658', *English Historical Review* 23 (1908), pp. 734–6.
56 *State Papers Thurloe*, VII: 18 October 1658, pp. 447–9.
57 *Mercurius Politicus*, 14–21 October 1658. An engraving from *Some Farther Intelligence of the Affairs of England* (1658), p. 9, shows the crown resting on a cushion on a chair. See also *The True Manner of the most Magnificent Conveyance of His Highnesse Effigies* (1658).
58 Sherwood, *Court*, pp. 110–11.
59 *Mercurius Politicus*, 9–16 September 1658.
60 Ludlow, *Memoirs*, II, p. 48.
61 Sherwood, *Court*, p. 126.
62 E. A. B. Barnard, *A Seventeenth-Century Country Gentleman: Sir Francis Throckmorton, 1640–80* (Cambridge: Heffer & Sons, 1944), p. 53.

63 John Milton, *A Publick Plea* (1659).

64 John Milton, *Considerations touching the Likeliest Means to Remove Hirelings* (1659); also see Martin Dzelzainis, 'Milton and the Protectorate in 1658', in *Milton and Republicanism*, ed. David Armitage, Armand Himy and Quentin Skinner (Cambridge: Cambridge University Press, 1995), pp. 181–205.

65 John Milton, *Pro Populo Anglicano Defensio* (1658).

66 Jonathan Richardson cited in *The Early Lives of Milton*, ed. Helen Darbishire (London: Constable, 1932), pp. 289, 291.

67 *Letters of State written by Mr John Milton, To most of the Sovereign Princes and Republicks of Europe . . . To which is added, An Account of his Life* (1694), p. xxxvi. Also see William Poole, *Milton and the Making of Paradise Lost* (Cambridge, MA: Harvard University Press, 2017).

68 The *Works of John Milton*, ed. F. A. Patterson, 18 vols (New York: Columbia University Press, 1931–8), XII, p. 103.

69 John Milton, *Paradise Lost*, ed. Alastair Fowler (London and New York: Longman, 1971), I, ll. 25–6.

70 *Paradise Lost*, III, ll. 99, 124.

71 *Paradise Lost*, IX, ll. 351–2.

72 *Paradise Lost*, II, ll. 477–8.

73 *Paradise Lost*, II, ll. 256–7.

74 John Milton, *The Readie and Easie Way to Establish a Free Commonwealth* (1660), 2nd edition, p. 37.

1659

1 Thomas Rugg, *Mercurius politicus redivivus, or, A collection of the most materiall occurances and transactions in public affaires since Anno Domini 1659*, published as *The Diurnal of Thomas Rugg, 1659–1661*, ed. William L. Sachse (London: Royal Historical Society, 1961; repr. 2009), p. 1; William Prynne, *The Republicans and Others' Spurious Good Old Cause Briefly and Truly Anatomized* (1659).

2 *Clarke Papers*, III, 'An Account of the Fall of the Protector, Richard Cromwell, in a Letter from Nehemiah Boure', p. 211.

3 *ODNB*, 'Sir Henry Vane, the younger'; Vane, *A Healing Question* (1656).

4 Hutton, *Restoration*, p. 35.

5 Burton, *Diary*, III, 1 February 1659; *CJ*, VII, 1 February 1659, p. 596.

6 Burton, *Diary*, III, 9 February 1659.

7 Burton, *Diary*, III, 8 February 1659.

8 Burton, *Diary*, III, 14 February 1659.

9 Burton, *Diary*, III, 8 February 1659.

10 Burton, *Diary*, III, 9 February 1659.

11 Burton, *Diary*, III, 11 February 1659; 18 February 1659.

12 *Clarke Papers*, III, p. 179.

13 *England's Confusion* (1659); *The Humble Representation and Petition of the General Council of the Officers of the Armies of England, Scotland, and Ireland*, printed in *The Publick Intelligencer*, 11–18 April 1659.
14 Vane, *A Healing Question* (1656), postscript.
15 For a thorough account of the role of the army see Godfrey Davies, 'The Army and the Downfall of Richard Cromwell', *Huntington Library Bulletin* 7 (1935), pp. 131–67; Austin Woolrych, 'The Good Old Cause and the Fall of the Protectorate', *Cambridge Historical Journal* 13 (1957), pp. 133–61. Also see Jonathan Fitzgibbons, *Cromwell's House of Lords: Politics, Parliaments and Constitutional Revolution, 1642–1660* (Woodbridge: Boydell Press, 2018).
16 *Clarke Papers*, III, p. 190: 'Yesterday the House was resolved in a grand committee for considering upon the speedy payment of some moneyes to the army' (21 April).
17 *Clarke Papers*, III, p. 213, Appendix.
18 Ludlow, *Memoirs*, II, p. 69.
19 Burton, *Diary*, IV, 21 April 1659; see footnote no. 15.
20 *Correspondence of Henry Cromwell*, p. 516, 17 May 1659.
21 *Correspondence of Henry Cromwell*, p. 515.
22 *State Papers Thurloe*, VII, 20 October 1658 (Henry to Richard).
23 *Clarke Papers*, III, pp. 3–6, 'Letter from the Officers in England to General Monck and the Officers in Scotland', 3 May 1659.
24 Davies, 'The Army and the Downfall of Richard Cromwell'; Hutton, *Restoration*.
25 Ludlow, *Memoirs*, II, pp. 50, 74.
26 Milton, 'To Sir Henry Vane' (1662), *Complete Works of John Milton*, III: *The Shorter Poems*, p. 291.
27 *A Healing Question* (1660 [1659]). Brewster would later be tried and punished for publishing seditious books, in 1663. Brewster, in a note at the end of the 1659 edition, says that former copies had all sold and he had been asked by many people to produce more, since it proved very 'seasonable' in this new time.
28 Henry Vane, *A Needful Corrective or Ballance in Popular Government* (1659).
29 *Vanity of Vanities: Or Sir Harry Vane's Picture* (1660).
30 See, for example, R. Fitz-Brian, *The Good Old Cause Dress'd In It's Primitive Lustre* (1659).
31 *Clarke Papers*, III, p. 3.
32 *The Faithfull Scout*, 27 May–3 June 1659.
33 *To the Right Honourable The Lord Fleetwood, to be Communicated to the Officers of the Army, The Humble Representation of divers well-affected Persons of the City of Westminster and parts Adjacent* (1659), p. 2.
34 *Some Reasons Humbly Proposed to the Officers of the Army, for the Speedy Re-admission of the Long Parliament* (1659), p. 4.
35 Ludlow, *Memoirs*, II, p. 63.
36 Ludlow, *Memoirs*, II, p. 74.

37 Hutton, *Restoration*, p. 40.
38 *A Declaration of the Officers of the Army, Inviting the Members of the Long Parliament, Who Continued Sitting till the 20th of April, 1653. to return to the Exercise and Discharge of their Trust* (1659). *CJ*, VII, 7 May 1659; *Clarke Papers*, III, p. 8.
39 *The Faithfull Scout*, 6–13 May 1659.
40 *Correspondence of Henry Cromwell*, p. 515.
41 *CJ*, VII, 25 May 1659, pp. 664–5.
42 Butler, *Richard Cromwell*.
43 *ODNB*, 'Thomas Belasyse, first Earl Fauconberg'.
44 Mowl and Earnshaw, *Architecture without Kings*, p. 116. Wisbech Castle no longer exists, but there is a painting of it in nearby Peckover House, Cambridgeshire, National Trust Collections.
45 Evelyn, *Diary*, III, pp. 229, 228.
46 On 7 November, Evelyn's 'bold Apologie for the King' was published: *Diary*, III, p. 225.
47 *CJ*, VII, pp. 665–6, 662–3; Ludlow, *Memoirs*, II, p. 83.
48 *Diary of Sir Archibald Johnston of Wariston*, III: *1655–60*, ed. James D. Ogilvie (Edinburgh: T. & A. Constable for the Scottish History Society, 1940), p. 122: 1 July 1659.
49 *Diary of Wariston*, III, p. 106.
50 *Diary of Wariston*, III, p. 113.
51 *The Humble Petition and Addresse of the Officers of the Army, to the Parliament of the Common-wealth of England* (1659).
52 *Vanity of Vanities: Or Sir Harry Vane's Picture*.
53 Rachel Hammersley, *James Harrington: An Intellectual Biography* (Oxford: Oxford University Press, 2019), p. 247: 'Haselrig is so fixt to Mr Harrington's commonwealth, that he will lose all his ill purchased estate in defence of it.'
54 *Portrait of James Harrington*, after Peter Lely, *c.* 1658, NPG.
55 Aubrey, *Brief Lives*, pp. 124–7.
56 James Harrington, *The Commonwealth of Oceana and A System of Politics*, ed. J. G. A. Pocock (Cambridge: Cambridge University Press, 1992), p. 123. On democracy during the 1650s, and Harrington, see Peltonen, *The Political Thought of the English Free State*, Chapter 5.
57 James Harrington, *Pour Enclouer le Canon* (1659): 'though the people be twenty to one for monarchy'.
58 James Harrington, *A Discourse upon this Saying: The Spirit of the Nation is not yet to be trusted with Liberty; lest it introduce Monarchy, or invade the Liberty of Conscience* (1659).
59 James Harrington, *The Armies Dutie or, Faithful Advice to the Souldiers* (1659); Hammersley, *Harrington*, p. 234.
60 Henry Vane, *A Needful Corrective or Ballance in Popular Government Expressed in a Letter to James Harrington, Esquire, Upon Occasion of a Late*

Treatise of His, and Published as Seasonable in the Present Juncture of Affaires (1659). Harrington's treatise being responded to by Vane is his *Prerogative of Popular Government*.

61 See also, by followers of James Harrington: *A Proposition in Order to the Proposing of a Commonwealth or Democracie* (1659); *A Model of a Democraticall Government, Humbly Tendered to Consideration, by a Friend and Wel-wisher to this Common-Wealth* (1659).

62 *The Diurnal of Thomas Rugg*, p. 10.

63 *A Character of Coffee and Coffee-Houses by M. P.* (1661), p. 1.

64 Aubrey, *Brief Lives*, p. 125.

65 *Clarke Papers*, IV, p. 43; Marchamont Nedham, *Interest will not Lie. Or, a View of England's True Interest* (1659).

66 Pepys, *Diary*, 20 February 1660; 9 January 1660.

67 Aubrey, *Brief Lives*, p. 125.

68 *Clarke Papers*, IV, p. 31.

69 *Clarke Papers*, IV, p. x; *The Lord Lambert's Letter to the Speaker concerning the Victory over the Rebels under Sir George Booth* (1659); *A True Narrative of the Taking of Sir George Booth* (1659). Also see Hutton, *Restoration*, pp. 57–9.

70 *The Humble Petition and Proposals of the Officers under the Command of the Right Honourable Lord Lambert in the late Northern Expedition* (1659).

71 *CJ*, VII, 23 September 1659.

72 Hutchinson, *Memoirs*, p. 268; *The Humble Representation and Petition of the Officers of the Army to the Parliament of the Commonwealth of England. Presented to them Wednesday the 5th of October, 1659 by Maj. General Disbrowe [Desborough]* (1659).

73 Hutton, *Restoration*, p. 66.

74 *A True Narrative of the Proceedings in Parliament . . . from 22 September untill this Present* (1659).

75 George Monck to the Speaker, 18 June 1659, *Clarke Papers*, IV, pp. 22–3.

76 *State Papers Thurloe*, VII, 23 November 1658.

77 *ODNB*, 'George Monck, first duke of Albemarle'.

78 Hutton, *Restoration*. *Clarke Papers*, IV, on letters to Monck, and Monck's furious response; *The Parliamentary or Constitutional History of England*, XXII, pp. 4–7 on Monck's letters dated 20 October to Fleetwood and Lambert. Monck assured Fleetwood of his adherence to the good old cause and the establishment of a free commonwealth and warned Lambert that England would not 'endure any abitrary power' (p. 6). To Lenthall he wrote as a 'true Englishmen' and 'to stand to and assert the Liberty and Authority of Parliament' (p. 7) and that the 'asserting of a Commonwealth is the only Intent of my Heart' (p. 7).

79 *Diary of Wariston*.

80 *The Character of the Rump* (1660), p. 1; *The Resurrection of the Rump, or Rebellion and Tyrany Revived* (1659); *A New Year's Gift for the Rump* (1660).

81 *The Diurnal of Thomas Rugg*, p. 23.

82 *ODNB*, 'George Monck'.
83 *Clarke Papers*, III, p. 176.
84 Slingsby Bethel, *A True and Impartial Narrative of the most Material Debates and Passages in the Late Parliament* (1659), p. 3; *Fourty Four Queries to the Life of Queen Dick* (1659). See George Bate, *The History of the Rise and Progress of the Civil Wars in England* (1688); Mark Noble, *Memoirs of the Protectoral House of Cromwell*, 2 vols (1787), on closet Royalism; and Francois Guizot, *History of Richard Cromwell and the Restoration of Charles II*, 2 vols, trans. A. R. Scoble (London, 1856). *Fourty Four Queries to the Life of Queen Dick* (1659) – first appearance of 'Queen Dick'. 'Tumble-down Dick', cited in Hutton, *Restoration*, p. 41.
85 Kevin Sharpe, *Image Wars: Promoting Kings and Commonwealths in England, 1603–1660* (New Haven, CT, and London: Yale University Press, 2010), pp. 531–3.
86 Peacey, '"Fit for Public Services"', p. 257.

1660

1 *Mercurius Politicus*, 2–9 February 1660.
2 *A letter of General George Monck's, Dated at Leicester 23 Jan. and directed unto Mr Rolle to be communicated unto the rest of the Gentry of Devon: occasioned by a late Letter from the Gentry of Devon dated at Exceter 14 Jan. and sent by Mr Bampfeld to the Speaker to be communicated unto the Parliament* (1660), p. 5.
3 *The Letter-Book of John, Viscount Mordaunt*, ed. Mary Coate (London: Royal Historical Society, 1945), pp. 157, 174.
4 *The Diurnal of Thomas Rugg*, p. 29; S. R. Smith, 'Almost Revolutionaries: The London Apprentices during the Civil Wars', *Huntington Library Quarterly* 42 (1978–9), pp. 313–28.
5 *The Diurnal of Thomas Rugg*, p. 13.
6 *The Publick Intelligencer*, 28 November–5 December 1659; 5–12 December 1659. *The Remonstrance of the Apprentices in and about London* (1659).
7 *The Diurnal of Thomas Rugg*, pp. 34–5.
8 *The Publick Intelligencer*, 6–13 February 1660.
9 *The Parliamentary Intelligencer*, 6–13 February 1660.
10 'The Road to Restoration', in Hutton, *Restoration*; Woolrych, *Britain in Revolution*, pp. 761–3.
11 Pepys, *Diary*, I, p. 1, 1 January 1660.
12 Pepys, *Diary*, I, p. 22.
13 Pepys, *Diary*, I, p. 51.
14 Pepys, *Diary*, I, p. 62.
15 Whitelocke, *Diary*, p. 570.
16 Hutton, *Restoration*, p. 107.
17 Pepys, *Diary*, I, p. 74.
18 *The Diurnal of Thomas Rugg*, p. 77; *CJ*, VII, 25 April 1660.

19 Hutton, *Restoration*; Paul Seaward, *The Cavalier Parliament and the Reconstruction of the Old Regime, 1661–1667* (Cambridge: Cambridge University Press, 1989).
20 Pepys, *Diary*, I, p. 79.
21 Pepys, *Diary*, I, p. 121.
22 Evelyn, *Diary*, III, p. 243; *CJ*, VIII, 1 May 1660.
23 *The Diurnal of Thomas Rugg*, p. 80.
24 Pepys, *Diary*, p. 136.
25 Pepys, *Diary*, p. 155.
26 *The Diurnal of Thomas Rugg*, pp. 88–90.

Epilogue: Restoration

1 Alice Hunt, '"All Forms Accustomed": Ritual, Precedent and the Past at the Coronation of Charles II', in Lloyd Bowen and Mark Stoyle, ed., *Remembering the English Civil Wars* (Abingdon: Routledge, 2022), pp. 101–21; Pepys, *Diary*, II, p. 82.
2 On Fairfax's horse see Hunt, '"All Forms Accustomed"', p. 105. Accounts of the coronation include John Ogilby, *The Relation of His Majestie's Entertainment Passing through the City of London, to His Coronation: With a Description of the Triumphal Arches, and Solemnity* (1661); expanded illustrated edition: *The Entertainment of His Most Excellent Majestie Charles II, in his Passage through the Citie of London to his Coronation . . . to These Is Added a Brief Narrative of His Majestie's Solemn Coronation: with his Magnificent Proceeding, and Royal Feast in Westminster Hall* (1662); Edward Walker, *A Circumstantial Account of the Preparations for the Coronation of His Majesty King Charles the Second* (London, 1820); 'The Manner and Solemnity of the Coronation of King Charles II, 23 April 1661', BL, Add. MS 6338, fols 1–60.
3 Elias Ashmole, *A Brief Narrative of the Solemn Rites and Ceremonies Performed upon the Day of the Coronation of Our Sovereign Lord King Charles II Happily Celebrated upon the 23d. Day of April, being Saint Georges Day* (1661).
4 *A Sermon Preached at the Magnificent Coronation of the Most High and Mighty King Charles the IId King of Great Britain* (1661).
5 Marvell, 'An Horatian Ode', l. 82.
6 *From Republic to Restoration: Legacies and Departures*, ed. Janet Clare (Manchester: Manchester University Press, 2018).
7 Clare Jackson, *Devil-Land: England under Siege, 1588–1688* (London: Allen Lane, 2021), p. 504.
8 Montesquieu, *The Spirit of the Laws* (1748), trans. Anne M. Cohler (Cambridge: Cambridge University Press, 1989), p. 70.
9 Aubrey, *Brief Lives*, p. 125.
10 Hammersley, *Harrington*.
11 *The Readie and Easie Way to Establish a Free Commonwealth* (1660), p. 107; *Paradise Lost*, VII, ll. 32–3.

Bibliography

Select Newsbooks

The Faithfull Scout
The Kingdomes Weekly Intelligencer
The Man in the Moon
Mercurius Elencticus
Mercurius Politicus
Mercurius Pragmaticus
The Moderate
The Moderate Intelligencer
A Perfect Diurnall
The Publick Intelligencer
Severall Proceedings in Parliament
Severall Proceedings of State Affaires in England, Ireland and Scotland
The Weekly Intelligencer of the Commonwealth

Calendars and Papers

Acts and Ordinances of the Interregnum, 1642–1660, ed. C. H. Firth and R. S. Rait, 3 vols (London, 1911), British History Online

Calendar of the Clarendon State Papers Preserved in the Bodleian Library, 5 vols (Oxford, 1869–1970)

Calendar of the Proceedings of the Committee for Compounding, 1643–1660, ed. Mary Anne Everett Green (London, 1889–92)

Calendar of State Papers: Colonial, America and West Indies, Volume 1 1574–1660 (London, 1860), British History Online

Calendar of State Papers Domestic Series Preserved in the State Department [Commonwealth, 1649–60], 13 vols, ed. Mary Anne Everett Green (London, 1875–86)

Calendar of State Papers Relating to English Affairs in the Archives of Venice, vols XXVIII–XXXII, ed. Allen B. Hinds (London, 1929), British History Online

A Collection of the State Papers of John Thurloe, 7 vols, ed. Thomas Birch (London, 1742), British History Online

Journal of the House of Commons (London, 1802–3), British History Online

Journal of the House of Lords (London, 1767–1830), British History Online

Primary Works

For early sources the place of publication is London, unless otherwise noted.

Abbott, Wilbur Cortez, *Writings and Speeches of Oliver Cromwell*, 3 vols (Cambridge, MA: Harvard University Press, 1939)

Adams, John, *The Works of John Adams, Second President of the United States*, ed. Charles Francis Adams (1851; repr. Cambridge: Cambridge University Press, 2011), III, p. 394.

Allein, Toby, *Truths Manifest* (1658)

Another Victory in Lancashire (1651)

The Armies Vindication (1649)

Articles of Peace Made and Concluded with the Irish Rebels, and Papists by James Earle of Ormond, For and in behalfe of the late King (1649)

Ashmole, Elias, *A Brief Narrative of the Solemn Rites and Ceremonies Performed upon the Day of the Coronation of Our Sovereign Lord King Charles II Happily Celebrated upon the 23d. Day of April, being Saint Georges Day* (1661)

Aspinwall, William, *A Brief Description of the Fifth Monarchy or Kingdome, that shortly is to come into the World* (1653)

Aubrey, John, *An Essay towards the Description of the North Division of Wiltshire*, ed. T. Phillipps (1838)

———, *Brief Lives*, 2 vols, ed. Andrew Clark (Oxford: Clarendon Press, 1898)

———, *Brief Lives, Edited from the Original Manuscripts*, ed. Oliver Lawson Dick (London: Secker and Warburg, 1949)

———, *Three Prose Works*, ed. John Buchanan-Brown (Fontwell: Centaur Press, 1972)

Austen, Ralph, *A Treatise of Fruit-trees* (1653)

Bagshawe, William, *Living Water, or Waters for a Thirsty Soul Drawn out in Severall Sermons upon Revelation* (1653)

Barbon, Praisegod, *Good Things to Come, or, a Setting Forth some of the Great Things that will contemporize and take place when our Lord Christ shall come again* (1675)

Bate, George, *The Lives, Actions, and Execution of the Prime Actors, and Principall Contrivers of that Horrid Murder of our Late Pious and Sacred Soveraigne King Charles the First* (1661)

———, *Elenchus Motuum Nuperorum in Anglia: or, A Short Historical Account of the Rise and Progress of the Late Troubles in England* (1685)

———, *The History of the Rise and Progress of the Civil Wars in England* (1688)

Baxter, Richard, *A Holy Commonwealth* (1659)

———, *The Autobiography of Richard Baxter*, abr. J. J. Lloyd Thomas and ed. N. H. Keeble (London: Everyman, 1974)

———, *A Holy Commonwealth*, ed. William Lamont (Cambridge: Cambridge University Press, 1994)

ben Israel, Menasseh, *The Hope of Israel* (1650)

———, *The Hope of Israel . . . Whereunto are added, In this Second Edition, Some Discourses upon the point of the Conversion of the Jewes by Moses Wall* (1652)

———, *Vindiciae Judaeorum* (1656)

Bernard, Nicholas, *The Fare-well Sermons of Comfort and Concord preached at Drogheda in Ireland* (1651)

Bethel, Slingsby, *A True and Impartial Narrative of the most Material Debates and Passages in the Late Parliament* (1659)

Birkenhead, John, *Two Centuries of Pauls Church-yard* (1653)

Blount, Thomas, *Boscobel: or, The History of His Sacred Majesties Most Miraculous Preservation After the Battle of Worcester, 3 Sept. 1651* (1660)

Boate, Gerard, *Irelands Naturall History being a True and Ample Description of its Situation* (1657; first published 1652)

Boyle, Robert, *New Experiments Physico-Mechanicall, Touching The Spring of the Air, and its Effects, (Made, for the most part, in a New Pneumatical Engine) Written by way of Letter To the Right Honorable Charles Lord Vicount of Dungarvan, Eldest Son to the Earl of Cork* (1660)

———, *The Works of the Honourable Robert Boyle*, 6 vols, ed. T. Birch (1772)

———, *The Early Essays and Ethics of Robert Boyle*, ed. John T. Harwood (Carbondale, IL: Southern Illinois University Press, 1991)

———, *Robert Boyle by Himself and His Friends*, ed. Michael Hunter (London: Routledge, 2020)

———, *The Correspondence of Robert Boyle, 1627–1691*, 6 vols, ed. Michael Hunter, Antonio Clericuzio and Lawrence M. Principe (London: Routledge, 2022)

Boyle, Roger, *Parthenissa, A Romance in Four Parts* (1655)

———, *Parthenissa, That most Fam'd Romance. The Six Volumes Compleat* (1676)

———, *A Collection of the State Letters of the Rt Hon. Roger Boyle, the first Earl of Orrery*, ed. Thomas Morrice (Dublin, 1743)

Bunyan, John, *Grace Abounding to the Chief of Sinners* (1666)

———, *The Pilgrim's Progress*, ed. Cynthia Wall (New York and London: W. W. Norton, 2009)

Burnet, Gilbert, *A Sermon Preached at the Funeral of the Honourable Robert Boyle; at St Martins in the Fields, January 7, 1691/2. By the Right Reverend Father in God, Gilbert Lord Bishop of Sarum* (1692)

Burton, Thomas, *Diary of Thomas Burton Esq*, 4 vols, ed. John Towill Rutt (London, 1828), British History Online

By the Protector, A Proclamation Giving Encouragement to such as shall transplant themselves to Jamaica (1655)

Carlyle, Thomas, *The Letters and Speeches of Oliver Cromwell with Elucidations*, 3 vols, ed. S. C. Lomas (1904)

Carpenter, Andrew, ed., *Verse in English from Tudor and Stuart Ireland* (Cork: Cork University Press, 2003)

Cartwright, Johanna, *The Petition of the Jews for the Repealing of the Act of Parliament for their Banishment out of England* (1649)

Cary, Mary, *The Resurrection of the Witnesses, and Englands fall from (the mystical Babylon) Rome* (1653)

The Causes of a Publick Fast, and Humiliation, to be kept with all convenient diligence: by all the Members of this Kirk and Kingdom (Aberdeen, 1650)

Cavendish, Margaret, *Poems and Fancies* (1653)

———, *The Philosophical and Physical Opinions* (1655)

———, *The World's Olio* (1655)

———, *A True Relation of My Birth, Breeding and Life*, appended to *Natures Pictures drawn by Fancies Pencil to the Life* (1656)

———, *The Description of a New World, Called The Blazing World* (1666)

———, *The Life of the Thrice Noble, High and Puissant Prince William Cavendishe, Duke, Marquess and Earl of Newcastle* (1667)

Channel, Elinor, *A Message from God [by a dumb woman] to his Highness the Lord Protector… (recorded by Arise Evans)* (1654)

The Character of the Rump (1660)

Charles Rex. His Majestyes Declaration, to all his Loving Subjects of his Kingdom of England and Dominion of Wales (Aberdeen, 1651)

Child, Josiah, *Brief Observations Concerning Trade and Interest of Money* (1668)

The Clarke Papers: Selections from the Papers of William Clarke, Secretary to the Council of the Army, 1647–1649, and to General Monck and the Commanders of the Army in Scotland, 1651–1660, 4 vols, ed. C. H. Firth (London: Camden Society, 1901)

A Collection of Several Passages Concerning his late Highnesse Oliver Cromwell, In the Time of his Sickness; Wherein Is Related many of his Expressions upon his Death-Bed (1659)

A Complete Collection of State Trials and Proceedings for High Treason and Other Crimes and Misdemeanors, 21 vols, ed. T. B. Howell et al. (1816)

The Constitutional Documents of the Puritan Revolution, 1625–1660, ed. S. R. Gardiner (Oxford: Clarendon Press, 1906)

The Correspondence of Henry Cromwell 1655–1659: From the British Library Lansdowne Manuscripts, ed. Peter Gaunt (Cambridge: Cambridge University Press for the Royal Historical Society, 2007)

The Court and Kitchin of Elizabeth Commonly called Joan Cromwel, the Wife of the late Usurper (1664)

Cowley, Abraham, *Davideis: A Sacred Poem of the Troubles of David* (1656)

———, *The Third Part of the Works of Mr Abraham Cowley being his Six books of Plants* (1689)

———, *Abraham Cowley: The Essays and Other Prose Writings*, ed. Alfred B. Gough (Oxford: Oxford University Press, 1915)

Cranford, James, *The Teares of Ireland wherein is lively presented as in a map a list of the unheard off [sic] cruelties and perfidious treacheries of blood-thirsty Jesuits and the popish faction* (1642)

Cromwell, Oliver, *The Letters, Writings, and Speeches of Oliver Cromwell*, 3 vols, gen. ed. John Morrill (Oxford: Oxford University Press, 2022)

Culmer, Richard, *The Ministers Hue and Cry* (1651)

———, *A Parish Looking-Glasse for Persecutors of Ministers* (1657)

Davenant, William, *A Proposition for Advancement of Moralitie, by a New Way of Entertainment of the People* (1654)

———, *The First Days Entertainment at Rutland-House* (1656)

———, *The Siege of Rhodes* (1656)

Deacon, John, *The Grand Impostor Examined: Or, The Life, Tryal, and Examination of James Nayler, The Seduced and Seducing Quaker with The Manner of his Riding into Bristol* (1656)

———, *An Exact History of the Life of James Naylor with his Parents, Birth, Education, Profession, Actions, & Blaspheemies* (1657)

A Declaration by the Lord Lieutenant of Ireland Concerning his Resolutions for the Peace and Safety of Ireland (Dublin, 1649)

A Declaration of a Day of Solemn Fasting and Humiliation (1655)

A Declaration of his Highnesse, by the Advice of his Council, Shewing the Reasons of their Proceedings for Securing the Peace of the Commonwealth, Upon Occasion of the Late Insurrection and Rebellion (1655)

A Declaration of the Army of England upon their March into Scotland (1650)

The Declaration of the Lord Generall, and his Councell of Officers, shewing the grounds and reasons for the dissolution of the Parliament, April 20. 1653 (1653)

A Declaration of the Officers of the Army, Inviting the Members of the Long Parliament, Who Continued Sitting till the 20th of April, 1653. to return to the Exercise and Discharge of their Trust (1659)

A Declaration of the Parliament of England, Expressing the Grounds of their Late Proceedings, and of Settling the Present Government in the Way of a Free State (1649)

A Declaration of the Parliament, of the Commonwealth of England, Relating to the Affairs and Proceedings between this Commonwealth and the States General of the United Provinces (1652)

A Deep Sigh Breath'd Through the Lodgings at White-hall, Deploring the Absence of the Court, and the Miseries of the Pallace (1642)

A Dialogue Betwixt the Ghosts of Charls the I, Late King of England: and Oliver the late Usurping Protector (1659)

Denham, John, *Coopers Hill, a poem* (1643)

The Diurnal of Thomas Rugg, 1659–1661, ed. William L. Sachse (London: Royal Historical Society, 1961; repr. 2009)

Doyley, Edward, *A Narrative of the Great Success God hath been Pleased to Give His Highness Forces in Jamaica against the King of Spains forces* (1658)

Dury, John, *A Case of Conscience, Whether it Be Lawful to Admit Jews into a Christian Commonwealth. Written to Samuel Hartlib* (1656)

Eikón Basiliké the Pourtraicture of his Sacred Majestie in his Solitudes and Sufferings (1648 [1649])

England's Confusion (1659)

Englands Slavery, or Barbados Merchandize Represented In a Petition to the High and Honourable Court of Parliament, by Marcellus Rivers and Oxenbridge Foyle (1659)

Evans, Arise, *Light for the Jews, or, The Means to Convert them in Answer to a Book of theirs called The Hope of Israel* (1656)
Evelyn, John, *An Essay on the First Book of T. Lucretius Carus De Rerum Natura* (1656)
———, *A Character of England as it was lately presented in a letter to a noble man of France* (1659)
———, *Silva, or a Discourse of Forest-Trees* (1664)
———, *The Diary of John Evelyn*, 6 vols, ed. E. S. de Beer (Oxford: Oxford University Press, 1955)
———, *The Letterbooks of John Evelyn*, ed. Douglas D. C. Chambers and David Galbraith (Toronto: Toronto University Press, 2014)
Feake, Christopher, *A Beam of Light, shining in the midst of much darkness and confusion* (1659)
Fell, Margaret, *The Call of the Jewes out of Babylon* (1656)
Felltham, Owen, *A Brief Character of the Low Countries* (1652)
Fire from Heaven (1649)
Fisher, Payne, *Veni, Vidi, Vici. The Triumphs of the most Excellent & Illustrious, Oliver Cromwell* (1652)
Fisher, Samuel, *Christianismus Redivivus* (1655)
Fitz-Brian, R., *The Good Old Cause Dress'd In It's Primitive Lustre* (1659)
The Forme and Order of the Coronation of Charles the Second, King of Scotland, England, France, and Ireland (Aberdeen, 1651)
Fourty Four Queries to the Life of Queen Dick (1659)
Fox, George, *The Journal of George Fox: A Revised Edition*, ed. John L. Nickalls (Cambridge: Cambridge University Press, 2010; first published 1952)
Fox (formerly Fell), Margaret, *A Brief Collection of Remarkable Passages and Occurrences Relating to the Birth, Education, Life, Conversion, Travels, Services, and Deep Sufferings of that Ancient, Eminent, and Faithful Servant of the Lord, Margaret Fell* (1712)
Fox, George and James Nayler, *Saul's Errand to Damascus* (1653)
Fuller, Thomas, *The Church History of Britain* (1655)
A Further Narrative of the Passages of these Times in the Common-Wealth of England (1658)
Gage, Thomas, *The English-American his Travail by Sea and Land, or, A New Survey of the West Indias* (1648)
Gell, Robert, *Noah's Flood Returning* (1655)
The Government of the Common-Wealth of England, Scotland, and Ireland, And the Dominions thereto belonging; As it was publickly declared at Westminster, the 16. day of December 1653 (1654)
Graham, James, *Memoirs of the Most Renowned James Graham, Marquis of Montrose. Translated from the Latin of the Rev. Dr George Wishart* (Edinburgh, 1819)
A Great and Wonderful Victory obtained by the English Forces, under the Command of General Pen and Gen. Venables (1655)
A Great Victory by the Blessing of God, obtained by the Parliaments Forces, against the Scots Forces (1651)

Greengrass, M., M. Leslie and M. Hannon, *The Hartlib Papers*, published by the Digital Humanities Institute, University of Sheffield, 2013. Last accessed 16 May 2024 (http://www.dhi.ac.uk/hartlib).

Halkett, Anne and Ann Fanshawe, *The Memoirs of Anne, Lady Halkett and Ann, Lady Fanshawe*, ed. John Loftis (Oxford: Clarendon Press, 1979)

Harrington, James, *The Prerogative of Popular Government* (1657)

———, *The Armies Dutie or, Faithful Advice to the Souldiers* (1659)

———, *A Discourse upon this Saying: The Spirit of the Nation is not yet to be trusted with Liberty; lest it introduce Monarchy, or invade the Liberty of Conscience* (1659)

———, *Pour Enclouer le Canon* (1659)

———, *The Commonwealth of Oceana and A System of Politics*, ed. J. G. A. Pocock (Cambridge: Cambridge University Press, 1992)

Hartlib, Samuel, *Englands Thankfulnesse* (1642)

———, *A Rare and New Discovery of a Speedy Way, and Easie Means . . . For the Feeding of Silk-Worms* (1652; repr. 1655)

Heath, James, *A Brief Chronicle of the Late Intestine War in the Three Kingdoms of England, Scotland, and Ireland* (1661)

———, *Flagellum* (1663)

Henry, Philip, *Diaries and Letters of Philip Henry*, ed. Matthew Henry Lee (London, 1882)

Herbert, Percy, *The Princesse Cloria: or, the Royal Romance* (1665)

Herrick, Robert, *Hesperides, or The Works both Humane & Divine* (1648)

Heylyn, Peter, *Aerius Redivivus: or The History of the Presbyterians* (1672)

Higgingson, Francis, *Brief Relation of the Irreligion of the Northern Quakers* (1653)

Hobbes, Thomas, *The Correspondence of Thomas Hobbes*, ed. Noel Malcolm (Oxford: Clarendon Press, 1994)

———, *Leviathan*, ed. J. C. A. Gaskin (Oxford: Oxford University Press, 1996)

———, *The Clarendon Edition of the Works of Thomas Hobbes*, X: *Behemoth, or the Long Parliament*, ed. Paul Seaward (Oxford: Oxford University Press, 2009)

———, *Leviathan*, ed. Noel Malcolm (Oxford: Clarendon Press, 2012)

Hooke, Robert, *Micrographia* (1665)

Hubberthorne, Richard, *The Cause of Stumbling Removed* (1657)

The Humble Petition and Addresse of the Officers of the Army, to the Parliament of the Common-wealth of England (1659)

The Humble Petition and Proposals of the Officers under the Command of the Right Honourable Lord Lambert in the late Northern Expedition (1659)

The Humble Petition of divers wel-affected Women inhabiting the Cities of London, Westminster, the Borough of Southwark, Hamblets, and Places adjacent (1649)

The Humble Representation and Petition of the Officers of the Army to the Parliament of the Commonwealth of England (1659)

Hutchinson, Lucy, *Memoirs of the Life of Colonel Hutchinson*, ed. N. H. Keeble (London: Everyman, 1995)

Huygens, Lodewijck, *The English Journal 1651–1652*, ed. and trans. A. G. H.

Bachrach and R. G. Collmer (Leiden: Brill/Leiden University Press, 1982)

Hyde, Edward, *A Brief View and Survey of the Dangerous and Pernicious Errors to Church and State in Mr Hobbes's Book Entitled Leviathan* (1676)

———, *The History of the Rebellion and Civil Wars in England Begun in the Year 1641*, 6 vols, ed. W. Dunn Macray (Oxford: Clarendon Press, 1888)

I. D., *Concordia rar Sonorum, Or a Poem Upon the Late Fight at Sea* (1653)

I. S., *A Brief and Perfect Journal of the Late Preceedings and Successe of the English Army in the West-Indies* (1655)

J. H., *An Elegie upon the Much Lamented Death of his Highnesse Oliver the Late Lord Protector* (1658)

Jenner, Thomas, *Londons Blame if not its Shame: Manifested by the Great Neglect of the Fishery* (1651)

Johnston, Archibald, *Diary of Sir Archibald Johnston of Wariston, III: 1655–60*, ed. James D. Ogilvie (Edinburgh: T. & A. Constable for the Scottish History Society, 1940)

Josselin, Ralph, *The Diary of Ralph Josselin, 1616–1683*, ed. Alan Macfarlane (London: British Academy, 1976)

King Charls his Speech made upon the Scaffold at Whitehall-gate (1649)

King Charls his Tryal: or A Perfect Narrative of the Whole Proceedings of the High Court of Justice in the Tryal of the King in Westminster Hall (1649)

Laing, David, ed., *Correspondence of Sir Robert Kerr, First Earl of Ancram and his Son William, Third Earl of Lothian*, 2 vols (Edinburgh, 1875)

The Last Great and Bloudy Fight in Ireland on Wednesday last, being the 29. of August, 1649. between the Marq. of Ormonds forces, and the Lord Governour Cromwels (1649)

A Letter from Holland relating the Designes of the Scotch Presbyter (Rotterdam, 1650)

A Letter of General George Monck's, Dated at Leicester 23 Jan. and directed unto Mr Rolle to be communicated unto the rest of the Gentry of Devon: occasioned by a late Letter from the Gentry of Devon dated at Exceter 14 Jan. and sent by Mr Bampfield to the Speaker to be communicated unto the Parliament (1660)

Letter to His Highness the Lord Protector from Captain Unton Crook signifying the totall Defeat of the Cavaliers in the West under the command of Sir Joseph Wagstaffe (1655)

Letters and Papers Illustrating the Relations between Charles II and Scotland in 1650, ed. S. R. Gardiner (Edinburgh, 1894)

Letters and Papers Relating to the First Dutch War, 5 vols, ed. S. R. Gardiner and C. T. Atkinson (Navy Record Society, 1898–1912)

Letters from Dorothy Osborne to William Temple, 1652–54, ed. Edward Abbott Parry (Cambridge: Cambridge University Press, 2013)

Letters from Ireland Relating the several great Successes it hath pleased God to give unto the Parliaments Forces there (1649)

Letters from Roundhead Officers written from Scotland, ed. J. Y. Akerman (1856)

The Letters, Speeches and Declarations of King Charles II, ed. Arthur Bryant (London: Cassell, 1935)

Lilburne, John, *Englands New Chains Discovered* (1649)

———, *Foundations of Freedom; or An Agreement of the People: proposed as a rule for future government in the establishment of a firm and lasting peace* (1648)

———, *The Hunting of the Foxes from Newmarket and Triploe Heaths to Whitehall* (1649)

———, *An Impeachment of High Treason* (1649)

———, *A Preparative to an Hue and Cry* (1649)

———, *The Second Part of Englands New Chaines Discovered* (1649)

———, *An Hue and Cry after the Fundamental Lawes and Liberties of England* (1653)

Lilburne, John, Thomas Prince and Richard Overton, *The Picture of the Councel of State, held forth to the Free People of England* (1649)

Lilburne, John, William Walwyn, Thomas Prince and Richard Overton, *The Agreement of the Free People of England, tendered as a Peace-Offering to this Distressed Nation* (1649)

Lilly, William, *Merlini Anglici Ephemeris: Astrological Predictions for 1652* (1651)

———, *Annus Tenebrosus, or The Dark Year or Astrologicall Judgements upon two lunar eclipses, and one admirable eclips of the sun, all visible in England* (1652)

———, *Merlini Anglici Ephemeris: Astrological Predictions for the Year, 1658 (1658)*

———, *Mr William Lilly's History of his Life and Times: from the year 1602, to 1681* (1715, 2nd edn)

The Lord General Cromwel's Speech Delivered in the Council-Chamber, upon the 4 of July, 1653 (1654)

The Lord Lambert's Letter to the Speaker concerning the Victory over the Rebels under Sir George Booth (1659)

The Loyall Subjects Jubilee or Cromwels Farewell to England, being a poem on his advancing to Ireland (1649)

Ludlow, Edmund, *The Memoirs of Edmund Ludlow, Lieutenant-General of the Horse in the Army of the Commonwealth of England, 1625–1672*, 2 vols, ed. C. H. Firth (Oxford: Clarendon Press, 1894)

M. P., *A Character of Coffee and Coffee-Houses* (1661)

The Marquesse of Ormonds Proclamation Concerning the Peace concluded with the Irish Rebells (1649)

Marvell, Andrew, *The First Anniversary of the Government under H. H. the Lord Protector* (1655)

———, *The Poems of Andrew Marvell*, ed. Nigel Smith (Harlow: Pearson, 2003; rev. edn, 2007)

Matthews, W., ed., *Charles II's Escape from Worcester: A Collection of Narratives Assembled by Samuel Pepys* (London: G. Bell, 1967)

McRae, Andrew and John West, ed., *Literature of the Stuart Successions: An Anthology* (Manchester: Manchester University Press, 2017)

Melancholicus, Mercurius, *Craftie Cromwell, or Oliver Ordering our New State. A Tragi-Comedie* (1648)

———, *The Second Part of Crafty Cromwell or Oliver in his Glory as King. A Trage Commedie* (1648)

Memorials of the Great Civil War in England from 1646–52, 2 vols, ed. Henry Cary (London, 1842)

Menasseh ben Israel's Mission to Oliver Cromwell: Being a Reprint of the Pamphlets Published by Menasseh ben Israel to Promote the Re-admission of the Jews to England, 1649–1656, ed. Lucien Wolf (London: Macmillan, 1901)

Milton, John, *Of Education. To Master Samuel Hartlib* (1644)

———, *The Tenure of Kings and Magistrates* (1649)

———, *Eikonoklastes, in Answer To a Book Intitl'd Eikon Basilike, the Portrature of his Sacred Majesty in his Solitudes and Sufferings* (1650)

———, *Pro Populo Anglicano Defensio* (1658)

———, *Considerations touching the Likeliest Means to Remove Hirelings* (1659)

———, *A Publick Plea* (1659)

———, *The Readie and Easie Way to Establish a Free Commonwealth* (1660, 2nd edn)

———, *Letters of State written by Mr John Milton, To most of the Sovereign Princes and Republicks of Europe . . . To which is added, An Account of his Life* (1694)

———, *The Works of John Milton*, ed. F. A. Patterson, 18 vols (New York: Columbia University Press, 1931–8)

———, *Complete Prose Works of John Milton*, 8 vols, ed. Don M. Wolfe et al. (New Haven, CT: Yale University Press, 1953–82)

———, *Paradise Lost*, ed. Alastair Fowler (London and New York: Longman, 1971)

———, *The Complete Works of John Milton*, III: *The Shorter Poems*, ed. Barbara Kiefer Lewalski and Estelle Haan (Oxford: Oxford University Press, 2012)

———, *The Complete Works of John Milton*, VI: *Vernacular Regicide and Republican Writings*, ed. N. H. Keeble and Nicholas McDowell (Oxford: Oxford University Press, 2013)

A Model of a Democraticall Government, Humbly Tendered to Consideration, by a Friend and Wel-wisher to this Common-Wealth (1659)

Monarchy Asserted, to be the Best, most Ancient and Legall Form of Government, in a Conference had at Whitehall, with Oliver late Lord Protector and a Committee of Parliament (1660)

Monck, George, *A Letter of the Surrender of Sterling-Castle* (1651)

Moore, John, *Protection Proclaimed* (1655)

Mordant, Viscount, *The Letter-Book of John, Viscount Mordaunt*, ed. Mary Coate (London: Royal Historical Society, 1945)

Morley, George, *A Sermon Preached at the Magnificent Coronation of the Most High and Mighty King Charles the IId King of Great Britain* (1661)

Mr Hobbes Considered In his Loyalty, Religion, Reputation, and Manners. By way of Letter to Dr Wallis (1662)

Musarum Cantabrigiensium (1658)

Napier, Mark, *Memoirs of the Marquis of Montrose* (Edinburgh, 1856)

The Narrative of General Venables, with an Appendix of Papers Relating to the Expedition to the West Indies and the Conquest of Jamaica, 1654–1655, ed. C. H. Firth (London: Longmans, Green & Co., 1900)

A Narrative of the late Parliament, (so called) Their Election and Appearing (1658)

A Narrative of the Late Proceeds at White-hall, Concerning the Jews (1656)

Naylier, John, *The Foxes Craft Discovered* (1649)

Nedham, Marchamont, *The Case of the Common-wealth of England Stated* (1650)

———, *Interest will not Lie. Or, a View of England's True Interest* (1659)

A New Year's Gift for the Rump (1660)

Nicoll, John, *A Diary of Public Transactions and other Occurrences, chiefly in Scotland, from January 1650 to June 1667*, ed. D. Laing (Edinburgh, 1836)

No Age like unto this Age: or, Times Unparallel'd Oppression, Oppression, Oppression Being the Cries in Kent against the Great Oppression of Tythes (1653)

Noble, Mark, *Memoirs of the Protectoral House of Cromwell*, 2 vols (1787)

———, *The Lives of the English Regicides*, 2 vols (1798)

Ogilby, John, *The Relation of His Majestie's Entertainment Passing through the City of London, to His Coronation: With a Description of the Triumphal Arches, and Solemnity* (1661)

———, *The Entertainment of His Most Excellent Majestie Charles II, in his Passage through the Citie of London to his Coronation . . . to These Is Added a Brief Narrative of His Majestie's Solemn Coronation: with his Magnificent Proceeding, and Royal Feast in Westminster Hall* (1662)

Original Memoirs, Written during the Great Civil War: Being the Life of Sir Henry Slingsby, and Memoirs of Capt. Hodgson, ed. Walter Scott (Edinburgh and London, 1806)

Ormondes Breakfast or A True Relation of the Salley and Skirmish performed by Collonell Michaell Jones and his Party, against the Marques of Ormonde (Dublin, 1649)

Osborne, Dorothy, *Letters to Sir William Temple*, ed. Kenneth Parker (London: Penguin, 1987)

Owen, John, *The Shaking and Translating of Heaven and Earth* (1649)

———, *Complete Collection of the Sermons of the Reverend and Learned John Owen, D. D.* (1721)

Pagitt, Ephraim, *Heresiography, or, a Description of the Heretickes and Sectaries Sprang up in these Latter Times* (1654)

The Parliament under the Power of the Sword (1648)

The Parliamentary or Constitutional History of England, 24 vols (1751–61)

Penn, Granville, *Memorials of the Professional Life and Times of Sir William Penn*, 2 vols (London, 1833)

Penn, William, *William Penn: Political Writings*, ed. Andrew Murphy (Cambridge: Cambridge University Press, 2021)

Penruddock, John, *The Triall of the Hon. Col. John Penruddock, of Compton, in Wiltshire, and his Speech* (1655)

Pepys, Samuel, *The Diary of Samuel Pepys*, 9 vols, ed. Robert Latham and William Matthews (London: HarperCollins, 1971)

A Perfect and Particular Relation of the Severall Marches and Proceedings of the Armie in Ireland, from the taking of Drogheda, to this Present (1649)

The Perfect Politician Or, A Full View of the Life and Action (Military and Civil) of O. Cromwel (1660)

Peter, Hugh, *A Word for the Army and Two Words for the Kingdom* (1646)

Petty, William, *The Advice of W. P. to Mr Samuel Hartlib for the Advancement of some Particular Parts of Learning* (1648)

———, *The History of the Survey of Ireland: Commonly Called the Down Survey 1655–6*, ed. T. A. Larcom (1851)

Philipps, Fabian, *The Royall Martyr* (1660)

The Picture of a New Coutier drawn in a Conference between Mr. Timeserver and Mr. Plain-heart (1656)

The Picture of the Council of State Held forth to the Free people of England by Lieut. Col. John Lilburn, Mr Thomas Prince, and Mr Richard Overton, now Prisoners in the Tower of London (1649)

Poole, Elizabeth, *A Vision: Wherein is Manifested the Disease and Cure of the Kingdome* (1649)

Potter, William, *The Key of Wealth, Or a New Way of Improving Trade* (1650)

Prestwich, John, *Prestwich's Respublica, or, A Display of the Honors, Ceremonies & Ensigns of the Common-wealth under the Protectorship of Oliver Cromwell* (1787)

Price, Laurence, *Here's Jack in a Box* (1656)

A Proclamation of his Highness, Prohibiting the Disturbing of Ministers and other Christians in their Assemblies and Meetings (1655)

A Proposition in Order to the Proposing of a Commonwealth or Democracie (1659)

Prynne, William, *A True and Ful Relation of the Armies forcible seising of divers Eminent Members of the Commons House* (1648)

———, *A True and ful Relation of the Officers and Armies forcible seising of divers Eminent Members Of the Commons House* (1648)

———, *A Brief Memento to the Present Unparliamentary Juncto* (1649)

———, *A Short Demurrer to the Jewes* (1656)

———, *The Republicans and Others' Spurious Good Old Cause Briefly and Truly Anatomized* (1659)

The Rebels Looking-glasse: or, The Traytors Doome (1649)

The Remonstrance of the Apprentices in and about London (1659)

A Remonstrance of his Excellency Thomas Lord Fairfax, Lord Generall of the Parliaments Forces. And of the Generall Councell of Officers Held at St Albans the 16. of November, 1648 (1648)

The Resurrection of the Rump, or Rebellion and Tyrany Revived (1659)

Robinson, Henry, *Brief Considerations, Concerning the Advancement of Trade and Navigation* (1649)

———, *The Office of Addresses and Encounters* (1650)

———, *Certain Proposalls in Order to the Peoples Freedome and Accommodation* (1652)

[Rooth, Richard], 'Richard Rooth's Sea Journal of the Western Design, 1654–55', ed. John F. Battick, *Jamaica Journal* 5.4 (1971)

The Royal Miracle: A Collection of Rare Tracts, Broadsides, Letters, Prints and Ballads Concerning the Wanderings of Charles II after the Battle of Worcester, ed. A. M. Broadley (London: Stanley Paul & Co., 1912)
Rushworth, John, *Historical Collections of Private Passages of State*, 8 vols (1721)
Russell, Thomas, ed., *The Works of John Owen* (London, 1826)
Sadler, John, *The Rights of Kingdom* (1649)
Samuel Hartlib his Legacie: Or An Enlargement of the Discourse of Husbandry used in Brabant and Flaunders (1651)
Saumaise, Claude, *Defensio Regia, Pro Carolo I* (Leiden, 1649)
Selden, John, *Mare Clausum and Of the Dominion of the Sea, or, Ownership of the Sea*, trans. Marchamont Nedham (1652)
Severall Proposals for the Generall Good of the Common-Wealth (1651)
Sexby, Edward, *Killing Noe Murder* (1657)
Shawe, John, *Britannia Rediviva: or the Proper and Soveraign Remedy for the Healing and Recovering of these three Distracted Nations* (1649)
Shirley, James, *Cupid and Death, A Masque, As it was Presented before his Excellencie, the Embassadour of Portugal* (1653)
Sidney: Court Maxims, ed. Hans W. Blom et al. (Cambridge: Cambridge University Press, 1996)
Simmonds, Martha, *A Lamentation for the Lost Sheep of the House of Israel* (1655)
———, *When the Lord Jesus came to Jerusalem, he beheld the city, and wept over it* (1655)
———, *O England, Thy Time is Come* (1656)
Slater, Samuel, *A Rhetoricall Rapture As Composed into a Funeral Oration At the Mournfull Moving of His Highness Stately Effigies from Somerset-House* (1658)
Some Farther Intelligence of the Affairs of England (1658)
Some Reasons Humbly Proposed to the Officers of the Army, for the Speedy Re-admission of the Long Parliament (1659)
The Speech of the Right Honourable the Lord Fiennes, Commissioner of the Great Seal (1658)
The Speeches of Col. Penruddock, Col. Jones, Mr John Dean and Mr Lucas (1655)
Spittlehouse, John, *An Explanation of the Commission of Jesus Christ* (1653)
———, *The Army Vindicated, in their Late Dissolution of the Parliament* (1653)
———, *A Warning-piece Discharged* (1653)
Sprat, Thomas, *The History of the Royal Society* (1667)
Strangways, John, *The Commonplace Book of Sir John Strangways, 1645–1666*, ed. Thomas G. Olsen (Tempe, AZ: Arizona Center for Medieval and Renaissance Studies, 2004)
Stubbe, Henry, *An Essay in Defence of the Good Old Cause* (1659)
———, *Malice Rebuked, or a Character of Mr Richard Baxters Abilities* (1659)
Sydney Papers, Consisting of a Journal of the Earl of Leicester, and Original Letters of Algernon Sydney, ed. R. Blencowe (1825)
The Taking of Wexford, a Letter from an Eminent Offcer in the Army, under the Command of the Lord Lieutenant of Ireland (1649)

Thornton, Alice, *Book 2: The First Book of My Widowed Condition*, Durham Cathedral Library, GB_0033–CCOM 7

Thorowgood, Thomas, *Jewes in America* (1650)

To His Highnesse the Lord Protector of the Common-wealth of England, Scotland, and Ireland. The Humble Addresses of Menasseh Ben Israel, a divine, and doctor of physick, in behalfe of the Jewish nation (1655)

To the Parliament of the Common-Wealth of England. The Humble Petition of Divers Afflicted Women, in behalf of M: Jo hn [sic] Lilburn Prisoner in Newgate (1653)

To the Right Honourable The Lord Fleetwood, to be Communicated to the Officers of the Army, The Humble Representation of divers well-affected Persons of the City of Westminster and parts Adjacent (1659)

To the Supream authority of this Nation, the Commons assembled in Parliament: The Humble Petition of divers wel-affected Women Inhabiting the Cities Of London, Westminster, the Borough of Southwark, Hamblets, and Places adjacent (1649)

Tradescant, John, *Musaeum Tradescantianum: or A Collection of Rarities. Preserved at South-Lambeth neer London* (1656)

Trapnel, Anna, *The Cry of a Stone or a Relation of Something Spoken in Whitehall* (1654)

The Travels of Peter Mundy in Europe and Asia, 1608–1667, ed. R. C. Temple, IV (1639–47) (Cambridge: Hakluyt Society, 1925)

The True and Perfect Relation of the Taking of Captain James Hind (1651)

A True Catalogue, Or, An Account of the Several Places and most Eminent Persons in the Three Nations, and Elsewhere, Where, and by whom Richard Cromwell was Proclaimed Lord Protector of the Commonwealth of England, Scotland, and Ireland (1659)

A True Copy of A Petition Signed by very many Peaceable and Well-affected People, Inhabiting about the City of London (1658)

A True Copy of the Journal of The High Court of Justice, for the Tryal of K. Charles I . . . Taken by J.Nalson (1684)

A True Description of Jamaica, With the Fertility, Commodities, and Healthfulness of the Place (1657)

The True Levellers Standard Advanced (1649)

The True Manner of the Crowning of Charles the Second King of Scotland (1651)

The True Manner of the most Magnificent Conveyance of His Highnesse Effigies (1658)

A True Narrative of The Examination, Tryall, and Sufferings of James Nayler (1657)

A True Narrative of the Manner of the Taking of Sir George Booth (1659)

A True Narrative of the Proceedings in Parliament, Councell of State, Generall Councell of the Army, and Committee of Safetie; from the 22. of Septemb. untill this Present (1659)

The True Speeches of Colonel John Penruddock and Mr Hugh Grove, delivered on the Scaffold at Exeter Castle (1655)

Two Great Fights in Ireland, on Sunday, Munday, Tuesday, & Wednesday last, between the Marq. of Ormonds forces, and the Lord Lieut. Cromwels, at the two strong garrisons of Tredah and Dundalke (1649)

Two Letters one from Dublin in Ireland, and the other from Liverpoole (1649)
The Unparalleld Monarch, or The Portraiture of a Matchless Prince (1656)
Vane, Henry, *A Healing Question Propounded and Resolved* (1656)
———, *A Healing Question Propounded and Resolved* (1660 [1659])
———, *A Needful Corrective or Ballance in Popular Government Expressed in a Letter to James Harrington, Esquire, Upon Occasion of a Late Treatise of His, and Published as Seasonable in the Present Juncture of Affaires* (1659)
Vanity of Vanities: Or Sir Harry Vane's Picture (1660)
Vaughan, Henry, *Olor Iscanus* (1651)
Violet, Thomas, *The Advancement of Merchandise* (1651)
———, *A Petition Against the Jews* (1661)
Walker, Clement, *Anarchia Anglicana, or the History of Independency. The second part* (1649)
Walker, Edward, *A Circumstantial Account of the Preparations for the Coronation of His Majesty King Charles the Second* (London, 1820)
Walker, Henry, *A Sermon Preached in the Chappell at Sommerset-House in the Strand, on Thursday the 27 day of June 1650* (1650)
Waller, Edmund, *Panegyrick to my Lord Protector* (1655)
Waller, Edmund, John Dryden and Thomas Sprat, *Three Poems Upon the Death of His Late Highnesse Oliver Lord Protector of England, Scotland and Ireland, written by Mr Edm. Waller, Mr Jo. Dryden, Mr Sprat* (1659)
Walton, Izaak, *The Life and Death of Dr Donne* (1640)
———, *The Compleat Angler or the Contemplative Man's Recreation* (1653)
Webster, Charles, ed., *Samuel Hartlib and the Advancement of Learning* (Cambridge: Cambridge University Press, 1970)
Whitelocke, Bulstrode, *Memorials of English Affairs from the Beginning of the Reign of Charles I to the Happy Restoration of King Charles II* (1682)
———, *Memorials of English Affairs from the Beginning of the Reign of Charles I to the Happy Restoration of King Charles II*, 4 vols (Oxford, 1853)
———, *The Diary of Bulstrode Whitelock, 1605–1675*, ed. Ruth Spalding (Oxford: Oxford University Press for the British Academy, 1990)
The Whole Business of Sindercome (1657)
The Whole Triall of Mr Love, before the High Court of Justice in Westminster Hall (1652)
Wilkins, John, *The Discovery of a World in the Moone* (1638)
Williams, Roger, *The Bloudy Tenent of Persecution* (1644)
Winstanley, Gerard, *'The Law of Freedom' and Other Writings*, ed. Christopher Hill (Cambridge: Cambridge University Press, 1973)
Wither, George, *Carmen Eucharisticon: a private thank-oblation, exhibited to the glory of the lord of hosts, for the timely and wonderfull deliverance, vouchsafed to this nation, in the routing of a numerous Army of Irish rebells before Dublin* (1649)
———, *The Protector. A Poem Briefly Illustrating the Supereminency of that Dignity* (1655)

———, *Salt upon Salt: Made out of Certain Ingenious Verses upon the Late Storm and the Death of His Highness Ensuing* (1658)

Women Poets of the English Civil War, ed. Sarah C. E. Ross and Elizabeth Scott-Baumann (Manchester: Manchester University Press, 2018)

Worsley, Benjamin, *The Advocate* (1651)

Wright, Thomas ed., *Political Ballads Published in England During the Commonwealth* (1841)

Secondary Works

Adamson, John, *The Noble Revolt: The Overthrow of Charles I* (London: Weidenfeld and Nicolson, 2007)

Akkerman, Nadine, *Invisible Agents: Women and Espionage in Seventeenth-Century Britain* (Oxford: Oxford University Press, 2018)

Amussen, Susan and Mark Kishlansky, ed., *Political Culture and Cultural Politics in Early Modern England: Essays Presented to David Underdown* (Manchester: Manchester University Press, 1995)

Angell, Stephen W. and Pink Dandelion, ed., *Early Quakers and Their Theological Thought* (Cambridge: Cambridge University Press, 2015)

Armitage, David, 'The Cromwellian Protectorate and the Languages of Empire', *Historical Journal* 35 (1992), pp. 531–55

Armitage, David, Quentin Skinner and Armand Himy, ed., *Milton and Republicanism* (Cambridge: Cambridge University Press, 1995)

Ashley, Maurice, *Cromwell's Generals* (London: Cape, 1954)

———, *Financial and Commercial Policy under the Commonwealth and Protectorate* (2nd edn, London: Routledge, 1972)

Aylmer, Gerald, *The State's Servants: The Civil Service of the English Republic, 1649–60* (London: Routledge & Kegan Paul, 1973)

———, *Rebellion or Revolution: England 1640–1660* (Oxford: Oxford University Press, 1986)

Aylmer, Gerald, ed., *The Interregnum: The Quest for Settlement, 1646–1660* (London and Basingstoke: Macmillan, 1972)

Bagehot, Walter, *The English Constitution*, ed. Miles Taylor (Oxford and New York: Oxford University Press, 2001)

Baker, Philip, ed., *The Levellers: The Putney Debates* (London: Verso, 2007)

Baker, Philip and Elliot Vernon, ed., *The Agreements of the People, the Levellers, and the Constitutional Crisis of the English Revolution* (Basingstoke: Palgrave Macmillan, 2012)

Barber, Sarah, *A Revolutionary Rogue: Henry Marten and the English Republic* (Stroud: Sutton, 2000)

———, *Regicide and Republicanism: Politics and Ethics in the English Revolution, 1646–1659* (Edinburgh: Edinburgh University Press, 2020)

Barclay, Andrew, 'The Lord Protector and his Court', in Little, ed., *Oliver Cromwell: New Perspectives*

———, *Electing Cromwell: The Making of a Politician* (London: Pickering & Chatto,

2011)

Barnard, E. A. B., *A Seventeenth-Century Country Gentleman: Sir Francis Throckmorton, 1640–80* (Cambridge: Heffer & Sons, 1944)

Barnard, T. C. [Toby], *The English Republic, 1649–1660* (Harlow: Longman, 1982; 2nd edn 1997)

———, *Cromwellian Ireland: English Government and Reform in Ireland, 1649–1660* (Oxford: Clarendon Press, 1975; new ed. 2000).

———, *Making the Grand Figure: Lives and Possessions in Ireland, 1641–1770* (New Haven, CT: Yale University Press, 2004)

Bennett, Martyn, *The Civil War Experienced: Britain and Ireland, 1638–1661* (London: Routledge, 2000)

———, *Oliver Cromwell* (London: Routledge, 2006)

Bennett, Martyn, Ray Gillespie and R. Scott Spurlock, ed., *Cromwell and Ireland: New Perspectives* (Liverpool: Liverpool University Press, 2021)

Booy, David, ed., *Autobiographical Writings of Early Quaker Women* (Aldershot: Ashgate, 2004)

Bowen, Lloyd, 'Oliver Cromwell (alias Williams) and Wales', in Little, ed., *Oliver Cromwell: New Perspectives*

———, 'David Underdown, Royalist Conspirators and the Character of English Politics', *History Compass* 2 (2013), pp. 341–51

Braddick, Michael, *Parliamentary Taxation: State Formation in Early Modern England c.1550–1700* (Cambridge: Cambridge University Press, 2000)

———, *God's Fury, England's Fire: A New History of the English Civil Wars* (London: Penguin, 2009)

Braddick, Michael and David Smith, ed., *The Experience of Revolution in Stuart Britain and Ireland: Essays for John Morrill* (Cambridge: Cambridge University Press, 2011)

Bradstock, Andrew, *Radical Religion in Cromwell's England* (London: I. B. Tauris, 2011)

Brooks, Douglas, ed., *Milton and the Jews* (Cambridge: Cambridge University Press, 2008)

Brotton, Jerry, *The Sale of the Late King's Goods: Charles I and His Art Collection* (London: Macmillan, 2006)

Bryant, Arthur, *King Charles II* (London: Longmans, Green & Co., 1932)

Buckeridge, Bainbrigg, *An Essay towards an English School of Painters* (1706)

Butler, John A., *A Biography of Richard Cromwell, 1626–1712, The Second Protector* (Lampeter: Edwin Mellen Press, 1994)

Calladine, Amy, 'Public Ritual and the Proclamation of Richard Cromwell as Lord Protector in English Towns, September 1658', *Historical Journal* 61 (2018), pp. 53–76

Capp, Bernard, *The Fifth Monarchy Men: A Study in Seventeenth-Century English Millenarianism* (London: Faber, 1972)

———, *Cromwell's Navy: The Fleet and the English Revolution, 1648–1660* (Oxford: Clarendon Press, 1989)

———, *England's Culture Wars: Puritan Reformation and its Enemies in the Interregnum, 1649–1660* (Oxford: Oxford University Press, 2012)

Childs, Jessie, *The Siege of Loyalty House: A Civil War Story* (London: The Bodley Head, 2022)

Clare, Janet, ed., *Drama of the English Republic, 1649–1660* (Manchester: Manchester University Press, 2002)

———, ed., *From Republic to Restoration: Legacies and Departures* (Manchester: Manchester University Press, 2018)

Coffey, John, 'Puritanism and Liberty Revisited: The Case for Toleration in the English Revolution,' *Historical Journal* 41 (1998), pp. 961–85

Coffman, D'Maris, 'Towards a New Jerusalem: The Committee for Regulating the Excise, 1649–1653', *English Historical Review* 128 (2013), pp. 1418–50

Collins, Jeffrey R., *The Allegiance of Thomas Hobbes* (Oxford: Oxford University Press, 2005)

Colvin, H. M., D. R. Ransome and John Summerson, *The History of the King's Works*, IV: 1485–1660, Part 2 (London: HMSO, 1975)

Cooper, J. P., 'Social and Economic Policies under the Commonwealth', in Aylmer, ed., *The Interregnum*

Cooper, John P. D. and Jago James, 'Picturing Parliament: The Great Seal of the Commonwealth and the House of Commons', *Antiquaries Journal* 101 (2021), pp. 369–89

Covington, Sarah, *The Devil from over the Sea: Remembering and Forgetting Oliver Cromwell in Ireland* (Oxford: Oxford University Press, 2022)

Coward, Barry, *Oliver Cromwell* (Harlow: Longman, 1991)

———, *The Cromwellian Protectorate* (Manchester and New York: Manchester University Press, 2002)

Cunningham, John, 'Oliver Cromwell and the "Cromwellian" Settlement of Ireland', *Historical Journal* 53 (2010), pp. 919–38

———, 'Divided Conquerors: The Rump Parliament, Cromwell's Army and Ireland', *English Historical Review* 129 (2014), pp. 830–61

Cust, Richard and Ann Hughes, ed., *Conflict in Early Stuart England: Studies in Religion and Politics, 1603–1642* (London: Longman, 1989)

Damrosch, Leo, *The Sorrows of the Quaker Jesus: James Nayler and the Puritan Crackdown on the Free Spirit* (Cambridge, MA: Harvard University Press, 1996)

Dandelion, Pink, *The Quakers: A Very Short Introduction* (Oxford: Oxford University Press, 2008)

———, *An Introduction to Quakerism* (Cambridge: Cambridge University Press, 2011)

Darcy E., A. Margey and E. Murphy, ed., *The 1641 Depositions and the Irish Rebellion* (London: Pickering & Chatto, 2012)

Darley, Gillian, *John Evelyn: Living for Ingenuity* (New Haven, CT and London: Yale University Press, 2006)

Davidson, Peter, ed., *Poetry and Revolution: An Anthology of British and Irish Verse, 1625–1660* (Oxford: Oxford University Press, 1998)

Davies, Adrian, *The Quakers in English Society, 1655–1725* (Oxford: Clarendon, 2000)

Davies, Godfrey, 'The Army and the Downfall of Richard Cromwell', *Huntington Library Bulletin* 7 (1935), pp. 131–67

Davis, J. C., *Oliver Cromwell* (London: Hodder, 2001; repr. London: Bloomsbury, 2010)

Dawson, Hannah, *Life Lessons from Hobbes* (Basingstoke: Macmillan, 2013)

Dickson, P. G. M., *The Financial Revolution in England, 1688–1756* (London: Macmillan, 1967)

DiMeo, Michelle, *Lady Ranelagh: The Incomparable Life of Robert Boyle's Sister* (Chicago: University of Chicago Press, 2021)

Donoghue, John, *Fire under the Ashes: An Atlantic History of the English Revolution* (Chicago: University of Chicago Press, 2013)

Dow, F. D., *Cromwellian Scotland, 1651–1660* (Edinburgh: J. Donald, 1979)

———, *Radicalism in the English Revolution, 1640–1660* (Oxford: Blackwell, 1985)

Durston, Christopher, *The Family in the English Revolution* (Oxford: Blackwell, 1989)

———, 'Puritan Rule and the Failure of Cultural Revolution, 1645–60', in Durston and Eales, ed., *The Culture of English Puritanism*

———, *Cromwell's Major-Generals: Godly Government During the English Revolution* (Manchester and New York: Manchester University Press, 2001)

Durston, Christopher and Jacqueline Eales, ed., *The Culture of English Puritanism, 1560–1700* (Basingstoke: Macmillan, 1996)

The Early Lives of Milton, ed. Helen Darbishire (London: Constable, 1932)

Edmond, Mary, *Rare Sir William Davenant* (Manchester: Manchester University Press, 1987)

Farr, David, *John Lambert: Parliamentary Soldier and Cromwellian Major-General, 1619–1684* (Woodbridge: Boydell & Brewer, 2003)

Fea, A., *The Flight of the King after the Battle of Worcester* (London: J. Lane, 1897)

Finkelstein, A., *Harmony and the Balance: An Intellectual History of Seventeenth-Century English Economic Thought* (Ann Arbor: University of Michigan Press, 2000)

Firth, C. H., 'A Letter from Lord Saye and Sele to Lord Wharton, 29 December 1657', *English Historical Review* 10 (1895), pp. 106–7

———, 'The Battle of Dunbar', *Transactions of the Royal Historical Society* 14 (1900), pp. 19-52

———, *Oliver Cromwell and the Rule of the Puritans in England* (1900; repr. London: Putnam, 1947)

———, 'Cromwell and the Crown', *English Historical Review* 17 (1902), pp. 429–42

———, 'Cromwell and the Crown', *English Historical Review* 18 (1903), pp. 52–80

———, 'Sir William Davenant and the Revival of Drama during the Protectorate', *English Historical Review* 18 (1903), pp. 319–21

———, 'A Speech by Richard Cromwell, 14 October 1658', *English Historical Review* 23 (1908), pp. 734–6

———, *The Last Years of the Protectorate, 1656–1658*, 2 vols (1909; repr. New York: Russell & Russell, 1964)

———, 'The Expulsion of the Long Parliament', *History* 2 (1917), pp. 129–43
———, 'The Expulsion of the Long Parliament (continued)', *History* 2 (1918), pp. 193–206
Fitzgibbons, Jonathan, *Cromwell's Head* (Kew: National Archives, 2008)
———, '"Not in Any Doubtfull Dispute"? Reassessing the Nomination of Richard Cromwell', *Historical Research* 83 (2010), pp. 281–300
———, 'Hereditary Succession and the Cromwellian Protectorate: The Offer of the Crown Reconsidered', *English Historical Review* 128 (2013), pp. 1095–128
———, 'Reconstructing the Debates of the Protectorate Parliaments: The Pitfalls of J. T. Rutt's Edition of "Thomas Burton's" Diary', *Parliamentary History* 35 (2016), pp. 221–41
———, 'The Definition of Treason and the Offer of the Crown', in George Southcombe and Grant Tapsell, ed., *Revolutionary England, c. 1630–c. 1660: Essays for Clive Holmes* (London: Routledge, 2017)
———, 'Rethinking the English Revolution of 1649', *Historical Journal* 60 (2017), pp. 889–914
———, *Cromwell's House of Lords: Politics, Parliaments and Constitutional Revolution, 1642–1660* (Woodbridge: Boydell Press, 2018)
———, '"To Settle a Government without Something of Monarchy in It": Bulstrode Whitelocke's Memoirs and the Reinvention of the Interregnum', *English Historical Review* 137 (2022), pp. 655–91
Fraser, Antonia, *Cromwell: Our Chief of Men* (London: Weidenfeld & Nicolson, 1973; repr. 2002)
Furedi, Frank, *Authority: A Sociological History* (Cambridge: Cambridge University Press, 2013)
Gardiner, S. R., *History of the Commonwealth and Protectorate, 1649–1656*, 4 vols (London: Longmans, Green, 1894–1901)
———, *Cromwell's Place in History* (London, 1897)
———, *Oliver Cromwell* (London, 1899)
Gaunt, Peter, *The Cromwellian Gazetteer: An Illustrated Guide to Britain in the Civil War and Commonwealth* (Stroud: Sutton, 1987)
———, *Oliver Cromwell* (Oxford: Blackwell, 1996)
Gaunt, Peter, ed., *Cromwell: Four Centuries On* (Huntingdon: Cromwell Association, 2013)
Geiter, Mary, *William Penn* (Harlow: Longman, 2000)
Gentles, Ian, *The New Model Army in England, Ireland and Scotland, 1645–1653* (Oxford: Blackwell, 1991)
———, *Oliver Cromwell: God's Warrior and the English Revolution* (Basingstoke: Palgrave Macmillan, 2011)
———, *The English Revolution and the Wars in the three Kingdoms, 1638–1652* (London and New York: Routledge, 2014)
Gentles, Ian, John Morrill and Blair Worden, ed., *Soldiers, Writers and Statesmen of the English Revolution* (Cambridge: Cambridge University Press, 1998)

Graham, Elspeth, Hilary Hinds, Elaine Hobby and Helen Wilcox, ed., *Her Own Life: Autobiographical Writings by Seventeenth-Century Englishwomen* (London: Routledge, 1989)

Greengrass, Mark, Michael Leslie and Timothy Rayler, ed., *Samuel Hartlib and Universal Reformation: Studies in Intellectual Communication* (Cambridge: Cambridge University Press, 1994)

Greenspan, Nicole, *Selling Cromwell's Wars: Media, Empire and Godly Warfare, 1650–1658* (London: Pickering & Chatto, 2012)

Gregg, Pauline, *Free-born John: A Biography of John Lilburne* (London: Harrap, 1961)

Guizot, François, *History of Richard Cromwell and the Restoration of Charles II*, 2 vols, trans. A. R. Scoble (London, 1856)

Habbakuk, H. J., 'Public Finance and the Sale of Confiscated Estates during the Interregnum', *Economic History Review* 15 (1962), pp. 70–88

Hammer, Jane Ross, *Protector: A Life of Richard Cromwell* (1997)

Hammersley, Rachel, *James Harrington: An Intellectual Biography* (Oxford: Oxford University Press, 2019)

Hardacre, Paul, 'William Boteler: A Cromwellian Oligarch', *Huntington Library Quarterly* 11 (1947), pp. 1–11

Harris, Tim, *Restoration: Charles II and his Kingdoms, 1660–1685* (London: Penguin, 2006)

———, *Revolution: The Great Crisis of the British Monarchy, 1685–1720* (London: Penguin, 2007)

———, 'Revisiting the Causes of the English Civil War', *Huntington Library Quarterly* 78 (2015), pp. 615–35

Haskell, Frances, *The King's Pictures* (New Haven, CT: Yale University Press, 2013)

Hattaway, Michael, ed., *A Companion to English Renaissance Literature and Culture* (Oxford: Blackwell, 2000)

Hause, E. M., *Tumble-down Dick: The Fall of the House of Cromwell* (New York: Exposition Press, 1972)

Healy, Jonathan, *The Blazing World: A New History of Revolutionary England* (London: Bloomsbury, 2023)

Healy, Simon, '1636: The Unmaking of Oliver Cromwell?', in Little, ed., *Oliver Cromwell: New Perspectives*

Helmers, Helmer J., *The Royalist Republic: Literature, Politics and Religion in the Anglo-Dutch Public Sphere, 1639–1660* (Cambridge: Cambridge University Press, 2015)

Hill, Christopher, *Puritanism and Revolution: Studies in Interpretation of the English Revolution of the Seventeenth Century* (London: Secker & Warburg, 1958)

———, *God's Englishman: Oliver Cromwell and the English Revolution* (London: Penguin, 1970; repr. 1990)

———, *The World Turned Upside Down: Radical Ideas during the English Revolution* (London: Temple Smith, 1972; repr. 1991)

———, *Change and Continuity in Seventeenth-Century England* (London: Weidenfeld & Nicolson, 1974)

Hinds, Hilary, 'Introduction', in Anna Trapnel, *The Cry of a Stone*, ed. Hilary Hinds (Tempe: Arizona Center for Medieval and Renaissance Studies, 2000)

Hirst, Derek, 'The Failure of the Third English Reformation', *Past and Present* 132 (1991), pp. 33–66

———, 'The English Republic and the Meaning of Britain', *Journal of Modern History* 66 (1994), pp. 451–86

———, 'Locating the 1650s in England's Seventeenth Century', *History* 81 (1996), pp. 359–83

Hirst, Derek and Steven Zwicker, *Andrew Marvell, Orphan of the Hurricane* (Oxford: Oxford University Press, 2012)

Holberton, Edward, *Poetry and the Cromwellian Protectorate* (Oxford: Oxford University Press, 2008)

Hopper, Andrew, *'Black Tom': Sir Thomas Fairfax and the English Revolution* (Manchester and New York: Manchester University Press, 2007)

———, *Turncoats and Renegadoes: Changing Sides during the English Civil Wars* (Oxford: Oxford University Press, 2012)

Hopper, Andrew and Philip Major, ed., *England's Fortress: New Perspectives on Thomas, 3rd Lord Fairfax* (Farnham: Ashgate, 2014)

Horspool, David, *Oliver Cromwell: England's Protector* (London: Allen Lane, 2017)

Hughes, Ann, *The Causes of the English Civil War* (Basingstoke: Macmillan, 1998)

Hunneyball, Paul, '"Cromwellian Style": The Architectural Trappings of the Protectorate Regime', in Little, ed., *The Cromwellian Protectorate*

Hunt, Alice, 'The Monarchical Republic of Mary I', *Historical Journal* 52 (2009), pp. 557–72

———, '"All Forms Accustomed": Ritual, Precedent and the Past at the Coronation of Charles II', in Stoyle and Bowen, ed., *Remembering the English Civil Wars*

Hunter, Michael, *Science and Society in Restoration England* (Cambridge: Cambridge University Press, 1981)

Hutton, Ronald, *Charles the Second: King of England, Scotland, and Ireland* (Oxford: Clarendon Press, 1989)

———, *The Restoration: A Political and Religious History of England and Wales, 1658–1667* (Oxford: Oxford University Press, 1993)

———, *The British Republic, 1649–1660* (Basingstoke: Palgrave Macmillan, 1990; 2nd edn 2000)

———, *The Making of Oliver Cromwell* (New Haven, CT and London: Yale University Press, 2021)

Jackson, Clare, *Devil-Land: England under Siege, 1588–1688* (London: Allen Lane, 2021)

Jardine, Lisa, *The Curious Life of Robert Hooke: The Man Who Measured London* (London: HarperCollins, 2003)

Jensen, Freyja Cox, *Reading the Republic in Early Modern England* (Leiden: Brill, 2012)

Katz, David S., *Philo-Semitism and the Readmission of the Jews to England, 1603–1655* (Oxford: Clarendon Press, 1982)

———, *The Jews in the History of England, 1485–1850* (Oxford: Oxford University Press, 1996)

Keay, Anna, *The Restless Republic: Britain without a Crown* (London: William Collins, 2022)

Kelsey, Sean, *Inventing a Republic: The Political Culture of the English Commonwealth* (Manchester: Manchester University Press, 1997)

———, 'Staging the Trial of Charles I', in Peacey, ed., *The Regicides and the Execution of Charles I*

———, 'Constructing the Council of State', *Parliamentary History* 22 (2003), pp. 217–41

Knoppers, Laura Lunger, *Constructing Cromwell: Ceremony, Portrait, and Print, 1645–1661* (Cambridge: Cambridge University Press, 2000)

Kunze, Bonnelyn Young, *Margaret Fell and the Rise of Quakerism* (Basingstoke: Palgrave, 1993)

Law, E., *The History of Hampton Court Palace, Stuart Times* (1885)

Lay, Paul, *Providence Lost: The Rise and Fall of Cromwell's Protectorate* (London: Head of Zeus, 2020)

Lewalski, Barbara Kiefer, *The Life of John Milton: A Critical Biography* (Malden, MA and Oxford: Blackwell, 2000; rev. edn 2003)

Lincoln, Margarette, *London and the 17th Century: The Making of the World's Greatest City* (New Haven, CT and London: Yale University Press, 2021)

Little, Patrick, *Lord Broghill and the Cromwellian Union with Ireland and Scotland* (Woodbridge: Boydell Press, 2004)

———, 'Monarchy to Protectorate: Re-drafting the Humble Petition and Advice, March–June 1657', *Historical Journal* 79 (2006), pp. 144–9

———, ed., *The Cromwellian Protectorate* (Woodbridge: Boydell Press, 2007)

———, ed., *Oliver Cromwell: New Perspectives* (Basingstoke: Palgrave Macmillan, 2009)

Little, Patrick and David Smith, *Parliaments and Politics During the Cromwellian Protectorate* (Cambridge: Cambridge University Press, 2007)

MacGregor, Arthur, ed., *The Late King's Goods: Collections, Possessions and Patronage of Charles I in the Light of the Commonwealth Sale Inventories* (London and Oxford: Alistair McAlpine, 1989)

Mack, Phyllis, *Visionary Women: Ecstatic Prophecy in Seventeenth-Century England* (Berkeley and Los Angeles, CA: University of California Press, 1992)

Mahlberg, G., *Henry Neville and English Republican Culture in the Seventeenth Century: Dreaming of Another Game* (Manchester: Manchester University Press, 2009)

Mahlberg G., and Dirk Wiemann, ed., *Perspectives on English Revolutionary Republicanism* (Farnham: Ashgate, 2014)

Major, Philip, 'Sir Thomas Fairfax's "The Thoughts of Eternity"', *Modern Language Review* 107 (2012), pp. 1019–32

Major, Philip, ed., *Literatures of Exile in the English Revolution and its Aftermath, 1640–1690* (Farnham: Ashgate, 2010)

Malcolm, Noel, *Aspects of Hobbes* (Oxford: Clarendon Press, 2002)

Markham, Clements R., *A Life of the Great Lord Fairfax* (London, 1870)

Martinich, A. P., *Hobbes: A Biography* (Cambridge: Cambridge University Press, 1999)

Mayers, Ruth, *1659: The Crisis of the Commonwealth* (Woodbridge: Boydell, 2004)

McDowell, Nicholas, *The English Radical Imagination: Culture, Religion and Revolution, 1630–1660* (Oxford: Clarendon Press, 2003)

———, 'Urquhart's Rabelais: Translation, Patronage and Cultural Politics', *English Literary Renaissance* 35 (2005), pp. 273–303

———, *Poetry and Allegiance in the English Civil Wars: Marvell and the Cause of Wit* (Oxford: Oxford University Press, 2008)

———, 'Marvell Among the Cavaliers' and 'Marvell Among the Cromwellians', in *The Oxford Handbook of Literature and the English Revolution*, ed. Laura Lunger Knoppers (Oxford: Oxford University Press, 2012)

———, *The Poet of Revolution: The Making of John Milton* (Princeton, NJ: Princeton University Press, 2020)

McElligott, Jason, 'Cromwell, Drogheda, and the Abuse of Irish History', *Bullán: An Irish Studies Review* 6 (2001), pp. 109–32

McElligott, Jason and Smith, David L., ed., *Royalists and Royalism during the Interregnum: Politics, Culture and Society in Early Modern Britain* (Manchester: Manchester University Press, 2010)

Millar, O., ed., *The Inventories and Valuations of the King's Goods, 1649–1651, Volume of the Walpole Society* 43 (1970–2)

Mills, Jane, ed., *Cromwell's Legacy* (Manchester: Manchester University Press, 2012)

Mintz, Samuel, *The Hunting of the Leviathan: Seventeenth-Century Reactions to the Materialism and Moral Philosophy of Thomas Hobbes* (Bristol: Thoemmes Press, 1996)

Moore, Lucy, *Lady Fanshawe's Receipt Book: The Life and Times of a Civil War Heroine* (London: Atlantic Books, 2017)

Morrill, John, *The Impact of the English Civil War* (London: Collins & Brown, 1991)

———, *Oliver Cromwell* (Oxford: Oxford University Press, 2007)

Morrill, John, ed., *Oliver Cromwell and the English Revolution* (Harlow: Longman, 1990)

———, ed., *Revolution and Restoration: England in the 1650s* (London: Collins & Brown, 1992)

Morton, A. L., *The World of the Ranters: Religious Radicalism in the English Revolution* (London: Lawrence and Wishart, 1970)

Moshenska, Joe, *Making Darkness Light: The Lives and Times of John Milton* (New York: Basic Books, 2021)

Mowl, Timothy and Brian Earnshaw, *Architecture without Kings: The Rise of Puritan Classicism under Cromwell* (Manchester and New York: Manchester University Press, 1995)

Nadler, Steven, *Menasseh ben Israel: Rabbi of Amsterdam* (New Haven, CT and London: Yale University Press, 2018)

Nelson, Eric, *The Royalist Revolution: Monarchy and the American Founding* (Cambridge, MA: Harvard University Press, 2014)

Neufeld, Matthew, *The Civil Wars after 1660: Public Remembering in Late Stuart England* (Woodbridge: Boydell and Brewer, 2013)

Norbrook, David, *Writing the English Republic: Poetry, Rhetoric and Politics, 1627–1660* (Cambridge: Cambridge University Press, 2000)

Ó Siochrú, Micheál, *God's Executioner: Oliver Cromwell and the Conquest of Ireland* (London: Faber and Faber, 2008)

Ollard, Richard, *The Escape of Charles II after the Battle of Worcester* (London: Constable & Robinson, 2002)

Parker, Geoffrey, *Global Crisis: War, Climate Change & Catastrophe in the Seventeenth Century* (New Haven, CT and London: Yale University Press, 2013)

Parker, Matthew, *The Sugar Barons: Family, Corruption, Empire and War* (London: Hutchinson, 2011)

Peacey, Jason, *Politicians and Pamphleteers: Propaganda during the English Civil Wars and Interregnum* (Farnham: Ashgate, 2004)

———, 'The Protector Humbled: Richard Cromwell and the Constitution', in Little, ed., *The Cromwellian Protectorate*

———, '"Fit for Public Services": The Upbringing of Richard Cromwell', in Little, ed., *Oliver Cromwell: New Perspectives*

———, 'The Street Theatre of State: The Ceremonial Opening of Parliament, 1603–60', *Parliamentary History* 34 (2015), pp. 155–72

Peacey, Jason, ed., *The Regicides and the Execution of Charles I* (Basingstoke: Palgrave, 2001)

Peck, Imogen, *Recollection in the Republics: Memories of the British Civil Wars in England, 1649–1659* (Oxford: Oxford University Press, 2021)

Peck, Linda Levy, *Consuming Splendour. Society and Culture in Seventeenth-Century England* (Cambridge: Cambridge University Press, 2005)

Peltonen, Markku, *Classical Humanism and Republicanism in English Political Thought 1570–1640* (Cambridge: Cambridge University Press, 1995)

———, *The Political Thought of the English Free State, 1649–1653* (Cambridge: Cambridge University Press, 2023)

Penruddock, C., 'Mistress Jane Lane', *Wiltshire Archaeological and Natural History Magazine* 26 (1892), pp. 1–38

Pestana, Carla Gardina, *The English Atlantic in an Age of Revolution, 1640–1661* (Cambridge, MA: Harvard University Press, 2004)

———, *The English Conquest of Jamaica: Oliver Cromwell's Bid for Empire* (Cambridge, MA: Belknap Press, 2017)

Peters, Kate, *Print Culture and the Early Quakers* (Cambridge: Cambridge University Press, 2005)

Pincus, Steven, *Protestantism and Patriotism: Ideologies and the Making of English*

Foreign Policy, 1650–1668 (Cambridge and New York: Cambridge University Press, 1996)

Piper, David, 'The Contemporary Portraits of Oliver Cromwell', *Volume of the Walpole Society* 34 (1958), pp. 27–41

Pocock, J., *The Machiavellian Moment: Florentine Political Thought and the Atlantic Republican Tradition* (Princeton, NJ: Princeton University Press, 1975)

Poole, William, *Milton and the Making of Paradise Lost* (Cambridge, MA: Harvard University Press, 2017)

Popkin, Richard, 'Hartlib, Dury and the Jews,' in Greengrass et al., ed., *Samuel Hartlib and Universal Reformation*

Prendergast, John, *The Cromwellian Settlement of Ireland* (London: Longman, Green, 1865)

Purkiss, Diane, *The English Civil War: A People's History* (London: Harper Press, 2006)

Rahe, Paul, 'The Classical Republicanism of John Milton', *History of Political Thought* 25 (2004), pp. 243–75

———, *Against Throne and Altar: Machiavelli and Political Theory under the English Republic* (Cambridge: Cambridge University Press, 2008)

Ramsey, Robert W., *Richard Cromwell, Protector of England* (London: Longmans, Green & Co., 1935)

Ravenhill, W. W., 'Records of the Rising in the West, AD 1655', *Wiltshire Archaeological and Natural History Magazine*, 13–15 (1872–5)

Raymond, Joad, 'An Eye-witness to King Cromwell', *History Today* 47 (July 1997), pp. 35–41

———, *Pamphlets and Pamphleteering in Early Modern Britain* (Cambridge: Cambridge University Press, 2003)

Raymond, Joad, ed., *News, Newspapers and Society in Early Modern Britain* (London: F. Cass, 1999)

———, ed., *Making the News: An Anthology of the Newsbooks of Revolutionary England, 1641–1660* (Moreton-in-Marsh: Windrush Press, 1993)

Rees, John, *The Leveller Revolution: Radical Political Organisation in England, 1640–1660* (London: Verso, 2016)

Reilly, Tom, *Cromwell: An Honourable Enemy* (London: Weidenfeld and Nicolson, 2001)

———, *Cromwell Was Framed: Ireland 1649* (Alresford: John Hunt, 2014)

Roberts, Michael, trans. and ed., *Swedish Diplomats at Cromwell's Court, 1655–1656: The Missions of Peter Julius Coyet and Christer Bonde* (London: Camden Society, 1988)

Roots, Ivan, *The Great Rebellion, 1642–1660* (London: Batsford, 1966)

Roseveare, Henry, *The Financial Revolution, 1660–1760* (London: Longman, 1991)

Ross, Isabel, *Margaret Fell: Mother of Quakerism* (2nd edn, York: Ebor Press, 1984)

Rowe, Violet, *Sir Henry Vane the Younger: A Study in Political and Administrative History* (London: Athlone Press, 1970)

Russell, Conrad, ed., *Origins of the English Civil War* (London: Macmillan, 1973)

Rutherford, Emma, and Bendor Grosvenor, eds., *Warts and All: The Portrait Miniatures of Samuel Cooper*, exhibition catalogue (London: Philip Mould, 2013)

Schama, Simon, *The Embarrassment of Riches: An Interpretation of Dutch Culture in the Golden Age* (London: Harper Press, 1987)

———, *Landscape and Memory* (London: Fontana, 1996)

———, *Belonging: The Story of the Jews, 1492–1900* (London: Vintage, 2017)

Scott, Jonathan, *Algernon Sidney and the English Republic, 1623–1677* (Cambridge: Cambridge University Press, 1988)

———, *England's Troubles: Seventeenth-Century English Political Instability in European Context* (Cambridge: Cambridge University Press, 2000)

———, *Commonwealth Principles: Republican Writing of the English Revolution* (Cambridge: Cambridge University Press, 2004)

Scurr, Ruth, *John Aubrey: My Own Life* (London: Chatto & Windus, 2015)

Seaward, Paul, *The Cavalier Parliament and the Reconstruction of the Old Regime, 1661–1667* (Cambridge: Cambridge University Press, 1989)

———, *The Restoration, 1660–1688* (Basingstoke: Macmillan, 1991)

Shapiro, James, *Shakespeare and the Jews* (New York: Columbia University Press, 1996)

Sharpe, Kevin, *Remapping Early Modern England: The Culture of Seventeenth-Century Politics* (Cambridge: Cambridge University Press, 2000)

———, *Image Wars: Promoting Kings and Commonwealths in England, 1603–1660* (New Haven, CT and London: Yale University Press, 2010)

———, *Rebranding Rule: The Restoration of Revolution Monarchy, 1660–1714* (New Haven, CT and London: Yale University Press, 2013)

Sheridan, Richard B., *Sugar and Slavery: An Economic History of the British West Indies, 1623–1775* (Jamaica: Canoe Press, 1974; repr. 1994)

Sherwood, Roy, *The Court of Oliver Cromwell* (London: Croom Helm, 1977)

———, *Oliver Cromwell: King in All But Name* (Stroud: Sutton, 1997)

Skinner, Quentin, *Hobbes and Republican Liberty* (Cambridge: Cambridge University Press, 2008)

Slack, Paul, 'The Politics of Consumption and England's Happiness in the Later Seventeenth Century', *English Historical Review* 122 (2007), pp. 609–31

———, *The Invention of Improvement: Information and Material Progress in Seventeenth-Century England* (Cambridge: Cambridge University Press, 2014)

Smith, David, *Oliver Cromwell, Politics and Religion in the English Revolution* (Cambridge: Cambridge University Press, 1991)

Smith, Nigel, *Literature and Revolution in England, 1640–1660* (New Haven, CT and London: Yale University Press, 1994)

———, *Andrew Marvell: The Chameleon* (New Haven, CT and London: Yale University Press, 2010)

Smith, S. R., 'Almost Revolutionaries: The London Apprentices during the Civil Wars', *Huntington Library Quarterly* 42 (1979), pp. 313–28

Sommerville, C. John, *The Secularization of Early Modern England* (Oxford: Oxford University Press, 1992)

Spalding, Ruth, *The Improbable Puritan: A Life of Bulstrode Whitelocke, 1605–1675* (London: Faber and Faber, 1975)

Spence, Joseph, *Anecdotes* (London, 1820)

Stoyle, Mark, *Loyalty and Locality: Popular Allegiances in Devon during the English Civil War* (Exeter: Exeter University Press, 1994)

———, '"Memories of the Maimed": The Testimony of Charles I's Former Soldiers, 1660–1730', *History* 88 (2003), pp. 204–26

Stoyle, Mark and Lloyd Bowen, ed., *Remembering the English Civil Wars* (Abingdon: Routledge, 2022)

Strickland, Agnes *Lives of the Queens of England* (1865)

Thomas, Keith, 'The Levellers and the Franchise', in G. E. Aylmer ed., *The Interregnum: The Quest for Settlement, 1646–1660* (London and Basingstoke: Macmillan, 1972)

Thornton, Peter, *Seventeenth-Century Interior Decoration in England, France and Holland* (New Haven, CT: Yale University Press, 1978)

Thurley, Simon, *Whitehall Palace: An Architectural History of the Royal Apartments* (New Haven, CT: Yale University Press, 1999)

———, *Hampton Court: A Social and Architectural History* (New Haven, CT: Yale University Press, 2003)

Tinniswood, Adrian, *The Verneys: A True Story of Love, War and Madness in Seventeenth-Century England* (London: Vintage, 2008)

Townshend, Lee Porcher, 'Some Account of General Robert Venables of Antrobus and Wincham, Cheshire . . . Together with the Autobiographical Memoir or Diary of his Widow, Elizabeth Venables', *Chetham Miscellanies*, Volume the Fourth (1872), pp. iii–28

Tuck, Richard, *Hobbes: A Very Short Introduction* (Oxford: Oxford University Press, 2002)

Uglow, Jenny, *A Gambling Man: Charles II and the Restoration* (London: Faber and Faber, 2009)

Underdown, David, *Royalist Conspiracy in England, 1649–1660* (New Haven, CT: Yale University Press, 1960)

———, *Pride's Purge: Politics in the Puritan Revolution* (Oxford: Clarendon Press, 1971)

———, *Revel, Riot and Rebellion: Popular Politics and Culture in England, 1603–1660* (Oxford: Oxford University Press, 1985)

———, *Fire from Heaven: Life in an English Town in the Seventeenth Century* (New Haven, CT and London: Yale University Press, 1992)

Vallance, Edward, *A Radical History of Britain: Visionaries, Rebels and Revolutionaries* (London: Little, Brown, 2010)

von Maltzahn, Nicholas, 'Making Use of the Jews: Milton and Philo-Semitism', in Brooks, ed., *Milton and the Jews*

Walsham, Alexandra, *The Reformation of the Landscape: Religion, Identity and Memory in Early Modern Britain and Ireland* (Oxford: Oxford University Press, 2011)

Watkins, Stephen, 'The Protectorate Playhouse: William Davenant's Cockpit in the 1650s', *Shakespeare Bulletin* 37 (2019), pp. 89–109

Webb, Stephen Saunders, *The Governors General: The English Army and the Definition of Empire, 1569–1681* (Chapel Hill: University of North Carolina Press, 1979)

Webster, Charles, *The Great Instauration: Science, Medicine, and Reform, 1626–1660* (London: Duckworth, 1975)

Wedgwood, C. V., *The Trial of Charles I* (London: Collins, 1964)

———, *A King Condemned: The Trial and Execution of Charles I* (1964; repr. London: I. B. Tauris, 2011)

Wennerlind, Carl, *Casualties of Credit: The English Financial Revolution, 1620–1720* (Cambridge, MA: Harvard University Press, 2011)

Wilcher, Robert, '*Eikon Basilike*: The Printing, Composition, Strategy, and Impact of "The King's Book"', in Laura Lunger Knoppers, ed., *The Oxford Handbook of Literature and the English Revolution* (Oxford: Oxford University Press, 2012)

Wilson, John, *Fairfax: A Life of Thomas, Lord Fairfax, Captain-General of all the Parliament's Forces in the English Civil War, Creator & Commander of the New Model Army* (London: John Murray, 1985)

Wolf, Lucien, 'Crypto-Jews under the Commonwealth', *Transactions of the Jewish Historical Society of England* 1 (1893–4), pp. 55–88

———, 'The First English Jew', *Transactions of the Jewish Historical Society of England* 2 (1896), pp. 14–46

Woodford, Benjamin, *Perceptions of a Monarchy without a King: Reactions to Oliver Cromwell's Power* (Montreal: McGill-Queen's University Press, 2013)

Woolrych, Austin, *Penruddock's Rising, 1655* (London: G. Philip for the Historical Association, 1955)

———, 'The Good Old Cause and the Fall of the Protectorate', *Cambridge Historical Journal* 13 (1957), pp. 133–61

———, *Commonwealth to Protectorate* (Oxford: Clarendon Press, 1982)

———, *England without a King, 1649–1660* (London: Methuen, 1983)

———, *Soldiers and Statesmen: The General Council of the Army and its Debates 1647–8* (Oxford: Clarendon Press, 1987)

———, 'The Cromwellian Protectorate: A Military Dictatorship?', *History* 75 (1990), pp. 207–31

———, *Britain in Revolution, 1625–1660* (Oxford: Oxford University Press, 2004)

Worden, Blair, *The Rump Parliament 1648–1653* (Cambridge: Cambridge University Press, 1974)

———, 'The "Diary" of Bulstrode Whitelocke', *English Historical Review* 108 (1993), pp. 122–34

———, 'Marchamont Nedham and the Beginnings of English Republicanism, 1649–1656', in D. Wootton, ed., *Republicanism, Liberty, and Commercial Society, 1649–1776* (Stanford, CA: Stanford University Press, 1994)

———, *Roundhead Reputations: The English Civil Wars and the Passions of Posterity* (London: Allen Lane, 2001)

———, *Literature and Politics in Cromwellian England: John Milton, Andrew Marvell, Marchamont Nedham* (Oxford: Oxford University Press, 2007)

———, *The English Civil Wars, 1640–1660* (London: Weidenfeld & Nicolson, 2009)

———, *God's Instruments: Political Conduct in the England of Oliver Cromwell* (Oxford: Oxford University Press, 2012)

———, '350 Years On: Cromwell and the Expulsion of the Long Parliament', in Gaunt ed., *Cromwell: Four Centuries On*

Zagorin, Perez, *A History of Political Thought in the English Revolution* (London: Routledge & Kegan Paul, 1954)

Zaret, David, *Origins of Democratic Culture: Printing, Petitions and the Public Sphere in Early Modern England* (Princeton, NJ: Princeton University Press, 2000)

Zurcher, Amelia, *Seventeenth-Century English Romance: Allegory, Ethics and Politics* (New York and Basingstoke: Palgrave Macmillan, 2007)

Zwicker, Stephen, *Lines of Authority: Politics and English Literary Culture, 1649–1689* (Ithaca, NY: Cornell University Press, 1993)

Acknowledgements

Writing this book has, mercifully, not always been a lonely endeavour. I am very grateful to family, friends, colleagues, scholars, librarians and archivists who have helped me along the way. Thank you to the Leverhulme Trust for funding a period of invaluable early research, to the Society of Authors for a work-in-progress grant and to the University of Southampton for enabling me to take regular research leave. My colleagues in English and History at Southampton, and at the Centre for Medieval and Renaissance Culture, have been consistently supportive. I am particularly grateful to John McGavin for reading and commenting on the book at all stages, and for his mentorship over the years. I am indebted, too, to Mark Stoyle for his invaluable feedback on the early chapters, and for many a helpful and thought-provoking conversation. Peter Middleton also read and commented on early draft chapters, and Stephen Bending, Maria Hayward and Philip Hoare always asked the right questions. Beyond Southampton, I am immensely grateful to Bernard Capp, who read the final manuscript in its entirety, and whose expertise and sharp eye have made this book sounder; any mistakes are, of course, my own. Thank you, too, to Susan Doran, Paul Hammond, Thomas Healy, Greg Walker and the late Justin Champion.

I am fortunate to be represented by Catherine Clarke at Felicity Bryan Associates. Her advice has been invaluable and her support – and that of all the team at FBA – unwavering. It has been a privilege and a delight to be published by Faber. I am indebted to Neil Belton for buying this book in the first place, and hugely grateful to my friend and erstwhile publishing colleague Louisa Joyner for steering it through to publication with characteristic positivity, intellectual verve and patience. Fiona Crosby has been an attentive, rigorous and reassuring editor: thank you. Thank you, too, to Robert Davies for his judicious copyedit, and to Anne Owen, Jo Stimfield, Tara McEvoy and Henry Petrides (for his witty cover design) at Faber.

Friends have sustained me more than they know. I am not sure I would have a career without Anna Whitelock, who has supported my hunting around in republics for many years now. There is not an aspect of this book, or of life in general, that I have not talked through with her. I am grateful too to the following for valuable friendship, excellent advice and good humour during the writing of this book: Hannah Breeze, Ben and Julia Cairns, Emma Clery, Ita Mac Carthy, Natasha and Olly Montagu, Richard Scholar, Charlotte Scott. Particular thanks to my friend Toby Mundy, who has taught me so much about publishing and writing.

Finally, I would like to thank my family: my parents, David and Kate Hunt, and my siblings for their encouragement. They, together with my parents-in-law, Robin and Gwen McConnachie, have each enabled me to combine work and motherhood, and provided spaces in which to write. I would also like to acknowledge my late grandfather. He owned an engraving of Robert Walker's portrait of Cromwell, which I walked past endless times as a child and which I am now pleased to own. My largest debt is to my husband, James – my best friend, and by far my best reader and critic – and to our three children: Florence, Mary and Jem. They have all lived with this book for a long time, and have brought me joy while putting up with much. *Republic* is dedicated to them.

Index